Longevity Revolution

# Other Books by Theodore Roszak

THE DISSENTING ACADEMY
(EDITOR)

THE MAKING OF A COUNTER CULTURE
Reflections on the Technocratic Society and its Youthful Opposition

WHERE THE WASTELAND ENDS
Politics and Transcendence in Postindustrial Society

MASCULINE/FEMININE
Readings in Sexual Mythology and the Liberation of Women
(COEDITOR WITH BETTY ROSZAK)

SOURCES
(EDITOR)

UNFINISHED ANIMAL
The Aquarian Frontier and the Evolution of Consciousness

PERSON/PLANET
The Creative Disintegration of Industrial Society

THE CULT OF INFORMATION
A Neo-Luddite Treatise on High Tech, Artificial Intelligence, and the True Art of Thinking

THE VOICE OF THE EARTH
An Exploration of Ecopsychology

ECOPSYCHOLOGY
Restoring the Earth, Healing the Mind
(EDITOR)

AMERICA THE WISE
The Longevity Revolution and the True Wealth of Nations

THE GENDERED ATOM
Reflections on the Sexual Psychology of Science

PONTIFEX

BUGS

DREAMWATCHER

FLICKER

THE MEMOIRS OF ELIZABETH FRANKENSTEIN

# LONGEVITY REVOLUTION

As Boomers Become Elders

Theodore Roszak

BERKELEY HILLS BOOKS
BERKELEY, CALIFORNIA

Published by
Berkeley Hills Books
P. O. Box 9877
Berkeley, California 94709
www.berkeleyhills.com
(888) 848-7303

Comments on this book may also be addressed to: jpstroh@berkeleyhills.com

Cover design by Elysium, San Francisco.

Manufactured in the United States of America.
Distributed by Publishers Group West.
ISBN: 1-893163-50-4

### Library of Congress Cataloging-in-Publication Data

Roszak, Theodore, 1933-
  The longevity revolution : as boomers become elders / Theodore Roszak.
    p. cm.
Rev. ed. of: America the wise. 1998.
Includes bibliographical references and index.
  ISBN 1-893163-50-4 (alk. paper)
  1. Aging--Social aspects--United States. 2. Longevity--Social
aspects--United States. 3. Baby boom generation--United States. 4. Old
age assistance--United States. 5. Social change--United States. 6.
Caring. I. Roszak, Theodore, 1933- America the wise. II. Title.
  HQ1064.U5 R666 2001
  305.26'0973--dc21
                              2001001373

There is no wealth but life. Life, including all its powers of love, of joy, and of admiration. That country is richest which nourishes the greatest number of noble and happy human beings.

— John Ruskin

I am indebted to many people for interviews and consultations. All of the following helped wrap some flesh around the demographic bones of this study: Paul Kleyman, Dr. Allen Harnish, Martin Schiffenbauer, Robert Schutz, Roxanne Lanier, Harold Gilliam, Tyrone Cashman, Sally Bingham, Rachel Remen, Connie Lynch, Lucy Scott, Sue Brand, Royda Crose, Barbara Weiss, Irving Kermish, Betty Soldz, Kerstin Joslyn Schremp, and Robert Giusti. Judy Clarence's research help was especially appreciated.

# Contents

*For little Lucy Castle*
*my granddaughter,*
*a very new person whose future*
*depends on the kindness of elders.*
*Will they measure up to the job?*

# INTRODUCTION

## THE APPROACHING SENIOR DOMINANCE

Longevity held no interest for me until I realized I had a reasonably good chance of living beyond the age of sixty. Like many others of my generation, having lived through an era dominated by an ebullient youth culture, I was inclined to wait as long as possible before I turned my attention to those chapters on old age that wait at the end of one's life story. I had no reason to believe I would find much to interest me there. Dogged for many years by serious illness, I was not even sure there would be much to add to my autobiography beyond middle age.

Then, in the late 1980s I underwent a grueling medical crisis that nearly cost me my life. The disease was rampant ulcerative colitis, a disease that stands a good chance of turning malignant after so many years. I came within inches of that fate. Thanks to a remarkable new surgery that was able to redesign my insides, I was able to rid myself of that threat. More astonishing still, when the ordeal was over, I discovered I was in better health than I had known in thirty years. But most remarkable of all, something was missing that had been haunting me for decades: the grim certainty that I would die young. That had departed with the disease. One morning, much to my amazement, I awoke realizing that I might very well reach old age and had best start thinking about it.

In the crisis I experienced, I was lucky enough to find my way to a medical counselor whose practice included all those aspects of disease and surgical trauma that are left unattended by conventional medicine — the fear, the existential trembling, the blank despair. I recall being told, "People like you — ambitious, competitive professional types — don't stop until you get hit right between the eyes. That's what has happened. You've been hit in a way you can't ignore. Nothing else would do it. Now you know.

You are very, very sick. You might die. So … what are you going to make of that?"

If the disease itself had not brought my life to an abrupt halt, those words would have done the job. I suddenly realized that this was another way to understand my situation. Instead of fleeing from it, which was useless, I might try taking hold of it and staring it in the face.

*You might die. What are you going to make of that?*

Poorly prepared as I was, I decided to make all I could of it. You have to be on the receiving end of that question to understand how frightening and how liberating it can be. For one thing, it permits you to put everything in your life on the back burner because what really matters any longer when you stand in the shadow of death? I laid aside my work, took a leave of absence from my job, emptied my schedule, learned a few basic meditation techniques, and began to attend to a great deal of unfinished business. I was astonished to discover that every aspect of my life changed in magnitude and urgency. Some insights were small, but important. I recalled a remark I had read: "Nobody on his death bed ever regretted that he had not spent more time at the office." How true, how *obviously* true. Why had I never realized that before?

Nothing cuts the ego down to size like a close encounter with death. I came to see that there was actually very little that I *had* to do, very little in all the world that depended on me and me alone. I could not think of anything on my usually busy agenda that could not be left to somebody else to do. I stopped playing the decision-maker who had to make everything work, stood back, and gazed at my life with as much objectivity — and mercy — as I could. It was a memorable episode.

I soon realized that I was passing through a sort of forced early retirement. I had time on my hands. Pure, empty, aimless time. No place to go, nothing to do. I heard that many people have no idea what to do with themselves after they retire. Well, I decided to use my retirement to get serious about life. Had I not been serious before this, during my first fifty years? No, I had simply been *busy.* I had been overscheduled, anxious, job-career-and-money worried. I had been attending conferences, giving lectures, writing articles, penciling in appointments, as if all these things mattered. In brief, I had been a passably normal adult … meaning I had been a troubled soul. If some of what I had spent my time doing was of value, I had nevertheless been doing much of it in the wrong spirit and so had diminished its significance. I had spent fifty years getting older, but not much wiser.

Eventually, the crisis passed, thanks to state-of-the-art surgery. That was another revelation. For the first time in my life, I found myself taking medicine seriously, as a matter of life and death. *My* life, *my* death. Surgeons and nurses had done what no priest or therapist had ever succeeded in doing. They had, without realizing it, forced me to find the meaning of my life.

The years rolled forward. I was a survivor. I would grow old. At this point, I cannot honestly say I am still vitally in touch with the crisis that brought me such penetrating insights. The fact that I had a job to go back to and a pending literary contract made it difficult to hold on to the moment of truth. That was also something I learned: if we look aside for a moment, if we stop staring death in the eye, the distractions of daily life close in upon us like weeds in a garden. Vanity has its strategies. In the Middle Ages, teachers of the *ars moriendi* — the art of dying — would have called these the temptations of the world, the flesh, and the devil. I would not phrase it quite like that, but temptations they were nonetheless.

Then just a few years ago my wife went through an even riskier medical crisis that would surely have taken her life twenty years before. Thanks to another surgical miracle, she survived. In both our cases, I was struck not only by the medical daring and skill that had come to our rescue, but by how utterly casual the doctors were about these ingenious procedures. This was simply what they did all day every day for scores of patients. "Have you performed many bypass surgeries?" I asked the surgeon who was about to open my wife's chest, hold her heart in his hand, and rework her circulatory system. "Hundreds," he replied with a smile and a shrug. He did the job and he did it well. A familiar routine for him. Yet doctors like him were saving lives — my life and my wife's — that would have been lost not so long ago.

After my wife's operation, she and I joined a cardiac rehabilitation program in which, though now in our early sixties, we were among the youngest members. All around us were companions in their seventies and eighties who were actually *improving* their health. Some were in better shape than we were. As a group, we come from many backgrounds, but all of us are united by the same good feeling: being there, simply *being there* to enjoy one another's company. We sing "Happy Birthday" whenever anybody in the class grows a year older. We know how much that means. One more year that might not have happened.

This mixture of risk, awe, and gratitude started me thinking about the dramatic changes in life expectancy that have occurred in my time. Those thoughts grew more searching when, as of the mid-1990s, the media began to issue warnings about the disasters that longevity was threatening to visit upon our society in the years ahead. Social Security ... Medicare ... how could we possibly afford these fiscal horrors? The "horrors" that pundits seemed to have in view included my survival and my wife's. They seemed to be saying we had no right to survive and be alive. *We cost too much. All old people cost too much.*

I winced to hear so many people, many of whom I knew to be smart and well-read, repeating the same words of doom. Up ahead in the twenty-first century, they saw all these *old people* devouring our national wealth — old people who, apparently, would never include *them*. They talked about how we were burdening our children — as if our children might not one day live to be even older than we had. I came upon newspaper editorials blaming our cowardly leaders for not *doing something* about this impending crisis. Next to the editorials there might be cartoons that showed a crocodile labeled "Entitlements" swallowing a poor little bird labeled "Balanced Budget." Balanced Budget was the victim. Entitlements was the villain.

The dissonance between these two things — long life and fiscal fear — was enormous. It stretched my mind to the point of pain. The conventional wisdom of the day seemed to be at war with life itself as it might now be enjoyed by millions.

Clearly, there was something wrong with seeing things that way — as if money mattered more than life. As if there was something else we needed this money for that was more valuable than life. How had we become so confused about the most fundamental values? And how might we see the matter with greater clarity and humanity?

Quite naturally, I viewed these questions with a historian's eye — and discovered I had a few good insights to offer. After all, the aging population that was now supposedly darkening the future was the same population I had once written about in their youth. The baby boomers. I had called them then a "counter culture," young people who, in surprising numbers, had once bravely questioned the authority of all received ideas.

The media seemed to be surprised to discover that they had not vanished in a puff of smoke in 1975 — though there were certainly those on the political scene who were pretending they had. But here they were, two or three decades further along in life, causing a different kind of cultural disruption by the very act of staying alive a good long time.

People who are surviving into what they now know will be a long old age have begun to come to grips with longevity as a personal challenge. They are seeking ways to make creative use of their time, to plan their retirement, to keep their minds sharp and well-informed, and, not least of all, to face the advance of death with courage. But as a society, we have not yet begun to grasp the implications of mass longevity as a social phenomenon. In the pages that follow, we will explore the many contours of this demographic frontier. Most significantly, we will trace our social values, so long dominated by the dynamism of the young and middle aged, as they shift toward the needs of an older society. Be warned: My conclusion will be jarring. I will try to convince you that aging is the best thing that has happened to the modern world, a cultural and ethical shift that looks a lot like sanity.

Choose any statistic that defines modernity. The number of automobiles or computers in the world, the amount of electricity used, the number of flights arriving at airports around the world. None of these is as remarkable or as valuable a sign of progress as the growing life expectancy of people in the industrial societies. Nothing should be a more decisive measure of what it means to be an underdeveloped society than a life expectancy of only forty or fifty years.

Longevity is here to stay and it is destined to increase. We are headed for a future in which we may expect to see streets and shops and public places crowded with older people, but where the sight of a child will become steadily rarer. Nobody has ever lived in a world like this. Few people saw it coming. Fewer still know how to plan for it, because almost nobody has found the moral imagination to say the two things that need most to be said about longevity.

It is inevitable.

It is good.

The aging of the American public is not some stroke of unaccountable bad luck. Although nobody seemed to notice it until the day before yesterday, *all* industrial societies are aging with the momentum of a biological necessity. Industrial societies *have* to age. That is the logic of progress. Unless we can imagine the modern world giving up entirely on medical science and technology, then progress toward ever greater longevity is *inevitable* — as inevitable as the continuing refinement of computers and telecommunications. And unless we can imagine people giving up on life and health as common-sense goals, then longevity is *good* — as good as any humane concern that enjoys a total popular consensus.

Both words are important. "Inevitable" is what you cannot sensibly fight *against*. "Good" is what you fight *for* in life. Put "inevitable" and "good" together, and you have a historical movement, a longevity revolution, as the gerontologist Robert Butler has called it.

In the modern world, nothing inspires people to greater deeds than belonging to a movement, especially if they believe they are riding the wave of the future. For the past two centuries, revolutionary spirits have asserted their claim to the future loudly and violently, as if they were not really certain about their destined success. In the twentieth century, we have seen some very ugly politics grow out of movements that insisted *their* nation, *their* race, *their* class, *their* economic system, owned the future. The movements have come ... and gone, marching away into the past, often leaving a bloody trail behind them. We have learned to treat movements with skeptical caution.

But there is one movement that has secretly owned the future all along. A quiet, gentle, life-enhancing movement called longevity. Few have recognized its cultural importance because its power springs from the simplest of the heart's desires, a prayer to which all but the most despairing have given voice.

*Let me live another day.*

That was the movement I joined on the day I eluded the disease that might have killed me at age thirty, or forty, or fifty. With millions of others, I find myself animated by this stubborn, insistent impulse that meets the doctor's skill with affirmation, guides medical science to its goal, and gives healing a meaning larger than survival.

As a historian, I tend to see human affairs as stories spread out across time, tales that take twists and turns, offer us heroes and villains, and include narrow escapes, heartbreaking losses, moments of triumph. All this is true of the longevity revolution. In my special field of industrial history, that revolution has been fighting its way forward against enormous odds for two centuries. Though the media may only recently have discovered it, longevity has long roots. They reach back to that early industrial world of "dark Satanic mills" where life was brutish and short and living one more day was more than many people dared to hope for. In a very real sense, we can only now read the *real* history of the industrial period, its essential but long hidden direction.

The past two centuries have been a troubled era. No period in history has been more tormented than ours has been by the trials of modernization. We have looked evil in the face. Behind us lie the horrors of world war, racial strife, industrial upheaval, revolutionary violence, imperialist competition, and class warfare. We have lived through a time that added the terms "genocide," "balance of terror," "wage slavery," "death camps," "final solution," "ethnic cleansing," "global warming," "the death of the seas" to our political vocabulary. And yet ... more people are living longer. Who would have expected so bright a prospect to emerge from so dark a period? I cannot help but believe that those whose lives were cut cruelly short by war or persecution would expect us to make the most of this great victory over despair.

My viewpoint on the aging of industrial society, then, is simple but radical in its implications. Our task is to stop resisting the inevitable and to embrace the good.

We are the first generation of the senior dominance. The century that has just ended will be remembered as the last in human history in which the young outnumbered the old. As the beneficiaries of a revolution in life-extending medicine and public health, those of us who are now entering the second half of our lives possess more political influence, greater wealth, more vitality than any older generation before us. When our children become seniors, their life expectancy will have reached one-hundred. By then, grandparents, once the least important people in modern society, will wield the power to determine the fate of nations. Let us hope they will be *good* grandparents, willing to take on responsibilities no older generation has ever been big enough and powerful enough to assume.

The discussion of those responsibilities begins now, with the people of the baby boom generation. The values we choose to live by as we cross into an unexplored demographic frontier cannot help but be a commanding influence in shaping the century to come.

## Some Thoughts for the Second Edition

A large part of this book appeared in 1998 under the title *America the Wise*. The title, more to my publisher's liking than mine, was meant to convey the stately maturity appropriate to old age. The title I preferred, *Longevity Revolution*, was rejected as both too spirited and forward-looking for a book about "the elderly," as my publisher kept referring to the people I was writing about. (As far as I could tell, there was no one on the editorial board who was older than forty-five.) That was my first lesson in the denial that continues to surround the subject of aging in our society. Whoever "the old" may be, they apparently cannot include the baby boom generation, and certainly not anybody who is up and coming in the publishing world.

Under its new title, this book has been substantially revised, not only to update some statistics that have changed along the way, but also to take advantage of all I have learned as an author in writing about aging — and especially the aging of the baby boomers. It is a subject that requires special handling because it is grounded in paradox.

The paradox is this: We live in a world dominated by baby boomers who are growing more senior with each passing day. Yet the baby boom generation continues to be surrounded by an aura of youthfulness, much of it the invention of the mass media whose marketing practices were shaped during the 1960s when boomers were just emerging on the historical stage.

The period known as the baby boom is the unexpected interval of high fertility that stretches from 1946 to 1964. During those years, women in a number of Western nations and in Japan reached a record-breaking birth rate. During the peak years of the boom, American families were running an average of nearly four children, usually born in rapid succession, the high point being 1957 when 4,332,000 babies were born in the United States. That is a veritable Third-World level of reproduction. A population surge of such dimensions could not help but radically change the nation's perception of its identity. Though it made no sense, we began to think of society as growing younger. Who cared about people over fifty ... or even forty? The hot topic was youth. What were young people doing? What did young people want?

Widely shared as it was — I once came close to believing it myself — this may rank as one of the most ignorant views of history on record. Until the post World War II period, it was commonly accepted that all modern societies were growing older as the birth rate dropped steadily. That had been the dominant demographic fact for over two centuries. Seen against that background, the Great Depression was all the gloomier, since the joblessness of the period made the aging parents of younger workers far more of a burden than they would have been in prosperous times.

In 1939, writing in a pioneering anthology on problems of aging, the American social philosopher John Dewey observed with some urgency,

> It is now becoming evident that the changes that have brought about great reduction of infant mortality and the lengthening of the span of life for those who survive the hazards of infancy have had important social effects so that social conditions have been created which confront civilization with issues of the most serious nature.[1]

Then came World War II and the baby boom.

Within a year following the end of the war, women in the United States, Europe, and Japan started reproducing in record numbers and continued doing so for the next nineteen years. How to account for this amazing reproductive outburst? Perhaps it was a spontaneous collective response to the years of depression and war, an assertion of life after so many years of hard times and mass destruction. Whatever the reason, for a period of nearly two decades, America, along with several other industrial countries, seemed destined for eternal youth — as if nobody who had been young in the sixties could ever be expected to grow old. After all, in the mid-sixties, could anyone have imagined that the Rolling Stones would one day be gray and bewrinkled, yet still performing for fans who would bring their children (and eventually their grandchildren) to hear the good old songs?

With the benefit of hindsight, we can see that the boomers have simply been more raw material for the long-term, global trend toward aging. But as they join that trend, they carry with them the image and the reputation they created for themselves in a time of high spirits, youthful protest, and spreading affluence. In the eyes of opinion-makers who found the boomers intolerably self-absorbed and abrasively irreverent as young people, they remain a population deserving hard knocks, a hedonistic "Me Generation" that needs to be taken sternly in hand by their more responsible elders.

But of course this makes no sense. Time marches on, and as it does, boomers have marched on to become the next older generation; they are now our society's elders. Taken together with their children and with their parents, for whose medical and nursing care boomers are now beginning to pay the bills, they have become the population of the industrial world. They define its cultural mainstream just as fully as the generation of the Great Depression and World War II defined the world of the thirties and forties. Spanking boomers amounts to castigating what contemporary America, and indeed the modern world as a whole, has chosen to become: an international order of dynamic market-based economics, high consumption, rapidly developing technology, proliferating media, compulsive travel, frenetic global entrepreneurs, ever more liberated women, ever more extravagantly indulged children, and ever more troubled would-be patriarchal political leaders.

For better or worse, this is who we are today in the high industrial societies; this is the world most underdeveloped societies are struggling to join. As of the year 2000 there has been an effort to polish the image of the boomers' parents — the so-called "greatest generation" — which is fair enough. But the greatness of that generation was a matter of suffering, not choosing. It had depression and war visited upon it. The story of the boomers is quite different. Their destiny has been to act and choose. Born into an unprecedented level of affluence and power, theirs has been the task of sharing the abundance, controlling a runaway global economy, and achieving a sustainable industrial order. Atop the affluence so many among them have known, they now inherit the longevity revolution. How will long life and good health be shared fairly? How will this gift of life be put to use? Other generations have formed their character by bearing up under pressure. The boomers will shape their character by the choices they make.

The baby boom remains an unassimilated historical episode. Boomers often talk about themselves with a certain defensiveness, as if history has given them a reputation they must either live up to or live down. They have surely known more than their share of mean-spirited controversy. Lambasted in their youth as spoiled brats and rebels without a cause, they have grown up to be called other unflattering names: "grabby boomers," "state-of-the-art hypocrites," "the most selfish and irresponsible generation this country has ever produced." Following the 2000 census, the *Chicago Tribune* ran an editorial applauding the fact that boomers would now be dying off more rapidly. Good news for all those who are "irked at the boomers' collective influence and self-centeredness." Boomers, the *Tribune* reminded its readers — most of whom must be boomers — "were noisy and demanding children and adolescents. They have been noisy and demanding adults ... and they promise to be noisy and demanding codgers." Boomers even badmouth themselves. Upon turning fifty, the humorist Dave Barry declared that "we are the self-absorbed, big, fat loudmouth of generations."

Perhaps those who make the accusations have some valid case in point — an incident, a trend, a person or two, a few slogans or graffiti they recollect with rancor. But when we set out to judge something as large and amorphous as a generation, we are rather like the blind men who tried to describe an elephant. Each had a piece of the truth, but only a piece. They were each a little right and a lot wrong.

In writing about any social group, but especially about something as large and ill-defined as a "generation," it is important to avoid casual generalizations. As they move into their senior years, boomers remain as socially and culturally diverse as they were in their youth. Not everybody on the college campuses of the 1960s joined a protest movement. Most did not. Countercultural youth of the 1960s both in the United States and elsewhere around the world were a minority within the minority of young people who went to college. For that matter, in the United States, contemporary conservatism — including its evangelical wing — traces its current following back to boomers who were offended by the dissent of that period.

Diversity will continue within the ranks of boomers as they go into retirement. Those who characterize the over-sixty-five population as a monolithic bloc of voters are indulging in political fantasies — whether to spread fear of a selfish gerontocracy, or to magnify the importance of older voters and their organizational leadership. Both motives are in play in senior politics, and both exaggerate the unity of the older population.

But social diversity, which must always be assumed of any generation, need not rule out the possibility that there are certain experiences that unite people and make them more than a chaotic mass. Out of the turbulent mix of the past fifty years, I have isolated in these pages a single demographic factor that strikes me as the least well-understood, yet potentially the most promising development from the viewpoint of humane social values: the aging of modern society.

This book is predicated on the possibility that the experience of aging changes the tone and quality of life in ways that are as important as any more superficial political differences. People may finish by holding divergent political values, but they may hold them in ways that make them more willing to question their convictions, more capable of bending and adapting in the face of suffering and injustice. I think of that difference of tone as the virtue we call wisdom, and I take it to be one of the gifts that comes with age. Combine that with the common historical experience that boomers share, and one has, at least, the grounds for making an appeal that stands a chance of being heard.

Boomers are the generation that brought the global industrial hegemony to its climax; they are the first generation to pass into their senior years with the power and the savvy to challenge that hegemony. With them, we reach a point of astonishing contradiction.

*The modern world is aging beyond the values that created it.*

Like most historians, I assume that every generation is a mixed bag made up of people who are bravely improvising their lives by the passing hour, hoping to get as much of it right as they can, often falling short of their own highest expectations. Upon closer scrutiny, every generation reveals vices among its virtues, virtues among its vices. If I did not think there was a wealth of idealism and a willing spirit in the people I write for and about, I would not have started this book in the first place. Rather than laying still another judgment upon them, I offer an appeal.

In the years ahead, an increasing number of us will be living decades longer than our parents or grandparents. Imagine, then, adding together all those *extra* years of life. Think of those years as a *resource* — a cultural and spiritual resource reclaimed from death in the same way the Dutch reclaim fertile land from the waste of the sea. During any one of those years, somebody who no longer has to worry about raising a family, pleasing a boss, or earning more money will have the chance to join with others in building a compassionate society where people can think deep thoughts, create beauty, study nature, teach the young, worship what they hold sacred, and care for one another. Once we realize that, we should have no difficulty understanding the most important fact about the longevity revolution. It has given this remarkable generation the chance to do great good against great odds.[2]

---

# CHAPTER ONE

# BOOMERS' DESTINY

A single fact overshadows our entrance into the twenty-first century, a demographic statistic that is simply stated and undisputed. *More people are living longer.* Never before has so large a part of the population been older than sixty as we find today in the industrial societies. Never before has the ratio of age to youth been so high. Half of all the people who ever managed to live to the age of sixty-five in the whole of human history are alive today.

As we enter the twenty-first century, there is one person over the age of sixty for every child below the age of four. Move ahead fifty years. By 2050, there will be ten people over sixty for every three children below the age of four. And that ratio will continue to extend with each passing generation: more people over the age of seventy ... more people over the age of eighty ...

Even stated as unadorned statistics, numbers like this carry formidable cultural implications — and not only for those who are moving into their senior years. Like all major demographic changes, whether plagues or famines, baby booms or great migrations, mass longevity will shape the course of history for generations to come. Even now, it is radically altering political power and social relations.

We are becoming accustomed to seeing cheery or worrisome facets of our changing demographics featured in the news of the day, in reports on the health or the wealth, the foibles and fashions of the senior generation. Some are heartening, even amusing — like the grandmothers' basketball league in southern California whose members, all over seventy and many with hip replacements, remain spirited competitors. Others are filled with an ominous pathos — like the wistful effort by a Denver health center to deal with Alzheimer's disease, a condition that may cost our nation as much as $1 trillion by the middle of the twenty-first century. There the staff has rigged up a mock Norman Rockwell Main Street where Alzheimer's patients, their minds already adrift in time, may roam freely among the familiar sights and sounds of their still-remembered youth: soda fountains, a Bijou movie house, Glenn Miller favorites on the jukebox.

But longevity is far more than a human interest item; it marks not only a massive change but a permanent one. The aging of industrial society is irreversible; now that this demographic current has started, the only direction in which it can run is toward greater senior numbers. Even if there should be other smaller baby booms or "echoes" along the way, the certain destiny of every future generation is to grow older than the one before. By the middle of the twenty-first century, those who fail to reach the age of one hundred (unless by reason of accident) are apt to fall into a new medical category: *premature death*.

This is how longevity appears stated as a bald census statistic. But now add some cultural contours to our new demographic landscape and the century ahead takes on intriguing possibilities.

Never before have people over the age of sixty controlled so much wealth or exerted so much political influence. In contrast to times past, when the elderly were marginal and powerless, seniors have become a coveted voting bloc and a potentially lucrative market.

Never before have people approaching their senior years enjoyed the advantage of so much education and travel. Nor have they ever bulked so large in the popular culture of the nation. They are avidly pursued for university coursework and museum shows, they are the most reliable season-ticket audience for the opera and symphony, they are a highly prized market for book clubs and the lecture circuit. For the first time in modern history, the senior population is beginning to be treated as if its tastes and interests matter.

Never before has the population aged seventy, eighty, and even ninety included so many physically and mentally active people. Most obviously, this is because no older generation has ever had so much access to health care. But there is also the fact that no previous generation has been so health- and fitness-conscious; today's seniors are eager to participate in caring for their own health by exploring alternative medicines and making radical changes in their habits of living. By fits and starts they are revolutionizing the way in which nations distribute and pay for health care, making it a major item in economic policy, an ever richer source of income and profit, an ever more important focus of investment and invention.

Never before has a senior generation possessed enough technical skill, professional training, and intellectual astuteness to consider staying on the job well beyond the legal retirement age. Nor have people over the age of sixty-five ever looked so much like a viable and sizable workforce, a labor pool that may be better equipped to compete for jobs than the younger generation.

Never before have so many people entered their senior years by way of a medical crisis, a contemporary rite of passage that brings them face to face with their own mortality. The cultural and political importance of that increasingly commonplace and widely shared experience should not be overlooked. Death, if one survives its first call, is a great awakener of conscience and a summons to serious reflection. The folk wisdom of World War II had it that there were no atheists in foxholes. Similarly, few people come out of intensive care wards less philosophically inclined than they went in. I have found in talking to people who have had such a brush with death what is clearly a sense of gratitude, as if the experience, terrifying as it was, had suddenly deepened their lives and given them a welcome occasion for radical reappraisal.

Finally, add one more factor to this generational profile, a defining feature of the baby boom generation. Never before has an older generation been conversant with so many divergent ideas and dissenting values. These are, after all, the people who, in their teens and twenties, lived through a time of principled protest that seemed determined to subject every orthodoxy, every institution, every received idea in our society to critical inquiry. It is the generation whose cultural repertory blithely mixed and matched western political ideology with Asian religions, Native American lore with high tech, psychotherapy with psychedelic drugs. It questioned authority on the basis of sources and insights that had no precedent in the modern western world. I have sometimes suspected that the effort made by many pundits to diminish the importance of that period stems from their fear that, in age as in youth, the boomers represent an unpredictable force for sweeping change.

Then (as now) those of a more conservative temperament were understandably concerned that so irreverent an attack upon authority could erode civility and weaken conformity. They were at least half right. Youthful dissent often produced upheaval and disrespect. But the right wing of American politics may have worse to worry about in the years ahead. Elder insurgency may prove to be far more unsettling than rebellion among the young. In a society where numbers and power are destined to gravitate steadily in the direction of age, one cannot write off the views and values of the senior generation as mere youthful effervescence; nor can one simply wait for the insurgents to grow up and move along in life. The future belongs to maturity.

## SINCE THE SIXTIES

This last point is especially important for me. When I wrote *The Making of a Counter Culture* in 1969 (the subtitle was *Reflections on the Technocratic Society and its Youthful Opposition*) I included this observation: "The ethos of disaffiliation is still in the process of broadening down through the adolescent years, picking up numbers as time goes on. ... Generational conflict will not vanish when those who are now twenty reach thirty, it may only reach its peak when those who are now eleven and twelve reach their late twenties."[1]

Given my age and perspective when I wrote the book — a young academic living and working among a strange new breed of student on the country's university campuses — I could not imagine anybody radically changing the course of history except the young, unless it was the younger still. By "generational conflict" I meant the struggle of the then-young against the then-old in behalf of a more humane, more tolerant, more intellectually adventurous society.

But in the years since then, I have come to see that the very notion of change permeating that study was a young man's way of seeing life. To believe that change comes from ideological fervor, that history is made by imposing bright, untested ideas on life, is a sad, though all too common, misunderstanding — whether the ideas are liberal, radical, or conservative. It takes some growing up and some growing old to learn that life-affirming and enduring change comes not from theories or principles ("headtripping," as we once called it) but from a wisdom of the heart — by which I mean the truths people learn from a full and well-examined life.

So my prediction was wide of the mark, if for no other reason than that it paid too little attention to living history. Like many another social critic, I failed to see the obvious. The big boomer generation that was in its teens and twenties in the 1960s was not destined to disappear when it ceased to be a "youthful opposition." If at some point boomers passed through a "big chill," there would be plenty of time for the chill to thaw. They would live on to become fifty, sixty, seventy, still there on the stage of history, battered perhaps by the years but better prepared to change the world than they were in their high school and college years. And given their need to defend and expand the nation's entitlements programs, they might feel an even more urgent need to transform their society than they had in their youth.

Meanwhile — and how ironically! the next younger generation I had in mind when I wrote that passage were destined to have a very different course of life than I foresaw, one that made them more timid, more bewildered, more stymied than I would have thought possible. The children of the baby boom generation began reaching their teens and twenties at the height of the Reagan presidency, during a conservative backlash of historic proportions. They came of age during a militant campaign to denigrate everything the protest movement of the 1960s and 1970s had championed. Throughout the 1980s, conservative think tanks vilified the counter culture of that day for challenging parental authority and for all that presumably followed from that challenge: movements for racial equality and social justice, women's and gay liberation, the ideal of participative democracy, a heightened environmental consciousness. Almost as if the social upheaval of the 1960s had fatigued America to the bone, protest went into hibernation to be replaced by what the historian Sidney Blumenthal has called a "daydream decade, when wish fulfillment became national policy."

I now believe that a far more promising future — at least from my dissenting viewpoint on urban industrial society — depends not upon the youth of the nation, but upon the initiative of those who are reaching their fifties and sixties as of the beginning of the twenty-first century. Not only is the older population of our day larger in numbers, but it constitutes *a different kind* of older population. Nothing we assumed about age in the past will fit these people. That is why we seem to be having some difficulty finding an appropriate name for them. Those who take up the subject of the baby boomers (or even of seniors already retired as of the 1990s) seem reluctant to call them "old," much less "elderly." As for the cute "gold," "gray," and "silver" euphemisms that were coined for our grandparents, all these have become cloying enough to set one's teeth on edge. Labels like these, freighted with an outmoded sense of fatigue and dependency, are terms we once used for a population that clung to the shadowed margins of life, *there* but not importantly there.

Polling the baby boomers for fun or profit has become a favorite Sunday supplement topic over the past decade. Their tastes, their values, their ways with marriage, money, and careers are subjects of endless fascination to advertisers and editorial writers. But one need only make a cursory personal survey of the over-fifty population we find around us — including yourself if you are in that category — to see the striking difference between past-old and future-old. How many are stereotypic cranks and codgers whom life has passed by? What one more and more commonly finds are hungry minds, physical vitality, keen perception, lively tastes, political know-how, even ambition: people who fully expect to get a lot older before they admit to being *old*, people not to be dismissed or treated with condescension.

Of course, they are not superhuman; time still takes its toll on mind and body, if at an increasingly later age. Though some among them may be delivered by their genes into the cruel ravages of dementia, not many will become doddering, senile incompetents. Like so many other social roles — male, female, black, Hispanic, Native American, gay — "old" is being radically redefined in our time by people themselves. Age is becoming varied to the point of unpredictability, and so it is becoming interesting to study. And even more interesting to experience.

THE EXPANDING SENIOR SPECTRUM:
FROM FIFTY TO ONE HUNDRED

As longevity assumes the dimensions of a second lifetime, we must be more precise about its demographic definition. The terms "seniors," "elders," "retired" — all of which I use in these pages as the context dictates — run the risk of blurring more than they clarify. Just as we have learned, in dealing with youth, to distinguish childhood from adolescence and adolescence from young adulthood, so we must begin making more refined distinctions about the senior years, distinctions that have less to do with calendar age and physical condition and more to do with sociology or culture. The greatest mistake one can make about age is to see it as a fixed social identity rather than as a spectrum encompassing a wide range of diversity and creative improvisation.

Throughout this book, I suggest that the longevity revolution requires a new *cultural demographics* that draws upon aspects of mind and value even more than on physical condition. Age needs to be surrounded by history. We will want to know what people have lived through and what vision of life they carry with them into an ever extending seniority. For example, the entire population we will be studying here might, by way of a rough historical classification, be thought of as *World War I seniors*, *World War II seniors*, and *Vietnam War seniors*. In each case, the upheaval of war was the defining moment of their generation. But the wars were very different wars, and the experience they provided dictated very different values.

Within this historical-biographical continuum, the baby boom generation is one of three senior "cohorts" — as demographers call them — that differ significantly yet share a common fiscal interest and potentially a common electoral force. At times I will distinguish them as *senior old*, *middle old*, and *boomers*. Each of these groups is a cross-section of the society at large; nothing I say here about age is meant to discount the role that class, race, ethnicity, and religion play in defining and dividing people. But age, as it grows more politically empowered, is an increasingly important social identity, one that may become a stronger bond between people in the years ahead as they have more time to be old together. Above all, one must remember that these cohorts are interrelated by family ties. That means they share problems in ways that social classes or races do not.

So, for example, what aging may bring to the middle old — medical expenses, nursing home costs, Alzheimer's Disease — are as much problems of their midlife boomer children as of themselves. And in turn, those in their later midlife have to begin thinking seriously about their retirement well before they reach sixty-five. In this way, aging creates a political constituency that may unite people from age forty to age eighty. The sense short-sighted teens and twenty-somethings may hold that aging is not relevant to them is best seen as an aberrant and transient belief they will soon outgrow.

## THE SENIOR OLD

Now in their eighties, nineties, and over one hundred, the senior old are also known as the "oldest old," a term coined for the age eighty-five-plus population by the American Association for the Advancement of Science in 1984. The distinction had an admitted political purpose. It was meant to call attention to the fact that gerontologists regard the over-eighty-fives as a special demographic category with needs and problems all its own that should not be confused physiologically or sociologically with those of the younger old, especially where questions of intergenerational equity are concerned.[2]

The 3 million senior old, whose lives have spanned much of the century, arrived at old age before any of the social-psychological changes we review in this book took place. The oldest among them, the 50,000 centenarians (85 percent of them women), lived out their youth in the aftermath of the first war to be called a "world war." The America they grew up in was the society Norman Rockwell was drawing for covers on the *Saturday Evening Post*. They remember the great boom of the 1920s and the crash that followed. They were young adults when the phrase "Age of Anxiety" was coined; they became parents in time to send their children into another and bloodier world war.

The senior old can remember when Social Security was created as a favor to the elderly. They may not be entirely certain that they are really "entitled" to such entitlements. Many among the senior old accepted the status of "old" in the 1960s and 1970s when the elderly were expected to retire from life in every sense of the word. When Robert Butler made his classic study of them in 1975, he began by calling "old age," as they knew it, a "tragedy." He titled his book *Why Survive?* and did not come up with an encouraging answer.

Brave survivors though they are, many of the senior old have spent their final years haunted by the stereotype of senility. Often lacking the benefits of adequate health care, they may be finishing out their lives as the most restricted of our nursing home population. In that respect, they have been used ideologically to raise the daunting prospect that our society will be overwhelmed by a growing population of chronically ill, hopelessly demented basket cases. As of the year 2000 it is estimated that the national doctor's bill for the senior old is running about $80 billion. There would be good reason for such fears if the health of our older population as a whole were not improving so rapidly. Some estimates predict between 20 and 40 million people will be aged eighty-five or older by 2040, perhaps as many as 4 million of them centenarians.[3]

As Robert Binstock observes, the oldest old could become a means of scapegoating the entire aging generation for the rising cost of health care. "It is more than possible that the subgroup of persons aged 85 and over will become subject to stereotyping on the basis of multiple old-age categories. 'The oldest old,' in contrast with 'the aging,' could well become a common label for extreme conditions of frailty, disease, disability, and social dependency among the elderly."[4]

It will be a major point of this book that the medical history and comparative political timidity of the senior old belong to the past. The senior old are "old" in a sense that is vanishing from society. Their place is already being taken by a different breed.

Yet while decades separate centenarians from baby boomers, there is a curious bond across those years. People half the age of centenarians have begun to see their future in these aging faces. As we seek to unlock the secrets of longevity, the 100-plus population is receiving more professional attention than ever before, as if they have important secrets to teach us. Far from being the social curiosities they once were, the very old are, in effect, modeling an old age the rest of us can more and more realistically expect to reach. We take courage from all we learn about their often remarkable capacities, but we also have more to fear in what we see of their inevitable decline. More of us can now expect to reach their age and to live longer with whatever burdens the oldest old. Scholars and medical researchers around the world now study the oldest old to find out how they got to be one hundred, how they see the world, what their powers and limits may be. All this has become a matter of great fascination to a public reading paperbacks with titles like *DARE to Be 100, Stop Aging Now!, You're Not Old Until You're 90, How to Live to 100.*[5]

One hundred is coming to be seen as a feasible life expectancy — but (so we hope) with a far higher standard of vitality and self-respect.

## THE MIDDLE OLD

The middle old, now in their sixties and seventies, are well along in the project of changing the body and the soul of aging. Not only do they have more years ahead of them than any previous generation, but they *know* they have those years and are out to make the most of them. At senior centers where I lecture and in my history courses at the university, I continue to be impressed by the number of retirees I meet who display none of the mental or emotional hallmarks of age. Thanks to the organizational and lobbying efforts of groups like the National Council of Senior Citizens, the Gray Panthers, and the American Association of Retired Persons (AARP), and to the publications and programs that have grown up around those groups, the middle old realize vividly that they are part of a significant demographic transition.

The middle old include among their number the better-off, more active retirees of the post-World War II boom who have become a substantial market for upscale vacations, spas, aerobics classes, university extension courses, investment seminars, growth center programs, and retirement communities. These are the people we see in television commercials dancing the night away aboard a cruise ship.

Inevitably, the wealth controlled by the middle old, whether in the form of personal savings or their claim to entitlements, has drawn some treacherous attention. The financial community has tried to persuade the richest among them to abandon Social Security and Medicare in favor of privatized medical insurance and a stock market portfolio. So far, the middle old have proven to be wary, heeding the warnings of mainstream seniors' organizations like the AARP that depositing the Social Security nest egg in a national 401(k) plan would, at best, benefit only the well-to-do few who have money enough to risk and who may possess more experience as investors. Indeed, the real purpose behind the effort by budget-minded conservatives to entrust Social Security to Wall Street may be to divide the senior generation by driving a wedge between the more affluent and those of modest means, so that the latter can be cut back to the minimum. Social Security currently provides over 80 percent of income for Americans in the lowest 20 percent of the U.S. population. It provides only 17.7 percent for those in the highest 20 percent. As Binstock observes, "Some older persons have much more at stake than others do in policy proposals that would reduce, maintain, or enhance Social Security benefit payments."[6]

The strategy may work, But it could also have an unforeseen outcome. It may unite the entire older generation against the entitlements critics. Nothing builds solidarity among people as effectively as a shared sense of danger and injustice.

Our first full-fledged "entitlements generation," the middle old have been politically targeted from more than one direction. Conservative critics have called them "greedy geezers," including those who have saved enough of their own money to retire in comfort. More liberal political activists have castigated the middle old in states like Florida, California, and Arizona for voting to defeat bond issues and social programs that would benefit children and adolescents. As these critics see it, the entire older population — senior old, as well as middle old — is pursuing an "anti-youth agenda" in favor of "Aid to Dependent Seniors."[7]

Minority group leaders have charged that the nonwhite poor, concentrated in an "immigrant belt" that includes California, New York, Texas, and Illinois, are especially burdened by the costs of "publicly subsidized welfare" for seniors. In the coming century, they foresee "the prospect of young minority workers supporting the mostly white elderly." One demographer goes so far as to predict a "coming war" over entitlements dollars between states dominated by the "old white" and the "young diverse."[8]

Among the senior groups most often singled out for voting its selfish interest on issues like school bonds is the Silver Haired Legislature, a Florida lobby that has been described as a "political powerhouse."[9] Yet as of the 1990s, there is no good evidence that senior Americans have as yet gelled into any kind of a predictable voting bloc. "Diversity among older persons," Robert Binstock observes, "may be at least as great with respect to political attitudes and behavior as it is in relation to economic, social, and other characteristics."[10] Gerontologists have found very little statistical support for the "senior power model" of politics in any country — at least when it comes to some knee-jerk response in defense of social programs like the American entitlements. In a recent thorough survey of senior voting habits, Binstock concludes

There is no sound reason to expect that a birth cohort diverse in economic and social status, labor force participation, gender, race, ethnicity, religion, education, health status, family status, residential locale, political attitudes, partisan attachments, and every other characteristic in American society — would suddenly become homogenized in self-interests and political behavior when it reaches the old-age category. ... Moreover, if some older voters primarily identify themselves in terms of their age status, this does not mean that their self-interests in old-age policy issues are the most important factors in their electoral decisions. Other policy issues, altruism, the characteristics of specific candidates, long-standing partisan attachments, and many other stimuli in an electoral campaign can be of equal or greater importance.

Binstock places the senior power model in the category of "electoral bluff," which is not to deny it any influence since that bluff might be used by skillful politicians.[11]

Only the AARP, of all senior organizations, comes close to having serious political influence. But under scrutiny, the AARP, so often cited as the authoritative voice of senior America, reveals significant internal divisions and has been charged with being considerably more liberal than seniors who come out of the business community.[12] All of which is not to say that senior power could not become a significant factor in the years ahead, perhaps as powerful as organized labor once was. True, even when all the boomers have reached retirement age, the total senior vote will amount to only one-quarter of the eligible voting public. But older Americans are the country's most reliable voters; their turnout vastly outweighs younger voters. Nearly 70 percent of eligible voters over age sixty-five turned out in the elections of 1996 and 2000. Moreover, it is not as if age sixty-five is a clear line of political demarcation. With effective organization and education, senior interests may influence the voting patterns of their middle-aged children, who have a stake in the entitlements that provide their parents with financial independence. In any case, political power cannot be wholly gauged by voting. There is also the time, the energy, the money, and the leg work that the next older generation may be willing to put into election politics.

All the more reason to recognize the burden of conscience that lies on the middle old. If they continue to be portrayed as the grasping beneficiaries of a "racial generation gap," they will surely see their entitlements and those of future seniors come under ever more severe attack. As I suggest in chapter five, the worst course senior politics could take, both ethically and economically, would be to limit itself to a narrow, entitlements-based agenda that assumes there is not enough wealth in the nation to provide generously for young and old alike.

Until the baby boom generation moves into retirement, the public image and moral character of senior America rests heavily on the shoulders of the middle old. Some students of senior sociology have already called for retired Americans to face up to that responsibility. For example, Gerald Larue, who has created the field of "geroethics," argues poignantly for an "ethical elderhood."

> Like all ethical elders, I am naturally concerned with events, policies, and programs that affect the well-being and health of those in my

own bailiwick. But that is not enough. That worldview is too small, too limited. We elders have moved beyond the world we inherited sixty-five and more years ago and have been instrumental in developing global awareness. ... Our concerns for one another must be familial, bridging racial, ethnic, territorial, and all other gaps that today separate us.[13]

I would expect views like this to become more prominent as the middle old give way to the growing numbers and influence of the boomers, whose political strength should make them far more secure about their own interests.

## AND FINALLY ... THE BOOMERS

The baby boom generation now entering its fifties and early sixties is most clearly characterized by not feeling old at all, and, often enough, not looking it or acting it. A more refined analysis divides the boomers into a "leading edge" (born 1946-1954) and a "trailing edge" (born 1955-1964). But both these groups are allied in not quite feeling their age. "Funny, We Don't Feel Old," proclaims a band of Americans aged fifty to seventy pictured on the front cover of the March 7, 1997 *New York Times Magazine.* Their stories are personal accounts of undiminished ambition and bustling activity, a style called "productive aging" that we will want to investigate in chapter seven.

Whether with enthusiasm or trepidation, everyone agrees that the boomers will be a senior generation of great consequence. For some, the nearly 80 million boomers are the source of fiscal nightmares. But a simple head count with a price tag attached is hardly sufficient to tell their story. These are the children of a deeply transformative episode in American culture. Just as their parents were marked by the Great Depression of the 1930s, so the boomers were shaped by Great Affluence of the postwar decades. What they learned about abundance and scarcity, wants and needs, from that remarkable episode in our history will be an indispensable part of the debate over entitlements.

Expecting more out of life than their parents, they will not easily be guilt-tripped into surrendering their share of the national wealth. If politicians think the middle old have been pushy about their rights, wait until they have to deal with the next senior generation. There is already a lively awareness among boomers that their independence in retirement is closely connected to their *interdependence* with the rest of the community. Boomer women, destined to be their generation's majority gender, have already grasped their role as "agents for change" in American life. They have wisely come to see ageism within the same spectrum of prejudice as sexism and racism.[14]

When, in 1972, Maggie Kuhn, a gentle but tough older woman from a YWCA and Quaker background, found herself unhappy with the existing style of senior politics, it was an omen of things to come. Then in her mid-sixties, she decided to rally her peers to play a nobler role in the boisterous politics of her time.

> We wanted to go beyond the national groups for "senior citizens" that had already been established, the highly successful American Association of Retired Persons and the National Council of Senior Citizens. These organizations, we felt, didn't encourage older people to take control of their lives or to concern themselves with large social issues. Fighting for services and privileges for their members, many organizations for the old fell into the special interest pit, as if the old were saying to the young, "We worked damned hard and we're going to get ours."

Kuhn's vision was more daring. "The old, having the benefit of life experience, the time to get things done, and the least to lose by sticking their necks out, were in a perfect position to serve as advocates for the larger public good."[15] The organization she founded fancifully took the name Gray Panthers. A small, feisty group that continues to welcome intergenerational membership, the Gray Panthers have outlasted the Black Panthers and continue to pursue justice for elders with an eye to the community at large.

If I were asked to guess what direction boomers will take when they become the next senior generation, I suspect a number of them will choose something rather like Maggie Kuhn's vision, a reassertion of the ideal of community and the politics of advocacy. One sees that prospect emerging in industrial societies everywhere as the "women's agenda," a compendium of liberal social programs that emphasizes education, child-care, welfare, health and safety, and the environment. There is one thing more to be said in favor of the Panther style: Maggie Kuhn's way points toward adventure. And choosing adventure is the one best way to stave off what age has meant at its most melancholy, namely that one stops growing and gives up on the future.

But there may be more in store for boomers besides social action as we have known it in the past. Especially as the discussion of our national wealth unfolds in the minds of a senior generation in search of life's higher values, we may see our politics grow more searchingly philosophical than anyone could imagine when entrepreneurial values ruled the world. It promises to be a distinguishing quality of the longevity revolution that great questions of fate and purpose will force themselves upon our awareness and into the political realm.

## Opening a Demographic Frontier

This book works from the assumption that the baby boom generation is pioneering a demographic frontier where every aspect of our culture — politics, the arts, work, love, family, education, the media, the marketplace — will experience great change. Yet, at this point, the way into that vast, unknown terrain is through the narrow door of a single heated social issue. Entitlements. Understandably, what has first come to our attention about the longevity revolution is the senior generation's growing need for secure subsistence and costly medical care. As that need begins to shape our economic priorities, far-reaching political choices are being forced upon us. In the years ahead, those choices will no longer be made as they were in the past. Instead of being made *for* seniors, they will be made *by* and *with* seniors, and most decisively by the boomers, the most adventurous, assertive, astute senior generation we have known. In time, they will colonize the demographic frontier as a whole, making their needs ever more central. Surviving longer than seniors before them, they will eventually become the oldest old — but in unprecedented numbers, leaving behind them a new, activist identity for seniors who follow.

This is what makes the entitlements issue a key ideological battleground. As a matter of bread-and-butter daily necessity, the 40 million Americans now living on entitlements are the largest component of the welfare state. They will soon be joined by another 80 million Americans as the baby boom ages into retirement. It is as if life itself in this era of longevity were recruiting tens of millions for a political orientation that undermines conservative opposition to big government. Hence the shrill urgency surrounding discussions of Social Security and Medicare.

In 1997 the ultra-conservative Paul Tsongas Project held a national public forum dedicated to "Generational Responsibility: The Future of Social Security and Medicare." It called for swift action "before the baby boom becomes the senior boom." It identified that interval as "the window of opportunity." Apparently the hope is that citizens in their forties and fifties will prove unable to imagine living to retirement age and will conveniently rush to act against their own interests, as well as those of their parents.

Senior citizens have proven to be odd political animals. As the stereotype would have it, they supposedly become more hidebound and cautious as they grow older. Thus, they are usually thought of as natural allies of the conservative right: property-conscious, backward-looking, and fearful of change. Yet no group is more dependent upon the big federal programs that conservatives are out to dismantle. If it were not for the entitlements programs, anti-government conservatives might have little trouble riding roughshod over every social program in the federal budget.

If expensive government programs are what conservatives have in mind when they revile the evils of liberalism, then, existentially speaking, the senior citizens of this country are the most deeply entrenched liberals on the political landscape. As every politician who stumps America's retirement communities discovers, seniors are apt to be tough-minded about the stake they hold in the nation's wealth. They are not easy to slap down. What have they got to lose that can be legally taken away from them? "Retirement," as the Gray Panthers say, "is like being rich. Nobody can fire you."

More than any mere fiscal consideration, that fact explains the panic that now dominates the entitlements debate. The strident concern that conservative critics display is much more than budgetary. What they fear is the growing power of the one group in our population that is best placed to question market values and competitive individualism. Not only are these numbers large and growing, but they are predominantly female — the constituency least likely to support individualistic and macho social values. As one gerontologist put it to me, "The future belongs to estrogen. That's what the conservatives are afraid of, especially when it comes at them in the form of millions of assertive older women who vote."

There may be something about the senior population that business and political leaders fear even more. *Wisdom*, the hard-won result of experience and reflection. Business elites who are working so feverishly to transform the planet into a hard-charging global economy demand an unquestioning obedience to the laws of the marketplace. To that end, they are committed to the smooth manipulation of taste and the engineering of consensus. The last thing they want is a searching discussion of the meaning of life, its highest values and ethical responsibilities. In effect, they cannot afford wisdom. But questions that lead to wisdom are what fill the minds of people as they grow older.

In this there is a deep contradiction. People over fifty are with us in such numbers because of industrial progress; they are among the major beneficiaries of modern technology and medical science. Yet the values that come naturally with longevity are not the values that made that progress possible in the first place. In many ways, the values of the older generation may become exactly the opposite. Their beliefs may lead them to a penetrating critique of modernity as they age beyond its hectic pace and market-driven values.

One can see this contradiction in very human and graphic terms in any airport. Air travel is one of the hallmarks of modernity. Every airport in every major city is a thronging hive of busy people on their way to do something important that requires rush and bustle — even if it is meant to be a vacation. On all sides one sees intense executive types, their heads filled with money and worry, studying their watches and jabbering into cell phones as they career through the crowds to catch a connecting flight or find their waiting limo. The air is filled with announcements of departures for Tokyo, Cairo, Brussels ... And there, more and more often, one sees the elderly being slowly guided through the crowd in wheelchairs or electric carts, holding up the line, blocking the corridor, getting in the way. Airports were not built for them. That is why the airlines must hire more and more people to escort them to their seats, handle their tickets and luggage, or simply wheel them out of the way, a costly new service that will have to expand — for the old do indeed travel. They are customers no airline wishes to turn away. And yet ... what a trouble they are!

I confess that I have begun to take a certain perverse satisfaction in seeing these prime beneficiaries of progress "getting in the way." I watch the irritated expressions on the faces of those who must stand and wait. I think, "If you're lucky enough, one day you will be that elderly passenger, still traveling the world at the age of seventy or eighty and slowing that world down. But by then there may be more of you than of aggravated young onlookers. When that time comes, expect the elevators and escalators to run slower, the traffic lights to change at a more leisurely speed, the freeways to lose their fast lane. And if you find that irritating, write it off as sound medical advice. You might be paying a psychiatrist $200 an hour to tell you to slow down and lower the stress in your life."

That the elderly should drop away and dissent from the dynamic, world-beating ambitions of the young is not remarkable. But never before have elders possessed the social clout to make their values count in matters of policy and the distribution of wealth.

## "The Causes and Beginnings of Great Events"

> I publish and set forth these conjectures of mine, which make hope
> in this matter reasonable, just as Columbus did before that
> wonderful voyage of his across the Atlantic, when he gave the reasons
> for his conviction that new lands and continents might be
> discovered, which reasons, though rejected at first, were afterwards
> made good by experience, and were the causes and beginnings of
> great events.
> — Francis Bacon, *The New Organon*, 1620

Over the course of the last century, ever since futuristic thinkers began brainstorming "things to come," we have had many prophetic scenarios laid before us. Almost all of them have been obsessed with technology, committed to the idea that industrial development will continue onward and upward without limit. Futurologists continue to conjure up visions of space colonies and the exploration of galaxies far, far away. Yet among all these visions of power and plenty, nobody who has looked into the future has foreseen a world dominated — some would say burdened — by the needs and values of *old* people. Nothing would have seemed more unlikely and less welcome.

Industrial society, even under the leadership of politicians and entrepreneurs bent with years, has always been in spirit a society of youth, never of age, a society obsessed with the latest, the newest, the daringly innovative. Tough, old men — the alpha males I will discuss in chapter ten — may retain power in that society, but they dare not act their age, lest they seem too old to govern. Age, so the modern world assumes, belongs to the

40

past; it reeks of decrepitude, despair, and death. It is therefore given little voice in deciding the future. Nobody ever expected much of the old; they have rarely expected much of themselves. Now they will be with us in increasing numbers; their needs will claim an ever higher priority.

Someday our era, the era of the boomers, will belong to the past. Perhaps only with hindsight will people then realize that we have undergone a fateful transition. Historians may then look back and observe that this is where longevity began to make all the difference, this is where industrial society turned a corner and at last had the chance to catch its breath and reflect upon its greater human purpose. How will they record that transition?

Will it be seen despairingly as the time when our society defaulted on a promise to its senior population that it could not find the wit or the will to afford? Will it be the onset of a slump that blighted our brightest hopes? Will it be remembered as a war of the generations that pitted old against young and finally impoverished both?

Or will the aging of the boomers be remembered as the opening of a true postindustrial era in which the compulsive drive to get and spend lost its appeal? At this point, there is no certainty about how the matter will go. Our current crop of political leaders surely shows no certain grasp of the situation. In the summer of 1997, at the G7 summit of industrial nations, the growing population of retired workers was unanimously identified as a major crisis in the making, one that threatened bankruptcy. Drastic changes would have to be made — though nobody knew quite what. It occurred to no one that the number of healthy, secure senior citizens a society supports might be designated as *the new criterion of economic success*.

I will, in chapters four and five, turn to the economic aspects of longevity, seeking to show that there are many ways to handle the costs gracefully. But it makes all the difference in the world how we regard that cost. Context is everything.

Imagine, then, that we find ourselves transported back to the time of Christopher Columbus. The great explorer returns to announce what he has found beyond the edge of the sea. But, amazing to say, the decision-makers and opinion-leaders of his day take no interest. Instead, they drown him out in an angry dispute over docking fees! "Too expensive," they cry. "No more voyages like this! We cannot afford them!"

Had that happened, might we not expect that someone would have spoken up in exasperation, rather like this: "Here now, gentlemen! You are missing the point. There is a new world beyond the seas. That is the future. Remarkable things lie before you."

The image I use here, the voyage of discovery, holds a special place in the intellectual history of the modern world. It is the metaphor Francis Bacon invoked four centuries ago when he undertook to revolutionize Western thought. There are seas of the mind, he announced, that promise more riches than all the oceans that have yet been sailed. Among the intellectual discoveries he anticipated was the very science that has given us longevity as its greatest benefit. In his time, Bacon believed the worst barrier to progress was despair, so he presented his work as a "gospel of hope" in which readers would find "the causes and beginnings of great events."

This book has much the same purpose. A new world is opening before us — not across the seas, not in outer space, not in cyberspace, but in time. *Living* time. Longevity is our voyage of discovery. As we will see in later pages, that voyage is affordable by any rational accounting — so easily affordable, indeed, that money is the least interesting issue to address. Far more fascinating are the powers of the mind, the resources of the spirit, that wait to be explored.

_____

# CHAPTER TWO

# THE ATTACK ON ENTITLEMENTS

H ad you opened any newspaper in the United States at the beginning
of the twentieth century, you would almost certainly have come
upon a dire warning. It might have read something like this: "What possible defense has the white man against awakening and oncoming Asia?
Asiatics swarm by millions. They must not be allowed to overturn our
civilization, nor be permitted to turn us into Asiatics by ruinous economic
competition."[1]

Politicians took up the theme; churches and social groups spoke out
on the issue. Across the nation, the public was convinced that Western
society would soon be overwhelmed by the hungry hordes of Asia. The
issue combined fear with righteous indignation and added up to a good
hate — always a guaranteed political success.

It was called the Yellow Peril. A combination of false statistics and
racial bigotry, the campaign served to dictate Asian immigration policy for
decades to come.

## BEWARE THE GRAY PERIL!

Now, at the dawn of the twenty-first century, Americans are once
again hearing dark predictions of economic doom. This time the threat
arises much closer to home. The campaign is not racist, but ageist. The
menace is now the Gray Peril: the 40 to 50 million retirees who are drawing their entitlements under Social Security and Medicare, and whose ranks
will soon be augmented by 80 million baby boomers. Just as a century ago
the teeming masses of Asia appeared in political cartoons as scrawny, slant-
eyed vermin swarming across the Pacific to devour our national wealth, so
now we have similarly fearful caricatures of the elderly. Newspaper edito-

rial pages show potbellied, bewrinkled oldsters living it up on the golf course, presumably on their children's money. Or they are shown lounging atop a mountain of cash, feasting on the wealth of the nation. "The widespread failure to die in a timely fashion," as Richard Leone sardonically puts it, "has inspired countless predictions of political chaos and economic ruin in the industrialized countries."[2]

It is particularly unsettling to realize that the image of the senior as greedy geezer first emerged in the *New Republic* (the issue of March 28, 1988), on most issues a reasonably liberal publication. It appeared as part of a diatribe by Henry Fairlie against retired Americans. Castigated as a selfish burden to the nation, seniors were depicted on the cover of the magazine as an army of odious old parasites massing to defend their privileges as an undeserving leisure class. There was a strange irony to this accusation. It came upon the heels of a frantic effort during the 1980s to persuade the Reagan administration to raise the Social Security payroll tax. That had in fact been done in 1983 partly under the guidance of Alan Greenspan. And why had the tax been raised? Social Security is legally obliged to think ahead. The 1983 fix was in anticipation of what the baby boom generation would cost as it came due for retirement from 2008. Thus, the rising costs that entitlements critics were blaming on greedy geezers over the age of sixty-five were in reality the costs that would begin to register for the *next* retirement generation, the boomers. The people who least deserved to be blamed by fiscal conservatives for the higher Social Security tax — if indeed anybody deserved to be blamed at all — were Americans already in retirement during the 1980s.

But before the injustice of that accusation could be clearly recognized by the public, entitlements critics had found a marvelously effective way of confusing the issue still further. They had invented the "entitlements trick," as Dean Baker has called it. They had begun to amalgamate Social Security and Medicare into one big tax bill called "entitlements," even though these are different programs financed in different ways and with a different economic status. Social Security is so solidly financed that it is has been running a surplus since 1984. This is the very budgetary surplus in which President Clinton took such pride and which President George W. Bush would later talk about "giving back" to taxpayers. Medicare's far greater problems have to do with costs — including waste, overcharging, and illegality — that plague the entire for-profit health care industry in the United

States. Wrapping these two programs together as "entitlements" creates the impression that avaricious senior citizens are "getting" all the money in the package. Thus, speaking grimly of entitlements, the economist Paul Krugman argues that "the United States and other western governments have become engines for transferring income from workers to retirees."[3]

But Medicare reimbursements are not "income" for retirees. The money never passes into their hands. Like all health insurance reimbursements, Medicare is transferred directly to doctors, hospitals, nursing homes, insurance companies, and pharmaceutical houses. Most of these, as medical corporations of some kind, are run for profit; their shares can be found in the portfolios of the investing public. If Medicare is an income transfer engine, it is a pump that sucks taxes out of all of us and delivers them to some of the wealthiest people in America. If anybody is paying golfing fees out of Medicare, it is apt to be the CEOs of the nation's prospering HMOs. Medicine may cost, but those costs are not collected by the sick. Lumping Social Security and Medicare together has become the centerpiece of a conservative crusade based on skewed statistics and drawing on ideological venom stored up since the days of the New Deal.

Peter Peterson, an investment banker who was Secretary of Commerce under President Nixon, has been among the most influential of the anti-entitlements crusaders. As head of the Concord Coalition, a right-wing think tank, Peterson has been campaigning against entitlements since the 1980s. Anybody who believes the senior vote can have its way in American politics would do well to study what Peterson has been able to accomplish with a few well-placed millions from the brokerage community. Author of two book-length jeremiads on entitlements, Peterson has helped direct what may be the most effective lobbying effort since Prohibition, all of it based on egregiously biased statistics. As Dean Baker, the Social Security analyst at the Economic Policy Institute, has put it, "If there are any claims in Peterson's book that are not outright false or seriously misleading, I was unable to find them." Yet Peterson has had little difficulty commanding the generous and friendly attention of major American media, none of which seem to have had time to check his predictions with the Social Security Administration.[4]

In May 1996, for example, Peterson published a dire warning in the *Atlantic*. His argument was many-sided: Senior entitlements are unsustainable, undeserved, unprincipled, and unfair. But more striking than any statistic he offered were the illustrations the *Atlantic* chose to accompany the article. Seniors appear like an alien species of obnoxious, geriatric layabouts thronging the sunny shores of Florida, crowding their children out of the country, stealing the food from their mouths, and devouring the national treasury. One especially vicious cartoon depicts a cadaverous old man in a hospital bed on IV tubes; the substance being transfused lavishly into his arm is ... money. If anything, such an image tells us that for some critics money is the equivalent of our life's blood. When one is involved in spreading rumors of intergenerational warfare as many entitlements critics are, one might expect a bit more sensitivity. Pictures like these come dangerously close to the nasty propaganda imagery Dr. Goebbels might have employed in the 1930s to dramatize "the Jewish Menace."

The language evoked by the Gray Peril can be as frenzied as the pictures. As entitlements critics would have it, the old are becoming too numerous, they insist on living too long, but worst of all, they are just plain *bad,* a failed generation of weak, self-indulgent freeloaders. Peterson, for example, not only condemns entitlements as "a fiscal meltdown" but castigates the entire baby boom generation — the geezers to come — for its "unseemly" and "ruinously dysfunctional" way of life. He believes "we now face public budgets strained to the breaking point by demographic aging which will crowd out all forms of capital accumulation, private and public, material and human." As if he could imagine no worse fate for the nation, he asks how we would like to be living in "a nation of Floridas," amid a "gray wave of senior citizens that fills the state's streets, beaches, parks, hotels, shopping malls, hospitals, Social Security offices, and senior centers." The anti-immigration propagandists of the nineteenth century might have raised the same question about all those repugnant yellow people. "How would you like to live in a nation of Shanghais?"

In the case of the Yellow Peril, the usual proposal was to lock the intruders out or send them back where they came from. The dreaded gray wave offers no such options. Still, one shudders to imagine what entitlements critics have in mind for our senior population. Peterson is among those who have most forcefully proposed the rationing of health care. By this he means finding some way to deny dying seniors the expensive medical care that might keep them going another few weeks, months, or years at the expense of some health insurance company's profits. Given the insensitivity of Peterson's critique, this looks more like a "final solution" than a cost-benefit analysis.

## THE DISMAL SCIENCE OF GENERATIONAL ACCOUNTING

In a 1995 critique of entitlements, James P. Smith of the RAND Corporation, fretting that Social Security and Medicare are "draining the capacity and incentive of workers to save for their own retirement," insists that "loud alarm bells are ringing for the nation's future."[5]

Whenever those alarm bells start ringing, one can be certain the generational accountants have had a hand in setting them off. The creation of the economists Laurence Kotlikoff of Boston University, Alan Auerbach of the University of California, Berkeley, and Jagadeesh Gokhale of the Cleveland Federal Reserve Bank, generational accounting is the brains trust behind the conservative attack upon entitlements. A single-issue school of economics, its sole interest is the nation's senior dependency load, which it interprets to be the distribution of wealth between retired Americans and their working children.

Kotlikoff and his colleagues seek to estimate, in present-value terms, how much people born in any given year will pay the government over their lifetimes and how much they can expect to get back in entitlements.[6] Of central importance to their analysis is the ratio between net lifetime payments into and out of Social Security and Medicare. This yields a percentage that can be projected across future generations. Thus, Americans born in 1930 have paid a net tax equalling 30 percent of their income for what they have eventually received in return from entitlement benefits. Those born in 1950 will have paid 33 percent. If current policies continue, Kotlikoff estimates that children of the post-baby boom generation will supposedly be facing a net tax rate of 82 percent! "What that's telling you," he warns, "is that current fiscal policy is unsustainable and generationally unconscionable. We need to pay more and spend less today so our kids won't be taxed to death." Otherwise, the result will be a "fiscal train wreck."

In reaching these conclusions, Kotlikoff has been criticized for making some questionable assumptions. Like most entitlements critics, he plays the entitlements trick, conflating the cost of Social Security with the cost of Medicare. He then takes the cost of medical care in the United States at face value, giving no attention to the amount of fraud and waste the health care system, and especially Medicare, are presently carrying. He also assumes a rate of continuing inflation that would make *any* form of health insurance, whether public or private, unaffordable.[7]

In Kotlikoff's eyes, none of the entitlements reforms currently under discussion comes close to doing the job that needs to be done. He contends that even the most rigorous proposals for balancing the budget in the early twenty-first century will cost the next generation a crushing 70 percent of their income. And even then, he observes, those who are drawing on the Social Security trust fund, according to the Congressional Research Service, will, on the average, use up everything they contributed within the first ten years of retirement, including the employer contribution. After that, they are living off a subsidy from current workers.

Of course, the "subsidy" that generational accountants are talking about is rather like the subsidy those same retirees, as parents, once gave their children when they fed them, clothed them, put a cozy suburban roof over their heads, built schools, playgrounds, and universities for them, hired teachers to educate them and doctors to medicate them. And with even a minimal sense of history, one might add that some previous generations suffered the Great Depression and two or three wars along the way, sacrifices that make paying one's taxes look like rather less than an ordeal by fire. The tie that binds the generations cannot be reduced to a neat fiscal formula. The discussion of entitlements is complicated by a biological fact that does not yield to a purely economic analysis. It is called "family," a category that has no standing among professional economists. The people who are giving and taking, earning and spending are relatives. And as nature would have it, with the passage of time the babies grow up, get old, and retire. Despite all the groaning and gnashing of teeth we hear from the generational accountants, it pays to remember that nothing worse is happening here than that life is going on. The demographic configuration changes, but the underlying obligation of kin to kin continues.

What we have in generational accounting is not really economics at all. It is a remarkably obtuse, if not deliberately misleading, political campaign. It would have younger Americans believe that balancing the budget is more important than providing medical care for their parents — or, at some point in the future, for themselves. It is as if we were being asked to send up a perverse prayer: *If only the twenty-first century looked more like the nineteenth century!* One would hardly be surprised to hear the generational accountants advocating that we bring back cholera and typhoid, the better to take advantage of the economies of early death.

Yet as deceptive and inhumane as the anti-entitlements campaign has been, opinion-leaders in astonishing numbers have compliantly accepted its argument at face value. Perhaps that is because the anti-entitlements movement has offered the media the one thing they cannot resist: a good scare. Tell the world that the sky is falling, and what might otherwise be a boring parade of actuarial numbers and fiscal priorities suddenly becomes top-of-the-hour news. But even if the sky were falling, it is falling very, very slowly. The entitlements "crisis," at its worst, is still thirty to fifty years away. What other issue in our lives is viewed on such a timeline? Education? Environmental clean-up? Public transportation? National defense? Extend any of these issues another generation into the future, and they too will look flatteningly expensive.

The rhetoric employed by the media in handling entitlements betrays a determined effort to dramatize to the hilt. Articles in leading publications find the future of entitlements "mind-boggling" and warn that we are sitting on a "demographic time bomb" (*Wall Street Journal*). Or entitlements are "a giant sponge soaking up so large a share of the federal budget that little will be left for anything else" (*New York Times*). Sporting a big "Uh-Oh!" on its cover, the *New Republic* announces, "Social Security is on the skids." *Time* magazine warns that we are facing an "entitlements monster that will consume the budget if left unchecked." Demanding rigorous cutbacks in senior benefits, *Time* addresses an editorial challenge to President Clinton under the title "No Guts, No Glory."

All these are stories written by journalists who simply believed the first thing they heard from a biased source. Had they picked up the phone and checked with the Social Security Administration — whose veracity is unquestioned even by anti-entitlements critics — they would have learned how false these fiscal horror stories are.

It is unlikely as smart a politician as President Clinton fell for the slippery arguments of the anti-entitlements crusade. But instead of arguing the fiscal details, he did something a lot more effective. He resorted to political *jiu-jitsu*. He took the alarmists at their word and agreed that Social Security was in trouble. That allowed him to become the savior of the system. "Save Social Security first," he proclaimed, and began reserving the budget surplus for that purpose. Instead of cutting taxes as the Republicans were so eager to do, he proposed paying down the national debt to prepare for the day when the boomers would claim their share of Social Security. The ploy left Clinton looking like a fiscal conservative. This is called hoisting your opponent on his own petard. It was a clever maneuver, but it unfortunately left Social Security looking endangered.

As Social Security actuaries have been at pains to point out, any program tied to demographic change will have to be fine-tuned from time to time, as indeed Social Security has been on several occasions in the past. Assessing the full impact of these adjustments would have to take into account, not only the rising number of dependent seniors, but the number of dependent children in the United States, which is declining here as in all industrial societies. We would also have to include the increasing capacity of older people to use the opportunities of our service-based, increasingly professionalized, high-tech economy to stay in the workforce longer.

In the current debate over entitlements, as early as 1993 the American Society on Aging published a set of corrective essays and statistics making such key distinctions as the proper way to calculate dependency ratios between young and old.[8] Working from such commonplace facts, Robert Ball, an advisor to presidents both Republican and Democratic and one of the nation's most trusted authorities on entitlements, has flatly stated that "there is no financial crisis in Social Security."[9] Similarly, the financial columnist Jane Bryant Quinn has struggled to inform her readers about Social Security in no uncertain terms. "Contrary to popular belief," she writes, "Social Security isn't going bankrupt. ... The problems are fixable, with incremental changes in benefits, taxes and, eventually, borrowing. ... But, hey — shouting 'bankruptcy' pays off politically."[10]

Adding a far larger body of research to the discussion, the co-authors Dean Baker and Mark Weisbrot, directors of the Center for Economics and Policy Research in Washington DC, have extensively documented "the phony crisis" in Social Security. They have explained that over the next several years, a relatively modest set of adjustments that might include a gradual rise in the Social Security tax will keep the system solvent well into the twenty-first century.[11]

If currently predicted tax surpluses come through, the Social Security Administration estimates that it can meet all its commitments until the year 2035. If we were to do absolutely nothing between now and 2035, Social Security would still be able to pay three-quarters of the pensions it owes, which is not quite what "going broke" implies. In short, the program would at that point have to be cut — which is what entitlements critics would have us do *now*. But why would we simply wait and do nothing? When Social Security has required adjustments in the past, we have made them. And we will make them again.

Thus, if between now and 2035, we gradually raise the FICA payroll tax by a bit more than 2 percent (half to be paid by employees, half by employers) the system will remain solvent at the present level throughout the century. The tax increase might be even less if Social Security were to absorb the pensions of several million state and local employees who are not now covered, or if capital gains were to be included under the Social Security tax, which now falls only on payroll earnings. When pundits tell us how "painful" it will be to save Social Security, that is the measure of the pain: a 2 percent increase in the payroll tax phased in over several years. Unless one works from the assumption that taxes must never, never, *never* be raised, which may indeed be the viewpoint of some fiscal conservatives, none of this looks either extreme or arduous. It is not nearly as strenuous a change as we will surely be asked to make over the next fifty years in the areas of energy policy, military weaponry, transportation, or repairing our industrial infrastructure.

But critics are not persuaded. Throughout the 1990s, largely on the basis of polemical materials artfully assembled and vigorously disseminated by conservative groups like the Concord Coalition and the Cato Institute, entitlements doomsayers managed to make themselves the most vociferous and widely quoted viewpoint in the United States on the future of Social Security and Medicare. And overwhelmingly, the media were prepared to believe what these sources told them, which is analogous to accepting whatever defense contractors tell us about the military budget. In late 1997, Alan Greenspan, head of the Federal Reserve Board, went on record supporting the need to restructure entitlements. Deciding beforehand that a tax increase was unthinkable and brushing aside other modest adjustments, he too proclaimed the program to be "unsustainable" and recommended stringent cuts plus some degree of rapid privatization.

Other critics, playing upon public ignorance, invoke a scenario that might have been written for the *X-Files*. They insist that the system is *already* bankrupt; the government has been covering up the truth for half a century. Open up the Social Security trust fund and look inside. What will you find? Nothing but U.S. treasury bonds, worthless pieces of paper in the opinion of anti-entitlement critics. It is as if they expect to find all the money collected for Social Security sitting idle under some big mattress in Washington. Would they expect their bank to keep all their savings deposits untouched and unused in a vault? All money circulates. It gets used. The money in the trust fund is loaned out to the federal government to pay for any number of current programs that have been voted by the Congress. If the government did not borrow at a bargain rate from the trust fund, it would have to borrow in the financial markets at a much higher rate, which, in turn, would have to be paid for out of taxes as part of the national debt. Nevertheless, Peter Peterson uses this skewed interpretation of the trust fund as evidence for charging that the Social Security system is a fraudulent operation little short of a "Ponzi scheme."[12]

True, there is no piggy bank somewhere in Washington containing everybody's pension funds marked by name. Nobody ever said there would be. No insurance anywhere in the world works on such a basis. Insurance is always made up of a certain amount of money on hand surrounded and buttressed by a fiduciary responsibility, meaning a promise to live up to one's obligations — as Social Security has since it began. The system expresses our sense of national community. It is based on something more valuable than money in the bank: *conscience,* the ethical consensus among Americans as to how our national wealth shall be used.

## PRIVATIZING SOCIAL SECURITY: THE PHONY SOLUTION

Any social change that involves redistributing large sums of public money is bound to present a "problem" of some kind, whether we are discussing defense appropriations, welfare, education, or environmental protection. View that change on a seventy-year timeline, as the Social Security Administration is required by law to do, and the problem is bound to look bigger — meaning more expensive. Imagine trying to estimate the cost of maintaining the nation's streets and highways over the next century. Some would say the bill looked ... "unaffordable."

Sometimes we use the word "problem" for insoluble disasters; but sometimes "problems" are matters of intelligent adjustment. The problems raised by longevity are of the latter kind; they present an occasion for rationally reordering priorities. Every great public issue involves trade-offs, choices, and competing claims. That is what politics is all about. Thus, it is hardly beside the point that those who are campaigning against entitlements include financial interests that have a great deal to gain from the solution they propose: privatizing Social Security. That is also politics, and very profitable politics at that.

In the course of the next generation, privatizing Social Security could entrust as much as $1 trillion in mandatory savings to brokers and mutual fund managers who would collect handsome fees for supervising personal security accounts. Not only would privatization involve a costly transitional phase that would have to be covered by taxpayers as a higher Social Security tax, but it would result in investment portfolios that lacked any protection against inflation, the always unpredictable fluctuations of the stock market, opportunistic churning, and plain bad management. And, in contrast to Social Security, private pension plans would not include life insurance and disability insurance, benefits that have been estimated as worth $200,000 to $300,000 to workers and their survivors.

As most privatizers have formulated their proposal, those who suffer financial losses are promised that there will be a "safety net" to catch them — a sort of shadow Social Security system. For "safety net" read "bailout," to be paid for by the taxpaying public if brokers swindle their senior clients blind or if the market goes into a tailspin, as the Japanese stock market of the early 1990s did. Not since the great robber barons of the nineteenth century stepped forward to take over the building of the nation's railroads — on the basis of generous federal and state land grants and subsidies — has there been so self-serving a proposal. But even such a hypothetical safety net would not save one kind of retiree from disaster. It is now estimated that nearly 70 percent of those who hold private 401(k) pension plans close the plan out when they change jobs. Even though they must pay income tax on the money they withdraw plus a 10 percent penalty, most workers prefer to cash in for a lump sum. Among Gen Xers, those below the age of thirty, nearly 80 percent elect to spend their prospective retirement money. These are exactly the voters President Bush appealed to in his 2000 election campaign, offering them a plan for partially privatizing Social Security so they could get a "better rate of return." The result may be a future generation of workers who go into retirement with no pension plan of their own and diminished Social Security.[13]

Some brokers have shamelessly projected "can't lose" earnings of 10 and 12 percent on personal security accounts; the more common promise is about 7 percent. Given the now chronically massive fluctuations of the stock market, they hardly inspire confidence. Still, one might make a reasonable case for including private securities in the Social Security trust fund; many public pension funds allow for cautious, well-regulated investment and, like the California Public Employees Retirement System, are now among the biggest players in the stock market. Among the proposals produced by the 1997 United States Advisory Council on Social Security was one recommendation that all the equities be placed in the hands of the Social Security Administration itself, to be managed as cheaply and cautiously as possible. That is not a course that privatizers fancy; in the words of the *Wall Street Journal*, "this would put the economy into government ownership." It would amount to "socialism-by-acquisition."[14]

On the other hand, how much confidence can one have in the extravagant promises that are being made by those in the private sector who want to get hold of Social Security funds and invest them with no supervision or few safeguards? Stories of major bankers, brokers, and fund managers being sued, prosecuted, or imprisoned for blatantly chiseling the public are the news of the day. Morgan Stanley, Paine Webber, Merrill Lynch, Solomon Brothers, these and any number of minor operators have at one time or another been accused and convicted of playing fast and loose with their clients' funds. To cite an example: in December 1997, as part of a class-action lawsuit, the SEC fined twenty-four New York brokerage firms nearly $1 billion for bilking millions of investors by colluding to fix prices on the Nasdaq Stock Market between 1989 and 1994. The firms included just about all the major Wall Street players. Making the sleazy even sleazier, the brokers pleaded with the court to announce the fines on Christmas Eve, hoping that many readers would miss the story during the holiday rush.[15]

Who are these people, then, to offer themselves as more deserving of the public trust than Social Security? If the system were to be privatized, these are the firms to which novice investors would be entrusting their retirement nest egg. The result would doubtless provide *60 Minutes* with a steady stream of scam stories for the next generation.

There may be many elements of government that have forfeited their claim to the public trust. The military, CIA, FBI, IRS, Federal Reserve Board — all these have, at one time or another, blundered or lied, made serious mistakes or allied themselves to special interests. The Social Security Administration is not among those who deserve to be treated like culprits. Indeed, when it comes to handling money, its record is the best we can find in the land. Nothing very exciting or newsworthy happens at Social Security. Nobody has ever had to track down an erring administrator for fraud or embezzlement. The contrast with the record of the private financial community could not be clearer.

And yet, as recently as the 2000 elections, the policy assumptions and statistics of the nation's anti-entitlements forces were still being marshalled by Republicans in the presidential campaigns like articles of faith that must not be abandoned. The Bush campaign traveled the country telling younger people that "Social Security won't be there for you ... the system is going broke ... run for cover!" Then, having done their best to spread the false alarm, anti-entitlements groups report that large portions of the public are convinced that only the sweeping privatization of Social Security can save the nation from bankruptcy, as if that were further proof that the molehill is really a mountain.

Dean Baker and Mark Weisbrot understandably wonder, "How have we reached this sad state of affairs in which those who would throw millions of senior citizens into poverty and undermine the retirement security of all future generations have come to be regarded as courageous leaders, bold defenders of the national interest from the special interests of politics? Historians looking back on this period may well marvel at how we managed to regress from the War on Poverty to the war against the poor, the old, the sick, and the bottom half of the working population generally."[16]

Trudy Lieberman may have part of the answer. In a deft analysis of conservative think tanks, she shows how slanted statistics and the constant repetition of misleading catch-phrases have been used deliberately and effectively to panic the public. "The public has heard so often that Medicare is bankrupt and that Social Security won't be around in thirty years, many have come to believe it, paving the way for their acceptance of the right's prescription for change. Conservative organizations identified repetition in the media as a key media strategy faster than other groups, and exploited it more rigorously and energetically."[17]

If anything has put a damper on the drive toward privatization, it has been the budget surplus that the United States has been running since the mid-1990s. To be sure, the surplus would not exist if it were not for the money taken in by the Social Security payroll tax, which will, at some point over the next thirty years, have to be raised to cover the cost of retirement of long-lived boomers and succeeding generations. But the surplus has provided an insight. We have learned that a healthy economy with high employment can easily afford the cost of Social Security. The secret of affordability is healthy economic growth with plenty of jobs to go around. Rather than seeing entitlements as an inherent drag on the economy, the public has begun to see Social Security as an integral part of the economy, easily affordable when employment and productivity are high. Of course, the economy may not continue to generate so much wealth. There may be a slump. But if that happens, the stock market will be hit as hard as every other part of the economy, and those who hold personal security accounts will lose their nest egg. The economy is an interrelated whole; the stock market will not prosper in the absence of paychecks and purchasing power.

The entitlements debate has become so panic-stricken that it has driven otherwise humane and liberal thinkers to intemperate extremes. The economist Lester Thurow, for example, has called the elderly a "revolutionary class," but not in any good sense of the word. He charges that retired Americans are "bringing down the social welfare state, destroying government finances, altering the distribution of purchasing power, and threatening the investments that all societies need to make to have a successful future." Predicting that, "in the years ahead, class warfare is apt to be redefined as the young against the old," Thurow darkly hints that the grandparents of America may accomplish what no foreign foe has succeeded in doing. They will kill the democratic way of life. Democracy, he believes, "is going to meet the ultimate test in the elderly. If democratic governments cannot cut benefits that go to the majority of their voters, then they have no long-term future."[18]

That comes close to saying that the only way we can save the nation is by disenfranchising the retired. As the gerontologist Meredith Minkler observes, "When a leading liberal economist and former editorial board member of the *New York Times* can make these statements and get away with them, we need to be concerned."[19]

## THE WORLDWIDE RISE OF THE WRINKLIES

In understanding the issues raised by the longevity revolution, it helps to know that our aging population is not due to some peculiarly bad luck or faulty social planning. What we are facing results from the logic of progress in the modern world. Barring another Black Plague that carries off more of the old than the young, every industrial nation is destined to become something like "a nation of Floridas." If that looks like a threatening prospect, then all the other industrial societies would seem to be facing a bleaker future than the United States. They are aging every bit as rapidly as we are and paying even more to provide for their retired citizens.

By the year 2020, seniors over sixty will account for 25 percent of the population in the United States; in Japan, that figure will reach 30 percent. In Germany, 36 percent of the population will be above age sixty by 2035, the highest proportion in the European Union. Refine the analysis to focus on women who are leading the way toward a longer life expectancy, and the wave of the future comes into clearer view. As of the 1990s, over 40 percent of all French women and 30 percent of all American women are on their way to living past eighty. By the time those Chinese who were teenagers in the 1990s reach their middle age, their country will have one citizen over sixty-five for every child below fourteen.

Japan now leads in longevity statistics: Japanese women have a life expectancy of eighty-three; for the population as a whole, the average age is forty. At the same time, over the next decade the number of young workers under the age of thirty in Japan will fall by 25 percent. Economists frequently cite Japan as a bleak example of what the longevous future will bring. For example, the *London Observer* in a 1998 survey of the Japanese economy reported that "the shrinking [Japanese] family is a threat to productivity, pensions, and the welfare system, and in turn is being blamed for consumers' increasing tendency to save rather than spend — which worsens the current economic downturn."

The generational accountants have found a way to make the future appear especially catastrophic. They call what these nations owe their retired citizens "an unfunded pension liability," that is, the amount of their annual gross domestic product that will have to be set aside to pay for pensions. The United States would have to set aside 43 percent of GDP, Germany 160 percent, and Japan 200 percent. The Canadians would have to set aside an impossible 250 percent of GDP. Pushed to these limits, the tax burden for entitlements would absorb very nearly all the lifetime income of the working population.[20] But as we have seen, the generational accountants reach these awesome figures by making a number of assumptions, all of which betray a remarkable lack of confidence in the productivity of the capitalist system. Just as their early industrial ancestors, the classical economists, could see nothing in the future but misery for the millions, the generational accountants are telling the younger generation that it is destined for grinding poverty — unless it finds some way to turn life expectancy back to what it was during the Great Depression when few people were expected to live long enough to collect their Social Security.

On the other hand, there are countries that are struggling against formidable demographic odds. They include nations where capitalism has failed to pay off as promised. Among European nations, the former Soviet Union may be doing the worst job of dealing with its seniors as it fitfully makes the transition to a market economy. Previous socialist entitlements have been undermined before anything has emerged to take their place. It is reportedly a commonplace sight to find elderly Russians on the streets hawking the last of their personal possessions to buy food or peddling bootleg vodka. Entitlements critics might admire the way in which Russia is dealing with its older population. Instead of funding pensions, it has reverted to old-age indigence.

Prospectively the worst-case scenario for seniors in the century ahead will be in China, where the government is fiercely determined to develop the economy. In contrast to China's age-old veneration of its elders, the new industrial society has come to regard the old as a millstone around its neck. There, senior care has taken on a particularly menacing aspect, if only because of the magnitude of the problem. In 2025, when the over-sixty population doubles, it will amount to 400 million people, well over one-fifth of the population. By then China, which has mandated single-child families, may have halved its birth rate, but its fiscal problem will be more demanding than ever. Why? Because the portion of the population then on the increase, the elderly, will be more expensive to maintain, while the younger generation will follow the pattern of the longevity revolution and fall below replacement level. The Chinese government is already resorting to warehousing its seniors in substandard, urban "collection centers" that have a bad reputation for abusing their inmates. Judging by reports on the problem, one might almost conclude that the Chinese government wishes it could have edited medical science out of the Western technology it is borrowing.[21]

But where does one stop making grim demographic speculations like those that now govern public policy in so many industrial societies? At 2020 ... or 2050? After all, time marches on. If we extend the numbers a few decades further in any industrial society one cares to name, there are likely to be more retirees than workers. It would seem that the young, steadily diminishing as they are in relative numbers, are destined for lifelong generational serfdom. At least that would be the case if we looked at the future through the lens of generational accounting. But statistics, when they leave out the human and historical context, are profoundly misleading.

Consider a favorite statistical horror of the generational accountants: How many taxpaying workers will there have to be in the future to pay for the growing needs of the elderly? The numbers can seem staggering, especially if Medicare is lumped together with Social Security. To cover the cost of Medicare alone presently requires the taxes of 3.9 workers for every senior citizen. By 2015 there will be only 3.1 workers to carry the Social Security tax load; only 2.5 by 2025, and by 2050 the figure falls to two.[22] The result sounds as outrageous as it is forbidding. It almost suggests that working couples in the year 2050 will one day wake up to find a strange, old, sick person on their doorstep waiting to be taken in. If generational accountants really took dire predictions like this seriously they would be campaigning for eliminating all restrictions on immigration so that we might have more young workers to carry the load. Or they might start encouraging the young women of America to do as the mothers of the baby boom did.

What is the optimum ratio of workers to the retired? Ten to one? Twelve to one? Is there any economic calculus that will answer such a question? There is not, because this ratio, so often cited, is simply not a relevant statistic. One need only consider a truly poor country like Somalia, where, for every elder who cannot work, there may be twenty people toiling from dawn to dusk to scratch a living out of the arid soil. And still, despite the ratio, the dependent young and elderly starve because the economy cannot produce enough. On the other hand, think back to the 1940s and 1950s when the baby boom was just beginning. True, the ratio of workers to the retired was about eight to one. But in that period, when most families were living off a single paycheck, the wage-earner in every household — usually one working father — was supporting three, four, or five dependents, plus all the retirees on Social Security. Big families, many children: that is what it meant to have a *baby boom*. Had the generational accountants been on the scene when that boom was under way, they would no doubt have been warning us that the nation would soon be fiscally smothered in diapers or drowned in baby formula. After all, think of the cost of a baby boom. Think of all the medical and dental care those babies required. Think of the schools and school teachers, the universities, the day care facilities, the food that had to be put on the table, the new suburban housing that bigger families necessitated, the freeways that had to be built so that fathers could commute to work, and eventually the investment in job creation.

And yet the baby boom did happen and it did get paid for. In contrast to the postwar period, when families were so much larger, generations to come will have a diminishing number of young dependents. As that happens, the *total* dependency load carried by each working member of society — youth dependency taken together with retirees — will actually grow smaller. The Social Security trustees estimate that as of the year 2020, there will be .42 children below the age of twenty for every adult between the ages of twenty and sixty-five, a marked reduction in child dependency from .5 in 1995. In the United States as in all industrial societies, as the size of families shrinks, we will see healthy and educated elders, semi-dependents who can do ever more to pay their cost of living longer, replacing children, whose dependency is total. The ratio that matters when it comes to calculating any society's dependency load is that of *productive capacity* to dependents. And that continues to rise, thanks to our ever expanding industrial technology.[23] After all, what does it mean to say that there will be only two workers for every retired person in a society where those two workers may be running an entire automated factory which once employed thousands?

In any case, the business community has been quite opportunistic in dealing with the worker-to-retiree dependency ratio. Opposing even a modest tax increase to fund Social Security, it subscribes to the argument that we will soon have too few workers on the job to support the retired population. But it also wants to have a free hand to fire older workers who are willing, if not eager to stay on the job. One cannot have it both ways. Either older workers are kept employed, or they go on Social Security earlier than they might otherwise choose to.

Like so many fiscally conservative critics, Lawrence Kotlikoff makes the mistake of assuming that, if we eliminate a government program, the people who need that program will vanish in a puff of smoke. But consider what our situation would be if we did abolish entitlements and let "our children," for whom the generational accountants purport to have such concern, keep all their hard-earned money as discretionary income. Entitlements would be gone, but the people who depend on those entitlements would still be there.

And what would the position of the working population be? Presumably, each worker would still have at least one or two retirees to support:

they would be called Mother and Father, with, perhaps a few long-lived grandparents included in the load. Where would these people turn once they had left the workforce? And, if we followed the generational accountants in reducing Medicare, the cost of our parents' dependency would include all their medical bills as well as their basic necessities. Seen from that angle, entitlements look like rather a good deal. They are the arrangement we have made as a society for pooling a collective moral obligation and discharging it as practically, dependably, and fairly as possible.

## "FISCAL CHILD ABUSE"?

Perhaps the cruelest tactic used by the anti-entitlements campaign has been that of pitting young against old in generational conflict. In a consummate bit of parental guilt-tripping, the generational accountants have associated senior entitlements with greed, selfishness, irresponsibility, and self-indulgence — traits that make good mothers and fathers wince. Third Millennium, an advocacy group for twenty- and thirty-somethings, condemns Social Security as "a generational scam, fiscally unsound and generationally inequitable." The system is "robbing our children in order to indulge ourselves in the luxuries of a time gone by." It is little short of "fiscal child abuse." What would Third Millennium do about these evils? The government, it insists, must stop "invoicing future generations for today's spending sprees." It should raise the retirement age to seventy, means-test for pensions and health care, and "stop paying the greens-fee for well-heeled retirees."[24]

How justified are these accusations? Have seniors been greedy in accepting entitlements and in letting them be augmented through cost-of-living increases? If so, in many cases the benefits of their "greed" are being shared with their children. Consider the number of under-thirties who, in today's fluctuating job market, have been living at home, relying on parental room and board. These days jobs come and go at the whim of the global marketplace and the dot-com economy, but family ties hold strong. As early as 1987, sociologists began to report the phenomenon of "boomerang kids," the increasing number of insecure or downwardly mobile children who were returning home to live with their parents for lack of enough income to afford homes of their own.[25]

Cross-generational support is not limited to housing. As of the mid-1990s, economists believe more than 20 percent of all wealth in the United States was being passed from parents to adult children by way of gifts, and this did not include the cost of university education.[26] Shared family wealth explains the continued high level of consumer spending among younger, less affluent workers, as well as their otherwise puzzling acquiescence in declining wages and job security. To a worrisome extent, the new dot-com economy has developed the practice of paying its workers with stock options that are little better than gambling chips. As one Silicon Valley hacker has put it, "I own shares worth half a million bucks in this company, but meanwhile I'm living on Top Ramen every day of my life."

Money from home has been providing much of the ballast in our storm-tossed economic life. It has offset the growing amount of part-time and temporary employment, independent contracting, and general job insecurity that now characterizes working life in America. Until the bull market of the late 1990s took hold, the decade of the 1990s, as Frances Goldscheider observes, was "really a depression for young adults" relieved for many only by the families they could fall back upon when the job market turned against them — as it may again.[27] The global economy, certainly as it is reflected in the gyrations of the worldwide stock market, places little value on long-term stability.

What parent-child economics of the 1990s proved is that the family bank account has become an important, if unofficial, element in the national safety net. If the economic disparity between America's postwar and *fin-de-siècle* generations has not been as glaring as it might be, it is because a great deal of wealth is being informally transferred between the generations.

In September 1995, *Newsweek* ran a feature entitled "MediScare." It presented a cover picture of a young man struggling to hold his ailing, wheelchair-bound mother above his worried head. "Young vs. Old," the caption read. "Who will carry the burden?" Poor fellow! But the picture might have been closer to the truth if it were turned upside down. It might just as well show aging parents keeping an underemployed son or jobless daughter afloat in the swirling waters of the global economy.

Such parental generosity may not continue indefinitely. While some envious young adults like the members of Third Millennium characterize the senior generation as a population of cruise-ship sybarites, the inexorable pressure of medical needs is steadily eroding senior wealth. It is true that, thanks to entitlements, the over-sixty-five white population in America is living better than in any previous era.[28] And though they cannot eat or wear the homes they live in, some 600,000 elderly citizens own homes valued at above $100,000.[29] If anybody is going to gain any cash benefit from the parental home, it will be the children who one day sell it off after their parents die or go into nursing care. Other than that, the bequests that elders can leave to their children began shrinking as of the early 1990s, a fact that is bound to exacerbate generational friction.

Well-off though they may be in comparison with previous elders, as they survive longer all older Americans — the senior old, the middle old, and the boomers — risk outliving whatever resources they have set aside. Above all, they continue to be plagued by medical expenses beyond those that Medicare covers, especially as for-profit health care trims and cuts its coverage. These days some seniors display sassy bumper stickers on their cars that proclaim, "I'm Spending My Children's Inheritance." And so they are. But on what? Entitlements critics, assuming an austere Calvinist air, condemn retirees for spending as much as they do on "consumption." They omit to mention that, as time goes on, what seniors are primarily consuming is medical care. While they may be spending more relative to the younger generation of the 1990s, what they lay out goes increasingly to doctors, hospitals, pharmacists, and nursing homes — hardly the most enjoyable kind of spending.

Both the critics and the defenders of Social Security can produce mountains of statistics to support their cases. But sometimes numbers get in the way of the simple truth. Whenever we debate sharing the wealth of the nation, we are talking politics and ethics. Numbers help, but they can never decide the issue. Whether by taxation or the diversion of resources, nations will always manage to afford what they decide they must afford as a matter of necessity, glory, or honor. So too with the costs of an aging society. Originally created as a compassionate commitment to alleviate, if not end, old-age poverty, Social Security is an ongoing contract between the generations based upon the full faith and credit of the world's richest nation. It is grounded in our trust in ourselves.

As Justice Benjamin Cardozo put it in 1937 in delivering the Supreme Court's decision in favor of the Social Security Act, "The hope behind this statute is to save men and women from the rigors of the poor house as well as from the haunting fear that such a lot awaits them when journey's end is near." If we leave out the historical experience and the moral force that undergird Social Security, we have lost the entire meaning of the program and have become ethically poorer.

CHAPTER THREE

## The Coming Health Care Economy

T he first rule of the Hippocratic oath is to do the patient no harm. But until well into the twentieth century, even with the best intentions, medicine in the Western world frequently did more harm than good. That was why the village sawbones of the early industrial period often had to rely upon the comfort and consolation of their bedside manner. There was little else they had to offer the sick and dying. As for hospitals, they were understood to be the shortest way to the morgue, germ-ridden traps that increased one's risk of infection and death. Those who stayed away and used any folk remedy at hand were better off.

Since the invention of sterile surgery and antibiotics, the healing capacities of modern medicine have been revolutionized many times over. And there are revolutions still to come — in environmental, wholistic, and preventive medicine and in genetic therapy. All this stands behind the astonishing increase in longevity we now enjoy. And yet modern medicine is dogged by the limitations and failures of its past. Mention health care and, as if it were a conditioned reflex, people think loss, liability — even waste. Even now, when medical science can do so much to preserve health and save lives, we continue to list spending on health care as a debit, as if it were not buying us anything of value. And as the cost rises, people bemoan the fact ever more loudly. But does that make any sense?

### How Much is Too Much?

In September 1998, the Health Care Financing Administration estimated that spending for health care in the United States will reach $2.1 trillion by 2007, an average of $7,000 per person. That cost has been rising steadily at a rate vastly higher than inflation, in spite of the fact that more and more Americans are living without medical insurance and doing without care.

Is this simply because the nation is aging? Only in part. About one-third of rising medical costs can be traced to the needs of patients on Medicare. A far more important reason for the increasing cost of medicine is that we have more medicine for people of all ages — more procedures, more pharmaceuticals, more lab tests, more medical technology — to spend our money on than ever before and nobody, not patients, doctors, HMOs, or the government, has found a way to control that spending. Much of what we spend on, like treating AIDS, rescuing premature babies, caesarean child delivery, or providing major organ transplants, is highly expensive. Many would regard these as proud triumphs of modern medical science. And so they are; but they do not come without a price tag. People may gasp at the collective cost of health care, but when it comes to themselves and their families, how many will volunteer to demand less care than they need so that others will have more to spend at Walmart?

There are other reasons that make American medicine more expensive both in total and per capita cost than health care in any nation in the developed world. But these are reasons in which nobody can take pride. They include such items as misdiagnosis, substandard treatment, and above all plain fraud. Since the mid-1990s, a steady stream of reports from the media, the Justice Department, and the Congress has documented the amount of swindling that goes on under Medicare, as well as under private health insurance. The culprits have included such major players as Columbia/HCA, the largest for-profit health care conglomerate in the country.[1] The General Accounting Office has even found evidence that organized crime has been skimming hundreds of millions of dollars from Medicare and Medicaid by the creation of phantom clinics and phony patients.[2]

How much, then, of the $200 billion that Medicare spends annually as of the 1990s is being paid for good, necessary care, and how much for illegal billing and overpricing? Malcolm Sparrow of the Kennedy School of Government, who has made a study of Medicare fraud, believes that as much as 38 percent of billing in the system is dishonest — roughly $60 billion annually.[3] Estimates of fraudulent insurance billing in health care as a whole, private and public, run as high as $100 billion a year, far more than would be recovered by curtailing services or raising senior deductibles.[4]

Health professionals have begun to recognize these distressing facts.

In December 1997, two thousand Massachusetts doctors and nurses went on record in the *Journal of the American Medical Association* condemning "the dark side of market-driven health care." They even staged a replay of the Boston Tea Party by dumping the reports of HMO corporations into Boston Harbor as they issued a "Call for Action" to curb the fleecing practices of for-profit medicine in the United States. One interesting criticism of the effort came from the California Nurses Association. It commented that nonprofit hospitals can be just as exorbitant and wasteful as the for-profits.[5]

No question but that we should seek in every way we can to avoid wasting our medical resources. But where does that effort begin? Surely not with cutting back on Medicare coverage. We should, instead, start by cleaning up the incompetence and waste in the nation's health care system. Until we do that, we will not know with any accuracy how expensive senior medical care really is.

Ultimately the solution to the entitlements issue is not a matter of fiscal manipulation. It does not have to do with costs but with *values* — and not the value of money, but the value of life. When it comes to Medicare, or to health care in general, it is crucial to know what counts as a cost and what counts as a benefit. Disease costs, death costs, broken bones, bad teeth, and environmental pollution cost — and not only in dollars. They cost in physical suffering and emotional anguish, sleepless nights and anxious hours. Health and long life are the benefits that offset those far more serious emotional costs.

## LIFE EXPECTANCY: THE TRUE WEALTH OF NATIONS

How easily both economists and physicians overlook these simple truths.

Take, for example, a 1996 study of chronic illness done by the University of California at San Francisco. The results were released to the press with a note of alarm as presenting "startling, very large numbers." A veritable "epidemic" of chronic disease was sweeping the nation.

What terrible truth did the study find? "As the baby boom generation ages, the number of Americans with chronic illnesses is expected to swell, reaching nearly 150 million by 2030, costing the nation $798 billion a year in direct health care costs." In the 1960s, chronic illnesses cost about 60 percent of all health-related costs; now they total 70 percent of direct health costs alone, meaning doctors, hospitals, drugs, emergency services.[6]

The figures are worth noting, but are they all that alarming? Only if one views them within a strictly budgetary perspective that measures all the costs and none of the benefits. But if we view them from a positive angle, what are these numbers really telling us? They result from the fact that medical science is finding ways to prolong the lives of people who, a century ago, would have died early deaths of diabetes, heart disease, and cancer. Now people with these diseases survive years longer and often in surprisingly fit shape, with less pain and disability. These are the people we now expect to stay in the workforce longer, earn more, and pay more taxes. Of course prolonging their lives costs money. But is there some better use we ought to be making of that money? What might it be? Distributing it as discretionary income to buy more appliances, more cars, more CDs? But why would we do that unless we had somehow been induced to believe that life has less value than a cell phone in our economic calculus?

Today if one asks about the state of the economy, the answer may be framed in any number of ways. One might choose productivity as the key criterion, or profit, or price stability. Whatever one chooses is an expression of value, not fact. What we measure and how we measure it is an ethical matter.

Suppose, then, that we stopped thinking of longevity as a set of numbers in a debit column and came to regard it as a *benefit* — the main benefit for which we expend our wealth. To keep the economists happy, let us make the item rigorously quantitative. Add up the years by which we are extending life expectancy. Give the total an official name. Call it the NLE: national life expectancy. Let us agree that it is a useful and enjoyable long life that we want, not bare, vegetative survival. So let us include a quality-of-life adjustment based on money spent for doctors' visits, hospitalization, medication, and so forth. We might also calculate an index for the feeling of general physical well-being. After all, if we believe we can measure something called "consumer confidence," then why not the confidence people have in their health, so much more important than consumption? Let the NLE count for more in the index of leading economic indicators as a measure of the national wealth than the gross domestic product.

As long as the NLE keeps rising, let us celebrate that as prosperity — at least as warmly as we celebrate an uptick in the Dow-Jones average.

Then let us use whatever metaphor for good fortune we choose — we have scaled the mountain-top, we have crossed the finish line, we have won the war, we have struck it rich, we have hit the jackpot — but accept longevity *as* success and offer it to all who step forward to take it. We might even reward companies that make some significant contribution to the NLE, such as cutting back on auto emissions or finding a better treatment for diabetes.

It would not be impossible to produce formulas like these. If there seems to be a certain flippancy to this proposal, it stems from my skepticism about the entrepreneurial vision of reality that now governs our economy. Within that vision, nothing would seem to have value, not even life itself, unless it can be counted out in dollars and cents. Nevertheless, in the years ahead including the NLE in our economics may be the sort of radical reappraisal we will have to make once we accept the fact that there is nothing we can do about longevity but accept it, enjoy it, and value it.

## THE HIGHEST STAGE OF INDUSTRIAL DEVELOPMENT

It is one of the ironies that the costliest adventures in human history go undebated or even unnoticed. They roll forward with so mighty a consensus that they seem to be destined. Mass migrations, the settling of continents, the creation of vast irrigation systems, the founding of great cities, the building of empires ... Who could begin to set a price upon such grand episodes? Yet they did cost and cost dearly. We quibble over the cost of school lunch programs or the price of sending a letter through the mail. But was there ever the slightest question raised about the cost of building the continental water system that has turned the deserts of the American southwest into arable land and major cities? That feat, which cost trillions of dollars, seemed simply to happen as if by divine decree.

The same is true of the great waves of technological innovation that sweep through modern times. At first we cannot imagine them at all, then suddenly we cannot imagine doing without them no matter what they cost. At the beginning of the twentieth century, few people foresaw that in another generation the United States would become an automotive economy devoting most of its industrial power to building bigger, faster cars and ever more sprawling highway and freeway networks. Nobody except for science fiction writers could have predicted the high tech and aerospace that would dominate our economy in the latter half of the century. Nobody would think now of asking if they have turned out to be worth what they cost. We have come to assume that cars, computers, and space shuttles are the grand climax of industrial development.

But that may be wrong. Ahead of us may lie a still higher stage of industrialism in which health care and biotech will absorb the lion's share of our resources, capital, labor, and skill. Few who now see the possibility that we are headed toward a health care economy welcome that prospect. On the contrary, that is precisely what economists and political leaders have in mind when they lament the rising national medical bill and warn that it may devour all other forms of growth and investment. So, when economists register what health insurance adds to the price of American manufactured goods, they bemoan this cost as a regrettable expenditure that undercuts our competitiveness in world markets. Employers hasten to replace expensive full-time employees with part-timers or independent contractors who work without benefits. Or they outsource the work to cheaper labor markets. In short, they simply externalize the cost of health as if it were of no value to them.

This is not sound economics; it is simply a myopic management style. Even in strict economic terms, skimping on the nation's health benefits nobody except those who collect short-term profits on lower prices. What we spend in the United States on health care is *somebody else's* profit or paycheck: doctors, nurses, lab technicians, hospitals, laboratories, paramedics, pharmaceutical houses. Are these not also part of our business society? If they prosper, in what sense is the economy suffering? Suppose a company buys a new truck. Has the company grown poorer? Has the economy suffered? Or has money simply changed hands? Now suppose a company pays a laboratory to screen its employees for cancer and saves several lives. Has the company lost money? Has the economy grown poorer? Or again, has money simply changed hands, and in the process produced some good result? What some see as a "cost" in transactions like this is simply capital and resources shifting to another sector of the economy. At some point in the past, money that formerly went to blacksmiths began to flow to car mechanics; at another point, money that was once paid out to telephone operators was diverted to those who build, sell, and service direct dialing systems. Taking the economy as a whole, where was the loss in this? After all, every economy spends most of its wealth on *something*.

Currently, health care absorbs about 15 percent of GDP in the United

States. Some experts warn that this figure may grow to 20, 30, 40 percent over the next generation. Well, suppose that happens. Which is of greater value: adding another one hundred megahertz to a microprocessor or adding another ten years to the national life expectancy? On what basis do we answer such questions? There is surely no law of the marketplace that dictates that General Motors or Microsoft must make more money than Kaiser Permanente or Merck Labs. As Jonathan Cohn, editor of the *New Republic* argues, "As a nation we are creating more wealth — wealth that can easily be directed to health care rather than to, say, sport utility vehicles, either in the form of higher insurance premiums or (heaven forbid!) higher taxes."[7]

In an incisive analysis of the coming health care economy, Charles Morris calls into question the "counting conventions" that bias our view of service industries and of health care in particular. "There is a brawny illusion about manufacturing and other goods-producing industries that makes them seem more 'real' than services. ... When an older person gets a hip replacement ... it does not appear so obviously on the radar screen as an increase in wealth." He concludes: "the argument that a continued shift away from traditional heavy industry toward health care will somehow impoverish the country is a compound of nonsense."[8]

It may be that the long-standing association of medical care with age contributes to this peculiar prejudice. A healthy economy is, supposedly, made up of healthy, preferably young people; it reflects their needs, not the needs of the old. But as far as raw statistics are concerned, the economy is neutral. These are simply different consumer groups spending their money on different goods. One group spends on designer jeans, the other spends much more on cataract surgery. As boomers shift more of our money toward their needs, we will come to recognize that a healing economy can be as prosperous as any other.

As a basis for our long-term industrial future, an economy based on health care offers many advantages. It is intensely technological and so puts our best technical brains to work on obviously necessary tasks like saving lives. It is labor-intensive, hiring people at both the skilled and unskilled levels at jobs that cannot be exported. As for productivity, one might consider the "product" of caesarean surgery to be one human unit, but the very idea is absurd. At some point, plain common sense must intervene to tell us that health care makes a more defensible use of capital and resources

than the high-definition (and high-expense) television we are under increasing pressure to fund. If health care raises the nation's tax bill, people
will adjust in exactly the same way they once got used to paying for clean
drinking water and street lighting. They will spend less on something else
in order to have a safer, healthier life. Perhaps families will cut back on
season tickets for the local baseball team. And what great harm will that
do? Money that now pays a mediocre shortstop several million dollars per
season will flow toward nursing home workers, nurse practitioners, or brain
surgeons.

Morris, along with the MIT economist Paul Krugman, believes that
by the middle of the twenty-first century we could very well be spending
30 percent of GDP on health care. When that time comes, we may see
more of our scientific brainpower at work in biotech than in high tech.
There may be more caregivers in our economy, tending to the needs of the
sick and elderly, than aerospace engineers. Hospitals and hospices may be
taking in more money than theme parks. We may then wake up to the fact
that health and longevity are, at last, the highest stage of industrial development. Rather than regarding healing as a costly liability, we will accept
what physicians and physical therapists, aerobics teachers and pharmaceutical researchers, dietitians and psychiatrists offer us as the supreme value
in life. By the time the longevity revolution has run its course, we may look
back upon all that came before, from heavy industry to high tech, as a dark
age of deplorable waste when people did not know what really mattered.

## Maintaining Mamie

I learned my most persuasive lesson in health care economics from a
woman named Mamie. I had just finished a lecture at a California retirement community. She was the first person to come up and shake my hand.
She was eighty-four years old, bright eyed, smiling, and looking not the
least bit burdened by her years. "Thank God somebody finally recognized
how much I'm worth," she exclaimed. "What you see is a high-mainte-
nance body. There must be fifty people making a living off of me. Why,
I'm a walking medical goldmine."

My lecture subject for the day was the rising cost of health care. No
news to this audience, which was used to hearing economists and politicians lament what the senior population is already costing us and how
much more the retiring baby boomers will add to those costs. But I came

that day with a different message. When I hear that the nation's medical bill is going up, my deliberately provocative response is: "So what?" Who wants to live in a society where life expectancy is declining? The only problem I see about longevity is that the billions we pay to live longer and stay healthier are not buying fair access to good medicine for everybody. Would that the projected 20, 30, or 40 percent more we will be paying for health care in the future bought all of us 20, 30, or 40 years of extra life and reasonably good health. I would regard that as the best bargain in sight.

Mamie saw my point. She blithely rattled off her medical record. Cataract surgery, hearing aid, dentures, quadruple heart bypass, double hip-replacement, gall bladder removal, podiatric care, arthritis ... I had to admire her sense of humor. It showed that she was glad to be alive, despite the ailments. And I was glad she was alive too, because, as she went on to tell me, she spends most of her retirement time at volunteer activities with children and shut-ins, valuable community service for no pay. Calculated by the hour at a fair wage, she is probably paying back a lot of her doctor bills.

As the Mamies of the world multiply, America, along with all the industrial nations, is going to become a health care economy. It will happen with just the same spontaneous consensus that led us to span the continent with railroads. Money spent on and money made from health care is already fast becoming a major economic indicator; in the future it may become *the* major indicator. Caring for Mamie will account for more and more paychecks. Providing the medical miracles, pharmaceuticals, prosthetic equipment she needs will earn more and more businesses and investors fat profits. Discovering ways to solve the tricky biological problems of aging will become a primary attraction for our best scientific and technological talents.

For that matter, it is not just the elderly who are transforming us into a booming health care economy. Young and old, we are in this together, wanting ever more of what modern medicine can give. Recently, it was discovered that CAT scans can locate cancer at a very early operable stage. Some physicians now think mass scanning for everybody above the age of thirty might be a good idea. The only drawback? Cost. But can anybody doubt that, once the word gets around, life-saving cancer scanning will come to be seen as a medical necessity worth more to most people than sport utility vehicles?

As of 2001, New Jersey, under a Health and Wellness Promotion Act, has mandated that HMOs provide free annual physical examinations to every adult in the state. The testing includes pap smears, mammograms, blood tests, and sigmoidoscopies. The program will result in higher taxes to cover the costs, money that will be paid to health professionals for their services. It will also result in all the health care costs that New Jersey residents will incur by living longer because of the tests. After all, without the program, many of them would have died sooner rather than later, some of them well before they got to their retirement years. Is this a better or worse way to use the wealth of New Jersey residents than building a new sports stadium? Does it make the state richer or poorer?

When we were a youthful, suburbanized society always on the move, we voted with our pocketbooks to buy gas-guzzling cars, build freeways, and pump petroleum. Soon the same boomers who spent to repair their cars will spend more to repair their physiques. The "raw material" of our economy will be ailing and aging bodies; the "product" will be better health, longer lives. And if for-profit HMOs will not pay for that product willingly, they are likely to be forced to do so — if necessary to the point of driving them out of the business of life and health.

Like every other economy, health care obeys the first law of money, which is that "money keeps moving." Having most of our money moving through the hands of doctors and nurses, physical therapists and pharmacists, hospital administrators and nursing-home attendants frankly makes more sense to me than spending on cars or computer games. It is both environmentally sustainable and morally defensible. The people of the United States now spend $630 billion annually on casino and lottery gambling, a figure three times higher than the amount we spend on Medicare — and that does not factor in the possibly billions more that Americans funnel into illegal gambling for the benefit of organized crime. A January 2001 report on *60 Minutes* estimates that as much as $400 billion may be wagered each year on professional football, much of it by way of Internet web sites. In the near future, the amount spent on "gaming," as it is euphemistically called, will rise as more concessions are made across the country to Native American casinos. Bear in mind that whenever you hear worried reports about the rising cost of Medicare, no figure you hear quoted is likely to catch up with what we feed into slot machines over the next few generations.

In the course of this century, we may spend most of the nation's wealth keeping millions of Mamies in good working order — if for no other reason than that the Mamies will vote to make sure we do. But then, I cannot imagine any thoughtful person begrudging them all they need to live a full, active life. After all, these are the people we call Dad and Mom, Grandma and Grandpa. There may be twenty-somethings who would rather spend our national abundance widening the fast lane or exploring galaxies far, far away. But until under-twenties, only a quarter of whom turn out to vote, become a significant constituency, nobody is going to pay much attention to their whims and wishes. In any case, we must be patient with them. By the time they reach their forties, they will start thinking more like Mamie.

CHAPTER FOUR

---

## ENTITLEMENTS AND THE ETHICS OF AFFORDABILITY

I f we were to believe the conservative think tanks that are providing so much ideological firepower to the campaign against entitlements, we might almost assume that Social Security and Medicare were foisted upon an unsuspecting nation in the dead of night by a conspiratorial gerontocracy. The truth is quite the opposite. Until the Great Depression, elderly Americans had little voice in our political life; their power and organization did not compare to that of the business interests that bitterly opposed all publicly-funded pension plans.

Even in the boom years of the 1920s, the American business community openly celebrated the "fearsome prospect of old-age dependency" as a character-building force. It saw social *insecurity* as the "chief discipline in the interest of wholesome living." As one conservative economist of the period insisted, "the ultimate test of the wisdom of the various forms of public provision for destitute old age must be, not merely the comfort and gratification of the individual concerned, but the influence on the moral fiber of the community."[1] When at last the Roosevelt New Deal introduced a pension program — a modest one in comparison to those in other industrial nations — FDR's right-wing critics hastened to warn that Social Security was "begging the unfit to be more unfit." The plan, they argued, removed "one of the points of pressure which has kept many persons up to the strife and struggle of life."[2]

THE SILENT VICTIMS OF "PROGRESS"

Whenever seniors hear themselves portrayed as an invincible vested interest in our electoral system, they should look to their history for the truth of the matter. In our time, older Americans, especially if they have retired into a comfortable middle-class status, may not think of themselves as victims. Nevertheless, they share with all older people a long, sad history of bleak mistreatment they would do well to remember. For generations they have suffered wrongs inflicted on them often by their nearest and dearest. With the exception of some traditional societies where elders may be honored — if for no other reason than that there are so few of them around — not many societies have treated their seniors as more than troublesome dependents who are expected to stand aside and let life pass them by. That has certainly been the case in the modern Western world, where the old have been seen as the claim of the dreary past upon the busy forces of progress.

The new industrial economies of the nineteenth century took an especially savage toll among older workers. The men burned out early at the heavy and dangerous work they did in the factories and mines, on the railroads, in the oil and timber fields. The women grew old before their time in the sweatshops and mills. Even if older workers kept their health and strength, industrial accidents, for which there was no compensation or adequate medical care, might take them off the job at any point. During the early generations of the industrial revolution, the aged, unless they belonged to the propertied classes, ordinarily ended lives of hard labor assimilated to the status of "the poor." Even if they had worked all their lives, they were expected to die as marginal paupers. If the elderly wished to avoid the humiliation of public assistance, they had no place to turn for care after they left the payroll but to their children. They might be classed among the "impotent" or "deserving" poor, but they were still viewed as a burden. If they suffered, they suffered in silence.

Social Security came late to the United States, long after the welfare state was taken for granted in Europe. It was a step forward, though a small one. Yet twenty years after the first Social Security check was sent out in 1941, "old" almost invariably still implied "poor." In his classic 1963 study of American poverty, *The Other America*, Michael Harrington placed the elderly population of the United States near the bottom of the social order. He observed what was already becoming the great demographic irony of modern times. "Only a society of abundance could produce such a high proportion of old people. We can afford them, we can create them, because we are so rich. But ... these human products of abundance [are] denied its fruits. We tolerate them as long as they are poor."

76

Harrington estimated that half the Americans over the age of sixty were living below "minimum standards of decency," somewhere near the level of America's inner-city minorities and rural slum-dwellers, with whom they overlapped as the poorest of the poor. Their poverty rate was three times higher than that of any other group in the nation. The main reason for their declining status was the obvious one: sickness. The rapidly rising cost of good medical care and adequate health insurance — if the elderly could find it at all — was impoverishing them. And lacking medical care, they were trapped in a downward spiral. As Harrington put it, "We have ... a storage bin philosophy in America. We 'maintain' the aged; we give them the gift of life, but we take away the possibility of dignity. Perhaps one of the most basic reasons why America has such problems with its elderly men and women is that America really doesn't care about them."[3]

## WHO'S ENTITLED?

While Medicare was under consideration in 1963 as part of his Great Society, Lyndon Johnson convened a Presidential Council on Aging. Among its tasks was to draw up a profile of the typical sixty-five-year-old American. The council's picture was dismal in the extreme. "Americans of that age were typically unemployed and without adequate income, lacking a high school education, living off a Social Security check, but with no private pension and spending most of their income on housing."[4]

The AARP and, even more so, the National Council of Senior Citizens, an adjunct of organized labor with two and a half million members, played a key role in passing the landmark Older Americans Act of 1967, and an even more crucial role in supporting Medicare against the opposition of the American Medical Association. This was the first significant show of senior political power in our history since the Townsend Plan of the 1930s, the grass roots political movement led by Dr. Francis Townsend that became the model for the Social Security program adopted by the Roosevelt New Deal. At the time, the press was quick to note the growing senior electorate. Even conservative leaders of the time like Senator Barry Goldwater and Richard Nixon began to court the votes of older Americans, who had been seen since the days of FDR as the voting property of the Democratic party.[5] But in truth, beyond their potential voting power, seniors were still not a powerful lobby that politicians needed to view with respect. Perhaps the most important contribution made by the Great Society reforms was that they were grouped together with Social Security as "entitlements," a label that could be turned into a cause.

The motivation behind the Great Society programs was as much to serve the interests of the younger as of the older generation. The Johnson agenda for the elderly was welcomed as a way to free footloose, upwardly mobile children from being tied down by the needs of their aging parents. The journalist Max Frankel, who was present when President Johnson signed Medicare into law, relates a telling anecdote. He recalls saying to the president, "My mother thanks you." To which Johnson replied, "No, it's *you* who should be thanking me." One of the complicating features of the current debate over entitlements may be the fact that younger people have grown less aware of how valuable Social Security and Medicare are to them. "How many young people," wonders the social historian Edward Berkowitz, "give even passing consideration to the economic burden lifted from their shoulders by having their parents and grandparents on Social Security?" And, one might add, even more so Medicare.

Given the affluence of postwar America, the younger generation of that prospering period voted enthusiastically to pack their parents off in mobile homes or to retirement communities. One might almost argue that the principal financial beneficiary of Medicare was the medical industry, which has cashed in on the program ever since — and not always by the most ethical means when it comes to accurate billing. How else could the elderly afford the wonders of life-extending medicine? Writing just a decade after Medicare was inaugurated, one scholar concluded that Medicare

had been bitterly opposed by conservatives as a form of "socialized medicine." But the result has not been socialism at all — rather, a corrupt medical form of state capitalism, which has combined the vices of both ideological worlds without the virtues of either. The American health system has encouraged physicians to become medical entrepreneurs — except that it is the patient who assumes the risk and the physician who takes the profit. Proprietary hospitals and nursing homes have become business corporations more profitable than Exxon or United States Steel. Drug companies have driven up the prices of medicine by conspiracy and collusion. No other society in the world has tolerated a system of medical care which was so expensive and so corrupt.[6]

In short, entitlements entitled more than the elderly. Doctors felt entitled to be paid their fees; pharmaceutical companies felt entitled to fatten their profits; children felt entitled to have their own independent family lives and lucrative careers. In the 1960 census 80 percent of American households headed by people over sixty-five years old claimed to be financially "independent." That was surely an improvement upon the old-age indigence of the 1930s. But that statistic can be read another way. It also meant that the young marrieds of the baby boom generation were going to be just as "independent" of their aging parents. They could plan their lives without assuming their impoverished mothers and fathers would one day be moving in with them.

Despite Medicare and steady improvements in Social Security, poverty among seniors remained intractable through the supposedly spendthrift 1960s. Yes, people were living longer; the world was in fact experiencing what Robert Butler called an "elderly population explosion." But, Butler asked,

> ... is it all worth it? The truth is that we cannot promise a decent existence for those elderly now alive. We cannot house them, employ them or even feed them adequately. ... We talk earnestly about our "senior citizens," but we do not provide enough for them to eat. We become angry with them for being burdens, yet we take for granted the standard of living that their previous work has made possible for us. Neglect is the treatment of choice. The old are in the way, an ironic example of public health progress and medical technology creating a huge group of people for whom survival is possible but satisfaction in living elusive.[7]

Bear in mind: Butler's grim description was written in 1975 ... not 1875. As he sadly observed, "all too many old people have been brainwashed and pacified into believing they are powerless."

## LOST IN THE CROWD: NURSING HOMES AND WORSE

> "It is like wartime," Miss Taylor remarked.
> "What do you say?"
> "Being over 70 is like being engaged in a war. All our friends are going or gone and we survive amongst the dead and dying as on a battlefield."

She is wandering in her mind and becoming morbid, thought
Dame Lettie.

— MURIEL SPARK, *Memento Mori* (1959)

Those who see the elderly as selfish opportunists and view their programs as a crushing liability of the welfare state blind themselves to the
true pathos that many Americans still find awaiting them in their senior
years. Entitlements critics convey the misleading impression that Social
Security represents a ticket to the golf course surrounding a Miami Beach
condo. But of course that is not so. The economist Paul Elkins comes closer
to the truth when he observes that we live in a society where "old people
die of hypothermia while the shops overflow with videos and computer
games."

Nobody lives high on a Social Security check if that is all they have to
fall back on in retirement. One-quarter of working- and middle-class retirees receive nearly all of their monthly income — as of the 1990s, a maximum of $1500, and an average of $750 — from Social Security. About
one-seventh have no other income at all, and about one-tenth fall well
below the official poverty line. For many, retirement puts an end to a decent paycheck but not to work. As of the early 1990s, 5 million Social
Security recipients still held meagerly paid, part-time jobs as crossing guards,
stadium ushers, parking lot attendants, or night watchmen in order to
make ends meet. For these Americans — and their numbers will grow
steadily — Social Security is all the difference between the deck and the
sea. The great majority of recipients have a poor to moderate living standard or are dependent on relatives to stay alive.

As for the 2 million elders who reside in America's growing number of
for-profit nursing homes, their plight is dismal enough to deserve the attention of some good muckraking journalism. As of the year 1999, the
nursing home industry in the United States was doing $87 billion worth of
business annually, 75 percent of that amount paid for out of Medicare and
Medicaid. What is the public getting for its money? In an investigation of
what he calls "the nation's longest-running experiment in privatization,"
Eric Bates concludes that illegal billing, substandard service, short-staff-
ing, and outright elder abuse are the norm of the industry. "Horror stories
involving nursing homes have become almost commonplace," he reports.[8]

Bates is not alone in reaching this troubling conclusion. Several state governments have gone after nursing home entrepreneurs on a variety of charges, from violating health and safety laws to criminal negligence. In California, the year 2000 started off with a legislative initiative aimed at cracking down on glaring deficiencies in the state's nursing homes. Placing an Aging with Dignity Act before the legislature, California Governor Gray Davis cited a report by the United States General Accounting Office that documents neglect so severe that it has cost the lives of elderly inmates. One in three of California's nursing homes ranked seriously below standard. Among other reforms, the governor has demanded higher wages for nursing home workers, money to train home-care workers, and more inspectors for nursing homes. The situation across the country has become so threatening to the health and survival of residents that in summer 2000 the Justice Department elected to join forces with state and local agencies to do spot checks of homes and to provide heavier penalties for those who neglect or abuse elders.

Even if the nursing homes of the nation can be brought up to a humane standard, not many of the elderly or their children can afford the costs. The United States has more indigent elders than any of the industrial nations: 12 percent of all Social Security recipients. They would have every right to demand more than they receive under the program. If from time to time they get a break on a cost-of-living adjustment, that is hardly a criminal offense, especially after a lifetime in the workforce. Who ultimately gets their Social Security money anyway? Their landlord, the supermarket, the electric company, the druggist and the pharmaceutical houses. Like all money given to the low-income strata, Social Security is a transfer payment on its way through the hands of the poor to merchants, entrepreneurs, and doctors.

We should remember that retirees who can afford the comfort of a sunny beach have saved up for that purpose. They are spending their own money. Would it be fair for these well-off seniors to be means-tested and given less? That may depend on where the line is drawn. A retirement income of $40,000 to $50,000 may seem like a lot at first glance. But what if some of that money is being siphoned off to job-worried children? And what if some of it is being used up by uncovered medical expenses? Reforms in Medicare's handling of prescription drugs have been the subject of anxious debate for over a decade, but until changes are made, seniors may be left to pay thousands of dollars for drugs, many of which are more highly priced for Medicare recipients than for people in other health care plans, especially those who live in other countries. Canadians, for example, pay well below the prices charged in the United States by the same pharmaceutical companies. As long as Medicare and Medicaid are under threat of drastic cutbacks, many seemingly well-off retirees may be putting money aside for future medical emergencies, especially nursing home care, to spare their children the expense. Ever since Social Security was put on the books by the New Deal, conservative elements have claimed that the program diminishes people's incentive to save during their working years. Yet seniors who did save for their retirement are now being used to paint a picture of all elders as parasitic freeloaders. Facing a critique like this is a no-win situation.

Images of greedy seniors are worse than insulting; they mask the true suffering that can still be found among the elderly. A 1995 report in the *Washington Post* offers us a bleak picture of what it means for the poorest to grow old in America. "They were the urban anonymous, living in the odd isolation of large apartment complexes or the modest homes they had clung to after the death of a spouse. Whatever the stories of their lives — their families, friends, and jobs, their triumphs and disappointments — when they died no one apparently knew or cared."

Who are these unfortunate people? They are the victims of the great Chicago heat wave of 1995. The total number of those struck down during that terrible summer was 591, the vast majority of them elderly. Most had somebody to bury them, but there were some forty, with an average age of sixty-seven, whose bodies went unclaimed. The report continues, "The heat wave struck hardest at the elderly who may have outlived family and friends and so were left to spend their final days alone, unknown or unnoticed even by their closest neighbors."[9]

"Lost in the crowd" — that was how the fate of these seniors was described by the local clergyman who has been coming to Homewood Cemetery each month to offer a brief burial ceremony for the city's abandoned dead.

Even when it comes to the supposedly ruinous cost of Medicare, we should bear in mind how modest a contribution it still makes to the lives of its less affluent recipients. The poor who go on Medicare (those who earn below $15,000) have far and away the greatest number of serious illnesses. They bring to Medicare a lifetime of the poor health practices endemic among those at the poverty line: bad diet, smoking, unattended chronic problems for which they could not afford to seek treatment. A 1997 survey estimates that three-quarters of the Medicare population earns below $25,000 a year. But the recipients in that category use over 80 percent of the costs, in contrast to the needs of the better-off. Those who earn above $50,000 in their senior years make minimal demands on the system.[10]

If the overwrought rhetoric of the generational accountants prevails in setting our nation's budgetary priorities, we are certain to be reading more stories like the Chicago heat wave in the years ahead, pitiful reports of forgotten senior citizens who have fallen into various black social holes. Yet even the most rugged individualist should find it difficult to write off the senior poor as chronically indigent failures. These are yesterday's working and middle classes, our parents and grandparents who built the economy we have inherited. Any savings they may have failed to lay aside for their retirement were most likely spent straightening teeth and providing a college education for today's taxpayers. Would their children love them more if they had saved for their retirement by depriving the next generation of the toys, the little league uniforms, the excursions to Disneyland, and the decent schooling on which American parents lavish so much of their income? Beyond that, they spent because they were good Americans — meaning good consumers. How harshly is anybody in America to be blamed for doing what the entire economic system of the nation — the merchants, the advertisers, the banks, and the credit card companies — wants them to do? Recall how often our political and business leaders tell us the economy must be "consumer driven" if we are to prosper. If savings is what the business community can honestly say it expects from the public, would it consider banning advertising from television or illegalizing credit cards? Demanding thrift in this wonderful land of brands is a counsel of perfection.

## THE DARK SIDE OF THE GOLDEN YEARS

As for those seniors who must accept whatever low-cost institutional care public authorities or private sources make available, they may be in for a risky time. "Elder abuse" is now a well-defined legal and sociological category. The harsh cuts in social services undertaken in the 1980s — part of President Reagan's militant campaign to "get the government off our backs" — led to widespread austerity in nursing homes. Complaints by the

frail elderly were many times met by punishment, intimidation, and violence — often enough indeed to produce scandals that reached the front
pages. The problem is not limited to professional caregivers; adult offspring,
who may be too burdened to handle the responsibility, may also resort to
physical and emotional abuse.

Or more surreptitiously, elder abuse may disguise itself as standard
medical care. My grandmother, who reached the age of 104, finished her
life on a steady regimen of Halcyon, a tranquilizer that was once routinely
used to relax and soothe the elderly. She began to turn seriously paranoid,
fearing her own children, behavior promptly identified as senility. At last
she refused to eat, one of the most common ways for the depressed and
desperate elderly to die. The death certificates for such cases usually give
heart failure as the cause. Only after her death did the truth about Halcyon
break into the news. The drug, it was discovered, produces severe emotional dislocation, primarily paranoia. Except for such intervals of unaccountable fear and suspicion in her last days, my grandmother, feeble as
she was in many ways, was mentally alert to the end of her life. The conventional medical treatment she received stemmed from her busy doctor's
conviction that the best he could do for her was to dope her up. After all,
she was such an old lady!

There is another, more sobering statistic that reveals what the true
facts of aging are for many Americans. The Centers for Disease Control
and Prevention report that as of the 1990s, elderly Americans have been
running the highest suicide rate in the nation. "They see it as a solution to
their problems," reports one counsellor who deals in depression among the
elderly.[11]

The statistics bring to mind the historical background to the Social
Security program in the United States. When Dr. Townsend launched his
campaign for old age pensions during the Great Depression, one of his
most urgent goals was to address the suicides that were becoming commonplace among elders who did not wish to burden their children. As he
described the situation in his memoirs, Townsend, a physician already in
his sixties who had just lost his job, was at his wit's end.

> Here were mother and I, both past sixty, both intelligent and
> experienced but not active enough to compete in the world of
> commerce and politics. Or was that true? Economics in America is

something controlled by politics — and politics by votes. We might
be too old to work, but we were not too old to vote. And there were
millions of others like us — too old to work but not too old to vote!
An idea came to me which might alleviate the hopelessness of the
aged people of our community. I had not thought it through as
anything else than that — just an idea which might restore hope![12]

The rest of the story reads like a Frank Capra movie. Townsend, who
had no political experience whatever, published a sketchy version of an
old-age pension plan in the Long Beach daily paper. The letter got syndicated and in short order, he was awash in correspondence from well-wish-
ers and supporters. He managed to beg some free office space from a friendly
landlord and hung out a sign: "Old Age Revolving Pension Headquarters."
He drew up a petition whose appeal was immediate. Townsend Clubs spread
across the country "like wildfire." At the movement's height, the petition
rounded up 25 million signatures from twelve-thousand clubs across the
country. This was the first show of senior power in the nation's history.

Townsend's plan was not much more than a proposal to raise a tax
that would pay $200 a month to retirees at age sixty. "Any aging citizen,"
Townsend argued, "whose life has been one of hard work, depressions,
rearing a family, being a good citizen and neighbor, living a life free from
habitual criminality ... should be entitled to a pension when his days of
physical productiveness have passed." Townsend described his plan as "work-
able Christianity." Leading media had other names. The prominent *Saturday Evening Post* lashed out at the "pension epidemic" that was sweeping
the nation. *Life* magazine saw Townsend's effort to organize "the old folks
of America" as a "grave economic menace," especially if the life span should
continue to rise, possibly reaching 120 years as some scientists then thought
possible.

Even Franklin Roosevelt, while acutely sensitive to Townsend's growing popularity, rejected his pension plan as a "dole." Two-hundred dollars
per month! That would give most Americans more money in retirement
than they had ever earned on the job. Though Townsend was mocked by
the experts, he held to his vision, arguing that it was "only incidentally a
pension plan." This is characteristic of senior politics; the programs proposed have always been quite sincerely understood as offering some larger
benefit to the society as a whole. In Townsend's case, pensions were to be
available only to those who gave up their jobs so that younger workers

might find employment. He spent considerable time lamenting the plight of the jobless young, assuming that his followers would share his paternal sympathies. As the doctor pointed out, with competition from the elderly eliminated, young workers would be able to demand better wages. Moreover, it was a basic feature of the plan that all the money given out in pensions had to be spent in the same month it was received, the better to prime the pump of the depressed American economy.

Social Security was literally a life-saver for the elderly. Between 1940 and 1980, the period that gave older workers wartime jobs and later saw the creation of the entitlements programs, suicide among seniors declined sharply. But from the advent of Reaganomics in 1980 through the early 1990s, suicides among those over sixty-five rose by nearly 10 percent to become the highest rate for any age group in the United States. Among the most heartbreaking stories of our time is that of the elderly couple who have run out of friends, relatives, and resources and who finish their lives in a double suicide.

In dealing with the lives of the elderly, we are up against an intractable existential dilemma. The young may simply lack the capacity to imagine the cold fear with which less than wealthy seniors face their final decades. Youth carries with it certain inherent, commonplace advantages: the ability to scuffle and change jobs amid bewildering economic fluctuations, to wait out the crises in one's life and go on to better days. That is exactly what age takes away. After a certain point, elders cannot easily get back into the workforce and find some way to supplement declining or lost income. Older workers, especially older men in lines of work that require agility and muscle, may find themselves under pressure to move out of their jobs in their late fifties — before they are injured and apply for extensive medical care and disability awards. Once they slow down, even if it is because the job hurts, they rapidly lose their value in the workplace.

Even if older workers hold up well for a good many years after sixty, they must always fear physical incapacity and with it the dependency that takes away all hope of "getting back on your feet." Think how it must feel, then, if the message seniors more and more frequently hear in the media is that they are an intolerable budgetary burden. Not all of them will find the courage to grow feisty and fight back.

Thanks to the fiscal panic that entitlements critics have helped to spread, playing upon the anxiety of the elderly is becoming a growth industry in the United States. Older Americans, living in isolation and on meager means, become easy targets for direct mail and telephone solicitors who inundate them with urgent announcements that their Social Security and Medicare benefits are about to vanish. One typical letter, marked "personal" and mailed in an official-looking express envelope, declares, "The liberal monster is primed to rip your Social Security to shreds. Enclosed is the one document that can protect your benefits." But that document has to be accompanied by a $75 contribution. There are nearly indigent seniors who have donated hundreds of dollars to fright-mail scams like this. Some say they lie awake at night dreading the loss of the only source of income they have.[13]

Just as there are issues that do not gracefully translate across the barriers of gender, race, and class, so too there are matters that do not easily cross the barrier of age. The world as one sees it looking back from age seventy or eighty is radically different from that same world seen looking forward from twenty. Family, work, wealth, security, love, faith, and hope are all transformed in the lens of age.

The modern world has not yet begun to talk frankly about the great issues that the longevity revolution brings with it, nor will we as long as we view the demographic changes of the twenty-first century through the eyes of Dickensian bookkeepers. A society that tilts as sharply toward the senior years as ours now does clearly needs to find a new measure of social progress that includes longevity itself among its highest values. Otherwise, we may be left to conclude that the gift of long life was more a curse than a blessing. Despair may then become the most lethal disease among the elderly, and the one for which the doctors can find no cure.

The longevity revolution brings us such fine possibilities for wisdom and compassion. But as we explore these high hopes, we must also remember that age can bring with it depths of fear and depression that the young cannot remotely imagine. The time may come when even the luckiest among us will have to look into those depths. In that moment, let us hope we have something better to offer one another than a desolate hour in the middle of the night, a cheap pistol, a bottle of barbiturates.

## But There Will Always Be a Ragged Fringe

In the course of this study, we will come upon many dazzling visions of our longevous future. They can be found at all levels of our culture, from specialists in the field to popular science magazines. The head of the American Academy of Anti-Aging Medicine announces that by the mid twenty-first century "physical immortality will be a reality." A popular magazine that reports on life-extension research and medications, carries on its banner the slogan "Living Longer, Extending Life Span, Reaching for Immortality."

But we must also take less exuberant possibilities into account. It may be that, in gaining the ground we have already won for life extension, we have used up most of the progress we can expect to make. Improved hygienic conditions, public health measures like vaccines, heroic forms of surgery, better diet, lifestyle changes, and environmental care may eventually leave us at the intractable boundaries of the physical organism. James Riley the medical historian has proposed an "insult accumulation theory," which holds that aging must of necessity contribute to the increasing morbidity rate. His gloomy conclusion is that older people carry a load of scars and blows into their later years; the traumas add up; the result is disease of some kind striking at a weakened organism. Many microbiologists believe that as the cells of the body grow older, their vulnerability to disease increases. Medical science may ultimately run out of measures to postpone that result.[14]

Whether at the age of thirty (as in paleolithic times) or at the age of 130, eventually the inherent frailty of the flesh enters its claim. Even if all of us could one day expect to become centenarians, somewhere not far beyond there may lie a physical barrier that we will never cross. This has led Anthony Smith to a gloomy conclusion. "Put at its crudest, the advances in medicine are enabling more and more of us to achieve senility."[15] Dr. Allan Roses, a Duke University specialist in the genetics of late-onset diseases, takes the same position. He believes that even if we eliminate all other causes of death, those who might then reach an age of about 140 will finally succumb to Alzheimer's disease. Our best hope in his eyes is that the disease can be delayed for more and more people until they pass the age of one hundred. But after that, he believes, "we are all moving toward Alzheimer's disease, but at different rates and ages."[16]

That is where the dilemma of the ragged fringe begins.

By "ragged fringe" I mean the inevitable vulnerability of the physical organism, the point at which we must find the wisdom that Sigmund Freud once called "acquiescence in fate."

We tend to see every advance in medical progress as a clear victory over death, as if we were driving back an enemy who will one day be defeated and sue for surrender. But the military metaphor misleads. Death is not a foe over whom we will ever gain a final victory. Every elderly person who does not simply drop dead after years of perfect health must at last slip away into some protracted state of physical decline, possibly requiring more and more care as life draws to its end. Death's strategy in the face of each new medical victory, if we must speak in these terms, is that of strategic retreat — until at last we, the "victors," are worn down and must give up.

This grim fact does not preclude continuing good news on the aging front. For example, the National Long-Term Care Survey, a 1996 federal study of some twenty thousand seniors over the age of sixty-five, concludes that a growing number of the elderly are now able to care for themselves. Incapacitating illness among the Medicare population has been dropping 1 to 2 percent each year since the survey started in 1982. Chronic diseases like high blood pressure, arthritis, and emphysema among those who reach sixty-five are steadily declining. One demographer estimates that these improvements alone, mainly due to better public health, nutrition, and hygiene, have saved Medicare $200 billion between 1962 and the mid-1990s.

Similarly, disabilities among the aged are being postponed more and more effectively. Estrogen supplements keep women in far better condition longer. Even the nursing home population has benefited from high-resistance strength training that doubles the power of quadriceps and makes those once bound to wheelchairs ambulatory.[17] The New England Centenarian Study at the Harvard Medical School has discovered that seniors who reach their nineties tend to be healthier than those in their eighties and seventies. Move ten years further along, and some 20 percent of surviving centenarians may still be alert and competent — some even holding intellectually demanding jobs.

All to the good. But at *some* point, durability and good luck give out. Our life span inevitably outruns our health span. Despite the resiliency of many in the ninety-plus population, half of those who reach that age can be found in nursing homes in deteriorating physical and mental condition. And what else would we expect? Keeping people in good shape into their seventies, eighties, and nineties only postpones the inevitable for another decade or two.

Few would question the value of those extra years. But somewhere not far beyond them waits expensive surgery and medication, the intensive care unit and nursing care — and with them rising medical bills. Thus, the more people who reach a healthy seventy or eighty or ninety years, the more people there will be moving into the ragged fringe. From each individual's viewpoint, an additional decade, even one more year of active life is a blessing; none of us would refuse the gift. But from society's viewpoint, it does not matter how long physical decline and incapacity are delayed; sooner or later, they appear and the costs mount.

There are gerontologists who have taken a strong position on this matter. Leonard Hayflick, for example, is "apprehensive about extending average life expectancy beyond age one hundred once the leading killers are resolved, because the result would be disease-free but nonetheless functionally weaker, still inexorably aging people. ... Old people will simply become older, condemned to the vicissitudes of a continuing aging process. And that outcome, I believe, is undesirable for most people."[18] Hayflick argues that we should round off longevity research when it has eliminated the current major killers — heart disease and cancer — and settle for a life span of about 120.

He may be right. The extra years that medical science adds beyond ninety or one hundred may not be worth living — as judged rationally and in the abstract. But that is rarely how this most vital of life and death decisions is made. Unless people are in great pain, they may cling to life out of fear or longing. Or they may build up false expectations about the years ahead as less than rational forces come to play an inordinate role in the coming elder culture.

In this sense, medical science is the victim of its own claims and successes. It has achieved so much that it is easy to believe its triumphs may continue forever. The very fact that new things keep coming to light — new techniques, new medications — encourages us to hang on longer. There will always be researchers who promise miracles: skin that will not wrinkle, eyes that will not dim, limbs that will not lose the vigor of youth. Estrogen is doing wonders both physical and mental for older women and may one day also be prescribed for men, who have already been promised drugs that will overcome baldness and impotence. Cosmetic surgeons are busily finding ways to put a good face on old age. The media are bound to play a key role in this, presenting uplifting reports of energetic seniors still climbing mountains or winning dance contests. Such stories encourage the belief that one's own senior years may yet benefit from unexpected discoveries.

At a certain point, matters of medicine overlap with matters of commerce. As we move through the longevity revolution, business interests are bound to work up an ever greater investment in merchandising hope. Retirement community entrepreneurs have an obvious reason to paint rosy pictures of their clients sporting on the green; cruise-ship and vacation firms are already populating their commercials with carefree seniors waltzing across the quarterdeck by moonlight. Pharmaceutical companies are certain to fill television and senior magazines with more and more tantalizing advertisements for pills and tonics guaranteed to revive the failing body. "It's a great time to be silver," announces a vitamin supplement firm, featuring a vignette of happy, active elders. As the senior market grows, others will find ways to exploit such wishful fantasies. The boomers may soon find themselves surrounded with treacherous illusions of eternal youth. Keeping the discussion of longevity real is going to be a struggle.

I count myself among those who doubt the value of adding a few more months of enfeebled life when the measures become heroic and exorbitant. Suppose we could choose in advance which procedures are worth their long-range cost; suppose we could agree what "worth" means in this context. Perhaps then we could close down certain lines of research before we had committed both our hopes and resources to them.

But that calculation is quite unrealistic. At first sight, *everything* that extends life looks desirable. Every breakthrough looks bright with promise. That is what the physicians behind every medical advance draw upon in winning public approval and funding for their research. People do not leap into the ragged fringe; they *edge* into it step by step as they accept each new medical marvel. *Hope is the bait.* It is only when they are already on the fringe that they and their doctors may learn that the life they have gained brings with it intolerable pain or disability and the need for more medical care than anybody anticipated. Until our culture provides some very different way of understanding death than as a defeat, what can we expect but that seniors and their families will gamble on survival?

And what will we do if the ragged fringe should one day be filled with millions of severely incapacitated nursing home inmates and Alzheimer's victims who are somebody's loved ones?

The answer is obvious: *We will care for them.* It will cost and we will pay the cost as the inevitable result of longevity. We will accept long-term care as our peculiar modern plight in the same way that our ancestors accepted what they could not change, whether plagues or famines or an infant mortality rate that took the life of every third child born. The full force of our religious and ethical heritage points us toward that decision. The struggle to keep the ragged fringe as distant and as narrow as possible will surely continue, but medical science may one day have to tell us that "living long and dying fast" is the best we can hope for. In that cruel interval between the "long" and the "fast" our society will be called to nobility. It will have to pioneer policies of altruism that have no precedent in human history. It will have to see the care we afford the old and the ill as a prime measure of our social character.

## MEMENTO MORI

In analyzing the cost of entitlements, one must make no rosy assumptions. Aging will not bankrupt us, but nonetheless the industrial societies of the world have been swept into a permanent and expensive demographic shift. We must accept as given that longevity requires a substantial reallocation of the national wealth. As of the 1990s, the total annual cost of medical care in the United States was over $800 billion (11 percent of GDP). As we have seen, the Health Care Financing Administration estimates that our national medical bill will mount to more than $2 trillion by 2007 (15 percent of GDP). Is that too much? Or too little? The President's Council of Economic Advisers cannot decide the matter for us. There is no iron law of economics we can invoke. Only we ourselves, working by what our hearts and consciences tell us and on the advice of the best ethical counselors we can find, can give the answer. Unless we find ourselves in some future cold war that brings with it an arms race as costly as that of the 1950s, 1960s, and 1970s, the cost of an aging population may indeed rise until it outweighs all other budgetary responsibilities. But, as I suggest in later chapters, the total benefits of longevity — cultural, ethical, and even economic, the gains it brings us in wisdom, compassion, and spiritual fulfillment — may far outbalance that cost.

Once we accept that perspective on the matter, we can face up to the fact that even many of the short-term economies that are being proposed for Medicare will not save money over the long run, not if we keep the dilemma of the ragged fringe clearly in view. No matter how many rabbits we pull out of the budgetary hat, demographic reality begins with the recognition of the one overriding fact we have taken as the basis for this study: More (and more) people are living longer (and longer). Combine that fact with the simple truth that few people stay healthy to the day they die, or die quickly when they do reach old age, and it becomes clear that, even with rigorous cost containment, the cost of senior medical care is bound to rise steadily. That is inherent in modern medical technology.

For example, the gerontologist Bernard Starr has wisely recommended greater use of preventive medical counseling as part of Medicare. He suggests that counseling be connected with a mandatory schedule of monetary incentives and disincentives. In a *Barron's* magazine article titled "This Longevity Is Killing Us," Starr points out that, "Despite our spending a greater percentage of gross domestic product on health care than any other country, a scant 3 percent of that spending goes for prevention." He advocates a number of reforms, among them: granting credits toward health services premiums for those who participate in fitness programs; requiring chronic smokers to do community service with patients dying from smoking-related emphysema; and assigning personal health-care counselors to the members of all health plans, including Medicare and Medicaid.[19]

Of course we should make the changes Starr suggests, because it makes perfect sense from each individual's viewpoint. But then let us factor in the true long-term costs. Testing and screening always produce a number of false warnings that require more expensive testing to check and confirm. On the other hand, if the tests are correct, they are apt to find problems early and result in higher costs at that point to treat patients who must finally develop *other* conditions that will eventually kill them when they are further out on the ragged fringe. Extending life is a worthy goal, but it does not save money.

Nobody conceived of Social Security and Medicare as object lessons in the high price of progress, but that is what these programs are turning out to be. They are forcing us to ask an unprecedented question: *What is life worth by the day, the week, the year?* When we say that life is infinitely precious, do we really believe that? Working from hearsay, early anthropological studies reported that the Inuit once left their elderly to starve on an ice floe when food was short in the community. Would we institute measures like that in a society where the hospital may be located within sight of the theme park and the shopping mall?

The science fiction film *Logan's Run* tells of a society where everybody is deceived into committing suicide at the age of thirty. Those who agree to self-immolation are promised safe passage into an ethereal land of ease and plenty. It is the only way the society can maintain its high investment in entertaining diversions and sybaritic pleasures. In another anti-utopian saga, *Soylent Green*, the elderly are encouraged to volunteer for painless euthanasia. In a hopelessly overpopulated world, they are encouraged to die the way Socrates supposedly died, dozing off peacefully after drinking hemlock. They can even choose the music they wish to have played in the background.

Unless we are prepared to dispose of our elders in some similarly economical way, all our thinking about the costs of longevity has to begin with sober acceptance of the fact that we are dealing with a responsibility that is here to stay and is going to rise in cost as more people experience the benefits of modern medicine. No honest study of longevity can avoid that fact.

*Memento mori.* Think upon death. That phrase, once carved on the walls of every medieval church, now finds a place in public policy. It reminds us that affordability is an ethical, not an economic, category. All of us, but especially the young and healthy, have to ask about that final stage of life: *What do I want to find waiting there for my parents, for my children, for myself?* The sooner we face that question, the easier our transition will be into the compassionate community we must become.

## ELDER INSURGENCY

> I am afraid to grow old — we're all afraid. In fact, the fear of growing old is so great that every aged person is an insult and a threat to the society. They remind us of our own death — that our body won't always remain smooth and responsive, but will someday betray us by aging, wrinkling, faltering, failing. The ideal way to age would be to grow slowly invisible, gradually disappearing, without causing worry or discomfort to the young.
>
> — SHARON CURTIN, *Nobody Ever Died of Old Age, In Praise of Old People, In Outrage at Their Loneliness* (1972)

What Curtin was sure we needed was "a revolt of old people." As she put it:

> Any real change will have to originate with the old themselves. I think it is time for old people to turn their energies toward discovering their common oppression, from thinking about safe, gracious living out in some planned community to a fight for self-respect and their right to a place in the larger community.

When Curtin raised that appeal, she saw nothing on the scene that remotely resembled a senior revolt. The AARP was in its infancy as a political lobby; seniors were still largely a marginalized constituency. As of the year 2000, we have still not seen a senior revolt. On those occasions when older Americans have flexed their voting muscle through the AARP, they have done little more than defend programs that guarantee them minimal independence. They have neither gouged the public treasury nor held the nation up for ransom. By no stretch of the imagination can lobbying for catastrophic medical insurance or defending a cost-of-living adjustment that permits a Social Security recipient to buy a better grade of beef be characterized as "self-enrichment."

Since the days of the Townsend Plan, the goal of senior political action has been to maintain a decent minimum standard of life without unduly burdening one's children. Those who raise such groundless fears about the recent electoral power of senior Americans are perpetrating an opportunistic deception. The clout of senior Americans hardly compares with that of any major financial interest or industrial lobby.

But all that may be about to change in ways no political philosopher could have imagined. As the conventional wisdom would have it, revolutionary upheaval arises from the dispossessed and wretched of the Earth. The obvious candidates for that role have been workers and ethnic minorities, but never the elders of the society. Perhaps that is because so few people survived into old age in the nineteenth century, and those who did arrived at that status depleted of resources and strength. Since they were no longer in the workforce, they were regarded as dependents of those who were. Their interests were those of the families that fed and housed them. Or, if they possessed material wealth, they were assimilated to the ruling class.

As for how and when and why radical change would take place, that has always been understood as a matter of ideology. If revolutions were going to happen, they needed a set of clear political principles that could be identified as some kind of "-ism." But as boomers move into their retirement years, they may invent a new kind of radicalism, a *physiological* radicalism, a force for change that arises from the needs of the ever-more-vulnerable body. It would be a nonverbal ideology written in EKG readings, cholesterol levels, and blood tests.

Older people need care. They need the services of health care professionals; some may eventually need to go into assisted-living households or nursing homes. Younger people also need help, if with nothing else, then with their aging parents and grandparents. As the number of those who need care grows by the tens of millions, pressure on every health care institution in society will increase. State and federal budgets will feel that pressure, but even more so the quarterly reports of non-medical corporations, which will increasingly find health care incompatible with high profits, or perhaps with any profits at all.

Already, the demand that Medicare recipients have raised in the United States for a "patients' bill of rights" is squeezing for-profit health care providers cruelly. On the surface, the bill of rights looks like nothing more than a reasonable desire to participate in decisions about medical treatment. But many insurance companies have no prospect of meeting the requirements of such a bill of rights if they still hope to make money for their shareholders. HMOs, especially those offering managed Medicare, once thought they could find all the profits they needed through cost control measures. They are discovering how wrong they were. As one report puts it, the rising demands of patients both young and old are "wreaking havoc on HMOs" by undermining their profitability and even driving many into bankruptcy.[20] As a consequence, managed Medicare plans are being abandoned across the country. By the time the boomers move into their Medicare years, there may be no alternative to having the federal government take full responsibility as the single-payer for the medical needs of the elderly.

In effect, by speaking out for health care rights, older Americans are defining the limits of market values when it comes to matters of humane social policy. They are proving, more effectively than any ideological movement of the past, that selfish interest is incompatible with the public good. And they are proving it as a matter of life and death. Because again and again in every emergency room and intensive care ward, that is what health care comes down to: deciding whether life means more than money. Will we save lives even when the patient cannot afford to pay? Will we tax ourselves to preserve the health of fellow citizens we will never meet? Will we make first-class medical care available to all, even if we must give up some purchasing power at the shopping mall?

Where decisions like these have to be made, profit can only be an obstacle. It will have to be sought in enterprises that are well removed from the realm of medical ethics. The patients' bill of rights may lack the elegance of great statements like the Rights of Man and the Citizen, but it is part of the same revolutionary impulse that first sounded the demand for liberty, equality, fraternity. Those who try to stand against that impulse are destined to become the *ancien regime.*

# CHAPTER FIVE

# RETIREMENT: HOW *NOT* TO

E ver since 1983 when Congress raised the age for Social Security eligibility to sixty-seven (to take effect as of 2017), it has become fashionable among political leaders and editorial writers to call for raising the retirement age still higher — to seventy ... seventy-five ... eighty. This is among the most frequently proposed changes for the system by entitlements critics who stubbornly insist that Social Security needs reform. The proposal seems superficially reasonable. After all, aren't people living a lot longer than they were in 1937 when the system was first created? Yes, they are. But retirement is not simply a matter of age; it is primarily a matter of the work we are retiring from.

Whenever I find myself talking to people who feel comfortable with proposals for raising the retirement age, I make a point of asking if they have ever *worked* for a living. They are usually as surprised as I was when I was asked that question some years back. At the time, I was complaining to a friend about the number of office hours my university expected me to keep. My lament brought a smile to his face. He asked, "When was the last time you worked for a living?" I asked what he meant and he told me. He meant *really worked.* Sweated, strained, flirted with rupture and backache, risked serious injury on the job, and finally finished the day dog-tired and dirty.

I had as a matter of fact worked like that getting through college. I held jobs in warehouses, factories, boiler factories — jobs I hated. University teaching was my way out of drudgery like that. An extra office hour or two was not much to complain about compared to a job that bores you senseless or leaves you bruised and hurting.

Most people believe they work hard for a living. There may be chief executive officers who collapse in their chauffeured limo after flying home from a heavy lunch in Brussels. But not everybody leaves their day's work with pulled muscles and broken fingernails, with lungs that have breathed toxins all day or ear-drums that have been battered by deafening noise. Few people who work at such jobs show up at conferences, congressional hearings, or panel discussions on retirement. Most of those who pontificate on the subject are academics, professionals, white-collar employees, or politicians who may put in a tiring day at the office, but whose worst physical pain is eyestrain or a stiff neck — people like myself, a professor of history who could go on lecturing until I reach one hundred. I love my work and will keep at it after some fashion for as long as students put up with me. But I know there are those who go to work each day muttering the lyrics to *Take This Job and Shove It* under their breath.

We hear much talk these days from pundits about the information economy. They often make it sound as if physical labor were a thing of the past. I wonder who they think pulls the crops out of the ground and collects the garbage, digs the ditches and cleans out the sewers. The people who work hardest to keep our society fed, housed, healthy, and on the move — the builders, oil drillers, miners, field hands, truckers, assembly-line workers, construction crews — earn their living from exhausting, often hazardous physical labor, work that takes years off one's life.

When should people retire? My father was a carpenter. He came home every day bone-weary and finally died of a heart condition at forty-seven. Advocating that the retirement age be raised to seventy for people who work like that is simply a tasteless joke. My father should have retired from hard labor at forty and been given the chance to find a job that would not kill him.

In this rich society, how much heavy-lifting do we want to expect from men and women over sixty? For that matter, how many seventy year-old pilots, air traffic controllers, police officers, or brain surgeons do we want to keep on the job simply because they cannot afford to retire? They may persevere at their work, but in some of these occupations it is surely best for the public safety to allow earlier rather than later retirement.

This, I suggest, is the key to any ethically searching discussion of retirement. Start with those who need the choice of retiring early as a matter of danger, fatigue, or pain. Recognize that their retirement is linked to the work they do: hard, risky work that stresses and strains and that may impinge on the health and safety of others. Start from the premise that all those whose work demands a certain high standard of physical, emotional, or mental stamina should be free to retire before they break down or endanger the well-being of others.

That should keep the discussion clearly focussed on the paramount ethical fact. *The quality of working life* has everything to do with determining if, when, how, and why people should stop working. Once we take that simple fact into account we may find it easier to accept the most basic rule about retirement, namely that it must be flexibly suited to the individual.

## THE ROAD TO SUN CITY

Adapting retirement to the individual is the very opposite of what retirement was originally meant to be. Today, when retirement has very nearly been elevated into a culture of its own, we forget that it was introduced in the late nineteenth century by efficiency-minded businessmen who took no interest in the security or the survival of those they dropped from the payroll. One simply got rid of the old in favor of younger, more agile workers. Thus, in the early years of the twentieth century, major employers like the railroads adopted mandatory retirement policies for older workers, but with no pension attached. Retiring meant getting fired and fading away into old-age indigence.[1]

It was not until the days of the Johnson Great Society, when an improved Social Security system and Medicare gave the elderly a chance — though just barely — to achieve financial independence, that retirement began to take on a more benign, if not always inviting look. By the 1960s more than 80 percent of Americans over sixty-five were living in self-supporting households. Even so, their lives were still based on a negative stereotype of aging. This was, after all, the high noon of the baby boom. The future seemed to belong to youth.

In response to this new, youthful ethos, senior Americans of the 1960s did their children an even greater favor than setting up independent households. They began to abscond from the scene and go into hiding as if the world must now be abandoned to the young. In 1962 the real estate entrepreneur Del Webb opened the landmark retirement community of Sun City, the most ambitious effort of its time to create an age-segregated design for living. Webb was overwhelmed by the response. Thousands more than he could accommodate showed up in the deserts of Arizona wanting to buy a home in his housing project. As much as insurgency on the college campuses, the flight of the elderly to secluded places stamped the society of that period with its youthful identity.

Sun City advertised itself as a new kind of utopia, a guarded community based on "active leisure." It promised a "year-round vacation." But the underlying spirit of the place was that of social misfits seeking a comfortable refuge from the bewilderingly youthful country they saw forming around them. "I'm an outcast because I'm sixty-seven years old," one Sun Cityite told a *New Yorker* journalist. "I think the whole damn bunch of us are outcasts who have found a way of living without impinging on anybody or bothering anybody."[2]

For the next thirty years, retirement communities patterned on Sun City became the goal for which older Americans saved and planned. For an increasing number of Americans over sixty-five, retiring to someplace patterned on that gated ghetto was the difference between success and failure in life. This is the image entitlements critics like Peter Peterson have in mind when they warn that we are becoming "a nation of Floridas." They are referring to a segregated, seemingly self-indulgent way of life focussed on the golf green and the bridge table. What Peterson overlooks is the fact that this style of retirement was born out of the baby boom years and is likely to vanish as boomers themselves reach retirement. In the words of Marc Freedman, Sun City reflected "the wasteland that was life for older Americans in the country at that point." Significantly, the Del Webb Corporation has decided to build no more Sun Cities. It expects the coming generation of older Americans to be work- and culture-oriented.

## REBOUND RETIREES

In the mid-1990s, the American Association of Retired Persons decided it was time to retire its title. It now refers to itself simply by its initials: AARP. The reason? With each passing year, fewer of its 30 million members are retired. That is especially the case with the baby boomers the AARP is now working hard to attract, but it is also true of an increasing number of Americans already above age sixty-five. The image of older Americans spending their days deepening their sun tan or perfecting their golf swing is becoming an even creakier stereotype than when it was invented somewhere in the early 1980s.

Whether on the lecture circuit or in private conversation, I meet very few people these days who intend to stop working and collecting a pay-check this side of age seventy. They may expect to leave their present job at sixty-five or so — or to be downsized into quitting well before that. But most expect to continue working at something for either love or money for a good number of years longer. For one thing, they feel physically and mentally fit enough to stay in the workforce. But more often they expect to be financially pushed by the cost of making it through a long old age.

When the retirement age was set at sixty-five, few people survived beyond that. Life expectancy in the United States in the 1930s was sixty-two. Now retirement is a long-term commitment with many more pitfalls along the way. Long before people can afford to stop working to pay their own cost of living, they may require a second income to finance their parents' nursing-home care. Little wonder that 80 percent of Americans in a 1998 AARP survey reported that they were planning to work well beyond the legal retirement age, a result confirmed in many other polls. Indeed, there are financial planners who specialize in showing people how *not* to retire. Stephen Pollan, for example, bluntly tells baby boomers, "Don't retire!" Pollan believes that retirement financed by any of the existing modes public or private is a bad risk: "a pyramid scheme ... you've no chance of winning [that] has produced a society ill at ease, full of contradictions, and unsuited for the next century."[3]

No society has ever seen so much of its skill and energy concentrated in its retired and otherwise unemployed population as the industrial econo-mies will in the twenty-first century. At some point after 2050, jobless adults in the world's industrial societies may outnumber the working popu-lation. This is especially apt to be so if we include the involuntarily retired, all those in their forties and fifties who have been technologically unem-ployed or downsized out of their jobs years long before they wish to leave the payroll. There have already been highly controversial court decisions that grant employers the right to fire workers under fifty as a matter of economic necessity. In a landmark decision in 2000, the Supreme Court upheld the right of states to fire state workers simply because they were "too old." There were legal technicalities to the case that permitted protec-tion for senior employees, but writing for the majority, Justice Sandra Day O'Connor sounded an ominous note. She reached the remarkable conclu-sion that it was logically impossible to discriminate against the elderly, at least as discrimination is covered by the equal protection clause of the fourteenth amendment. "Old age," she reasoned, "does not define a discrete and insular minority because all persons, if they live out their normal lives, will experience it." How then can the old be a minority? Moreover, she added, "Older persons ... have not been subjected to a history of purpose-ful unequal treatment," an observation that reminds us that some forms of discrimination have become so ingrained, we simply do not see them at all.

Some judicial decisions have allowed older workers — which may include people in their forties — to be fired for "economic" reasons. Since older workers tend to earn more, this leaves companies free to clear them from the payroll contending that they have acted for financial reasons, not on the basis of ageism. The courts are still in flux on issues of age. Litiga-tion on behalf of older employees is bound to continue, if for no better reason than that lawyers stand to make a fortune on age-discrimination suits.

Whatever position the law may finally take, those who leave the workforce, whether voluntarily or not, will include an increasing number of healthy, active, highly-skilled men and women. By the time they begin their retirement, boomers may even be the beneficiaries of breakthroughs in biotechnology that will bring them a life expectancy that stretches be-yond a hundred years. There they will be, retired by the millions, with nothing but time on their hands. Leaving so much skill untapped is the one cost of retirement that nobody is likely to regard as affordable. Finding ways to recycle this enormous pool of senior energy — one commentator calls it "quite possibly this country's only increasing natural resource" — is apt to become an industry in its own right and in fact, is already under intense study by social scientists and policy-makers.[4]

But keeping older workers on the job poses some special problems for our economy that are only beginning to register. Do younger workers re-ally want them in the workforce? After all, they represent a serious form of competition in the job market. An *ABC News* feature for February 10, 1998, reports that employees aged fifty-five to sixty-five are the fastest-growing segment of American labor. Indeed, the job boom of the 1990s in the United States was largely the result of recruiting retired workers, many of them at bargain-basement wages.[5]

Entitlements critics purport to be seriously concerned about "our chil-dren," but in seeking to beat down entitlements and push the retirement age ever upward, they may be working against the interests of the younger generation. Suppose they were to succeed in cutting Social Security and Medicare back and thus lowering the living standard of retired Americans. It would then hardly be surprising if many seniors felt compelled to augment their income by bouncing back into the workforce, seeking at least part-time work. Given the fact that the next senior generation will be the healthiest, best educated, and most skilled in history, these rebounding retirees would be eminently employable. In fact, many firms might find them more job-worthy than younger workers, who want secure, high-paying positions. Some firms are already showing a preference for older workers who, having no family life to distract them, can put in more hours and work on odd schedules.

Older workers who have been on the job continuously for twenty or thirty years at higher salary levels may look unaffordable to employers; they may even be squeezed out of jobs in their fifties. But forcibly retired workers who reenter the workforce for supplementary income may willingly take jobs that offer no benefits because they already have their entitlements; nor would they be as concerned about job security or advancement, since they would be on the other side of their careers. They might even prefer to hire on as temps or independent contractors. Bear in mind, these would not be the middle-old members of the senior population we know today; these would be baby boomers, many of them proficient in high-tech skills and professionally trained. They would, in short, be cheap, flexible, skilled, experienced, responsible employees, willing to work without benefits and with a minimal concern for long-term prospects.

*Is this not exactly the cheap, trouble-free workforce that corporate America is looking for in this era of the global economy?*

If so, those workers are waiting in the wings 80 million strong. And every over-sixty-five boomer who feels compelled to keep working will be taking a job away from the younger generation. That could become as great a threat to younger workers as the cheap labor of Mexico and Taiwan has become to blue-collar workers on the assembly lines. If a new employment pattern of this kind begins to take shape in the years ahead, we may find younger Americans wishing mightily that this was indeed a "nation of Floridas" where they could pack all the troublesome seniors off to anyplace well out of the job market.

## THE NEW POLITICS OF PENSION RIGHTS

In the 1990s, while conservative elements groaned over the rising public cost of our retired population, the United States was putting a mere 4 percent of its GDP into Social Security. France was contributing over 10 percent of its GDP to its national pension expenditures, Germany over 11 percent, Sweden nearly 12 percent, Italy over 13 percent, and Japan 14 percent. There have been voices raised in all these nations against the increasing cost of social services; critics make the same arguments that we hear in the United States. In response, there may be adjustments in pensions, but nobody expects that stringent cutbacks will come any time soon.[6]

Moreover, the support these nations give their older citizens comes on top of welfare-state programs that often include universal health care (including dental care, pharmaceuticals, eyeglasses), generous maternity leaves, longer paid vacations, substantial sick pay, and lump-sum payments at death. Yet all of these are prospering nations where more and more people live well. Some of them are offering the United States impressive competition in world markets and doing an effective job of infiltrating the American economy.

Does that mean the United States can use any of these societies — for example, the Scandinavian countries — as a model for revamping our entitlements programs? Conservative critics will surely say no, insisting that these nations are too different from us in history, culture, and politics. Yet conservative organizations like the Cato Institute and the Concord Coalition have been recommending another country as the model they believe we ought to adopt in reforming Social Security. Their unlikely choice is Chile, a country whose history and culture diverges from that of the United States far more than any European nation. Since 1981, Chile has had a privatized pension system; it was imposed on the nation by the Pinochet military dictatorship after labor unions had been suppressed. The system is less than a generation old and wholly untested. It is managed by regulated private investment houses and runs administrative costs far higher than Social Security. The individual retirement accounts held by workers have earned well off special high-yield government bonds based on high interest rates, but the system has yet to take a significant chance on the stock market. Reportedly, one quarter of the workforce prefers to evade making payments into the system. Is this, then, a model that has anything to teach a major industrial nation?[7]

In contrast to other, more welfare-state oriented societies, our business culture prefers to keep insecurity hanging over the heads of people like the wrath of the old Puritan God who rationed grace on the basis of the work ethic. So people do the best they can to provide for their later years. If there is one force that accounts more than any other for the big bull market of the 1990s, it is boomers rather desperately and often whimsically putting all they have into an investment portfolio they hope will provide them with a secure retirement.

What else can people rely upon for more than minimal Social Security support as, with each passing year, corporate America eliminates the fixed-benefit plans that accounted for three-quarters of employee retirement programs in 1975? Fixed-benefit plans, which once provided a guaranteed income for the retirement years, have all but departed the national scene. They belong to the era of the great American job that came to an end during the Reagan years. In their place, as of the year 2000, we have 401(k) investment plans on which nearly 50 million pre-retirees in the United States now rely. These plans, totaling over $1.7 billion, specify a defined contribution to be taken out of each paycheck, but make no promise of any future payoff. What they are worth depends wholly on the fluctuations of the stock market. They are, in short, a gamble. The worker takes the risk, with the result that every dip in the Dow Jones average —- as in fall 1987 or spring 1998 — can send boomers scurrying to replan their lives.

Even if the stock market remains relatively stable for another decade, there is a serious problem about using Wall Street as our main national pension fund. If millions of Americans have put their money in stocks for the purpose of retirement, then at some point they will have to pull that money out of the market. As that happens, equities can only lose value and continue to spiral downward as retirees sell off. Conservatives purport to be concerned about the long-term solvency of Social Security. But corporate America is blindly flirting with a stock market crisis that will come as early as 2010 when retiring boomers reclaim their investments to pay their bills.

Retirement, so baby boomers are fast learning, is a hot political issue that reaches beyond the current Social Security population. Led by such major firms as IBM, Kmart, and Lucent Technologies, several hundred corporations have been cannibalizing the pensions of older workers, slashing what they once promised to pay by as much as 50 percent. Often the techniques used to terminate pension obligations are shamefully underhanded, leaving workers uninformed until they are on the brink of retirement. The money creamed from company pension plans is then appropriated as profit. These ruthless tactics may lead to short-term gains, but they have already inspired a militant pension rights movement among employees who might otherwise be comfortable and complacent middle-class retirees.

As pension-plundering practices of this kind spread through the economy, boomers are discovering that they cannot trust the corporate community to provide them with a secure retirement. In effect, they are experiencing retirement as their great grandparents did in the days of the robber barons; they are being dumped off the job and left to fend for themselves while corporate earnings soar. But what else should one expect from a marketplace ruled by a social Darwinist ethic? Stop regarding secure retirement as a universal entitlement, and the result could be a steady drift toward the same old-age indigence that we knew in the United States before Social Security was passed into law.

But of course the demographics of the twenty-first century will not allow that to happen smoothly. In ever-increasing numbers, voting seniors will put political muscle behind their legitimate needs. If neither the stock market nor corporate pension plans can meet those needs, where else can they look but to the federal government? How else can the right to a dignified retirement be enforced?

## Affluence Revisited

Given the widespread historical illiteracy of our society, many are apt to see the fiscal dilemma raised by the approaching mass retirement of the baby boom generation as something new. But the entitlements controversy actually takes us back to a discussion that began in the 1940s. For a full generation following World War II, economists and politicians of every ideological stripe brainstormed schemes that would grant a basic subsistence to all citizens as a matter of right. Go back a half century and you will find the country immersed in plans to make something like life-long Social Security available to everyone, not simply to the elderly.

In the 1960s major American publications were running editorials and articles on the "guaranteed annual income," as it was most frequently called, all of them addressing the idea as realistic, if not inevitable. Dwight McDonald, writing in the *New Yorker* in 1970, was typical in advocating "the principle that every citizen should be provided, at state expense, with a reasonable standard of living regardless of any other considerations. ... The governmental obligation to provide, out of taxes, such a minimum living standard for all who need it should be taken as much for granted as free public schools have always been in our history."

Proposals like this were America's version of a worldwide moral transformation. It was called "the revolution of rising expectations," a spreading conviction that the human race was at last able to abolish the curse of scarcity. The substance of that hope was in fact the United States. Following the devastation of World War II, the United States was the standard of affluence everywhere. People looked to us to see how the abundance of a fully developed industrial society should be shared.

There were many variations on the theme. Liberals advocated an approach modeled on Social Security or other New Deal programs; conservatives preferred family allowances or, like the libertarian Milton Friedman, championed a negative income tax.[8] The latter was especially popular with opponents of big government; at one swoop the negative income tax would eliminate the crazy quilt of expensive, overlapping state and federal programs — aid to families with dependent children, farm price supports, welfare, public housing, Social Security — replacing them all with the Internal Revenue Service. The IRS would be empowered to send anyone whose income fell below a standard cost-of-living exemption a check to make up the difference. Friedman's proposal seems long forgotten now, but, in fact, it lingers on in a modest version as the earned income tax credit that the Clinton administration sought to build up as an alternative to welfare as we once knew it.

In his bid for the presidency in 1964, Barry Goldwater, a founding father of America's radical right, embraced Friedman's negative income tax as part of his platform. Goldwater lost the election, but his rival Lyndon Johnson at once launched the War on Poverty, which became the official centerpiece for new ideas about sharing the wealth. In 1966 Johnson summoned the National Commission on Guaranteed Incomes. The commission began a two-year series of hearings that finished by recommending "the adoption of a new program of income supplementation for all Americans in need."[9] By the time it reported back, Johnson's political future had been eclipsed by the Vietnam War.

The same year the National Commission began its hearings, the U.S. Chamber of Commerce, the leading voice of the American business community, convened a conference titled "The National Symposium on Guaranteed Income." The event assembled ranking economists of the day to discuss establishing a legal right to the necessities of life for all American citizens whether they held jobs or not. The conference agreed on no single program, but there was an overwhelming consensus that, whatever form it might take, the proposal was an idea whose time had come.[10]

The figure who did the most to publicize the fact of industrial abundance and explore its implications for economic theory was John Kenneth Galbraith. His 1958 book, *The Affluent Society,* named the period. Surveying the American scene from the vantage point of the great postwar boom, Galbraith wrote in amazement at the nation's productive potential. Here was wealth that might well spell the end of poverty. He was among the first in the intellectual-academic mainstream to recognize that America's affluence changed all the rules of the economic game. Hitherto, he observed, economic thought had been based on "poverty, inequality, and economic peril." That was the world of yesterday. "Poverty," Galbraith reminded his readers,

> was the all-pervasive fact of that world. Obviously it is not of ours. ...
> So great has been the change that many of the desires of the
> individual are no longer even evident to him. They become so only
> as they are synthesized, elaborated, and nurtured by advertising and
> salesmanship. ... Few people at the beginning of the nineteenth
> century needed an adman to tell them what they wanted.

If ours is the affluent society, why are we still haunted by insecurity? The problem, so Galbraith believed, was no longer scarcity but our inability to consume enough to keep our productive plant turning over and to keep people employed. The link between paychecks and production was now the key economic problem. In an age of abundance, people were still expected to work forty hours a week for wages, but on the production line their work only augmented the store of goods to the point that the system was constantly in danger of foundering in its own plenty. What was needed, Galbraith argued, was "a reasonably satisfactory substitute for production as a source of income. This and this alone would break the present nexus between production and income."

Accordingly, Galbraith proposed a modest variation on the guaranteed annual income. When the economy slumps and people lose their jobs, let them be given an "unemployment wage." Galbraith called it CGC:

cyclically graduated compensation. According to an official formula, CGC would increase in amount as the number of unemployed increased and decrease as full employment was approached. The more unemployment, the more pay each jobless worker receives. In this way, the unemployed would retain their self-respect and at the same time continue to discharge their necessary economic role as consumers.

Because he was seeking to rationalize a regime of continued high production, Galbraith envisioned a workforce that would fluctuate in and out of the job market. Thus, he missed a promising possibility. If it was proving ever more difficult to find work for everybody, why not simply buy people out of the workforce *permanently*. That is called "retirement." In his analysis, Galbraith did touch on Social Security as an aspect of public policy, but it never occurred to him to nominate *subsidized retirement* as a model for compensated joblessness.

Why did Galbraith overlook so obvious a solution? Perhaps because the longevity revolution had not yet become visible; entitlements were not yet major policy. It was left to Robert Theobald, one of the principal theorists of the guaranteed annual income, to see what Galbraith had missed. He observed that "Basic economic security can be best regarded as an extension of the present Social Security system to a world in which job availability will steadily decline." But by the time he wrote these words, Theobald feared that, "We shall fail to adopt those policies, such as the guaranteed annual income, which are essential in the new era we are entering."

What accounted for his pessimism? Like many others, Theobald saw forbidding signs of social disintegration on all sides. The "liberal dominance" of American politics was collapsing, and with it the belief that "existing structures could create the new programs required to deal with our new problem/possibilities." For that reason, "predictions about steady improvements in man's condition ... are both naive and dangerous. The only conceivable course for the immediate future is further fragmentation and this will result in further conflict willy-nilly."[11]

The year was 1970.

## Entitlements for Everybody

Early in the decade that followed, the lively national dialogue on the guaranteed annual income was closed down so completely that it requires an archaeological dig through the historical record to recover any trace of it. Today if one searches through out-of-print books and yellowing articles, one comes upon the concept like the remains of once opulent cities interred beneath the wasteland of contemporary economic thought. Mention the great postwar debate over a guaranteed annual income even to well-read people, to journalists, to economists, and the result is totally predictable. A blank stare tinged with amused incredulity.

The ignorance that surrounds the guaranteed standard of living is surely the most remarkable example of social amnesia one can name. How many who read these pages can remember that figures as prominent as those I have mentioned in this chapter once proposed *entitlements for everybody* from the cradle to the grave? It is as if we had lost all the accounts of the great voyages of discovery and people had gone back to believing that the Earth was as flat as a pancake.

Why was the discussion so abruptly terminated? Not for any economic or technological reason. The problem of finding enough work to go around continues to plague every industrial economy in the world. By the 1970s new automated systems were coming on line that made labor even less necessary. As that happened, technological unemployment was growing ever more entrenched, as it continues to be. In France and Germany, the unemployed have become all but a permanent organized movement, demanding their right to a share of the national wealth. The unskilled young as well as the retired old find no place in the workforce. Entry-level jobs have been steadily vanishing along with the assembly lines of the nation.

We are, in short, a more machine-productive, less labor-intensive economy than ever. Why then did the idea of the guaranteed annual income drop from the national agenda? The answer, as Theobald feared, was political. By 1970 the cities of the United States and Europe were boiling with protest. The American military industrial complex was at war in southeast Asia and with its own citizens in the streets of Washington. The countercultural assault upon parental values was at fever pitch. With the social fabric coming undone, neither our political leaders nor corporate America were of a mind to dream utopian dreams. The good society would have to be put on hold. Or better still buried forever and forgotten.

By now it should be clear that proposals like those of Friedman and Galbraith anticipated the debate over Social Security we find ourselves in today. Entitlements are simply a scaled-down replay of the guaranteed annual income.

Here then is a strategy for saving entitlements by taking the offensive, rather than narrowly defending the interests of the elderly. Those who wish to defend Social Security and Medicare would do better to return to the subject of affluence, and so reopen the discussion where it left off at mid-century. The boomers, children of the Great Affluence that flowed from World War II, were born into a searching public dialogue that asked how we should share our national wealth. With a neat philosophical symmetry, it is now their demographic destiny to retire into that same dialogue.

But this time it will not be possible to put the question on hold as it was in the 1970s. As boomers pass into retirement, there will be too many people involved and too many votes at stake. Boomers will usher in the senior dominance of our society. What they make of that dominance cannot help but be a major force in our national life.

Just as entrepreneurs, feverishly wheeling and dealing in the marketplace, have long determined the nature and quality of our lives by how they invest their money, soon the boomers will shape our society just as decisively by the way they invest their time, their wits, and their moral energy. They have the best model they could ask for before their eyes: the entitlements they have been given. Why should Social Security and Medicare not spread through the entire society?

## An Economy of Subliminal Abundance

Can we afford entitlements for everybody?

We are not apt to answer yes until we regain the same vivid sense of our true affluence that prevailed in the immediate postwar period. Our situation is once again as Galbraith saw it in his analysis of the American economy in the 1950s. He argued that the conventional wisdom of our leaders had not yet caught up with the reality of our industrial abundance. "Illusion," he warned, "is a comprehensive ill. The rich man who deludes himself into behaving like a mendicant may conserve his fortune although he will not be very happy."

Our political and business communities are still behaving like that "rich man," pretending that scarcity prevails. Astonishingly enough, that pretense continues just as stubbornly now when the federal government is predicting enormous budget surpluses as when the national debt was at astronomical levels. As if it made no difference how much the economy booms, political leaders and economists grimly carry on as if we were still living with constrained fiscal resources.

But in fact there is more affluence as well as more technological power available now than when Galbraith wrote *The Affluent Society*. If there is any reason for middle-class Americans to feel deprived these days, it is because they have so many more things on their family shopping list. As Plato said, "A poor man is a man who has many needs." Those who need cell-phones or sport utility vehicles they cannot easily afford, may feel hard pressed, but if that is privation, it is privation at a very high level.

Over the last generation, our industrial power has been many times multiplied by the cybernated systems that have revolutionized every aspect of our lives. The media are filled with exuberant talk about high tech, but the abundance it brings with it has become subliminal. "Subliminal" may seem like an odd term to use in this context. The word derives from psychology, not economics — specifically from the psychology of perception. It refers to a stimulus that fails to register on consciousness. What Galbraith referred to as "illusion" might better be seen as just such an odd quirk in the social psychology of industrial societies.

People tend over time to lose sight of how affluent they are. They drift away from experiencing luxuries as luxuries and at last experience them as "necessities" to the point of feeling needy in the midst of plenty. Finally, they conclude that we can neither accommodate the needs of the sick and disabled nor grant survival rights to the elderly. That quirk now allows conservative critics to argue that the nation cannot afford entitlements — or for that matter, anything that will have to be paid for by taxation. In the midst of overwhelming plenty, we persist in acting as if we were nearly bankrupt.

But how rich are we? Take one telling instance of subliminal abundance. The automobile. It is an example that has played a significant, even colorful role in the lives of the boomers: It should call to mind a number of fond, nostalgic episodes from their youth, such as the suburbanization of America that took place in the 1950s and 1960s, or the drive-in movie theaters of that day, and any number of cheery television commercials for the great chromium behemoths that dominated the road. Once upon a time, through the first thirty years of the twentieth century, the automobile was an obvious luxury. Those days were long gone by the time the boomers began rasing their own families. By then the car had evolved into a necessity that impinged upon jobs, shopping, and chores of all kinds.

From there, the car rolled steadily forward to displace cheaper, more practical forms of public transport, which were literally torn out of the streets of our cities at enormous expense during the Eisenhower 1950s as part of the new national highway program.

Today a busy suburban mother does not think twice before driving miles to the shopping center to buy a quart of milk; a father may use the car to drive still further to buy a washer for a leaking faucet. Neither mother nor father has any other practical way to buy the milk or the washer. Nor have they any other way to get to their jobs to earn the money to buy the milk and the washer. As a result, they no longer see commuting as extravagant. A pattern of life has taken shape around our daily transportation needs that would require us to redesign the working life of the nation and dismantle whole metropolitan areas in order to diminish our dependency on the car.

Yet, though we regard it as a necessity, the car is a dazzling manifestation of our excess social wealth. Simply look around you next time you are on any freeway; estimate what it costs to transport so many people, usually one person to each internal combustion engine. Calculate the cost of the cars, the fuel, the freeways, the city streets, the parking lots, the entire traffic control system, the insurance we must all pay, the medical care and litigation that follow accidents.

Jane Holtz Kay, a sharp critic of the American automobile economy, has sought to make just such an estimate. Along the way, she discovered that American taxpayers lay out hundreds of thousands of dollars for every mile of highway that must be paved and then repaved.[12] And that is only the beginning. As of the mid-1990s, her best approximation was that the car culture costs each of us $6,000 a year in direct expenses for owning, running, fueling, licensing, and insuring the vehicle. In addition, Kay has concluded that the "external" costs — the cost of parking facilities, traffic police, land use — range anywhere from $3,000 to $9,000 per citizen per year. At an even more subliminal level, Kay has further estimated that the price we pay each year for people stuck in traffic and off the job may total as much as $40 billion.

But we have long since stopped tracking these costs, just as we overlook the installment debt that people are carrying on their cars, which amounts to nearly half of all consumer debt in the economy. At a modest estimate, we are spending well above $1 trillion dollars a year on what Kay calls our "car culture," vastly more than the cost of welfare and senior entitlements combined.

The same commonsense analysis that we apply to cars could be carried out with respect to any number of necessities of life. Our supermarket pattern of buying food, the shopping mall pattern of buying clothes, the suburban pattern of housing, our way of dealing with refuse and sewage, our public health, our forms of entertainment and recreation ... none of these is any longer carried out in a direct, local, and low-cost way; all have become complex and convoluted, with maximum overhead and echelons of highly salaried intervening personnel to administer, supervise, and transport. There are forms of affluence in our society so enormous that asking people to estimate their dimensions would be like asking a flea to measure the size of the elephant it rides on.

We live in a society so rich in time and money that entertainment has become an "industry" whose profits rival the durable goods sector. Today CEOs who run theme parks and market computer games earn more money than the steel masters and railroad barons who built our industrial infrastructure. Even during recessions, the public has hundreds of billions of dollars to burn at gaming tables across the nation. The Pentagon, despite the end of the cold war, continues to spend hundreds of billions more on weapons systems with no enemy in sight. In 1997 it requested more than $300 billion to "upgrade" warplanes alone over the next two years. Somewhere waiting in the wings of Congress are exorbitant plans to build some version of Ronald Reagan's Star Wars anti-ballistic missile defense system, even though tests continue to show that the weapon would be useless. The abundance of the world's industrial systems rolls forward, but political philosophy and moral sensibility remain stalled in a market-based moral orthodoxy that insists people must still compete to hold their place in life.

It would be the supreme irony if the debate over entitlements were to open out into a renewed investigation of the guaranteed living standard, a public discussion that was broken off in the 1960s. America's baby boomers might then remember that entitlements are the single surviving remnant of affluence as we once knew it, a promise of security we thought might be universally shared.

# CHAPTER SIX

---

# THE COMPASSIONATE ECONOMY

The elderly were the first to experience the changing conditions of industrial life, though not in any way for which they could be grateful. They were the first to suffer the economic dislocation of labor-saving technology. Industrial economies have been steadily disemploying older working men ever since. Their labor was no longer needed, neither on the land nor in the factories. Their place had been taken by new technological processes.

In 1900 when life expectancy in the Western world was only forty-five, two out of three men over sixty-five were still on the payroll, still struggling to earn their daily bread. By the final decade of the century, only one in five were still employed, many of them working only part-time. As one sociologist puts it, whether by choice or necessity, "the old are forerunners of a future leisured society."[1]

As chapters four and five have shown, millions of working class and indigent elders find no leisure in retirement. They work on under the pressure of necessity. But there are now millions of others who have earned well or saved carefully and who do find time on their hands after they leave the workforce. For them, empty leisure can become a curse for as long as they have the physical stamina and mental acuity to work on. And so they do, but in innovative ways that are opening up new opportunities for more than seniors. By fits and starts, we will soon find ourselves improvising a postindustrial economy in which increasing numbers of people old and young will work voluntarily as the spirit moves them, at occupations — perhaps vital occupations — that are nothing like employment as we have known it. They will have only the most tenuous connections with standard hiring, ordinary scheduling, or a conventional paycheck.

Transferring over to so divergent a pattern of working life may take some painful adjustment, but in fact it should be seen as a sign of our economy's ever increasing productivity. Needing less labor to produce the necessities — let alone the wasteful luxuries of daily life — we have more leisure than we have yet learned to handle gracefully. The current generation of seniors, especially those in the middle-old range who have put aside some money, are already growing restless with a life limited to cruise ships or the golf course. As a sign of significant change, a distinctive new occupation has already grown up around that restlessness. It is called "volunteer vacationing."

Volunteer work has long been seen as a province of the elderly, whether as museum docents or hospital candy stripers. But the volunteering involved in this new form of vacation is of a wholly different order. Indeed, the term "vacation" obscures the reality. This is actually rigorous public service, but with a twist. These public servants *pay to work*. They often lay out a good deal of their own money to cover the cost of transport, lodging, food, and care. Environmental organizations like Earthwatch and the National Audubon Society, as well as government agencies like the U.S. Forest Service or the Fish and Wildlife Service have been making extensive use of senior volunteers. They now organize vacations that allow participants to do significant conservation work: repairing public facilities in wilderness areas, building trails, taking censuses of wildlife, planting and restoring parks. Sometimes the effort includes assisting on digs to find and catalog fossil remains or preserve native habitats.

There are also inner city vacations, like those of Habitat for Humanity, whose purpose is to build homes for the poor, and Third World vacations that demand substantial stamina. The American Hiking Society, for example, advertises vacations that involve "hard, manual labor in rugged, remote locations, many at high altitudes." Fortunately for older participants, the assignments are not always so rigorous. There are other opportunities for teachers, technicians, cooks, housekeepers, child-minders, and go-fers. But whether the volunteers are providing brains or brawn, clearly the satisfaction in vacations like these is very different from strolling the Champs-Élysées.[2]

## BE KIND TO OLD ANIMALS

Sometimes the chores that turn up for retired Americans are strangely specialized. Around the country, there is a growing movement on the part of zoological societies to engage retired volunteers in a strange new occupation: the often very painstaking care of overaged animals. The assumption is that aging creatures share a cross-species bond of sympathy with one another. If that is so, and if these programs result in better care and longer life for the animals, they may actually yield important gerontological findings. There have never been many very old animals in the world. "Sans teeth, sans eyes, sans everything," rhinos, tigers, and elephants in the wild fall victim to rivals, hunters, or predators. But in captivity they linger on whether they like it or not, developing the common diseases of the old: arthritis, diabetes, osteoporosis, even dementia and suicidal depression. The U.S. government has now retired scores of aged and sickly chimpanzees that were raised for the NASA space program or for laboratory experiments. After spending years in cages, some of the chimps have developed serious psychoses. Placed in zoos, they too are falling under the care of elders, who are expected to be infinitely patient with them.

Lurking in the background of these programs is the quaint notion that the animals might teach their human caretakers something about aging gracefully. That is how a commentator in an *NBC News* feature on the subject put it. He was impressed with how "uncomplaining" the old beasts are, how dignified in their decline. Was I wrong in detecting a subtext, a message to the elderly asking them please to cost less and make less trouble?

There is just the slightest touch of pathos, and perhaps condescension, in programs like this, as if to suggest that old animals and old humans have outlived their usefulness except to one another. There is also something of the lore of "second childhood" involved. As infants, humans play with stuffed animals; in their old age, they get real animals to entertain them. One could imagine a film comedy: how Wally the warthog teaches the grumpy old codgers to mellow out and die with dignity. But if one can see beyond their comic aspect, these programs reveal a curious and growing sense that the old have special gifts of patience, dedication, and compassion — even toward other species.

The old animals program is a marginal effort, but along with volunteer vacations, it distantly anticipates the elder economy we are even now beginning to build. The old are being credited with — or perhaps assigned? — a willingness to take time and be kind in the service of their community. Encourage people to be like that, praise and reward them for it, and they may become that way in increasing numbers. Even the usual admiration for those who take up such work is revealing. It is almost as if the old are becoming a blank screen on which the society projects its moral idealism — at the same time carefully segregating them from the demands of "real life." This, we seem to be saying, is how all of us would be proud of using our time — if only we had the chance. The translation might be: If we were not trapped in this constant struggle for status, fame, success, and money, then we too might have the chance to be fully human. In the Middle Ages, people thought of the monks in much the same way. They exemplified the moral standard of the community: a life of contemplation, spiritual fulfillment, and charity that others insisted they could not afford to choose.

## THE CARING IMPERATIVE

The volunteer task everybody associates most readily with retirement is caregiving. Whether in hospitals, nursing homes, or private homes, seniors can be found taking care of all those who are forced into dependency, including one another. Among the AARP's most successful efforts is its Long-Term Care Volunteer Ombudsman Program, which works in nursing homes protecting the rights of the frail elderly. But in effect, many boomers are already in training to take up society's caring imperative. They, especially the women, are being schooled in coping and kindness long before they themselves retire. When their retirement does arrive, many women of the baby boom generation will have emerged from one of the 25 million American homes that have been taking care of an elderly relative.[3]

The AARP estimates that three-quarters of the people looking after a sick or disabled family member in those households are women; others place the figure at 90 percent. Women have become the default caregivers of our society; they have been thrown into that role and forced to make the best of it. Theirs has been called the "sandwiched" life. No sooner do they finish raising their children than their ailing parents move in for care.[4] As of the early 1990s, the average age of women taking care of their parents was fifty-seven; more than a third were over sixty-five and were destined to spend more of their lives "parenting" their parents than they had spent caring for their children.

Imagine for a moment women in their fifties and sixties saddled with this role for most of the rest of their lives. When anti-entitlements critics step forward to speak for "our children," this is what makes their claim ring so hollow. Far from being helpless babes in arms, many of those "children" are themselves on the brink of retirement. And many more are already so burdened with home care that the last thing they want is to be "saved" from the "entitlements monster." As women demand help with this responsibility, our society will in a sense become more "feminized" in its values — though the real solution is to see acts of kindness as gender-neutral, as much the calling of men as of women. But that, in turn, calls for a reappraisal of gender roles, a project that I will address in chapter ten as among the highest priorities in a longevous society.

One characteristic of the boomers has often been satirized. They "workshop" everything. That is, they get "into" things, turning every experience into a study, from death and taxes to straightening up their desks. Identify something as a "problem" and, as if by magic, "experts" emerge and courses are scheduled at the university extension. It was inevitable that as care giving came to be an unofficial occupation expertise would grow up around it. The books, magazines, hotlines, websites, and counselors multiply by the year. The books bear names like *How Did I Become My Parent's Parent?*, *Caring for the Parents Who Cared For You*, *Caring for Yourself While Caring for Your Aging Parents*.[5]

As the titles suggest, much of the advice has that kind of frankness we have come to expect from a psychologically sophisticated — and saturated — society. It is directed as much to the needs of the giver as the receiver. This is both honest and practical. Nobody who has served in a worthy cause these days is unaware of burnout and the toll it takes. Burnout is the result of assuming any task without some psychological sensitivity to its burdens and liabilities. So the books advise caregivers to define the limits of what they can do, consider their own health, give themselves a break when they need it, let their frustrations show periodically, and seek assistance fast when they cannot cope.

Candor like this is a hopeful sign. What is bound to come of it is a prompt realization that the fiscally cheap solution of unloading elder care on families is not necessarily the best solution. This is saving money at the expense of middle-class and working-class families. Worse, it may be a way to destroy even the best-intentioned families by burdening them — especially the woman of the house — beyond endurance. The result of that will be not only poor care but resentment, hard feelings, strife, and abuse. As the elderly live longer, and as gerontological medical science advances, many of the problems of old age require more than amateurish, part-time attention. Caring for an ailing parent is no longer a brief stint; it may go on for ten or twenty grueling and expensive years.

The classic Victorian family dealt with aged parents by seating them by the fire, bringing them an occasional cup of tea, and waiting for them to die. The wait was usually not long. Maybe the love was there, but not the skill and patience that elder care now demands. Nobody in the past had to administer medication (injections, IV-feeding, dialysis), take blood, stool, and urine samples, give physical therapy, prepare special foods, offer aerobic exercise, groom, dress, and bathe a fragile body, tolerate dementia, and deal with depression — one's own as well as the parent's. And beyond all this there is the vexation that comes with paying bills and collecting reimbursements, processing paperwork and struggling with agencies and accountants. When it comes to the nitty-gritty details of elder care, it is hypocritical to envision it as anything but a hard, bankrupting job.

As all the elder care manuals emphasize, guilt is not the appropriate response for those who find themselves overwhelmed by an ordeal like this. The extensive care that the frail and infirm require is uniquely the result of modern medicine. Nobody in any previous culture was expected to handle demands of this magnitude and live a life of their own. We are keeping people alive well beyond any limit for which the family was designed to provide wholly self-reliant care. Most families still prefer to keep parents at home; they make the effort. But the sooner we recognize the emotional and financial limits of home care for the elderly, the sooner we will begin looking for better alternatives that are bound to take the form of public programs.

## CAREGIVER POLITICS

It is already possible to make a few confident predictions about the future of care giving. When enough people find themselves overloaded by prevailing home care arrangements, there will have to be changes. This is especially bound to be the case with assertive women who have been even remotely touched by feminist values. They could become a dominant electoral factor as politicians come to recognize where the votes are. As a matter of workaday practicality, the women's vote is a welfare state vote. Even arch-conservatives have had to face up to the importance of closing the gender gap by meeting the demands of a female electorate that demands more public money for schools, day care, safe streets, food inspection. As if by cultural default in what has long been a "man's world," women care about these realities of everyday life.

Nursing homes are already an issue. The nursing home scandals of the 1980s emerged as a bellwether issue in senior politics. The problem came to public awareness in 1985, when the media and congressional investigators revealed the amount of elder abuse that was taking place in the cheap, unprofessional facilities many families were forced to use.[6] As we saw in chapter four, the struggle to improve long-term institutional care and make it affordable continues. When in 1992 budget-balancing conservatives in Congress began talking about measures to place a lien on the family home to pay for long-term care, the proposal was quickly dropped as unacceptable — and indeed morally reprehensible.

Full-time, full-scale home care, a burden that is already the blight of many women's lives, is bound to become just as urgent an issue as women find themselves sinking ever deeper into the harsh responsibilities that come with longevity. They will demand relief — and they will get it. With more money allocated for elder care, the caregiving sector of the economy will expand. In turn, caring will become a prominent occupation, even a profession. I have met young people at retirement facilities specializing in elder care as gerontological doctors, nurses, counselors, and all-purpose helpers. It is not difficult to imagine this turning into a growth industry, a category of service employment that cannot be sent off-shore or technologically eliminated. In the twenty-first century, geriatric care may take the place of high tech as the unfolding frontier of opportunity.

Will professionalization of this kind compromise the spontaneous kindness that caregiving requires? Hardly. It will institutionalize compassion and reward it as it deserves to be rewarded — not primarily with money, but with recognition and appreciation. Like all jobs, caring takes talent; it requires certain qualities of character, an abundance of patience, an adult sense of responsibility. Above all it takes a gift for impersonal compassion. I have found those gifts in almost every nurse who has cared for me when I have been hospitalized. The caring sensibility they possessed was not trained into them, it was born into them. Nursing happened to be one of the few jobs that called upon that sensibility. In the future there are bound to be more jobs and better-paying careers for those who have that quality. The more compassionately gifted people we have employed full-time as caregivers, the more socially influential their qualities will become.

Children will recognize caregiving as a highly regarded vocation and choose it as a life's work, the signature profession of a mature industrial society. Imagine people blessed with the ability to give tender, loving care becoming as important to us as hackers in the era of the computer.

Caregiving is not simply a family affair, nor can it be restricted to a profession. As medical science keeps more sick people alive, caring has turned into a spreading, grassroots feature of our society. It is already transforming neighborhoods, since it is neighbors who often have to intervene in the lives of the seriously ill.[7] Much of this contact is casual and private: a simple understanding between friends that escapes public visibility, but the National Alliance for Caregiving estimates that over 22 million households are now caring for neighbors as well as relatives. One federally funded effort called Gatekeepers enlists mail carriers and delivery drivers to learn about the neighborhoods they regularly visit, especially the shut-ins and the elderly who may need their help. They become part of a watchful mobile network of caregivers. Another rough measure: the National Federation of Interfaith Volunteer Caregivers, which trains and supports those who reach out to neighbors, has grown since the mid-1980s from twenty-five local chapters to over six hundred. An important part of that increase has to do with the AIDS crisis in the gay community, taking on the role of traditional families for one another. That example has been appropriated for other forms of care, including elder care.

Increasingly the basic units for elder care, as well as the care of the homebound sick, are the apartment complexes and condos where people find themselves living as age and illness descend upon them. With a few modest arrangements — a doorman to carry groceries, a visiting nurse, some taxi service, a few neighborhood children to run errands — people often prefer to "age in place."[8] The AARP has discovered that our once-footloose baby boom population has begun to put down roots. Almost half the country's older population has lived in the same place for more than twenty years. Researchers have come up with a quaint formal name for such an arrangement — NORCs: naturally occurring retirement communities. NORCs may become as characteristic of the longevous society as the suburbs were of the early lives of boomers. But while suburbs isolated residents from one another and emphasized high consumption, NORCs and caring neighborhoods unite people and emphasize compassion.[9]

## The Aging Opportunity and the Third Sector

When President Lyndon Johnson was formulating Medicare in the 1960s, he also sought to create an Office of Aging at the Department of Health, Education, and Welfare. The office would have overseen seniors serving in hospitals as medical aides. The American Medical Association thought this was a bad idea and vetoed it. The department was instead transformed into a program called the National Senior Service Corps. In 1971 the Senior Corps was expanded into the Retired and Senior Volunteer Program (RSVP).

RSVP is a little-known, vastly underfunded operation that continues to perform scores of vital services. In the mid-1990s, over half a million seniors in RSVP projects served tens of thousands of sites across the country. They tutored in schools, assisted in clinics and courts, did some environmental watchdogging, participated in rehabilitation and telephone reassurance programs, served as companions for shut-in elders, and took part in numerous intergenerational projects. The contribution made by the Senior Companions Program is particularly valuable. In the mid-1990s, twelve thousand volunteers helped more than thirty thousand frail elders to live independently. With nursing home costs running as high as $35,000 a year, the estimated value of the companion service was $150 million.

Marc Freedman, who regards RSVP as a "hidden triumph" of the Johnson Great Society, has called this bare-bones beginning "the aging opportunity." He asks: Why not expand it in all directions as a comprehensive, well-funded national service program? He believes that with enough money behind it, RSVP — and similar state and local programs — could turn the retired into the "new trustees of civic life."[10] The possibilities are vast. Retired teachers could become mentors, retired physicians could become medical counselors, retired lawyers could become legal aides available for all the problems people have with employers, landlords, and welfare and entitlement programs. There is a frontier of work and service waiting to be staked out by retired Americans.

But at some point programs like this raise a question of principle. It has to do with the peculiar status of volunteerism in American society. Volunteering is invariably presented as a noble human act that rises above government and the marketplace. Former President George Bush, who once scored a campaign success by describing the volunteer spirit as a "thousand points of light," praised it as "America's greatness." Like love and motherhood, volunteerism lends itself to many sweet songs. But volunteerism is not politically neutral; it has always been closely linked to conservative values as the glowing alternative to mandatory government programs. Voluntary service is the rich man's substitute for the welfare state and is often falsely opposed to government, as if the two must be at odds. During his presidency, Ronald Reagan contended that the government, following World War II, had actually set out to usurp the fine, friendly things people would otherwise do "out of the goodness of their hearts."[11]

Some among the well-to-do have taken volunteering quite seriously as a personal ideal, but volunteerism can also function as a rhetorically effective riposte to liberal proposals for government relief, welfare, and public works. It can be a thinly disguised effort to squelch those who believe that major social problems go well beyond what sporadic, part-time contributions of time and money can handle. We should recall that volunteerism entered American politics as the pet project of President Herbert Hoover, who was convinced that all social problems could be solved by grassroots generosity. His high hopes revealed their limitations after the Crash of '29. By no stretch of the imagination could a disaster of such dimensions be solved by charitable efforts. It was at that point that the first federal entitlements were initiated under the Roosevelt New Deal.

Yet the very fact that Presidents Reagan and Bush turned volunteerism into a talking point on their domestic agenda has sparked ambitious social thought about what is now often called the "Third Sector." Here is where the interrupted dialogue over the guaranteed annual income continues. The Third Sector is the sum total of all volunteer work outside the marketplace, either by individuals or through nonprofit organizations. It would be the main locus of the volunteer work we might expect of retired seniors. When all the people, projects, and assets in the Third Sector are pooled, we arrive at some strikingly large numbers. In the mid-1980s, by one estimate, the money spent by voluntary organizations in the United States for social projects was greater than the gross national product of all but seven nations. As of the mid-1990s, we have more people working in the American Third Sector than in construction or transport or textiles.[12]

Economists give scant attention to the Third Sector, mainly because it tends to operate in informal ways that produce few statistics. It pays little in the way of taxable wages and it produces nothing that can be measured as "output." For precisely that reason, the Third Sector is a great challenge to economic theory. Here we have all the work, the funds, the resources that hold communities together in dealing with such basic needs as education, day care, health care, legal advocacy, drug rehabilitation, and sheltering and feeding the homeless. Yet one looks in vain for some recognition of its value in standard economic texts or on the financial pages.

In other lands, the situation is very different. In France, where, as in all the European nations, unemployment has been rising inexorably, the volunteer workforce is seen as one important way to put people to work in what is called the "social economy." The French have been willing to offer a guaranteed income to those who agree to contribute time to that economy. The idea is not far removed from the American welfare reform that puts people to work at community service jobs like cleaning up the streets and parks or wiping the graffiti off walls. But in the United States, such work often goes unpaid and so amounts to a form of servitude.

Conservatives like to see volunteerism as a private sector alternative to government. But the two could work in tandem, exchanging resources and inspiration. Government could empower the Third Sector, often in very simple ways. For example, it could channel what is now welfare money through nonprofit and voluntary organizations to allow them to expand their workforce in the community. It could create a "shadow wage" that allows tax deductions for the value of the time one contributes to volunteer work.

When we identify the retired as volunteers and assume that they are willing and able to work for nothing, we may be badly mistaken. For Social Security recipients who are dependent on family to pay their full cost of living, a paid job makes perfect sense. As we have mentioned, several million Social Security recipients must scramble to supplement their meager government stipend. What they find are usually catch-as-catch-can part-time jobs at meager pay. It would clearly make far greater sense to pay retirees to work at something they know or to assume long-term caregiving responsibilities for members of their own generation. But by far the neatest, least bureaucratic way to achieve that goal is simply to give them higher Social Security payments so they will be free to volunteer. Either way, this would run up the bill for entitlements. All the more reason to begin calling our subliminal abundance to public attention. We are rich enough to pay compassion the wage it deserves.

## THE WE GENERATION

If the senior entitlements, allied to a growing Third Sector, should become the model for a guaranteed annual income, we would have the basis for a mature industrial economy in the United States. Such a compassionate economy would lend ballast to our otherwise turbulent marketplace. It would put retired skills to work. It would provide entry level jobs for the otherwise unemployable young. It would put purchasing power in the hands of those who otherwise have little to spend. It would guarantee employment of last resort for all those who lose their jobs owing to global competition. As the pioneers of a robust Third Sector in the United States, boomers would be building a solid economic foundation for entitlements policy and the elder culture that rests upon it. Beyond protecting their own immediate interests in the entitlements debate, they would become the primary defenders of humane social values for all their fellow citizens, beginning with those who most clearly share the vulnerability of the elderly: the nation's children. It should be the highest priority on the senior political agenda to see the same right to a decent subsistence and full medical care granted to the young as to the old. As Maggie Kuhn once put it in calling for a Social Security commitment to children, "We must act as the elders of the tribe, looking out for the best interests of the future and preserving the precious compact between the generations."

A robust Third Sector, fully recognized in economic theory and accounted for in our official economic statistics, could make a substantial contribution to the way we understand the status of retired citizens. It would give economic value and moral dignity to their service in the community. But even so, given the growing size of the senior population, the longevity revolution will always cost the public treasury. At some point, retiring boomers will have to arrive at a consensus about entitlements. They will have to recognize that our country, like every other industrial society, requires a permanent, generously funded welfare state sector to help all those in need. Either that, or they must anticipate a constant battle to save the programs on which they depend for sustenance and medical care. From now on, every budget-cutting attack on programs created to help the indigent, the disabled, and the down and out is bound to impinge on entitlements. Either the cost of entitlements will be used to justify diminishing support to the needy, or continued funding of welfare programs for the needy will be used to justify cutting entitlements.

Since the Reagan and the first Bush presidencies, conservative leaders have done all they can to confuse "welfare" (temporary assistance to the unemployed and unemployable) with "welfare state" (Social Security and Medicare) in the public mind, two very different areas of policy that have different histories and goals. The aim of such deliberate obfuscation has been to create the impression that seniors are living off of "welfare" and should be ashamed to accept handouts. The very concept of "entitlements" is being called sternly into question by conservative ideologues who ask, "Is anybody *entitled* to anything they did not earn in the marketplace?" Sooner or later boomers will have to recognize that their political fate is allied to that of all those who are dependent on our common humanity.

As Horace Deets, director of the AARP, reminds us, there has always been another America besides hard-charging, entrepreneurial America.

> One reason for America's greatness is that through our history one generation has helped another. Sometimes it has been through direct family support. Other times, indirectly through programs like Social Security and Medicare, Guaranteed Student Loans or Head Start. With the many problems our nation faces, Americans of all ages must work together as never before. Those who try to divide us along age lines are doing us a great disservice.[13]

In the 1970s, mordant critics spoke of the baby boomers as the "me" generation, rather as if selfishness had previously been an unknown vice. When they leveled the charge, it was never clear what generation they had in mind as the more appropriate ethical baseline. But if that accusation was ever true, the dynamics of the longevity revolution are bound to lay it to rest. Before they leave the stage of history, the boomers, the first generation to face up to the challenge of creating an economics of permanence, may translate "me" into "we."

# CHAPTER SEVEN

## THE SENIOR FOLLIES

If there is one conviction that every senior in the world shares, it is George Bernard Shaw's melancholy quip: "Youth is wasted on the young." But if the truth be told, age is often wasted on the old.

In these pages I have set out to muster all that is hopeful about the longevity revolution. There is so much to encourage optimism, not least of all the simple fact of longevity itself. The increasing life expectancy of the modern world may be the only clear measure of progress all people can agree on. Given the fact that more people are going to live longer, it is time to start finding a good social use for those extra years. As a political project, that is a novel undertaking. It has been the task of manifestos or mission statements to point the way forward. The old have rarely been the audience for such appeals. The common assumption has been that if anybody has the energy and inclination to change the world, it is the young or middle-aged. Just as no utopian thinker ever looked over the historical horizon and saw a world of elderly people waiting to create the good society, no revolutionary ever looked for a following among the old.

But of course it is naive to believe that anything good is ever guaranteed in human affairs. The longevity revolution could go wrong in any number of ways. I have no doubt that, as our society grows more senior-dominant, conservative politicians who would delight in trampling entitlements into the ground will find ways to suggest that they are actually out to do older voters great favors. It is even more likely that there will be a concerted effort to incorporate everything that is deep and wise about the experience of aging into the dynamics of the marketplace. There may even be those who feel that coping with this great demographic transition is essentially a matter of turning the seniority of our citizens into a sales pitch — just that and nothing more.

No doubt there are boomers who would welcome becoming a business opportunity; in America, possessing discretionary income is a form of validation. Being worth money means one officially *exists*. That is, after all, how boomers assumed social importance in their youth. Before anybody identified them with dissent and protest, hucksters saw them as a marvelous merchandising opportunity: kids with a room of their own, a music of their own, tastes, clothes, and hairstyles of their own — in short, a market.

## Hyping the Generations

Previous generational history has something to teach us about the perils of striking out toward new social values across the great commercial wasteland. In times past, the media and other self-appointed moral authorities might have maligned, censored, or ignored those who made divergent choices in life. The 1960s and 1970s added a new hazard: *assimilation*, which can be a greater threat than repression. No previous protest movement ever had to face so treacherous a strategy. Throughout the period, the radical young themselves worried obsessively about the dangers of "co-optation." As they found themselves reflected in the fun house mirror of the media, they feared that their rebellion would be absorbed into the mainstream culture as Radical Chic.

The fears were well founded. Gestures of dissent became recognized as hot copy, the big story of the decade. The young were vibrant, innovative, sexy; they quickly became an amazing, wish-fulfilling spectacle. There was never a demonstration, a rally, a teach-in, a love-in, a be-in, but cameras and microphones were on hand. In San Francisco the tour buses soon included the hippies of the Haight-Ashbury District on their itineraries.

Those who were the objects of this attention sometimes resorted to extravagant tactics to defend the purity of their stance. People *tried* to look and dress and behave in ways that were unphotographable. It did no good. Grungy rags were soon transformed into grungy fashions. Before the decade was out, expensive Mao jackets were appearing in major department stores and automobile companies were promoting their cars as a "rebellion." Rock, including its various outlaw varieties, became the staple of the music industry. One radical magazine, wanting to make sure no store would display it on the rack, took the title *Fuck You*. At countercultural gatherings, money earned by a book or a record might be scattered to the winds like confetti. Some dissenting voices, especially the rock stars of the era, certainly earned more than enough to be corrupted and probably were. Money is the universal solvent of American society; it melts the toughest ethical armor. I have met few outsiders, radicals, or dissenters who could hold out against a publisher's contract or a network interview. All of us have ways of explaining that the money *we* earn from what *we* do is purer than the money that sellouts and schlockmeisters earn.

When the aged were few in numbers and low in income, nobody rushed to sell them anything except Serutan and funeral insurance. Now, as mass longevity takes hold, boomers are starting to present some attractive market demographics. And they arrive at elderhood with unresolved questions about youth and age that others will rush to answer — for a fee. Already we have a host of commercial interests waiting in the wings to cash in on all the senior follies they can merchandise — and on nothing more so than the flight from age. My local supermarket is devoting steadily more shelf space to handsomely packaged and extravagantly priced longevity potions, various combinations of ginkgo and ginseng, echinacea and chamomile liberally laced with antioxidants. Some carry highly creative copy about the lost lore and secret teachings that went into a rather small, expensive bottle of "rejuvenating infusions." "Age-conscious" producers are finding ways to acknowledge that older people are different, but not, so they hope, in ways that make a difference to business as usual.

The joys of youth — especially as memory wishfully embroiders them — are not easily left behind. Many boomers are displaying a clear ambivalence about their role in life. As reaching a healthy age sixty-five becomes commonplace, they are experiencing a peculiar, late-life identity crisis. Having made it that far, one can now envision another twenty or thirty years of life ahead. That is a much longer time to be "old" than most people in the past had to worry about. It takes a moment of concentrated reflection to realize what this means. At the age of sixty, we may now have as much time ahead as our grandparents could expect when they were thirty and in their prime. How shall those years be spent? A pressing question — especially for those who have enough money to make choices.

Boomers have been haunted since their childhood by the assumption that they can have it all: rebellion and security, dropping out and great jobs, careers and families, high principles and a healthy bank account. Is there any doubt that they will see these impossible expectations protracted into their later years? Boomer men have been targeted for make-overs and anti-aging cosmetics. Boomer women are being told they can ignore the biological clock and find motherhood well after menopause. This is surely going to be the generation that refuses to believe that good looks, hard bodies, high adventure, and careers beyond careers are the prerogative of youth.

That could be a big mistake.

## SURGICAL CHIC

There are more than enough huckstering voices that want people to believe they should spend their sixties and seventies being twenty or thirty all over again — starting with the physical semblance of youth. The means for doing so are readily available and temptingly proficient. The same ingenious medical science that can keep us vital and alive so much longer can also reshape the body in increasingly clever ways. As of the mid-1990s, the American public referred to by the cosmetic industry as "youth-obsessed boomers" was spending upwards of $2.5 billion dollars on aesthetic surgery. That paid for over 2 million procedures in 1995, mainly face-lifts, breast augmentation, and liposuction. The numbers are bound to rise; even oral surgeons are tooling up to enter the trade. Dental implants or even transplants are all but certain to replace dentures in the next generation for those who can afford the bill.

Some of the techniques becoming commonplace would have sounded frightening in times past; they still do, but they are now routine and fearlessly endured. In more elevated income brackets, where the cost of age defiance is no obstacle, surgical improvement is becoming a painful and costly seasonal routine; procedures are planned in preparation for first night at the opera, the spring round of parties, the year-end holidays, or various openings and galas. One must time the operations carefully to make sure the swelling has gone down before the event — unless the procedure is breast augmentation; then the swelling is regarded as a bonus. Some enhancements, like collagen injections to give lips that bee-stung look, may have to be renewed every two months. So too liposuction and skin peels. No longer one time jobs, enhancements that fade or fail need to be tended around the social calendar. Aesthetic surgery is becoming a form of maintenance.

Men, who now utilize the skills of cosmetic surgeons nearly as frequently as women, claim their need for age suppression has to do with their jobs. Males represent a growth market for face-lifts, eyelid tucks, and laser hair implants. More and more men feel that keeping their place in the firm and getting promoted has to do with looking young. But if everybody does the same, what will come of that? In the 1960s, there was a bit of radical folklore about the Maoist students' meeting where every member of the audience turned out to be an FBI undercover agent. Perhaps one day all the thirty-something-lookers around the conference table will really be sixty-somethings. Will they need to wear the mask of youth then?

We may be creating a new category of beauty in our culture: the beauty of those who have been artfully made over with every intention of showing it. That certain tautly plasticized look is becoming as common a sight among us as stretched lips among Ubangi women. A man or woman of sixty who might (at dusk, with the light shining from behind them) be taken for thirty is a makeover; everybody can tell. But perhaps that will matter less as time goes on; it may even become the point of it all. In his novel *The Bonfire of the Vanities*, Tom Wolfe has a category of well-dieted, upper-crust women he calls "social x-rays," ostentatiously lean to the point of emaciation, hoping that thin will pass for young. Similarly, in the anti-utopian movie *Brazil*, society ladies of the future hold parties to announce their surgery, which is meant to be proudly on display. Prussian officers once took pride in their duelling scars as evidence of their manhood. Boomers may one day find a similar pride in the lesions that prove their age-defying courage. Why hide the makeover when, in itself, it makes the important statement: *I intend to remain vital, active, alert, and competitive. I have suffered and spent heavily for this look. Treat me accordingly.* And if the surgery has been well done, perhaps it should be admired as a kind of living sculpture. Then there need be no serious attempt to deceive. The work may be signed, trademarked, and exhibited. The best surgical talents in the business will hold openings and soirees that are, in effect, living galleries of their art.

And then there are the fantasies, the products associated with vigor and high living. Television commercials are already featuring frisky seniors — perhaps a more acceptable stereotype than the cranky codger, but a stereotype just the same. The problem is a tricky one for advertisers, whose main interest is neither accuracy nor compassion. How they cope with the senior market is less important than how seniors deal with their newfound marketability.

At the extreme, we have the pursuit of age-reversal fads, some little more than the old snake oil decked out in new, scientistic terminology. The magazine *Life Extension* now features an updated "top ten" list of youth-restoring elixirs. Vitamin supplements alone make up a multibillion dollar industry. Sampling all the remedies, even reading the literature on the products, could easily absorb all the time one has left in life.

All of these pursuits represent understandable human foibles, rather than serious moral failure. Perhaps they would have become common in any society of the past if the aged had not been resigned to poverty, isolation, and early physical breakdown. A bit of hair coloring and cosmetic surgery need not get in the way of social conscience. But it is quite another matter if playing at youthfulness obscures the opportunity and responsibility for making wise use of one's years.

## THE PRODUCTIVE AGERS

The struggle to emulate youth overlaps with another treacherous distraction in the growing culture of longevity. It is called "productive aging." With the best intentions, the term was originated in the early 1980s by the gerontologist Robert Butler, who offered it as an antidote for the resignation that surrounded old age. Butler was among the first to recognize that America's senior population was becoming healthier, more active, more competent, and more politically important than politicians and opinion-makers had recognized. The older years were taking on vitality. "The capacity for curiosity, creativity, surprise, and change," he insisted, "does not invariably decline with age."[1]

As a counterbalance to ageism, productive aging may have value, but there are problems with the underlying concept. Productive agers can be seen as those who keep competing and achieving into their late senior years. They include those who run for office at seventy, launch successful businesses at eighty, climb high mountains at ninety, win literary prizes at one hundred. They stay on the job and in the race. These seniors are apt to take on great visibility; they have a special appeal to the media because their stories easily qualify as "feel-good" journalism, combining financial success and inspirational rhetoric. These are often moneyed folk with good social connections who drop all the right names, dress beautifully, and look good on camera — exactly what talk-show hosts are after.

Such competitive talents may not, however, be within the aptitude or taste of many others, who are seeking something more in their elder years than a second round of youth. As one group of older women put it in a study of "wise choices beyond midlife": "We are being urged to become politically correct about aging — anything is possible. The elderly Olympics are just ahead. Get Up and Go! ... Can we still find respect and support for contentment, tolerance, and reflection or for being at peace with ourselves, our friends, our families, and the world?"[2]

Betty Friedan, a commentator whose views have to be respected, is a great believer in productive aging. She was among those who helped Butler shape the concept in the early 1980s. She continues to feel it is the only alternative to the self-pity and condescension into which elders have tended to decline. She observes that "It was in terms of work that the issue of the personhood of women was finally and fully joined. ... I welcomed the opportunity to deal with age in such terms." She is impatient with those who do not "want to look at older people in terms of 'work' or 'productivity.'"[3]

Friedan's study *The Fountain of Age* is among the most incisive books on the subject of aging in America. Her intentions are the highest, but with respect to the word "productivity," I would suggest a change of vocabulary. This is language coined in the economic mainstream for purposes of competition and profit. Typically, an executive type who has never met his workforce and who has no idea what, for example, healing or education are all about will push nurses and teachers to increase their "productivity," which usually means demanding that they work harder so the firm can lift its profit margin.

"Productivity" derives from the making of products, and products are for selling. That is exactly what hucksters in the senior marketplace are out to do. So they gravitate to those who maintain an air of success and celebrity into their elder years. As a transitional phase in the unfolding saga of the baby boom generation, we can expect to see and hear a great deal more about productive aging or some variation on the concept in the years ahead: stories that feature later-life high achievers who might almost pass for thirty years old. This is homage to the cult of youth all over again. We are being told more and more wishfully that seniors can keep up with the young at any task. Viewing age this way only makes the phenomenon of the ragged fringe — the point at which physical stamina must inevitably fail — all the more frightening.

If boomers are to be something authentically new under the sun, competitive achievement cannot be their way of using longevity; it is certainly no form of elderhood. Elders must be a force for balance and discriminating choices in our culture, the voice of hard-won experience, not the same old thing in advanced years. On the other hand, calling competition into question and opting out of the race for celebrity and wealth — *that* is new and takes both courage and imagination. Friedan is closer to the key question when she wonders whether "there might be life beyond retirement from the power-sex race?" She is right in sensing that the pursuit of power and sex belongs to the market economy. To rise above the race, then, is the beginning of wisdom. But the correct measurement of wisdom is hardly "productivity," which always comes down to a quantitative result: *more* of something, rather than something better.

This is the issue that arises with urgent economic importance when financial entrepreneurs propose to privatize Social Security, turning the national nest egg into millions of speculative portfolios. Such a policy would tie the senior years to the marketplace in ways that would never allow one to detach and grow beyond it. If one's savings have been invested, then one must attend to the mutual funds, follow their progress, choose among them, watch the ups and downs of the economy with an eagle eye. It is retiring into a full-time business: the business of managing one's money. What a nightmarish retirement that could be, worrying around the clock about the fate of Microsoft and the stability of a half-dozen Asian currencies! Of course, fund managers offer to do that for us, but who can trust them to do the job honestly? Certainly not the productive ager who looks after his or her own needs.

The senior follies all trace to the same source: the effort to deny or defy aging, to continue worshiping at the shrine of youth. That sad desire ties us to the marketplace and its values: money, success, glamour, celebrity. Moreover, the denial of age is self-defeating, because eventually time takes its toll and that comes as a jolt if one has devoted years to fighting off its claim. If wisdom means anything, it means the ability to see through the illusions of youth. That is the most liberating aspect of age. It frees the mind and enlivens the soul. It is the belated beginning of the great Socratic adventure of knowing ourselves.

In one respect the senior follies are worse than merely embarrassing. If boomers lose themselves in trendiness and commercialized hype, they will fail in their prime moral obligation. They will become, not elders, but simply over-aged consumers and fashion plates, as much a part of the marketplace as any American who was ever persuaded to believe that social success is a matter of using the right mouthwash. There are ominous signs that such fantasies might be floating through the psyche of too many supposed adults. In the highly popular, Academy Award winning movie *American Beauty*, the male lead, a husband and father, rebels against the emptiness of his life by reverting to an adolescent charade. He finds happiness at McDonald's flipping hamburgers, turns back to rock and roll, and goes hunting for teenage dates. How many viewers subscribed to his pathetic adventure?

Elders are not made by doting upon youthful frivolities or by fleeing the responsibilities of age. There is far more at stake in these matters than the wistful longing of the old to be young again. That is hardly what we owe the young who need to grow up. And if ever a generation needed a commanding model of adulthood, it is the generation (and by now more than a single generational cohort) that has come into being since the early 1970s.

The very fact that we now think so much in terms of generations, a slippery historical unit if there ever was one, is the dubious aftermath of the 1960s, which played out as a conflict between older and younger Americans. The issues of that time assumed that shape, not because there was a neat line of demarcation between ages — there never is — but because the most heated issue, the war in Vietnam, saw one generation making life and death decisions about another at a time when those who were expected to fight the war did not even have the right to vote. Against the background of the civil rights movement, which had made voting a burning issue of the day, the injustice of so brutal an assertion of privilege was dramatically clear. As Country Joe and the Fish asked the mothers and fathers of America in their "Fixin' to Die Talking Blues," did they want to "be the first one on your block to bring your boy home in a box?" The debate could become that bitter.

Without planning it that way, the boomers in their youth visited upon our society a generationally based reading of history that can do more to distort than illuminate. The media now insist that there must always be a "generation gap"; they see this as an ongoing story. But, of course, the gap in which the media are interested cannot be about anything as substantive as matters of morality or value; they prefer to limit the story to sex, hairstyles, clothing, tastes in music. If these are the characteristics that are to define every generation's place in history, then we are involved in a trivial pursuit. Yet it is precisely this focus on trivialities that has persuaded many of the young who have come along since the 1960s to believe their primary task is to have "attitude," which means above all sticking one's thumb in the public eye.

So we have Generation-X, or the Blank Generation, or the Postponed Generation, or the Digital Generation, or the Slackers — all hastily concocted Sunday supplement imagery intended to grab attention. But being different for the sheer sake of the difference is a meager project; struggling to be the latest, the hottest, the newest is a waste of life. This is the stuff of fashion, not history. If all citizens have a first order of responsibility, it is to secure justice and to make life fulfilling. This is the project that matters, and it has nothing to do with attitude. In that common human business, we unite across all lines of potential division. It is the task of the young to grow into that role, and the task of elders to help them do that.

## Time to Retire the Inner Child

Relations between the generations are apt to be strained under the best of circumstances. There is one respect, however, in which boomers have introduced an odd kink into their capacity to be effective elders. They have invested a lot of time seeking the inner child.

The years following World War II ushered in a new style of child-rearing in the Western world. It is usually labeled "permissive" and connected with the ideas of Dr. Benjamin Spock. Because of the unusually liberal parent-child relations that developed during that first wave of permissive parenting, a good many baby boomers arrived at their adult years lumbered with a lot of unfinished emotional business — rather as if they were not sure when or whether their childhood was over. Permissiveness taught us all to take childhood seriously, to lavish attention on the young and do all we could to keep them happy. Raising children in that spirit cannot help but bring out narcissistic tendencies, the sort of intense concern for oneself that we associate with children raised as the only child of doting parents. That became the norm in many middle-class families. No society in history has ever run so large and consequential an experiment in raising a generation of narcissists as the United States middle class during the 1950s and 1960s.

Ours is a highly psychological era. We have learned about the penalties of repression; we know there is an alternative we can use to bring shameful truths to light for examination — psychotherapy. And with enough money to indulge themselves in therapy, more and more middle-class Americans have been able to take advantage of the standard advice for all personal problems: "Find professional help." That advice was once reserved for the monied few who could afford twenty years of grueling psychoanalysis, which might finally be less than fully successful. So the boomers hired professionals to help them contact the child they once were — and might still be.

Several schools of psychological thought have developed around the image of the child, starting with Freud. Freud's orientation was regressive and reductionistic. He tended to see childhood as a time of illusion and fantasy that must be outgrown. In his eyes, the main reason for unearthing childhood memories was to cauterize the sexual wounds one expected to find there. In contrast, Freud's disciple Carl Jung found something very different in childhood memories. He spent some years hunting for his own inner child, to the point of returning to the game-playing of his childhood. In the spirit of free play, he eventually built an entire toy village, never quite understanding what he was doing until he had completed the task. This playful search became one of the most important episodes in his career. He finally placed the Child among the most powerful of the healing archetypes, a grand "unifying symbol."[4]

In the 1940s, the Stanford University psychiatrist Milton Erickson found his way to "the child within" in much the same playful way and, again like Jung, discovered in his childhood recollections a wealth of rejuvenating new departures for his work. Erickson claimed that great ideas came to him while he leafed through old comic books left over from his boyhood. In his school of thought, contacting the child within is the pivotal moment of the therapeutic relationship. To make that moment as vividly emotional as possible, Erickson recommended the use of hypnosis.

Later, in the 1960s, child-based therapy found its most influential formulation in Eric Berne's school of transactional analysis, which took the "Child" to be a "phenomenological reality" based on the actual "playback" of data surviving as actual chemical traces in the brain. Berne believed that old experiences of frustration, rejection, and abandonment can be triggered and will replay in the present in ways that put the Child-self "in command." Hurtful memories seem most vivid, but besides such "not OK recordings of negative experiments," there are also memories of delight and deep satisfaction that wait to be discovered. A main purpose of the therapeutic encounter is to reexperience all the old predicaments.

Other schools of psychology took up the same project, sometimes in grueling ways. Primal therapy favored reliving childhood all the way back to a vivid recollection of the birth experience that issued forth in the "primal scream." In the 1990s, the popular television therapist John Bradshaw was still drawing overflow audiences to lectures whose theme was "reclaiming and championing your inner child." Bradshaw characterized his clients as "adult children" whom he invited to join him in "grieving our neglected childhood development dependency needs."[5] As much as the music, the politics, and the literature of the 1960s and 1970s, the search for the inner child was a sign of youthful times.

Among tougher-than-thou social critics, this preoccupation with one's buried childhood has been a favorite target for criticism. The image of grown up people gathering to weep and stew over distant childhood grievances is easy to ridicule. Like all psychological problems that are transcribed to the printed page, consulting with one's "wounded inner child" can be made to seem embarrassingly banal. A middle-aged woman, one of Eric Berne's clients, throws a small fit in her group over her childhood recollection of having to kiss an Aunt Ethel she loathed. The memory still rankles. "Get over it and grow up!" the critics say, as if that were easy to do.

James Hillman, among the wisest Jungian analysts, has concluded that the emphasis on childhood during the 1960s and 1970s returned people to their most helpless condition in life, a position that blocks active social involvement. Moreover, the inner child frequently connects with experiences of victimization that do more to undermine the adult ego than to heal old wounds. "The trip backward," Hillman observes, "constellates the 'child archetype.' Now the child archetype is by nature apolitical and disempowered — it has no connection with the political world. ... Twenty or thirty years of therapy have removed the most sensitive and the most intelligent and some of the most affluent people in our society into child cult worship."[6]

In fairness to transactional analysis, the school that did most to bring this form of therapy to public attention, the purpose of all the exercises is, in fact, to become a grown-up by resolving the emotional issues of earlier years. The "Child" in question is to be integrated with the Parent-self and the Adult-self. T. A., popularized as an affordable form of group therapy by Eric Berne, was designed as "a teaching and learning device rather than a confessional or an archeological exploration of the psychic cellars."[7]

From an unsympathetic perspective, this could look like easy-do, feel-better psychiatry, which is anathema to those who insist that introspection must be prolonged, heroic, and anguished. It should, however, be kept in mind that as far back as Freud and the Oedipus complex, working through the traumas of child-parent relations has been the focus of mental health. In that sense, modern psychotherapy has always tried to lead us back to the child within. That is what it means to undo repression. Far from being a trivial, self-indulgent preoccupation, digging back through one's childhood is among the central tasks of modern psychotherapy, as well as of the finest introspective literature of our time. I would not, therefore, be quite as quick as some critics have been to write that project off, unless one wishes to reject therapy entirely.

One might hope that mothers and fathers who have been put charitably in touch with their own childhood behavior will avoid the heavy-handed, moralistic parenting that was the blight of the traditional family. We should recall that in Victorian times parents were told to play the role of God to their children, asserting a flattening authority, especially when it came to self-expression and sexuality. Given that background in our culture, it is understandable that psychotherapy would at some point reexamine childhood in intense detail for all that had been lost there.

The remembrance of things past has always been at the heart of self-knowledge. Coping with the emotional lacerations of early family life might be the definition of growing up; not coping *well* might make a passable definition of neurosis. But in the past, people either wrote great literature about their flawed upbringing or simply buried the memory as best they could and soldiered on in life — until they had the chance to inflict the same damage on their own children. This is the long, sad story that lies behind what some today call "family values."

On the other hand, whatever their theoretical intention, all these schools run the risk of keeping people so preoccupied with their childhood that they might well fail to get on with their primary adult responsibility. It seems fair to observe that the peculiar infatuation middle-class Americans of the post-World War II generation with inner-child psychotherapy has left us with an unusual set of dysfunctional family issues. It has also left the task of becoming elders wholly undefined. Parents, loitering over their inner child too long, may have left an *outer* child or two of their own waiting for the benefit of wise, adult counsel.

The poet Robert Bly, a leading figure in the men's movement, has been especially worried about the inner child orientation. He reaches the melancholy conclusion that its influence has left us with a population of "half-adults" stranded between growing up and staying childlike. He thinks "people of all ages are making decisions to avoid the difficulties of maturity." He even raises the possibility that the neocortex of the parental generation, the locus of civilized values, has been left weakened by too much self-indulgence. Convinced that "the experience of austerity and the experience of maturity are connected," he believes that child-based therapy and the cultural values it induces appeal to "the greedy and lazy parts of the soul." Thus, instead of a normal, nourishing relationship between elders and children, we have a "sibling society" where nobody wants to pay the price and take the risk of growing up.[8]

Bly is surely right in believing that the worst of the senior follies would be to withdraw from the eldering role that no society can long do without. Elders retire *into* responsibility, not out of it. But the responsibility that comes with age is not that of the young entering upon adulthood. Elderhood is what a lifetime of adulthood matures *into*. That may require *outgrowing* adult values that block the way to wisdom. That, in turn, may involve one more critical transition in the later years, a rite of passage that we will examine in chapters to come.

## CROWDING THE YOUNG

A letter to *Parade* magazine in June 1996 from a California teenager:

I am 17 years old, and I am pessimistic about my future. The whole world is so messed up — just look at the news: You have parents beating kids. You have adults molesting and raping children. You have lots of kids on drugs and lots of depressed kids. Our whole generation, "Generation-X," needs help. The X is almost the end of the alphabet. Does that mean that we've come to the end and that we are the ones who will destroy everything? If so, it isn't because we created anything. Everything is already here for us to play with. The flower children grew up thinking that all you had to do is love everyone and smile, and the whole world would just fix itself for you. But Generation-X knows the truth: We are not able to have everything. The odds are against us. Technology is starting to take over America. Jobs are no longer stable. As kids in my generation see it, it's the world against us.

Yes, drug use and sexually active teens have always been around, but their numbers are rising. And now middle school students are having sex. Middle school girls are having abortions. Something's gone wrong. Children are killing each other and themselves. I have friends who have killed themselves. Children are raping other children. Either these things have always existed but were never discussed, or our whole generation was raised terribly wrong.

About one-third of our generation doesn't care about anything important. It's kind of like anything goes. We feel like everything's changing and we have nothing to do with it, so we'll just sit back and let it happen. We have nothing stable to grasp. No one to look up to. No one to believe in. No one to trust but ourselves.

One letter from one sad young person, but a revealing confession of powerlessness and anxiety. The vision one finds here of the baby boom generation as a suffocating presence taking up too much social space has merit to it. On the basis of numbers alone, the boomers were a big generation, and a privileged one. Now they are enjoying the unforeseen benefits of longevity and so will be around a good deal longer than their parents or grandparents. They are not clearing out and leaving an open field to a younger generation they trust.

These facts radically alter the role of eldering in our time. If generosity is the soul of eldering, then the long-term demographic dominance of the boomers makes generosity all the more difficult. In the past, elders were far fewer in number and marginal in status. Their wisdom was all they had to offer. They might have been valued for that, but they did not necessarily wield power. The young might have deferred to them, but they did not have to. The deference was based on respect and appreciation. Now "productively aging" seniors stay actively on the scene far longer. They have no intention of creeping meekly into nursing homes, though that may be the fate that finally befalls many of them. Retirement for this group and for all who follow them may grow increasingly problematical. If they are fit enough to continue working, and probably ambitious enough to do so, will they find retirement an attractive prospect? If so, what kind of retirement will that be?

Meanwhile, youth in their twenties and thirties will be scuffling to keep employed at *anything*, probably holding more than one job in an ever less secure job market, accepting employment or independent contracting without benefits, struggling to afford families. How favorably will they look upon seventy-year-olds who are doing all they can to stay on the pay-roll, not least of all for the "psychic income" that comes of feeling still vigorous, still competent, still competitive? As we have seen, retired seniors may soon turn into a reserve army of cheap labor that displaces younger workers.

When anti-entitlements critics propose raising the retirement age to seventy or seventy-two, they might ask what the young think about that. After all, the jobs at which people in their seventies are most likely to keep working — white-collar managerial and executive positions or other pro-fessional work — are the best-paid occupations around. What will the efforts these seniors make to keep fit and appear youthful look like to the young but a cruel trick played by a privileged class? Indeed, these condi-tions help explain the peculiarly stalled quality of successive younger gen-erations since the late 1970s.

Unless boomers find other places to turn that engage their best pow-ers, they are apt to keep crowding the young for another twenty or thirty years. The result may be an interval when generational conflict grows par-ticularly bitter. The senior generation will not be doing the one thing that could always be expected of it: leaving the stage. Nor, for that matter, will this be true of the boomers only. The generation to follow will do the same. Longevity will outlast the boomers. Each older generation from here into the indefinite future is going to stay around longer. The "young" may have no chance to take over until they are well into their middle years.

## ELDERS IN NEED OF GREAT ASSIGNMENTS

Those who lived through the peculiar cultural style of the 1960s and 1970s are having their healthy doubts about permissiveness and lifelong narcissism. In my university classes, I now meet students, mainly women returning to school in their late forties, who are struggling with new issues in child-rearing. The experience of their own upbringing has left them acutely aware that parenting is not a talent that one can take for granted. Some who grew up in heavily patriarchal families broke away to live highly rebellious, countercultural lives in their teens and twenties. Rebellion played a liberating, though sometimes bruising, role in their lives. Now they wonder how much latitude to permit their own young. The sort of sex life they knew has become lethally risky.

Others who were raised permissively by Spockian parents are uncertain how to deal with their own children, especially with respect to issues of sex and drugs. They worry about being too unstructured. The more thoughtful parents I meet are trying to steer a midcourse between the authoritarian parenthood they rejected in their youth and an ineffectual leniency that Dr. Spock himself never condoned. As one might have guessed, the remedy for therapy in America is the hair of the dog. In the 1980s a new school of psychology called parent effectiveness training (PET) sought to offer advice to postpermissive parents on questions like these. Essentially, PET has tried to rebalance the scale toward discipline and structure in the family and to give parents a firmer grip on their responsibilities.[9]

As difficult as these choices are to make, an even more demanding role awaits boomers as they reach their senior years. Beyond the dilemmas of parenting their own children lies the task of being an elder within the society at large. Psychology has not come remotely close to mapping this late stage of life. It may well be that many of us will find ourselves face to face with eldering before we have worked it all out with our inner child. Perhaps one day we will have a new school of psychotherapy that starts from the assumption that inner children are destined to remain unfinished business throughout a lifetime. There is a child inside all of us waiting to be cared for, but there is also an elder within waiting to be honored before time runs out.

Just as the 1960s and 1970s generated child-oriented psychotherapy, we are likely to see a plethora of elder-relevant therapy and counseling in the years ahead. One can only hope that this healthy interest does not evaporate into another New Age fad. The scholarly and psychological groundwork for the study of eldering as a distinct phase in human development is under construction. The psychiatrist David Gutmann, for example, working from comparative studies of aging in modern Western and Native American cultures, believes that traditional societies have a great deal to teach us. "In settings in which elders have the social leverage to arrange matters according to their own priorities, we find striking evidence of new development in both male and female personalities in later life." In traditional cultures, the old are often given "great assignments." They may be asked to face formidable "spiritual dangers." Elders, Gutmann argues, are present not simply by virtue of fortunate survival, but because healthy cultures *need* them. "We do not have elders because we have a human gift and modern capacity for keeping the weak alive; instead, we are human because we have elders."[10]

In his study of the male life cycle, Daniel Levinson makes eldering the centerpiece of the senior years. He tells us that in the third era of life (middle adulthood, from age forty to sixty-five),

> we are responsible not only for our own work, but also for the development of the current generation of young adults who will soon enter the senior generation. It is possible in this era to become more maturely creative, more responsible for self and others. ... Unfortunately middle adulthood is for many persons a time of progressive decline, of growing emptiness and loss of vitality.[11]

As eldering becomes more prominently respected, we can expect the media to feature a steady run of "discoveries" about the emotional contours of the later years of life. No doubt we will be seeing a succession of senior gurus on television and on the lecture-workshop circuit mass-marketing techniques for creative aging. But these schools of psychology may have a strange configuration. Will therapists of thirty and forty take on the job of counseling clients old enough to be their grandparents? Will they presume to know more about chronic disease, grief, and mortality than those who have spent a long lifetime getting to where they are? I suspect I would find it either depressing or aggravating to have someone half my age telling me what life is all about. Or will elders create their own style of peer counseling, forms of spiritual companionship that unite them in facing the great philosophical issues on which nobody is an expert?

# CHAPTER EIGHT

## Maturity and the Media

My morning newspaper brings me a puzzling bit of cultural news. The television networks have run their annual sweeps, the viewer ratings that determine advertising revenues in the season to come. CBS scored highest, but CBS is considered the loser. The winners are NBC and Fox. That is because they have done the best job of attracting the eighteen- to forty-nine-year olds ... or better still, eighteen- to thirty-four-year-olds, preferably male, the group that is "deemed the most valuable by the advertising community," as the paper reports. Poor CBS! At least during this sweeps season, it stuck with more mature programming. That may have given it more viewers, but they just were not worth much to the people who buy the time. What programs drew youth to NBC and Fox? Run-of-the-mill sitcoms and police procedurals.

So what does "younger" mean in this context? It means programs that feature more action and less plot, more sex and less dialogue, more gore and less thought. It means nobody is going to take too much trouble making the stories coherent or the script crisp. It means there will be more clichéd lines, more flabby reaction shots, more slack and vacuous scenes filling time between commercials, more running, chasing, kicking, punching, and shooting, more footage of cars pulling up or pulling away, more quick cuts to keep viewers from asking embarrassing questions about continuity. It means there will be more gross-out material, more toilet humor shot in the actual toilet, more graphic vomiting and dismemberment, more slow-motion montages of bodies spurting blood.

The story confirms what I was told recently by a friend who has been struggling to earn her living as a television writer. She was complaining about her difficulties in Hollywood these days. As the years pass, she finds it harder to get pencilled in for meetings with studio executives. "Once you're past twenty-seven, you're over the hill and out of sight," she lamented. On the other hand, those who are twenty-seven, especially if they are twenty-seven-year-old males, have an uncanny psychological leverage with networks and producers. Being young and male, they are assumed to be in touch with the only audience that matters: the young demographic that guarantees victory in the sweeps.

## THE CURIOUS TYRANNY OF THE YOUNG DEMOGRAPHIC

What we have here is an age-gap that works in favor of the young. In a society that is steadily aging, those who produce our popular culture insist that it is the antics and tastes of youth that interest ... or *should* interest the public at large. The action movies that cost so much to produce and receive the most promotional hoopla are obviously designed for adolescents with nothing more than mayhem on their minds; the television dramas, sitcoms, and soap operas rolled out each season are after an audience of young singles. Confronted with so much media-fare that seems stalled on Melrose Place or Sunset Beach, I find myself asking, "What's wrong with this picture?"

The answer would seem to be *everything.*

Our popular culture is at war with the United States Census Bureau. The audience of high-living twenty-somethings they seek to attract is becoming a phantom population. Singles under thirty are a steadily shrinking part of our society. The number of Americans turning age twenty-five peaked in 1986; there will never be that many people entering that age range again. In the twenty-first century, the population over sixty will ever more steadily outnumber the population under twenty-five. Although that has been a thoroughly predictable trend for decades, it was not until President Clinton turned fifty — in the mid-1990s — that the media suddenly registered the demographic facts of life. When, in March 1997, the *New York Times* devoted an entire issue of its Sunday magazine to the "Age Boom," it began by reporting that "America Discovers a New Stage of Life." Meaning, of course, that the *New York Times* had just discovered a new stage of life — and decided to compliment itself for so doing.

The word "discovers" underscores how demographically illiterate we have become. By simply glancing over the census figures or following the calculations of the Social Security Administration, one could have learned twenty years ago that ours was a rapidly aging society. "Discovering" that fact is like discovering that a plane flying due west from anywhere in the United States is getting closer to the Pacific Ocean. When facts like this have to be announced with banner headlines, it is not because they were so hard to see, but because those who make the announcement have been looking in the wrong direction.

Who would guess from watching what goes out over television these days that Americans over sixty are now the largest viewing audience in the United States? They report spending half their free time watching.[1] Perhaps they wish they had better things to do with themselves, but if the media and the advertising image-makers elect to continue ignoring such elementary demographics, that is not because they enjoy privileged access to some inviolable first principle of marketing science. It is, rather, an impressive indication of how embedded the stereotypes of youth and age are in the folklore, cultural symbolism, and wishful thinking of our society. So stubbornly embedded, in fact, that even when money — a great deal of money — is at stake, people who are otherwise single-mindedly preoccupied with profit cannot see the obvious: namely, that in our society as in the industrial world at large the numbers and the money belong to the old not the young.

## Generational Myopia

Before the advent of mass media that could be privately owned and exploited, popular culture was an accurate expression of what most people in a society believed, liked, and valued. "Popular" might mean commercial, but the quality of the cultural offering could range from P. T. Barnum's circus all the way up to Shakespeare's tragedies and the liturgy of the church. In any case, what people sought out and enjoyed was a direct reflection of their taste. With the growth of an "entertainment industry" in the twentieth century, we now have contingents of middle men and women who pursue high-paying careers brokering culture between the public, the advertisers, and the sprawling conglomerates that monopolize ever more of the means of communication.

What "popular" means in our time is decided in boardrooms by people who claim to be professionally equipped to know what the public wants and who can talk the polling statistics to prove it. They hold august titles (Vice President in Charge of Planning and Research, Head of Programming, Director of Corporate Advertising, Chief Media Coordinator) and have staffs of eager young assistants with university degrees in marketing and mass communications who review the microdata and shuffle the demographics. The problem is not that they cannot read the numbers, but that they have more than one master to please. Even when they work from supposedly reliable data, they may be trying to appeal to what a corporate client or sponsor thinks the public wants rather than to the public itself. So they trim and tweak their research to please the people who pay them — and doubtless they do a lot of guessing. More and more frequently, they guess wrong and then paper over with numbers. This is called lying with statistics, an easy thing to do if you work in an industry that refuses to believe that the young demographic is fast becoming a thing of the past.

In their adolescent and college years, the boomers were the stars of an ebullient and colorful youth culture that has left its mark on media and advertising. More than representing immense purchasing power, they appealed to a certain restiveness in the business community that wished to break free of the Organization Man conformity that had often stifled the liveliest new minds. Youth, even in so inane a formulation as the famous "Pepsi Generation" sales campaign, was the image that liberated these stymied energies. In his study of "business culture, counter culture, and the rise of hip consumerism," Thomas Frank chronicles this remarkable transformation of corporate America in the 1960s. "What happened in the sixties is that hip became central to the way American capitalism understood itself and explained itself to the public." And "hip" meant pushing the young demographic. "Suddenly youth became a consuming position to which all could aspire. ... The conceptual position of *youthfulness* became as great an element of the marketing picture as youth itself."[2]

For "conceptual position," read "stereotype." We all know the stereotype, do we not? Youth means, above all, sex: beautiful young people in situations where talk and thought matter not very much, but simply fill in while clothes are being removed. It means brash, wised up, and sassy. It means parties. It means music, very loud music. It means an obsession with weirdly stylish clothing. It means catch-phrases and buzz words. It means all those fleeting images of care-free, high-living that can be captured in ninety lightning quick cuts during a thirty-second spot commercial.

What Frank overlooks is that the young demographic of the 1960s was freakish, transient, and unrepeatable. Demographers remind us that the United States began growing collectively older as early as 1800. Nobody was taking serious note of the statistics then, but in Thomas Jefferson's time half the white European population was under the age of sixteen, a ratio of young to old that the country was never to see again. Throughout the nineteenth century, despite the demographic ups and downs that resulted from industrialization and the massive influx of impoverished immigrants vulnerable to killer epidemics, life expectancy grew slowly longer and the society grew steadily older.

By the 1930s the aging of industrial society had become a major social issue. At the time, with no end to the Great Depression in sight, the economic fate of the elderly looked bleak indeed. How could the modern world afford so large an elderly population? Conferences on aging were held, major professional research was funded. Studies of the subject spoke prophetically of the "increasing consciousness of the inevitability of a further rise in age level of the population." In his perceptive, 1937 overview of gerontology, John Dewey observed that

> Present society in Europe and the United States is now approaching a stabilized, even possibly a declining, total population with a larger older population, both absolutely and relatively, than any country in the world has ever known before. In the United States, with decrease of birth-rate and the limitation of immigration (which has been mainly of the young and vigorous) we now have an unprecedented situation.[3]

In this context, the baby boom stands out as the one great exception to the gradual, long-term aging of the modern world. During the years 1946-1964, the American fertility rate ballooned to 3.7 children per family. Then, almost immediately following that reproductive surge, as if in a fit of exhaustion, total fertility dropped off to reach a record American low of 1.7 in 1976 — well below the rate needed to replace mothers and fathers. Since then, as in many industrial societies, our rate of population growth has hovered around the replacement number, with immigration playing an ever greater role in our population growth.[4]

It is the unusual and unforeseen bulge of the baby boom that has obscured the long-term demographic trend. Within a larger historical context, we might almost say that what the baby boom produced was a massive contribution to the continued aging of the nation. As of the late 1970s longevity had more raw material to work upon than ever before. Yet as aberrant as the baby boom was, it induced a wishfully delusionary state of mind that continues to distort demographic reality.

The baby boom gave one last infusion of vitality to an age-old fascination with youth — and not simply because of the numbers involved. There was also the role played by politics, the media, and the marketplace. As early as the 1950s, middle-class children of the baby boom came to be recognized as a lucrative market; accordingly, advertisers skewed their appeal toward them. Then, as the babies grew up to become more politically obstreperous through the 1960s, the media paid them inordinate attention. They were identified as the prime indicator of changes blowing in the wind. Since then, in every institution, in every walk of life, it has become all but an automatic reflex to ask what the young want, what they are doing, thinking, buying. As much as the major media want the young demographic, so too publications want to attract young readers, arts organizations — theater, symphony, opera — want to draw the young audience, social and political groups want to recruit young members. Everybody seems to worry if they sense they are drifting out of touch with the younger generation. But why? Treating youth as the primary force for change is the cultural style of the past; the future belongs to the longevity revolution, a demographic shift in which both old and young are caught up.

It is not, of course, that the youth market has become unimportant. Even though boomers have opted for smaller families, their sheer size as a generation has guaranteed a sizeable younger population. Generation Y, as it is sometimes called, peaked in 1990 with about 4,200,000 births before dropping off sharply again. That is a reproductive burst that comes close to baby boom levels. This "baby bump" will keep the youth market going strong for another few decades. But there is a new factor to be considered. The parents and grandparents of the baby bump are not simply going to vanish. They are living on in better physical and financial health than ever before. And that trend will continue, as their children follow them into the longevity revolution.

The share of the national wealth held by Americans above the age of fifty vastly exceeds that of their children and grandchildren — a fact that one would assume to be of considerable interest to the media. The one-quarter of the American population over fifty years old as of the turn of the twenty-first century has an annual personal income approaching $1 trillion dollars. This age group controls half the disposable earnings in the country. That includes 75 percent of financial assets (worth over $8 trillion) and 80 percent of all savings and loans accounts. With a long life expectancy, the boomer generation will get richer as it gets older. It will inherit some $10.7 trillion from its parents.[5] There are still too many seniors who fall below the poverty line, but thanks to personal savings, Medicare, home ownership, and tax breaks, the Social Security Administration estimates that, as of the 1990s, Americans over sixty-five years of age have the largest amount of discretionary income in the nation — more than twice as much as that of young people between twenty-five and thirty-four.[6] Among postmenopausal women alone we have what the columnist Ellen Goodman calls "a marketeer's dream" — an alert, book-buying, culture-consuming population heading toward 50 million in the early years of the twenty-first century, many of them working women who have earned well in their careers.

In contrast, as we enter a new century, the eighteen to twenty-four year-old population will shrink by 4 million, down 15 percent from its 1990 total, and lose $3 billion a year in discretionary income. "There will always be a youth market," observes the editor of *American Demographics*, "but it won't always be powerful relative to other markets. In the future, American business has got to learn to love the middle-aged."[7]

The trend is clear. In every coming decade, the same population that is now fifty or sixty — minus an ever decreasing percentage who die along the way — will report in at an older age, still there, still numerous, still moneyed. Unless another baby boom occurs, and that is nowhere in sight, the ratios of old to young with respect to numbers and wealth will remain "senior-skewed." Eventually, of course, the people now in the eighteen- to forty-nine population whom advertisers want so desperately to reach will become affluent enough to respond to their messages, but by the time they do they will have moved on into the senior ranks. The marketing trend away from youth and toward age is irreversible.

A moment's reflection explains why things have turned out this way. Americans of fifty years and over are the chief beneficiaries of the Great Affluence, the greatest economic boom in history. That boom saw the wealth of the nation more generously distributed than any labor leader or social reformer of the past had ever thought possible. Now that privileged generation is carrying its wealth into its retirement years. Here, clearly, is where our society's financial center of gravity lies. These are the people who own homes, shop for luxury vacations and cars, and pay off their credit cards on time. Nevertheless, the media have long regarded them as "consumer zombies."

Why?

One team of marketing analysts describes the problem as "generational myopia," meaning a "shortsighted application of the values and attitudes of your own generation to the development of strategies for marketing to another generation." In other words, the over-fifty population is written off simply because it is not the youth market that once mattered. Instead of being an easy mark for glitzy goods and trendy novelties, older consumers — in this analysis called "matures" and "boomers" — are seen as a tough sell. The matures (with a Great Depression — World War II background) are "slow to embrace new products," and the boomers (Great Society background) want "the kind of sophistication and impertinence that has always appealed to them."[8]

In the *New York Times Magazine* special issue on the "age boom," a senior advertising copywriter observes, "To advertisers, youth is excitement and pizazz. It all goes back to one of those unwritten rules of marketing: Don't target consumers who are fifty and over because they're beyond reach."[9]

Of course they are "beyond reach." That is because they *know better* than to let themselves be too easily reached by commercial rhetoric and imagery. There is at least a bit more skepticism and a lot less gullibility to be found in older heads. So, by way of a self-fulfilling prophecy, older people are out of reach because advertising itself has placed them there. They pay less attention because the advertisers prefer lifestyle fantasies that have little to do with being postadolescent. And yet, though the job market may fluctuate by the season, the jobs available to most younger workers lacking the high-tech skills currently in fashion have been steadily trending toward lower pay and less security since the mid-1970s. Even when the job market was booming in the dot-com economy, the high-tech industries were importing cheaper foreign workers to beat down wages. The hard-bodied teens and twenty-somethings most avidly courted by the media are the same job-worried youth who sell us ninety-nine cent tacos and hamburgers. They are the youth who once thought of themselves as "slackers."

To be sure, one can always find youthful high achievers: Wall Street wheeler-dealers, million-dollar athletes, rock stars, genius hackers. The networks and the news weeklies routinely run stories about the hot young talent of the "digital generation" that is about to "take over" the world. It is the clichéd American success story that is meant to convince those who may be taking a hard hit from the economy that it must be *their* fault. But one need only look at the course of real wages in our economy to realize that the income of younger workers has been steadily downscaling to the cheap jeans and six-pack level. If these young people display nice teeth, you can be sure they were not the ones who paid for the orthodontics and caps.[10]

Is it possible that the media elite, now in their middle and senior years, cling to fond illusions of the lifestyle they most want to emulate: wrinkle-free skin, endless parties, easy (apparently AIDS-free) sex? An older television director interviewed in 1995 on the subject of the "Hollywood Greylist" contends that there is "an abnormal obsession with the young, white boy ... a male youth fantasy syndrome."[11] This is the "diaper brigade" of young producers and young audiences that accounts for the biggest film budgets, namely, those spent on action movies that lose any semblance of coherence after the first fifteen minutes.[12]

Besides the consolations of personal fantasy, there may be another explanation for this fixation on youth. The people who produce our popular culture may have certain inadmissible limitations. Those who have earned their living for so long selling silly products to mindless millions may have lost the capacity to deal with a more discriminating audience. Indeed, they may find an older audience daunting in comparison to the ditzy world of adolescent and young-adult tastes and fashions, where the attention span is so brief that few can track through thirty seconds of commercial sophistry. Perhaps it is easier to write off an older public that thinks twice about the cost and quality of what it buys and simply move on to less demanding targets.

There are now highly paid "coolhunters" who study the youth market in microscopic detail, reporting on trends in speech, dress, cosmetics, haircuts, entertainment, food, lifestyle — effluvia that come and go so rapidly that there may not be time for goods to reach the market before they have lost their cachet. Coolhunting clients include some of the largest corporations in the global economy: franchise food and clothing chains, software manufacturers, theme park operators, media producers. As clever as it is meant to be, coolhunting produces the same boring result over and over:

lists of arbitrary weird things observed on the streets or in the clubs of major cities. Teenagers wearing their pants backwards, dying their hair saffron, chewing tobacco ... a "trend" is anything done, said, worn, eaten, drunk, listened to, or laughed at by a twelve- to eighteen-year-old that nobody remembers hearing about before.

In this bizarre ambience, changes in sneaker and jeans design — for example, a switch from fake grease spots to pastels — inflate to cosmic importance. Age brackets are exquisitely refined into fourteen- to eighteen-year-olds, nineteen- to twenty-four-year-olds, twenty-five- to thirty-year-olds. Often what is "cool" is a revival of a period the youngsters know only from television reruns — something "totally fifties," "absolutely sixties." Even "old lady" clothing can be cool — if it is worn by girls of fifteen.[13]

These merchandising strategies are not limited to the United States. In Japan the business community has developed a fascination with the "ko-gal" population: teenage schoolgirls whose preferences are carefully monitored by the media. They have been identified as Japan's trend-setting consumers. Highly brand-conscious and willing to squander hundreds of dollars a month on ephemera like Fendi bags or Tamagotchi virtual pets, the girls are rounded up into focus groups and hired as temporary consultants on "what's hot." One marketing analyst calls the ko-gals "the incubator for any product boom." If they go for the item, it will be promoted first to twenty-somethings, and then to thirty-somethings before being rushed into the export market as a likely prospect. The girls are reported to be so addicted to consumption that a certain number of them stray into prostitution to find more money to spend.[14]

This is almost the stuff of comedy. One imagines that somewhere at the dizzy top of the global-corporate pyramid, serious-faced men in expensive suits meet with deeply-studied marketing specialists to plan the investment of billions. And what is the topic under discussion? The latest rage among fifteen-year-old schoolgirls: cell phones wrapped in panda skin, cone-shaped hamburgers, Beavis and Butthead underwear. There cannot be a single person in the meeting who does not know this is unworthy of grown-ups. But the profits are too great to sacrifice in behalf of mere self-respect.

Coolhunters ... ko-gals ... is this what Adam Smith, David Ricardo, John Stuart Mill had in mind when they hymned the glories of the free market?

Clearly, there are people who are brilliant at selling zany clothes and novelty soft drinks to adolescents. But those who have worked throughout their careers in so vapid a world may be in no position to retool and switch over to maturity as if it were simply another transient style. There is an easier way to save one's career. One cooks the statistics and pretends the audience out there is really still eighteen to forty-nine, as it was in the good old days. If that is the case, then "eighteen to forty-nine rules" only applies for as long as the media remain in the hands of people who cannot them-selves outgrow that age range. Others will have to take their place.

And in time that will happen. Money will make it happen. We may safely assume that the media will at last develop a marketing strategy aimed at a mature public. One already sees signs of the change: cover stories about "ageless beauties" in film and television, fifty-something superstars model-ing panty hose and lingerie, press-agentry about bringing back all the once-popular stars who have joined the Over-Sixty Club. Some advertising agen-cies already specialize in reaching senior consumers. At some point, there will be an accelerated shift, rather like an earthquake fault responding to pressure that has been building for years. Suddenly products and programs galore will surface for those who have the discretionary income to spend.

Tremors have already registered. Early in 1998 the Kellogg Company noted a sharp drop in the sale of its principal brand. Research revealed that the middle-aged female market the company was after was repulsed by the cute, young, size-four models the company was featuring in its commer-cials. How much cereal would a forty-five year-old woman have to eat to look like that? Kellogg ordered new commercials and new models. When enough sales resistance of this kind accumulates, advertising may even be forced to use intelligence and honesty to gain the attention of grown-ups — though that may be too much to hope for. If that happens, no doubt opportunistic industry leaders will rush to claim credit for waking up to facts that should have been apparent years ago.[15]

As the boomers make their presence known, we may expect to see the media adjust by fits and starts, trying this and that to cope with the un-precedented task of meeting significantly more mature standards. One can predict what the changes will be. There will be more stories about *old* law-yers, *old* cops, *old* teachers, *old* divorced singles starring comeback actors as aging studs, sexy moms, and randy grandmas; there will be tales that mix and match older men with younger women, younger men with older women. Age will become an advertising ploy for films and television movies starring actors and actresses above a certain age, as it was in the case of the 1999 movie *The Thomas Crown Affair*. The film featured an actress of forty-six in nude love scenes. Perhaps the audience turned out to see what a body that old looks like. The answer was, filmed from all the right angles and with the help of a body double when needed — not bad.

But does maturity mean that the next phase in popular culture will feature a cult of age to replace a less and less profitable cult of youth: older faces, older actors, stories about age and its problems? Let us hope not. The young, always touched with a certain adolescent narcissism, may be eager to see themselves constantly mirrored in the culture, but not so the older audience. What a truly adult audience wishes to find in books and films is a decent reflection of its judgment and experience: material that reflects knowledge, a sense of significance, coherence, imagination, a grasp of the way of the world. Otherwise, what have they to show for the years that take such a physical toll?

While maturity might mean wisdom at best, it must surely mean intelligence at least. Intelligence is a broad category; there is no limit to the cultural content that can fit within it. Certainly it is not dependent on the age of characters. *Huckleberry Finn, Alice in Wonderland*, and *Catcher in the Rye* are adult novels, as much so as *War and Peace*.

## M for "Mindless"

We need a new television ratings category. M for "Mindless — unsuitable for IQs above fifty." The networks need not fear. There is a lucrative audience down there below IQ fifty. It consists of all the little boys and ex-little boys who grew up on *Power Rangers* and *Mortal Kombat*. That audience would probably search to find the rating, willing to watch the shows all the way through, including the hamburger commercial where the cute babe drips the ketchup down her cleavage. And because they are *the* audience, the rest of us will be expected to watch what they watch — or turn off.

Maybe searching for maturity in the media is hopeless. Perhaps network television, like summer movies, is destined to be a preserve of whatever audience it can find in the lower intellectual depths. After all, the baby boomers have brought some 70 million children of their own into the world. They may not be as affluent as their parents, but for as long as they are in the eighteen- to thirty-four age range, they will be seen as an easy mark, meaning their tastes will continue to dominate the media.

Meanwhile, the authentically mature audience that is worth more both financially and intellectually drifts steadily away toward other sources of entertainment and education — public television, cable, videotapes, pay TV — and takes its money with it. The share of the eighteen to thirty-four television audience that major networks are squabbling over is a diminishing prize. The so-called mainstream, prime-time audience is shrinking by the year. But momentum keeps the system going; it is always easier to coast than to rethink and revise.

In chapter twelve, we will note how the boomers are opening up a promising educational frontier in our universities and colleges. It may well be that in the years ahead the major competition faced by popular culture purveyors who want grown-up dollars will not be the next television channel, but the lectures, book clubs, seminars, theater productions, symphonies, discussion groups, and museum tours that a mature audience finds far more worthy of its attention.

Can material of this quality be drawn into mainstream culture? That is what public radio and television were intended to do and still sometimes do, despite ever greater commercial incursions. But even before content can be revised, there is a more intractable issue to resolve. The greatest change our media-masters will have to make to attain maturity has nothing to do with quality of content. Given the state of our popular culture, something else needs to be talked about first, something that underlies and permeates content. Marshall McLuhan believed that the medium was more important than the message; I would rephrase the idea. *Context* is more important than content. And the context here is commercialism. *That* is the media's greatest offense to maturity.

Punctuated every eight and a half minutes by two minutes of spot commercials, even the best television drama or documentary becomes intellectual mush. No "in depth" news report that has to be wedged into the two minutes available before the anchor intones, "When we come back ..." can be more than a snippet. On television, commercials dictate the pace, the timing, the continuity, the emotional impact of everything. What is the effect, for example, of following a report on famine in Africa with a thirty-second spot for antacids or diet pills? What is the psychological impact of following a brutal rape on a police drama with a commercial featuring a pretty young woman modeling panty hose? If we are reading an article about endangered species or environmental crisis, what does it do to the moral quality of the report if magazine pages are sprinkled with screaming advertisements for lip gloss and running shoes?

Why did anyone ever think that such assaults upon attention, coherence, and meaning were acceptable? Clearly those who carry out the assault have never cared about content or continuity of any kind. The material between commercials is a nuisance to them, at best something to be used as bait. By now many of us may have become hardened to these witless intrusions. We are like those tribal people we see in the news who are inured to having flies creep over their faces; they no longer bother to brush the pests away. Nevertheless, in the midst of any honest effort to instruct, inform, or entertain, intrusive commercialism violates the adult intelligence of our society. It cuts a hole in our attention and inserts the unrelated, money-driven antics of hucksters. What could be more basically immature than that?

By commercialism I do not mean simply advertising. Advertising may be the major manifestation of the vice, but it at least declares itself for what it is. Worse, because less obvious, are the corrupting choices made behind the scenes on the basis of money: How many will watch, how many will come, how many will buy? How can we get another few dollars out of them? Rigorous marketing strategies that turn on questions like these are just beneath the surface of every cultural event that is out to make money, if only enough to pay for itself. It may be the symphony, the opera, a major art exhibit. We now have an entire profession of people trained at arts promotion. They study tie-ins and spin-offs that will sell T-shirts, toys, gimmicks. If they were not promoting Beethoven, they would be selling real estate. No blockbuster movie is *just* a movie any longer: It is a deal about hamburgers, soft drinks, and trinkets; the movie itself may be a mere adjunct. No art museum can do without its gift and souvenir shop. The result is an air of silliness and avarice that cannot help but permeate the event.

In the summer of 1997, a friend of mine returned from a trip that had taken her through Philadelphia, where she had managed to attend the year's biggest artshow success: the traveling Cézanne exhibit. As a lark, she had brought home a souvenir: a multicolored baseball bearing Cézanne's signature.

Cézanne's baseball. Doesn't that say it all?

## INFANTILIZING THE MILLIONS

Maturity in the arts or media means doing what one loves to do with the hope of excellence foremost, doing it all the way through with decent concentration and clear purpose. It means caring that the work is well done as an end in itself. This is a natural human behavior, an instinct of workmanship that can infuse cooking a meal or washing the dishes as well as painting a fresco. We are so sunk in commercialism that many have forgotten that this form of behavior was once as true of popular as of high-brow culture. Excellence is not elite; it is within the reach of everybody. The work may be a Brahms symphony; it may be a dance routine by Astaire and Rogers; it may be a Raymond Chandler detective story; it may be a Krazy Kat comic strip. The work can be done to make money, as most popular culture has always been done; Molière and Shakespeare worked for companies that turned a handsome profit. But the money does not have to crowd out the quality; the creator does not have to be lost in a promotional scramble that swamps the work.

Maturity means one does not adapt the work to the preexisting advertising copy; one does not fit the play between the commercials; one does not paint the picture with a view to how it will fit on a coffee mug. That, for example, is the difference between the clever and modestly inventive early creations of the young Walt Disney, and the schlock that rains down upon us under the Disney name today, all of it stamped with logos, franchised and syndicated to the hilt, wrapped up in deals concocted by agents and promoters for whom the movie is an afterthought.

A common complaint from media critics is that advertising tells lies. That was once true, but less so today since class-action law has found ways to hold companies responsible for their claims. Advertising still lies when it can get away with it, but that is no longer the preferred strategy. I can recall very few advertisements or commercials that actually said anything at all that might pass for an empirical fact. Effective lying, after all, assumes or encourages some degree of adult intelligence on the part of the person lied to. The ability to deal in lies appears well up on the evolutionary scale — from about the mental level of chimpanzees. To lie, one has to tell a story and back it up with claims and facts; one has to expect that the person being lied to can follow along and be persuaded.

But for advertisers, calling on even that much adult intelligence is hazardous. The safer tactic is not to awaken intelligence at all, but to lull it to sleep. There is a better way to sell a product than to lie about it. Simply steer clear of the mind and aim at rudimentary reflexes built up around simple commands like "need," "want," "buy." In brief, deal with the public the way we deal with babies.

The main move in contemporary advertising is to get attention — not an easy assignment given the amount of competition from other advertisers. Just as the sound level keeps rising in a restaurant as each person tries harder to be heard, we have come to expect advertising to assault us with noise, bright lights, and sensational or irritating images — in the same way we try to attract a baby's attention. On rare occasions, this is done cleverly. For the most part, however, television commercials begin with people making fools of themselves to get us to look at them. Whether cleverly done or not, it is always the same attention-grabbing move. And that move is inherently infantile. Children rush into a room uninvited, breaking the flow of conversation, shouting, "Look at me! Look at me!" and demanding to be heard, seen, responded to. We forgive children for being intrusive. Advertisers expect us to forgive them as well.

After that, all that remains is to lodge one's message firmly and portably in the audience's mind. How does one do that? First of all, by being so brutally simple that no intelligence whatever is necessary to register and retain the content. Indeed, often the message is nothing more than a logo or a slogan hammered into one's skull like a nail. Hit hard, be loud, repeat, repeat, repeat. This is not lying, this is imprinting, as with newly hatched birds. Some advertising is a bit more imaginative; it drives its message home by associating the product with an image that will win instantaneous approval. The images are selected from a small, obvious repertory: sexual delight, health, wealth, happiness, success, social acceptance, mastery.

The point is to leave the audience with a simple equation: Our product equals that image. For example: Here are happy people. Here is beer. You want happy? Buy beer! Since no intelligent human being will believe that happiness equals beer, advertisers have to play upon the lowest susceptibilities of people to present messages like this. Advertising has a vested interest in infantilizing its audience. It cannot work unless it is dealing with numb, passive, childish mentalities.

This is the real obstacle that the American media have in programming for a mature audience, and the reason why advertisers are apt to resist maturity as long as possible. Their work is predicated upon an audience of infants — or as close to that as one can come. Lose that audience and advertising becomes a very different project. The commercial media may be bonded to immaturity by irrational forces that cannot be overcome even when those forces make no financial sense. Thomas Frank's analysis of "the conquest of cool" leads him to just that conclusion. He believes that advertising and the media have been won over permanently to the young demographic. "Youth must always win," he tells us. "The new naturally replaces the old." "We will have new generations of youth rebellion as certainly as we will have new generations of mufflers or toothpaste or footwear." If he is right, then we will never have a truly mature popular culture unless the boomers succeed in closing down Madison Avenue.

The one alternative would be an advertising based not on novelty and fashion, but on the enduring quality of the product. Quality does not need to be lied about; it does not need to force itself on the attention. It actually suffers for becoming a silly spectacle. Quality can tell the truth; it is its own best advertisement. Advertising that sells quality can therefore be tasteful, courteous, honestly informative, intelligently balanced, and respectful of the content it sponsors. There is no such advertising in the world today. Maybe nobody knows how to do it. But if anybody finds the secret, there will be a market ready to hear and buy. One need only have the eyes to see it on the far side of the longevity revolution.

## WHAT IF SEX STOPPED SELLING?

> All of us who are aging, and particularly us aging women, will do
> well to listen to the young often and earnestly. But we must never,
> never listen to them on the subject of sex. They are useful on this
> subject only to one eager to gather information on esoteric
> techniques and not-altogether-usual practices.
> — CAROLYN G. HEILBRUN, *The Last Gift of Time: Life Beyond Sixty*
> (1997)

At the rear of my neighborhood video shop there is a cramped, airless little cubicle. The videocassettes that line the walls of this tiny den bear pictures of young women in various contorted sexual postures, leering, winking, drooling. Some wear leather and chains, some wear nothing at all. The sign above the door reads "Adult." It might just as well read "Abandon Intelligence, All Ye Who Enter Here." If a child wandered into a place like this, I suspect he might be traumatized by images of sexuality that offer no hint of love or pleasure. But he might be even more troubled by being told that this is what "adult" means.

Adult, mature ... like all age-related words in our culture, these too cry out to be redefined, especially as a category in our popular culture. In film or television, *mature* or *adult* programming refers to some combination of heavy-handed sexual titillation, excessive violence, endless profanity, and off-color jokes. Add smoking cigarettes and driving fast cars to the list, and we have "adulthood" as a twelve-year-old boy might understand it. Yet that is the mentality that now earns the most and spends the most in producing films and television. I have no way to prove the point, but I suspect there is one more reason the media and the advertisers flee from maturity, a matter that arouses a peculiarly deep anxiety. It has to do with the kind of sex on display in the room at the rear of my video shop.

The longevity revolution impinges on sex in a way that may secretly panic the media and those who buy their merchandising services. This may be the point where maturing boomers deliver their most decisive challenge to the ingrained habits of the marketplace. Sex, after all, is the most potent weapon in the arsenal of commerce, the one come-on that can sell anything — or so the advertisers hope. Sex sells cars, beer, clothes, movies, medicine. The business of advertising is very largely the business of manipulating sexual promises.

In my childhood, the sexual imagery in advertising, though just barely subliminal, was comparatively innocent. The pretty girl on the swing in the Coca-Cola ads of that day, her skirt wafted to the inner thigh, seems tame by contemporary standards. But she was still meant to offer a peekaboo thrill. These days the imagery is over the top and aggressively obvious, served up lavishly enough to suggest that its effect must be rapidly fading. So the dosage increases as the subjects build up tolerance.

In writing about Willa Cather's fiction, Hermione Lee once wondered how an author might "attach a heterosexual emotional life to a character whose strength comes from her transcendence of usual sexual roles." At the level of popular culture, that is what advertisers are up against as they find the society around them aging beyond the essentially adolescent sexuality that once provided commerce with sure-fire images and symbols.

Where would the media be if sex lost its power to sell? For all we know, the American economy would collapse. Perhaps the entire structure is supported by cheesecake. In fact, that kind of sex surely will wane in its influence, if not tomorrow, then soon and inevitably. As we will see in chapter ten, age deconstructs gender and reconfigures sexuality, possibly to the point where it ceases to function as a psychological hot button. Doubtless people of all ages entertain sexual fantasies and hidden desires, but it is insulting to assume that the fantasies never get beyond the mental age of fourteen, and that, in their grip, grown-up men and women lose all capacity for intelligent judgment.

One would expect advertising aimed at teenagers to be sexually saturated. But boomers, who are, along with their parents, the bulk of the spending public, are finding a very great deal more to occupy their attention and their energy. Life moves on and sexuality matures. I suspect that many in the media would feel their own sexual identity as well as their careers threatened by that fact. The images they deal in are apt first of all to be attuned to their own responses. Question those responses, and people fall into an anxiety that is both erotic and financial — a potent mix. If sex stops being a compulsively adolescent glandular reaction, how will they move all the merchandise? So they try harder, cranking the sexual signals up to maximum, never realizing that they are working against the demographic and cultural grain.

Sex has an odd political and commercial history in our time. The Western world spent most of the twentieth century freeing itself of sexual repressions that reach well back into our Judeo-Christian past. Getting out from under that dead weight has been a commendable struggle, not simply with respect to private sanity. As boomers learned in their youth, the shame that attaches to sex can be a powerful form of social control. Shame disempowers people and mutes their public voice. Defying sexual shame is therefore both personal and political. The guiltless, often startling playfulness with which young people of the 1960s surrounded sex had at the time a serious social purpose. Gay liberation especially had a significant relationship to the use political demagogues like Senator Joseph McCarthy once sought to make of homosexual shame. And women's groups of the time felt forced to demystify the female body in order to break down a range of sexist practices, something women could not do as long as they were expected to act like ladies.

We refer to all this as the "sexual revolution." But the sexuality which that revolution brought out into the open was *infantile sexuality*, highly charged erotic impulses that grow out of unresolved childhood frustration and the child's search for an adult identity. This was the sexuality that preoccupied Freud, and it was an explosive enough issue in its time. Liberating sex at that level shook the structure of families and marriage; it undermined gender roles and public authority. A significant historical turning point. But people pass on in life, and the cry of the wounded inner child steadily fades into the past. New needs arise that are more demanding.

There is now a clear consensus among psychologists and sexual counselors; it can be found reflected even in the countless how-to and self-help sex manuals in the bookstores. We are learning that sex as pure performance, as push-button pleasure, as macho/bimbo role-playing, is emotionally crippling. Everybody who purports to have studied the subject now speaks out in behalf of intimacy, depth of feeling, companionship, meaning. The consensus deepens as sexual counseling moves into the years beyond menopause, both male and female. Indeed, the discovery of the male menopause is a key insight in contemporary psychology, one I take up in chapter ten. What emerges from this growing body of psychological practice is a vision of sexuality that is complex, many-sided, and subtly related to the whole personality.

As the society grows more authentically mature, we are leaving behind the compartmentalization of sexuality, the notion that sex is a repertory of images and actions disconnected from the rest of life. But compartmentalizing the sexual response is exactly what merchandising requires: the programmed stimulus that never fails to catch the eye, grip the mind, trigger behavior. There may be a time in life when sex can be enjoyed as impersonal recreation and pursued as a succession of one-night stands. But if contemporary film and fiction are any measure, that kind of sex belongs in long, sad stories of alienated and fragmented lives. It almost invariably appears as the sex of very young, very confused, and very unhappy people.

Candor about sex deserves to be respected as one of the great transformations of our time. But being candid about sex has to include a possibility that few adolescents can imagine: namely, that sex isn't everything. Our popular media are in debt to commercialism, and commercialism is bound to the mentality and the sexuality of the very young. The longer that constellation remains intact, the greater will be the division between our cultural life and demographic reality.

CHAPTER NINE

# In the Absence of Elders

I nner-child psychology, the distinctive psychological style of the 1960s and 1970s, may pose a serious problem for the eldering responsibility of boomers. But another, more troubling obstacle has appeared that makes it even harder to define the relationship of youth to age in our time. The obstacle is a machine: the computer. In ways nobody could have foreseen, digital technology — or rather the way in which that technology is being marketed — is creating a culture in which elders are being made to seem of less and less importance. Even as our demographics shift in the direction of age, the old are being portrayed as steadily less relevant to the lives of the young.

There have, of course, been many periods when relations between the generations were strained. The boomers grew up through such a period. But even while countercultural youth of the 1960s took their parents to task, they still drew on older minds for guidance and inspiration. The achievements of earlier generations were mined for insight. If only facetiously, the term "guru" was adopted to refer to influential figures like Herbert Marcuse, Paul Goodman, Jean-Paul Sartre, Buckminster Fuller, Gregory Bateson, as well as to any number of Asian and indigenous spiritual teachers. It was simply assumed that the experience of elders mattered. There was no equivalent to the belief that nothing predating the computer can be of much value, or that all the younger generation needs is "information," which can be found by simply logging on to the Internet.

How often have you come across an advertisement like this message from Sony, announcing a new multimedia system? "Movie making so easy, even a grown-up can do it." These days, it is commonplace to hear anybody above the age of forty who is not a professional hacker say, "I'm so

167

stupid about computers." They are convinced that "young people are much better at it." That is more than a confession of some minor incapacity like being unable to use a skateboard. The computer has become a generational landmark. Behind it stands high tech, a multibillion-dollar industry and the signature technology of our time.

### GROWING UP ABSURD, HIGH-TECH VERSION

Since the early 1980s, when the personal computer began to sell in significant numbers, the high-tech industry has been touting it as an epoch-making invention comparable to the steam engine, if not the wheel. The young — the *very* young — have been the special target of this sales pitch. Some high-tech enthusiasts come close to identifying all children born since the early 1980s as a mutant generation of the Information Age. One of the first television commercials for the PC showed a bright-eyed baby reaching out in delight to stroke the keys. He might almost have been the Starchild who appears at the end of *2001*, finally midwifed into life by IBM.

Not only is high tech presented as inherently youthful, but the hackers and investors behind it are invariably identified as young — exuberant kids who caught the wave of the future and joined the ranks of what *Time* magazine calls "instant billionaires." The implication has been that children are now *born* computer-proficient — *and* that they are therefore leaving their hidebound parents and teachers far behind. The latter assumption is crucial. Blocking out parents and teachers is integral to the sales campaign. It is not enough for children to see themselves as innate hackers; they must also see the parental generation as technologically retarded.

In the 1960s Paul Goodman analyzed the problems of youth in the increasingly technocratic society of the post-World War II world and concluded that the young were "growing up absurd."[1] The substance of that absurdity was considerable. The contretemps between baby boomers and the older generation — as voiced in such sources as *Catcher in the Rye*, *Catch-22*, the Beat poets, *Mad* magazine, the satirical comedians of the day, the early Bob Dylan folk-protest songs — had to do with serious politics and the greater purposes of life. Parents were accused of failing as citizens by becoming the docile pawns of a military-industrial complex that was undermining basic American institutions. Given what the parents of that day had lived through — the Great Depression, World War II — the accusation was high-handed and hurtful, though to a significant degree true. It was at least an important line to draw across the culture. The very act of drawing that line had everything to do with becoming an adult and a citizen. In contrast, the current younger generation is being encouraged to draw a very different line of generational demarcation. Elders are now to be denigrated because ... they cannot defrag their hard drive.

With the passage of time, one might expect this marketing gambit to wear thin. The baby boom generation has, after all, been living and working with computers longer than their children have been alive. Even so a recent study of the "N-Generation" (Net Generation) cites research to tell us all over again that 85 percent of children aged four to twenty know more about the World Wide Web than their parents.[2] But what is there to "know"? One clicks, one scrolls, one stares. With a credit card, one buys. And with a slow modem, one waits and waits. Having little time to waste clicking, scrolling, staring, and waiting might be a working definition of being grown-up.

Those who trouble to probe the claims that lie behind this promotional propaganda might find that there are about as many children born computer-proficient as there are born violin-proficient — but nobody is seeking to turn the violin into mass merchandise. Why, then, are we being told that children take to computers the way ducks take to water? There is a treacherous sales strategy behind this claim. It plays upon the difference in intelligence between children and adults — but *at the expense of intelligence!*

Adults, assessing the personal computer with a reasonably mature eye, have seen the obvious. The technology is being vastly oversold. The machine's actual utility in the home falls far below what it is advertised to be. High-tech promoters have tried again and again to persuade the public to adopt the computer as a substitute for everything in their lives from television to the family dog. (The latter is no exaggeration. Consider the "virtual pet," a cunningly computerized novelty that needs care and feeding.) Hence the industry's desperate effort to invent problems for the computer to solve — like storing recipes or balancing the checkbook. If one believed the info-hucksters, people need computers to turn off the lights and start the coffee. The older one is, the more childish it seems to have a computerized interactive *something* intruded into every aspect of one's life. But kids, equipped with far less sales resistance, are an easier mark. They have time on their hands to chat online about dating, clothes, school. They see the blinking screen, they hear the bells and whistles, and they register the proper amazement. They become the market.

Meanwhile, the skepticism of their elders is written off as a generational liability, and the well-placed reservations of their teachers, who sometimes resist spending scarce dollars to wire the classrooms of the nation, are ridiculed for their stodginess. The young, as the high-tech industry would have it, may have to haul their parents and teachers kicking and screaming into the digital future.

What, then, is the subtext of this pitch? Clearly, that this buzzing box on the table has more to teach the young than real people speaking from living experience. Degrade the value of experience and elders have nothing left to offer.

## AT WAR WITH THE BOOMERS

The Internet, destined to play the role that radio and television played for earlier generations, carries a great deal of traffic from Generation-X, the Slackers, the Cyberpunks, the Ravers — newsgroups where those in the fourteen to thirty-five age range gather to exchange joys and sorrows.[3] If one samples what youth of the Information Age are doing with the computer power at their disposal, the experience is disheartening. Much of the problem is in the medium itself, which encourages a cyberbabble that becomes ever more barbaric — a patois compounded of abbreviations and catchphrases that has so little connection with structured language that it might as well be a system of runes. Many newsgroup messages are off-the-top-of-the-head outbursts hurled blindly into empty, impersonal space. On the screen they look like a chaos of sound-bite sized fragments, often laced with profanity in capital letters.

The Internet, where one can find a newsgroup on nearly every subject imaginable, may not be an adequate sample from which to generalize about an entire generation, but it reveals something of importance about a reasonably good-sized subculture within that population. Because online communications are so spontaneous, unstructured, and anonymous, they arrive on the screen as unguarded emotional outpourings, streams of consciousness at once cathartic and confessional. There is also much role-playing, which no doubt liberates schizophrenic tendencies and all that they reveal.[4] Hostilities flash out online, as do fears and insecurities, all bub-

170

bling up too rapidly for the keystroking fingers to bother with spelling, syntax, or coherence.

At its murkier depths, the Internet has rapidly gone from being a valuable communications asset of computer technology to a slough of youthful despond, featuring newsgroups like alt.life.sucks, alt.angst, alt.suicide, alt.bitterness, alt.depressed.as.fuck, and alt.galactically.pointless. Most troubling of all are the social animosities one finds there: nasty, frat-house swipes at women, gays, and — of special interest here — the boomers. Efforts by those who have come of age since the early 1980s to assert their historical identity often take the form of backlash against what they understand of the protest and countercultural experimentation that came before.

But their sense of history lacks depth; the issues that once provoked that protest are only dimly remembered. One would never guess from reading what young people have to say on the Internet that America of the 1950s and 1960s was a Jim Crow society, that the military-industrial complex had ever abused its power, that political dissent had to fight to make itself heard against McCarthyite witch-hunting, that thermonuclear annihilation was a serious threat, that there was a war in Vietnam. With no clear realization that dissent in America once related to real moral dilemmas, the younger generation has only a blurred perception of protest as a theatrical gesture, something done to gain attention, rather like an outrageous set at a rock concert. If, then, the young seek to be "different," either they opt for ever more shocking exaggeration, as if history were a contest judged by media-grabbing sensationalism, or they discount protest and just go slack. It is hard to say which choice is worse.

Thus, one twenty-four year-old writing to the editor of the *San Francisco Chronicle* in 1996 comments mordantly on the Slacker option. Observing that "misery has become a cottage industry" among members of his generation, he goes on to say,

> Any grunge rock concert or coffee shop will reveal thousands of young adults wallowing in self-pity and despair — and loving every minute of it. Faces chiseled in pain, these twenty-somethings sing along with lyrics attesting to their crushed dreams, worshipping at the altar of despair. ... It all adds up to one Mount Everest of Misery.[5]

A contributor to alt.bitterness strikes that very tone: "At 27, life is seen as it really is — too much damn work, pain, suffering, boredom, and maybe if you're lucky one or two good days a year. At this rate I should be fat, arthritic, toothless, old, and (if I'm lucky) dead within a year or two."

But just as often the tone is angry, as in this posting to alt.punk:

> I remember being excited around 1990-91 when I first started seeing books and articles about "us kids," just because nobody'd ever bothered to fucking care before — the media was so fascinated with the Baby Boomers, and noting their every pathetic milestone. Yeah, the Boomers had it better, and the whole country played, and continues to play, indulgent-parent-from-hell with them. Yeah, it sucked coming of age in the 80s. (I'm waiting for "THE BOOMERS CAN NO LONGER GET IT UP" issue of *Time*.)

It would be a mistake to write off rancor and self-pity like this as mere posturing. There is a resentment here that can be easily enlisted against the "Woodstockers." Nobody seems more eager to believe the generational accountants than Internet adolescents, with the result that they are more apt to identify the AARP as their enemy than the corporations that have mangled their wages and benefits. Accordingly, business-financed lobbies like Americans for Generational Equity, acting as stalking horses for private insurance companies that want to move in on Social Security and Medicare, have recruited younger voters by playing upon their sense of victimization.[6] "The baby boomers took all the jobs," complains one message posted to alt.society.generation-x, "polluted the Earth and left us with an enormous national debt and no Social Security."

One need not look far to discover where the younger generation has acquired distorted notions like these. Their fears and frustrations are being expertly fed by those who purport to defend their interests. A 1996 syndicated newspaper feature bearing the headline "Mind-Boggling Disaster Looms in Medicare, Social Security" offers the usual doom-laden scenario of our entitlements future. The principal figure in the story is, once again, Laurence Kotlikoff, leading voice of the generational accounting movement. When he was asked what he would say to the president of the United States if he had the chance, Kotlikoff replied, "How can you sleep at night, given the fiscal disaster you're constructing for the next generation?"[7]

The "next generation" will face no greater test of its political intelligence than seeing through corporate propaganda of this kind. Neither *Ya-*

*hoo!* nor *Encarta* will help with that job. A few good history books might, with a few basic economics texts, some sociology — plain words on the page, no links, no screaming multimedia, no animation.

## RL Is Getting Weirder

I am talking to a bright young woman who works for a slick New York magazine oriented toward an under-thirty readership. We are talking about high tech and the younger generation. She cautions me. "*My* generation wasn't much into computers. That's really the *younger* generation — like seventeen ... in high school. I don't understand *them*." She is, as of 1997, age twenty-five.

The generations seem to be passing more rapidly. Maybe they are being "archived" like the compressed data on computer disks. Certainly young people have become aware of fine distinctions among themselves; even more so the media, which need a new youth culture every other year to back up their regular cover story on the "takeover" generation. As the new century dawns, the teens and twenties young, taken as a whole, find themselves deeply conflicted both culturally and morally, especially those who are "into" computers. They — or at least the more sensitive among them — are torn between a near-mandatory optimism and an instinctive cynicism.

Optimism is the official cultural line that the high-tech industry has been disseminating to young Americans since the day they were born, it is a tale of amazing possibilities and limitless opportunity with the digital generation as star of the show. High tech, the young are told, is serving up a "techno-feast of goodies." It is "enabling and empowering" them; it is an "ultra-personalized intimate technology — everything made to order."[8]

But they — or many of them — seem less than fully convinced. They sense that the very technology that supposedly enables and empowers them is also the source of the alienation they reflect so vividly in their own youth culture. Some may even suspect that, if it were not for this technology on which they lavish so much time reaching out to one another. High tech functions as both devil and deliverer for the young in their uncertain future. For example, one young woman logs on to alt.bitterness to say, "I have no fucking idea what I want anymore. You begin to wish to join the fellowship of productive citizens once again, even if it means processing workman's compensation claims which your employer hopes to be able to get out of paying." And another, posting to alt.cyberpunk: "Is our one force to break free from the corporate monsters that try to control information going to be completely swallowed by that which we strive to escape? It all bores me to death. Maybe I lost the energy to search hard."

Another, realizing that were it not for this machine, he might be out in "RL" (real life), enjoying the sun and the moon and the sky, not to mention other people, posts his resignation to alt.angst: "I am now spending more time communing with my single, square-eyed brother than with any human type. No offense, but I like all of yous out there as he configures you for me on the screen better than if I had to meet any of you in RL. In fact, this **is** RL for me from now on."

There are, however, encouraging signs of discontent. Though they remain enthralled by the glowing screen, America's recent younger generations have gravitated toward movies, music, and literature that reveal serious misgivings about their high-tech destiny. Trapped between the ennui of the suburbs and the violence of the inner city, adrift in a world of menacing scale and intimidating power, some begin to suspect that, unless they are gifted hackers out of MIT or financial wizards out of the Harvard Business School, they will have to scheme, scuffle, and grovel to find even mediocre temporary jobs. Hence, from punk rock forward (through heavy metal, death metal, grunge rock, gangsta rap, and so on), the music that fills the clubs has grown steadily more anguished and ugly. One typical group bills itself "specialists in apocalypse, annihilation, psychedelia, immolation, loss of ego and vertigo." Even allowing for some theatricality in the advertising, one can surely expect neither hope nor tenderness in the music that speaks for the young. When the movies need a cheery tune or a love song these days, they have to reach back a long way back to find them.

The music of the young also grows progressively louder, unmistakably with the intention of *hurting*. One rock group called Biohazard actually begins its concerts by screaming at the audience: "Are you ready to receive your punishment?" The bands, sporting vile names (Cradle of Filth, Napalm Death, Slayer, Virginkillers) and vying with one another to be as gross and gruesome as possible — reach out toward ever more extravagantly amplified expressions of depravity and fury. At raves, teenagers, as if to go the boomers one better, deliberately dose on far more damaging drugs — and combinations of drugs — than anybody knew existed in the 1960s. Heroin, sniffed in near-lethal amounts, has become the suburban favorite.

A high school student preparing for the next rave posts a message to alt.rave, asking for advice from anonymous online experts about a narcotic recipe he is brewing:

> I have 3 questions which I hope somebody will answer before Saturday (but later is OK too). (1.) Did anybody try the "new" antidepressant called Aurorix (moclobemid) with LSD or Shrooms? This antidepressant is a reversible MAO Inhibitor. Would it work to potentiate the trip? (2) I'm taking 20 mg of Paroxetine and 75 mg of Anafranil. I know mixing TCAs with MAOIs is dangerous, but would 150 mg of moclobemid really be a risk? (3) Should I discontinue Paroxetine and/or Anafranil for any other reason (do they interact with LSD/Psilocybine)? If yes, how long does Paroxetine/Anafranil stay in the body?

Medical friends tell me these are lethal mixtures, yet such mad pharmaceutical improvisations are a prominent thread running across the Internet, as is advice about suicide. Among the most common themes is the "woe is me" morning-after lament for the aches, pains, and mental dislocations of masochistic self-medication. One is reminded of the late nineteenth-century decadents, who turned dissipation into a fine art. The current version all but amounts to a romance of brain damage.

A posting to alt.drugs:

> mushrooms make you sick as a fucking dog for a couple of hours, then you're home free acid is a great trip if you can stand the speedy/metal-in-the-veins feeling acid is a walk along the razor's edge with every step pushing the razor deeper into your brainstem interesting the way being raped is interesting

And another:

> i forget things that i'm trying to learn, they just won't stick. i don't have any new ideas anymore (if i ever did), every paper i've written this semester has been like self-inflicted brain-surgery, first, rooting around inside to find something that was still alive in all that dead tissue — then, finding the words to say it with — making the letters all hang together one after another so they look like english and lining the words up in the right order so they come out like a thought. pleeze! how is this done? i have a dim memory of once actually considering the kinds of things that should matter to a

college student who's supposed to want to go off to grad school at some point. all i know is that RL is getting weirder for me by the hour like messages in a language i never learned.

## THE FUTURE AS NIGHTMARE

I cannot say how typical this taste for punishing, life-endangering experience may be. I doubt that anybody can, because the cries for help from these troubled young go largely unheeded — except as occasional disciplinary or legal "problems" if they lead to riot, arrest, or front-page scandal. Some, like Tipper Gore, have sought to censor ugly and violent rock lyrics. I can understand why one would want to do that. But it is quite as important to ask why ugly and violent things are being said in the first place, especially when so many young people are saying them at the top of their voice or crowding by the thousands into concerts to hear them. The possibility that ugly and violent remarks are significant, if halting, statements about our cultural condition has yet to be widely appreciated.

I know of some concerned members of the liberal clergy in England and the United States who have provided advice and friendship by hosting "rave masses" for the young. Their hope is to win them away from their seemingly self-destructive and nihilistic tendencies by offering a drug-free, humane alternative. Matthew Fox, the maverick Catholic and now an Episcopal priest, has been hosting such gatherings in San Francisco since the mid-1990s. He calls his religiously eclectic rituals Techno Cosmic Masses; they are usually dedicated to "Gaia Our Mother." One small effort to provide responsible eldering and a sincere one, but there is something about the abrasiveness of such events, even in the absence of drugs, that needs understanding. Why the volume and the frenzy? Why the need to shock, batter, and brutalize the nervous system?

I think it is this: Rather than growing up absurd, many of the young seem to be growing up *numb* — as if there were some narcotizing process at work in the collective cultural consciousness that deadens the senses of those who were raised on television and constant commercial stimulation. Is this, possibly, a defensive response to the scale, pace, artificiality, and intensity of urban life, as well as to the "normally" delusionary state of mind the media induce? Psychologists have identified a neurosis for our times: the "highly sensitive person," someone who feels the stimuli of daily life too much.[9] Maybe more of the young than we realize are caught between feeling too much and feeling nothing at all. So they seek in the music, the mania, and the deadly drugs some way to spark a vital sensation and so awaken themselves to life.

Some raves try valiantly to promote themselves on the basis of "good vibes and positivity"; sponsors insist that the event will be about love and respect. There is also a Christian rock movement, which was deliberately launched to counter the widespread negativity. The music scene is becoming like a battleground for the souls of the young. Does the young man who posted this sad little message to alt.evil represent many or few? "Life holds nothing but pain and death, but don't look for love, there is none left. There is only Scum, Napalm Death." Bad enough if there were but a few who feel this way; I suspect from the size and dynamism and earnings of the rock music industry that there are many. The only numbers that indicate which way the audience is trending are ticket and CD sales. Everything seems to sell, but hard rock, as it continues to reach for the extreme beyond the extreme, outsells all its competitors.

Those who came to their adolescence in the 1980s are more fully integrated into high tech than any generation before; the technology has been hyped to them as "theirs" in ways that cut them loose of parental ties. For as long as they can remember, corporate America has been leading cheers for an Information Age that promises endless electronic stimulation — a thousand channels of television, the excitement of ever faster, ever more eye-popping World Wide Web sites with bandwidth galore, virtual realities beyond number, stereo that can be heard from here to the moon. And how do the young respond, at least in sufficient numbers to be of concern? They rush to offer themselves for emotional battering at the hands of sadistically oriented rock groups like Nine Inch Nails ... just to feel something *real*.

Here is a problem for which the high-tech industry seems not to have found a solution: *Why aren't these kids happy with all they have been given? Why don't they just quiet down and enjoy their nice electronic toys?*

It is no coincidence that young people whose lives have been radically shaped by high tech are telling us that they are going numb. The cyberpunk resistance is a desperate cry from those who feel the wave of progress closing over their heads. They may not have found more to do about their plight than to suffer and cry out, but thanks to some surviving organic instinct, they know that what the high-tech visionaries are pitching at them is a lie. When it comes, then, to imagining the future, what they find most credible is the antithesis of the world according to Microsoft and the Media Lab. They see the future — their high-tech future — as a nightmare.

## DOWN AMONG THE CYBERPUNKS

> Now he slept in the cheapest coffins, the ones nearest the port,
> beneath the quartz-halogen floods that lit the docks all night like
> vast stages, where you couldn't see the lights of Tokyo for the glare of
> the television sky, not even the towering hologram logo of the Fuji
> Electric Company, and Tokyo Bay was a black expanse where gulls
> wheeled above drifting shoals of white styrofoam. Behind the port
> lay the city, factory domes dominated by the vast cubes of corporate
> arcologies. ... By day, the bars down Ninsei were shuttered and
> featureless, the neon dead, the hologram inert, waiting, under the
> poisoned silver sky.
> — WILLIAM GIBSON, *Neuromancer* (1984)

There are cyberpunks who bristle when they are associated with punk rock. "Cyberpunks aren't about PUNK MUSIC," insists one highly upper-case contributor to alt.cyberpunk.movement. "Cyberpunks are about FREEDOM OF INFORMATION because INFORMATION IS POWER and by god — POWER TO THE PEOPLE." But in fact there is a significant overlap of sensibility between the groups. The shared word *punk* serves in both movements to reveal an identity born of victimization. Both punk rock and cyberpunk express a spirit of resistance; both are made up of those who see themselves as marginal insurgents in a culture gone wrong. Cyberpunk takes its cue from science fiction literature rather than rock music, but the literature is every bit as dismal and despairing as the music. Like the hyperamplified howls of anger and anguish that blare from the stage at a death metal concert, it reminds us that, besides the yea-saying techies at *Wired* who see an endless frontier of technological wonders and amazements ahead, there are the grunts, the malcontents, the delinquents of the high-tech workforce, the hacker proletariat working out of coffin-sized cubicles with their phone calls and e-mail monitored to ensure quality service. Their view of the future runs to alarm, if not desperation. Leave them out and the picture is incomplete.

The most influential of the cyberpunk authors is William Gibson. His jackhammer abrasiveness suits the harsh landscape of his world, a vista of monolithic multinational corporations where embattled anti-heroes can survive only as outlaws plotting clever ways to sabotage a system they cannot own or control. Gibson's cyber-cowboys are marginalized bottom-dogs so sunk in narcotic fantasies and hallucinatory worlds that they have no reality principle to cling to. They inhabit a fictive zone where nothing is certain and everything can be manipulated. Anybody they meet might be a hologram. Not even their minds are their own. What the powers of modern technology have finally brought them is ecological doom in an empire of unlivable cities dominated by the high-rise towers and emblazoned logos of the reigning corporate elite.

Gibson's cities are the private property of ruthless American-Japanese-German-French conglomerates. "Sprawls," as Gibson calls the urban eyesores of the future (BAMA sprawls from Boston to Atlanta), are as squalid as any factory town of the nineteenth century — yet they are congested with advanced technology. Nobody draws a breath or dreams a dream without the use of "derms," or "entertainment modules," or "simstim" implants. In the sprawls, an underclass of demoralized billions struggles to survive in conditions of hopeless moral degradation. For them, the media offer, at best, forms of sad, mind-blowing escape or, at worst, techniques of psychological control. People have themselves been reengineered from their DNA up; they have been transformed into near-cyborgs equipped with internal processors and microbiotic spare parts. It is a world where nothing is real, nothing is human, nothing is gentle, beautiful, or noble. The only love Gibson's cowboys find might be a few drug-laced hours with a company whore in an overnight sleeping coffin.

That is much the spirit in which a young man logs on to alt.cyberspace.rebels to utter a word of anguish. His entry may fall short of literary elegance, but he is giving a voice to the cyberpunk vision of things to come:

> LOOK at us and look out there we are living in the world
> dominated by corporate marketing machine. These guys eat up just
> every opponent out there Nothing is existed beyond corporate
> world. These guys are GOD. These guys have the real consciousness.
> These guys eat you and me. These guys slowly take over our
> existence and body and mind. We have no power to fight against
> these fascist gigantic monster ever created by human race.

Cyberpunk fiction's literary genealogy traces back to early anti-utopias like E. M. Forster's *The Machine Stops* (1905), the novel and film versions of *Metropolis* (1920s), and Huxley's *Brave New World* (1933). All these works saw the bright promise of science and industry being swallowed up by fanatical social engineering and profiteering interests. At that early stage, the future depicted in these works was, on the surface at least, clean and elegant. (One exception: In *Metropolis* the proletariat is inexplicably confined to a dingy underworld.) Cyberpunk redesigned anti-utopia by adding just the right touch of corporate philistinism and ecological disintegration. The films *Alien* (1979) and *Outland* (1981) helped embed images of futurist noir in the public perception. They show industrial life under the control of interstellar corporations reverting to the grubby drudgery of early Manchester. The cavernous and clanking space stations have lost their luster; they are lightless, dank, and dripping. Everything is built cheap and chronically malfunctions; underpaid technicians sweat, scowl, and grumble; cutthroats skulk along the garbage-strewn air shafts and docking bays. The style might be called "future brutal." That is what the world will look like if it is owned by the same forces that own it today.

It is a new and jarring insight — a hell of a different kind. In earlier anti-utopias — Zamyatin's *We* (1920) Orwell's *1984* (1949) — it was universally assumed that only the central state could ever be powerful enough to rule the world. The dehumanized future would be the product of collective planning. But there is another possibility. What if corporate elites, with their insatiable appetite for profit, shape our destiny? Then we will have regimentation, but without the least concern among these selfish, competitive giants for cleaning up the mess or preserving order. Under the hegemony of triumphant market forces, pleasure gardens for the rich may survive under heavy guard, but the rest of the world will become a garbage dump.

It was, above all, the 1982 movie *Bladerunner* (directed by Ridley Scott, based on the Philip K. Dick novel *Do Androids Dream of Electric Sheep?*) that most effectively exposed the decadent underbelly of corporate high tech. Both the film and the novel have since acquired a mythic stature on the Internet; there are three or four highly active *Bladerunner* web sites. *Bladerunner* envisions a future where quasi-human replicants — patented products of the Tyrrell Corporation, one of the industrial giants that rule the future — have more humanity to them than "real" human beings. The tale, played out in the thronging, smog-shrouded streets of a decaying megacity, is a study in the ultimate criminality of corporate power. The fact that younger people are learning these facts of life from science fiction rather than sociology should not undercut the validity of the lesson.

## ELDERS IN THE REIGN OF ANTI-LIFE

A sample of the preconcert harangue shouted from the stage by a death metal group whose performances usually end with riots in the mosh pit.

> Power, rage unbound because been pounded by the streets. Cyanide blood burns down the skyline. Hatred is purity. The bullet connects at last. Let freedom ring with a shot-gun blast.

Words howled by twenty-somethings at an audience of teen-some-things. Not teens who have suffered through a holocaust or the horrors of ethnic cleansing or thermonuclear war, but kids from suburban homes. The performance, with its super-amplification and programmed light show, is supremely high tech. But the audience is wearing T-shirts with slogans like "Get Up and Kill" and "Hail, Satan."

It is difficult to take young people seriously when they immerse themselves in a nihilism they have not earned and cannot fully understand. Yet, as presumptuous as the cyberpunk vision may be, it is an expression of the life impulse, still there, still struggling to make its way forward. If that impulse is left uneducated and given no creative means of expression, it will finish where it began — as a howl of indiscriminate rage that drifts toward the madness or suicide with which the young too much confabulate. Either that or it will become mere show business — a marketable act, tolerable because it has no target and no strategy.

The cyberpunk vision is so extreme that it is tempting to dismiss it and hope that it will simply be outgrown. But the first thing that one must say is how *true* that vision is. It has a great deal more history and culture behind it than the young realize. That in itself is a healing lesson, for it brings perspective. William Blake saw the smoking mills of his day as dark and Satanic. Were he around today, he would very likely see high tech as *sleek* and Satanic. He would surely recognize the same inhumanity and sacrilege at work in the most ingenious of Silicon Valley's achievements. He would also see the genius, for he celebrated the inventor's skill as much as the artist's.

I suspect much of the angst the young reflect in their online messages to one another stems from their sense of isolation — which also imbues their words with an annoyingly self-congratulatory sense of originality. That is an error of ignorance on their part. That is why seeking to make elders, if not the entire pre-high-tech past, obsolete is so crippling. These wrongs need the voice of experience. Misguided science, the abuse of wealth and power, technology in the wrong hands ... these are issues that connect to the countercultural movement of the 1960s and back at least as far as the Romantic artists. What the cyberpunks have done is to press those issues to new, histrionic extremes, as if to warn us that, like Hollywood's indestructible Alien, this thing is still *here*. Blake called it Urizen ("a shadow of horror"), Allen Ginsberg named it Moloch — a suitably ancient name that reminds us how old the horror is.

> What sphinx of cement and aluminum bashed open their skulls and
>     ate up their brains and imagination?
> Moloch! ...
> Moloch whose mind is pure machinery! Moloch whose blood is
>     running money!
> Moloch whose fingers are ten armies! Moloch whose breast is a
>     cannibal dynamo!
> Moloch whose ear is a smoking tomb!
>
> — *Howl* (1957)

Some of our children are having bad dreams about Moloch. With a prophetic clarity beyond their years, they see the monster now as the alien, the cyborg, the android, caricatures of humanity that cannot love or understand us. They see it as the Tyrrell Corporation, as the *X-Files'* cigarette-smoking assassin, as Darth Vader in any number of his sword and sorcery/science fiction variations.

The first step in effective eldering is to make common cause with the dread and disgust of the young. But we must also recognize that their despair is a measure of their immaturity. The nihilistic hysteria that fills their music and literature simply tells us that they cannot make their way alone. They need the competence of elders to find their way out of the bad dream we are in together. Left to their own devices, they come up with poor solutions. Some contributors to the cyberspace newsgroups spend much time exchanging ideas for a liberating "people's technology." But what they have in mind — railgun specs, bioluminescent LCD implants, perimeter defense droids — is just more science fiction.

Others identify a cyberpunk as "a highly intelligent person who likes to spend 120 percent of his available time in front of a terminal doing something to test his brain." Such people are losing all touch with real life. Robert Bly, speaking with a poet's wisdom, believes there will be no growing up in what he calls "the sibling society" unless children find their way beyond the machines and the systems and back into the sustaining natural world to learn from the trees, the stars, the beasts.

The elder who taught me the most through my college years about the use and misuse of technology gave Moloch another name, perhaps the best choice of all. Lewis Mumford called it "Anti-Life." Anti-Life was the psychic distortion that Mumford believed was at work behind megatechnics, seeking to replace all things organic with mechanical substitutes. The inventions of Anti-Life might be as modern as the latest computer program, but Mumford believed they traced back to the divine kings of the River Valley civilizations with their compulsive appetite for power over man and nature. His vision of our destiny under the dominance of Anti-Life was grave in the extreme, and more deeply studied than any cyberpunk fantasy. But he knew that the true measure of wisdom is hope, and hope is what the competence of elders brings to the dilemmas of the young.

> On the terms imposed by technocratic society, [Mumford observed] there is no hope for mankind except by "going with" its plans for accelerated technological progress, even though man's vital organs will all be cannibalized in order to prolong the megamachine's meaningless existence. But for those of us who have thrown off the myth of the machine, the next move is ours: For the gates of the technocratic prison open automatically, despite their rusty ancient hinges, as soon as we choose to walk out.[10]

CHAPTER TEN

LONGEVITY AND GENDER

The novelists never told us that in love, as in other matters, the
young are just beginners and that the art of loving matures with age
and experience. Furthermore, while many of the young believe that
the world can be made better by sudden changes in social order and
by bloody and exhausting revolutions, most older people have
learned that hatred and cruelty never produce anything but their
own kind. The only hope of mankind is love in its various forms and
manifestations — the source of them all being love of life, which, as
we know, increases and ripens with the years.
— ISAAC BASHEVIS SINGER, *Old Love* (1979)

As the folklore of the world would have it, age and sex are poles apart.
Almost by definition, the old are beyond passion as well as reproduction. The famous reports by Kinsey and by Masters and Johnson that did
so much to launch the post-World War II sexual revolution gave scant
attention to sex after sixty — as if there were little to be found. It is only
since the mid-eighties that the media, registering a growing senior audience, have discovered sex among the seniors, though usually with a certain
coy astonishment. Inevitably, as with all matters sexual in the United States,
there has been research on the subject; followed, just as inevitably, by workshops at the university extension, earnest documentaries on television, and
how-to manuals in the bookstores.

THE GAME OF SEX, THE RULES OF GENDER

As one might imagine in a popular culture still dominated by the
fascinations of youth, the focus of this belated attention has been almost
wholly on sexual techniques and habits. Frequently overlooked is the cru-

cial distinction that social scientists make between sex and gender. "Sex" — the biology of being male or female — is what we are born into; it is of the body. "Gender" is of the mind; it is learned from the culture and usually rigidly restricted to just two behavioral choices: masculine or feminine. If we think of sexuality as a game whose goal is reproduction, then gender lays down the rules of the game as enforced by the umpire called "society." Gender, for example, decides who initiates a sexual encounter, how courteously or aggressively, with how much mutual consent, under what circumstances, with what responsibilities, and with how much personal improvisation. Gender in fact prescribes an entire personality and way of life that might, paradoxically, make sexuality more of a chore than a joy. Gender as Victorian ladies knew it actually defined females as angelic beings who found sexuality distasteful.

Raw erotic energy may always be more insistent in hard, young bodies primed for reproduction, but when it comes to gender, the cultural amplification of sexuality, youth might be the last place to look for enlightenment. What goes unmentioned in most media surveys of senior relationships is the intriguing possibility that viewing gender from the other end of life may teach us how much we got wrong in our youth.[1]

The courting rituals of young love invariably exaggerate the dissimilarities of male and female, often seeking maximum contrast in clothing, hairstyles, makeup, and behavior. It seems to be universally part of the mating game for man and woman to see themselves as polar opposites, though there is reason to doubt that this tendency arises from some underlying glandular agenda. Homosexual love clearly does without such extremes of contrast. Whatever the reason, the role-playing and reproductive maneuvering that preoccupy the young all but obliterate the human continuities between feminine and masculine. Male and female become almost alien breeds, different in every possible aspect. The differences are mythologized until they take on cosmic proportions: all nature — the sun, the moon, the Earth, the heavens — oppose masculine to feminine.

Yet ironically, opposition, which can serve to heighten sexual appetite, is also the relationship that does most to produce fear. The line between can become dangerously fine. For all its exciting tension, gender opposition is a psychologically grueling way to see life — grueling because, as time and experience reveal, it is untrue. With the passage of years, perception has the chance to soften the contrast and blur the edges. Both the older woman who discovers that the girlish and eye catching fashions of the day are no longer being designed for her and the older man who discovers that he is no longer (and may never have been) a superstud are bound to rethink the stereotypes they have honored all their lives. Hard knocks, the ordeal of disease, the approach of mortality — facts of life that both sexes must face when careers and child-rearing have been left behind — offer men and women the chance to find their common humanity. They may begin to feel more comfortable with the idea that the genders are *adjacent* rather than opposite, a realization that opens the way for durable friendship and authentic intimacy. It is one of the rewarding discoveries of age that the other gender has the mind, the inner life, the aspiration of another human soul and is in all these ways very like oneself.

With so many healthier seniors pursuing love, sex, courtship, and even parenting decades later in life than anyone ever imagined possible, we might expect to find the youthful gender roles prolonged into deep old age as people strive to stay young longer. I have talked to therapists who tell me — with a sigh of resignation — that they are seeing clients in their sixties, women mainly, who are still struggling to keep up with the dating and mating game. At the same time, when it comes to matters of sex and gender, the boomers are a special generation. Exploring what it means to be a man or a woman returns them to a project that began in their youth. Challenging gender stereotypes was a staple part of countercultural teach-ins and love-ins, rallies and rock festivals, where young men and women came together in rebelliously unstructured encounters, eager to throw off the repressive parental culture. In those years, when it was a daring gesture for men to wear their hair long and for women to do without bras and makeup, they launched (and suffered) a sexual revolution that still roils our society.

In the 1960s, Mick Jagger performed onstage dressed in a skirt; in the 1990s, we have gay liberation parades in the streets and lesbian sitcoms on prime-time television. As far as we have pushed the envelope, we are still discovering unimagined sexual identities. Some sexologists now believe there are at least *five* physically defined sexes, including three hermaphrodite variations that have long been altered at birth to enforce gender orthodoxy. Accordingly, there has been an organized rebellion among "transgenders" and "intergenders" aimed at keeping everybody's sexual equipment just as it was originally furnished, on the grounds that androgynous infants have a right to their own gender orientation.

I can think of only one aspect of sex and gender that has not been explored over the course of the last generation. That is the role that age has to play in deepening sexuality and taking it to the threshold of mortality.

## The Six-year-Old Beauty Queen

If boomers finally succeed in bringing greater maturity to our understanding of gender, the contribution of women will vastly outweigh that of men. Even more than it has been changed by the struggle for racial justice, our society has been revolutionized by the redefinition of gender brought about by a women's movement that has transformed every institution in our lives.

And yet ...

Even as I write, the police are investigating a gruesome murder in Boulder, Colorado. Late in 1996, a six-year-old girl was found strangled in her home. As terrible as such a crime would be under any circumstances, this case took on a macabre twist that played across the front pages of the nation's tabloid press. The little girl was a "beauty queen." On television and in magazines, we have been treated to pictures of her tarted up to look like a teenage seductress. The story out-Lolitas Nabokov's *Lolita*. The child at the center of this story was raised to emulate that same helpless, utterly vulnerable sex-pot who filled the movie screens in my boyhood. A child mimicking women who are playing the role of overgrown children, she was the cult of youth and the female-as-victim rolled into one. Worse than functioning as a salacious male fantasy, she was part of something that still haunts the sexual psychology of women. The main role in promoting little girls as beauty queens seems to be played by their mothers, who are apparently living out a fiction of virgin-vamp sexuality through their daughters. All the toxic images of femininity that the women's movement has labored to expunge have survived like a resistant virus in some corner of our popular culture.

Every year Miss America walks the runway, bikini-clad and wobbling on stiletto heels. Gaunt and girlish supermodels dominate the pages of the fashion magazines that women still buy and peruse. Salesmen take their customers to lunch at strip clubs confident that they will find women at work enacting fantasies straight out of Victorian pornography. Books that tell us men are Martian hunters and women are Venusian homebodies still rank high on the best-seller list.

Writing in the *Washington Post* in November 1997, the columnist Maureen Dowd, bemoans the evidence of consciousness-lowering she sees among American women of the 1990s. She wonders if women's liberation has been replaced by a "bimbo feminism" that gives "intellectual pretensions to a world where the highest ideal is to acknowledge your inner slut. I am a woman, see me strip." Can we confidently predict that the next turn of the cultural tide will finally carry such sexist flotsam out to sea? Or will it wash in still more of the same? At the very least, it would seem that feminism has a long way to go in achieving its primary goal of deconstructing gender in order to bring women their equality.

Though they have accomplished much over the past generation, women, who make up the majority of boomers, have some unfinished business with the men in their lives. Age is at the core of that business. For their own good and the good of the culture, female boomers will have to help male boomers grow up as well as grow old. They have special qualifications for that role. By physiological default, aging belongs to women as it has not thus far belonged to men. Menopause announces a dramatic end to a woman's youth, and after menopause women live out a longer old age for reasons that cannot be wholly explained by genetics. Women, as the gerontologist Royda Crose puts it in her study of gender and life expectancy, are "winning the game of life." Not that it needs to be that way. "It's time," Crose believes, "for men to break out of the life-threatening bonds that traditional masculinity places on their lives and their longevity."[2]

If there is one clear reason why inherited gender stereotypes continue to plague our lives, it is the domineering self-image to which men, especially men of great influence, continue to cling. It is an image that constellates social power and wishful thinking. It promises status, but at the risk of sorrow and early death. Most treacherously, it promises youth, or at least the fond reminiscence of youth. But what it brings men is a life-threatening folly.

## THE PECULIAR PROBLEM OF THE ALPHA MALE HUMAN

In the late 1940s, the film star John Wayne was at a crossroads in his career. Approaching his mid-forties, he would soon find it impossible to continue playing a conventional leading man. He was in sight of the age at which romantic leads of that period either retired from the movies or segued into character parts. But as it turned out, Wayne's best years as a he-man lover were still ahead of him. In 1948 he appeared in a movie that would give him a second career; it would also introduce a new male type into our popular culture. In the Western *Red River*, Wayne plays a father, a brooding widower, and a successful cattle baron. A distinctly senior figure, he is nonetheless the domineering stud, possessed of potent sexuality and capable of awing younger males into submission. Wayne would play that role for the next thirty years, never once giving up his claim to glory, dominance, or women. At about the same time, the slightly older French matinee idol Jean Gabin was staking out a similar film persona for the remainder of his career: the lonely, hard-bitten, older male, the survivor of a dead wife or a hard divorce, perhaps a kingpin criminal who carries on with as much erotic power as ever, feared by the men around him, pursued by lovely younger women.

In the movie world, older actresses still tend to drop by the wayside after forty. If they survive into romantic roles, it is by way of some awkward concession to their age. Wayne and Gabin, however, created an enclave for over-age leading men that opened new possibilities well beyond the movie screen. They embodied a masculine fantasy that cast its spell over men in all walks of life: the patriarchal male who grows sexier and more formidable with age. Many others have followed in their footsteps: Clint Eastwood, Sean Connery, Paul Newman, Robert Redford, Anthony Quinn, perhaps most definitively Clark Gable, who died playing the part opposite an adoring Marilyn Monroe in *The Misfits*. Reportedly, Gable brought on the heart attack that killed him trying to wrangle wild horses as the script required his character to do, rather than having a stunt man do it for him. Macho to the end.

The strangest version of this normally he-man role is the film persona that Woody Allen has developed, the nerd-lover whom gorgeous young women — sometimes *very* young women — cannot resist. Watching actresses throw themselves at Allen is not actually an exercise in the willing suspension of disbelief. One simply recognizes that the man writes and directs his own movies — though in Allen's case the fiction has overflowed into whatever "real life" means in the movie world.

In primate groups, such dominant figures are called alpha males: grizzled, old veterans who monopolize the females and stand as a target for eager young males who must prove their selective advantage by overthrowing them. Freud had something like this in mind when he invented his fanciful notion of the prehistoric primal horde. He imagined there were once elder males who ruled by taking all the women into their harem and suppressing (Freud thought castrating) their rival sons. Working more from dramatic license than reliable anthropology, Freud thought this was the distant origin of the famous Oedipus complex. If the notion had any intellectual validity, it nevertheless had to wait for Hollywood to give it popular visibility and, at least for the men of the world, popular appeal.

As age-denying as our culture is, senior men obviously continue to wield great power in our politics and economics. We see them in the news of the day giving speeches, attending VIP conferences, making deals, announcing policy, getting richer. As heads of state and as high corporate chieftains, they have succeeded in moving the John Wayne image off the screen and into the real world, where they become the political equivalent of the old gunslinger, the veteran cop, the battle-scarred military hero. The prominence of this figure might seem a paradox in a society that grants age so little respect. Does it represent a significant exception to the long history of shabby treatment that the old have suffered?

Not at all.

Men who continue competing for power into their older years are more the problem than the solution to age discrimination. They are, in the area of age, what token women have been in government or corporate life. Women, in order to qualify for positions of leadership in institutions that are shot through with stereotypic masculine qualities, often must become honorary men. While it is now generally recognized that the positions women must compete to hold in the political and corporate worlds are saturated with masculine qualities, what often goes unnoticed is that these are *young* masculine qualities — very young. Like ambitious women, men who cling to power must also become "one of the boys." As Betty Friedan was among the first to observe, "In the debate about women and men, sex roles and sex, over the last thirty years, it is never pointed out that all our assumptions and definitions of masculinity are based on *young men*."[3]

Even when it is older men who play the role, they are enacting the part of adolescents. In the world of power, the "king of the mountain" game-playing that every boy learns in the schoolyard remains the rule. Like the wild boys in William Golding's *Lord of the Flies*, old men in the power elite continue to compete for supremacy as if to prove that they are not *really* old. They play the role of targets for the young men coming along and bucking for dominance.

In his approach to the psychology of older men, David Gutmann includes a comparative study of the alpha male in industrial society and elders in Native American cultures.

> The elder rulers of "advanced" societies are only older versions of successful young men, those who have laid down the bases for their economic and political power early in life. They receive little honor, title, or credit on the basis of their age alone. For the rest, for the majority of undistinguished older males who have not laid up power and riches in their early years, personal and social prospects can be bleak, making for a striking and disheartening contrast with the typical older man of the folk-traditional assemblage.[4]

Few men in their fifties and sixties have what it takes to be ideal alpha males — namely, a professional makeup artist, all the right camera angles, a stunt man to take over the running, jumping, and fighting, a director to call "Cut!" when your toupee slips, and a million-dollar publicity department. Nevertheless, all men to some degree feel the weight of that image. It stands over them like the looming threat of failure — as failure is judged by a cruelly unrealistic standard.

Women sometimes complain how unfair it is for men to fixate on nubile movie queens. It is as much of a heartache for men to be held up to the Sean Connery criterion. Sometimes the movies that created this image reflect upon its pathos in real life — though rarely. In the 1950 film *The Gunfighter*, Gregory Peck, as the old gunslinger, yearns to give up the game and reclaim his life as husband and father. But he cannot. Wherever he stops, younger versions of himself insist on calling him out to prove that they are the fastest gun in the West. And at last the old man is gunned down by his youthful successor. John Wayne finished his career with a similarly pathetic story in *The Shootist*.

There are signs that things are changing in the film world, slowly drifting toward greater reality as the society ages. Paul Newman, in his seventies, is exploring roles that rather gracefully combine maturity and subdued masculinity. In the films that are finishing out his acting career, Clint Eastwood openly shows his years; his declining physicality is worked into the story line. Of course, when the script requires it, he can still leap from windows, run a mile, and bed the female lead. But in *Absolute Power*, he announces his AARP membership as a sixty-six-year-old retiree and turns fatherly toward his estranged daughter.

A small glimmer of reality perhaps, but in the far more consequential world of business and finance, alpha males have yet to make even that much of an adjustment. There, pretensions of youthful vigor and agonistic prowess reign supreme. Just as little boys play compulsively at gory and sadistic video arcade games, hoping to set the record for wiping out more planets than anybody else in the universe, big boys play for money and titles and status.

They also play for women, a sure indication of the adolescent orientation of the game. "Power," as Henry Kissinger once said, "is the ultimate aphrodisiac." The successful sixty-something CEO with a twenty-something trophy wife on his arm (and perhaps a well-advertised mistress or two) is like the alpha male chimp who must constantly display sexual prowess to the adolescents of the pack lest he lose everything he ever fought to achieve.

From time to time we get listings of the current alpha male standings: CEOs who are ranked by salary, stock options, bonuses. A few years back, a box score in *Forbes* magazine reported that even Bill Gates of Microsoft, though not old enough at the time to qualify as an alpha male but well on his way, might be in danger of falling behind in the money race. "Asian Billionaires Gaining on Gates," cried the headline. There followed a list of the pursuers who might soon "dethrone" him, the "poorest" of whom had a personal fortune of $10.5 billion. One woman was listed, the usual token, identified as "heiress" to a cosmetics empire and thus not a self-made man. In any case, she lagged well behind the pack with a mere $5 billion.

What is the meaning of money like this? It is more than a man can spend and enjoy, more than his family needs to remain secure for centuries to come. Money in these obscene amounts is an abstract score, the grown-up version of a computer game like *Mortal Kombat*, meaningless points that simply tell the world who the lords of the universe are. Yet as silly as that ambition may seem when viewed in the clear light of mature judgment, the alpha male model of masculinity links Darwinian self-interest to sexual potency in a way that makes criticism too threatening to tolerate.

## THE MISSING MALE ELDER

Down among the primates, alpha masculinity is a sad role for an old ape to perform; many die playing it. It is their only way out of this world.

Sadder still to see alpha male humans playing that part as if it were instinctually mandated. Sad for the men, sad for the women, but saddest of all for the planet Earth.

In one of the first books to probe the psychological dimension of human ecology, the environmental philosopher Paul Shepard described the males of our society as "ontogenetically crippled." They grow from a protracted adolescence into a false adulthood saturated with "juvenile fantasies." At that point, "irrational feelings may be escalated into high-sounding reason when thrown up against a seemingly hostile and unfulfilling natural world. The West is a vast testimony to childhood botched to serve its own purposes, where history, masquerading as myth, authorizes men of action to alter the world to match their regressive moods of omnipotence and insecurity."[5] As the women's movement discovered early on, gender stereotypes have more than social consequences. They determine our relationship with the Earth itself. Real women groan beneath the power of the alpha male human, but even more so the woman called Mother Nature.

The new school of feminist psychology has done much to illuminate the structure of the "separative self," the typically stunted male psyche. Feminist psychologists most often describe the masculine ego as a tightly bounded, autonomous, self-regarding module that permits of no penetration, no union, no warmth of feeling. In Catherine Keller's words, men (and all psychological schools modeled on the masculine norm) "identify development itself with separation, and attachments appear as developmental impediments."[6] This is a character type that permits the maximum aggression, acquisition, dominance, and ruthless competitiveness.

In her science fiction novel *Woman at the Edge of Time*, Marge Piercy imagines the ultimate example of the male separative self. He — or more accurately *it* — is called a "cybo," a semirobotic, seven-foot-tall warrior that never removes its body armor, even when indulging in violent sex with the prostitutes provided by its employer. "Instead of a sex drive," we are told, cybos "have a basic killer instinct." The futuristic employer is, significantly, a global conglomerate called Chase-World-TT. "We embody the ideal," the cybo proudly announces. "We can never be deflected, never distracted."

This semi-mechanized, single-mindedly aggressive male is now a film standard: images of *Steel, Robocop,* and *The Terminator* fill young imaginations. I know that comic-book heroes played a major part in shaping my boyhood ideal of manliness; their literary quality was no higher. But I recall that Superman and Batman lived up to a certain chivalric ethic in their treatment of women. The cyborg has none of that. He — it — has evolved beyond sexual warmth and tenderness.

The separative self is the man that every little boy is encouraged to become as he breaks free of maternal influence. In the life of the male, the nonrelational ego is a thing-in-itself; it never becomes a person-in-relation that would lack identity outside of relationship. The feminist psychologist Jean Baker Miller puts it this way:

> The concept of a "self" as it has come down to us has encouraged a complex series of processes leading to a sense of psychological separation from others. From this there would follow a quest for power over others and over natural forces, including one's own body. ... Our tradition [has] made it difficult to conceive of the possibility that freedom and maximum use of our resources — our initiative, our intellect, our powers — can occur within a context that requires simultaneous responsibility for the care and growth of others and of the natural world.[7]

Mainly in response to the women's movement, a vigorous and many-sided men's movement has grown up since the late 1970s that seeks to meet the need that many males feel today for other identities. Unfortunately, this quest often continues to be haunted by patriarchal images. The Christian Promise-Keepers, whose leader insists that "God is a Man-with-a-capital-M," meet in numbers that can fill football stadiums. Their goal is to reimpose paternal authority in their homes — an unlikely prospect. Even in the evangelical community, women hold jobs and enjoy access to education. There cannot be many among them who will accept the subordination that an antiquated biblical ideal requires. Other men's groups place more emphasis on liberating the repressed emotional ("feminine") side of the male personality, allowing fear and kindness to show through. But even these movements are frequently based on images of the warrior and hunter, roles freighted with excess historical baggage, all of it having to do with some repertory of supposedly exclusive masculine traits. Typically, the literature of men's groups touches not at all on aging but emphasizes ways to maintain virility. Sometimes compassion is mentioned, but there is always much histrionic rhetoric about experiencing wildness and fire in the belly.

The problem with these efforts is that they remain age-biased and therefore will not last out a full lifetime. The age bias cuts deeper than the gender bias because it ties men to an essentially adolescent phase of life when their main psychological project was to differentiate from the mother — and from all that is identified as feminine. But as the lives of women come to include more social space, what is the point of that task?

There was a time when dominant males enjoyed privileges rooted in the control of property, political office, education, official authority. Stripped of that backlog, the alpha male role becomes a kind of pathetic macho-lite that is apt to wilt at its first confrontation with any self-possessed woman. I confess that I have found myself embarrassed to be in groups where men gather to search for "manly" ways to be sensitive or caring. Trying to find "the warrior within" sounds too much like situation comedy. But then I never found alpha male "manliness" all that appealing. At school I was the boy who ran for cover when fighting broke out in the schoolyard. And when I didn't run fast enough, I got beaten to a pulp and had to drag myself home in tears. I can still hear the cries behind me, "Mommy's boy! Mommy's boy!" Being manly always seemed to mean hurting or getting hurt. I hated that game and longed to be free of it. Of course, I envied the he-man movie stars of my time — the Clark Gables and Gary Coopers and Errol Flynns — but I always hoped the girls I wanted to impress would prefer the attentions of gentlemen like Leslie Howard or Ronald Coleman.

Alpha males, straining and thrusting to prove their warrior virtues long after any true grown-up would care about such nonsense, are the old guys who make age obnoxious to the young. They may grow old, but they are not elders. They are over-age adolescents, geriatric boys. They do not lead by virtue of wisdom, but by cunning and ruthlessness. The historical and mythic talents they draw upon are not those of the sage, but those of the hunter and the warrior. They may take pride in holding their own with the young blood, but in truth, clutching at power until it is torn from one's grip makes for an unbecoming end to life. If they were as wise and brave as their years should make them, they would long since have put the strenuous pursuit of salaries, status, and sexual dominance behind them and moved on to other, better things.

Not that it is obvious what those "better things" might be. In our society, where money controls so much of the media, it is inevitable that moneyed men will try to hold center stage, crowding out the alternatives.

What they want to see in the culture at large are reflections of themselves. To take a telling contrast: In the Hindu tradition, there is a stage of life, called the *sanyassin,* that is reserved for men who retire after their family and business duties are at an end. It is meant to be a phase of contemplation and completion, a time to put one's spiritual house in order. Since the near-demise of the monastic life in the Western world, our society has had no equivalent to such a phase of spiritual retreat. At the beginning of the modern period, that wise and gentle male identity was obliterated. It is difficult to imagine a society as dynamic as ours generating anything like it again, not for as long as the alpha male model remains dominant.

But then we need not assume that a man or woman needs to leave the world in order to become a true elder, especially at this point in our history. As we lay the foundations of a postindustrial moral order, it is essential for elders to assume a greater role in our affairs. That role ought not to be a mere extension of midlife getting and spending. Far more challenging is the task of remaining involved and responsible, but in a new key, one that sounds a note of gentleness and ethical responsibility.

There are now any number of books, many of them growing out of men's therapy groups, that reveal the soul-searching men have undertaken. *The New Man, The Sensuous Man, The Liberated Man* ... all focus on the cultivation of emotional warmth, counseling men to open to their feelings and risk being vulnerable in their relationships. Among counselors and therapists, there is a clear professional consensus that the role of the alpha male has become a burden that more and more men need to unload and want to unload. Alpha male masculinity has been blamed for the ruination of sexuality, marriage, family, and social conscience. It is also plain unhealthy for men to drive their aging bodies to keep up with a handful of wealthy business tycoons or with movie images of compulsive masculinity. If the pace and strain of the macho lifestyle does not kill them, depression and despair will.

Suicides among men over the age of sixty-five are several times more common than among women in their age group. Elderly white males have by far the highest suicide rate in the senior population; they are unique in being the only group of Americans more likely to die by their own hand than in an automobile accident. In contrast, the lower suicide rate for women over sixty-five has been traced to their greater flexibility and more developed coping skills. Women spend more time building the relationships they need for support.[8] Men can be so good at hiding their emotions that they conceal even suicidal despair from professional counselors. And unlike women, for whom attempted suicide can be a cry for help, when men elect to kill themselves, they use the means most likely to do the job: guns, hanging, or car accidents. "Men," as Royda Crose observes, "are more at risk of early death because they are taught to ignore weakness, illness, and health concerns. ... They not only don't listen to their bodies, but they are applauded for the denial of pain and discomfort."[9]

Men become especially suicide-prone after their wives die, an event that often leaves them with no close friends, nothing to occupy their time, nothing to give meaning. Like Willy Loman in *Death of a Salesman*, if they have not proven themselves to be a success in their careers, they give up on life, feeling they are worth more dead than alive. They have outlived the role that sustained them since adolescence. A psychiatric social worker I know tells me he once organized a widowers' support group for men who had recently lost their wives. Discovering that most of the men could not find their way around their own kitchens, he brought in a woman to teach some basic cooking. To his surprise, the men resented what he had done. They felt embarrassed to be taking lessons from a woman so late in their lives.

The search for a way out of this masculine trap has produced the quaint concept of the male menopause. Technically speaking, there may be no such thing as a male menopause that fully corresponds to a woman's later-life transformation, but emotionally, as a psychological stage of life, there is something very like it. Since menopause is not as decisively announced by the male body as it is for women, men have been able in the past to override the crisis. No longer. "Putting the men back in menopause," as one therapist cutely puts it, is now an established psychological and cultural project among the boomers. At its heart lies the search for intimacy, a word that always requires another to be intimate *with*. That other is usually understood to be a lover, in most cases female. But liberating the male capacity for intimacy may also awaken another male potentiality, one that has to do with other men — younger men. Becoming intimate in love may be the gateway to becoming an elder to one's children and to one's society.

In his studies of the human life cycle, Erik Erikson, among the first psychologists to see aging as "a stage in the growth of the healthy personality," coined the word "generativity" to refer to the eldering project of our later years: "The interest in establishing and guiding the next generation," as he defined it. When that important task is left unattended, "regression from generativity to an obsessive need for pseudo-intimacy takes place, often with a pervading sense of stagnation and interpersonal impoverishment." Erikson, however, saw generativity as primarily a parental responsibility toward one's children and gave little attention to the collective responsibility of the whole senior generation in society.[10]

That is precisely the orientation that Daniel Levinson has sought to provide in his broader study of male developmental psychology. Referring to eldering as "mentoring," Levinson takes this defining responsibility out into the society at large, where men must deal with one another in school or the workplace. It is a complex role, combining the function of teacher, sponsor, guide, exemplar, and counselor. "The mentor represents a mixture of parent and peer; he must be both and not purely either one." Significantly, Levinson regards mentoring as a social task that had best take place outside the parent-child relationship. Parents, he feels, are "too tied to their offspring's pre-adult development (in both his mind and theirs) to be primary mentor figures." At his most challenging, Levinson identifies mentoring as "a form of love relationship." But love between men, so long shadowed in our society by fears of homoeroticism, is a difficult emotion to cultivate, especially for the alpha male. Some cultures, like the Greeks in the time of Socrates, saw no problem. Ours does. The alpha male is compulsively heterosexual, needing what he hopes will be a yielding woman to validate his sexual domination.

Levinson believes the ideal age differential for mentoring is about a half-generation; but he adds "a person twenty or even fifty years older may, if he is in good touch with his own and the other's youthful Dreams, function as a significant mentor."[11] "Dream" has a special, technical meaning for Levinson. It is the self-chosen life task that ushers the adolescent into the world as a man or a woman. Not all young people form a dream; not all are allowed to have one of their own. But the job of the mentor is to connect with the passion of the dream and help make it real. The Jungian psychologist James Hillman echoes Levinson when he tells us that "mentoring begins when your imagination can fall in love with the fantasy of another."[12] So too the poet Robert Bly, who defines the "true adult" as "one who has been able to preserve his or her intensities ... so that he or she has something with which to meet the intensities of the adolescent." Both Levinson and Bly remind us that cynicism and despair make for the worst kind of old age; such negativity leaves us unable to nourish the lively aspirations of the young. The essence of youth is *beginning*. If those who have lived longest cannot resonate with the adventure of beginning, what will the young want to learn from them?

Bly has made eldering the principal focus of his highly influential male consciousness-raising work. He has concluded that the rampant wildness of young men, their difficulty with commitment and responsibility, has only one cure: Older men must show the way. "The fundamental problem in the continuation of a decent life everywhere in the world," he insists, "is this question of the socialization of young males. ... It is not women's job to socialize young males. That is the job of the older men." But, he wisely fears, "we are losing our ability to mature. ... We are always under commercial pressure to slide backward, toward adolescence, toward childhood. With no effective rituals of initiation, ... young men in our culture go round in circles. ... Observers describe many contemporaries as children with children of their own."[13]

The eldering task Bly and Levinson have in view is nearly impossible to carry out in a culture that has taken the alpha male as its model for social leadership. The inherent bad faith of the marketplace, its cynical strategies, bullying habits, and low opportunism cripple the power to mentor. The business community has nothing to do with gentle or loving qualities; it does not encourage men to be mentors, only winners. The "commercial pressures" Bly cites as an obstacle to maturity are the creation of world-beating entrepreneurs whose goal is running up a score measured in dollars. Their way promises wealth, power, and status for a few. Where values of that order are at stake, it takes more moral courage to stand *against* the alpha male than to *be* the alpha male.

Because the alpha male role licenses irresponsible uses of power on the part of men, reconfiguring gender is part of a larger social task. This, as the women's movement realized long ago, is the place where the personal and the political intersect.

## Learning from the Invisible Woman

Historically speaking, old age is very new. As far as we can tell from the bones they have left us, early humans rarely survived beyond the age of forty. "Life after forty," Daniel Levinson observes, "has been a significant part of man's collective experience for but a moment in our history." In the past, the relatively few men who outlived their active young male adulthood might, at best, carry on as alpha males for another few years, but the charade was soon over. They did not have to maintain the pretense for as long as twenty or thirty more years into deep old age. But however long their lives may last, alpha maleness has given men, whether in reality or fantasy, the option of eluding the facts of aging longer than women can. Older women may find that men their age are frequently a full stage behind in life, still seeking in women things that are fast passing, still seeking in themselves things that are not there. There are few studies by men seeking wisdom in age, but many by women.

The new run of men's magazines may spend more space on health, toiletries, and aesthetic surgery, but they are largely a disappointing spectacle. The tone must still be gruff, the content overwhelmingly concerned with sexuality. Literature for older men is largely mired in an unresolved postadolescent struggle with the women in their lives, as if men read them with their eighteen-year-old self looking over the shoulder and snickering. Even the more enlightened fringe of the men's movement is still trying to find better ways "to be men." Older women, on the other hand, have gone on to finding better ways to be human.[14]

A man can go to his grave still enacting some version of the alpha male role. But women have no equivalent of John Wayne or Sean Connery awaiting them in their senior years, and so no temptation to try holding off the great changes age brings with it. In that respect, popular culture has left them to think things through for themselves. What does age take from them, what does it bring them? Women, like it or not, have more experience with aging than men. Age comes to them with physical decisiveness and for most of them will last longer. In the past, when the unquestioned dominance of alpha males threw women into social eclipse, these were hardly advantages. In a patriarchal society, older women are devalued and invisible. But in our time these once invisible women are doing most of the thinking and discovering that will make longevity worthwhile.

In this they have some support from evolutionary history. The best explanation biologists offer for women's long life after menopause suggests that it enabled females in early human society to stop having babies and thus save their strength for raising the children they had already borne. But as the life span has grown, women's postmenopausal years have taken them well beyond child-rearing. They are left with time on their hands for other matters — something approaching what women of an early time would have considered a full lifetime. That punctuating event of menopause — a built-in rite of passage — prompts women to give serious thought about aging long before men have to think about it. A woman may be undergoing that transition while men her age are still fiercely on the job, battling it out with younger rivals, hopelessly immersed in a male stereotype that has no future.

If wisdom about sex and gender begins on the far side of the inherited male and female stereotypes, then it is clearly women who are doing most to create a wisely nongendered identity for boomers. "How do we *live our age* as simply a new time of our life, a new period of our humanness, a new stage?" Betty Friedan asks. "The clue lies in those individual differences that increase with age for both women and men. The clue is the *personhood of age.*" With age, we are, as she observes, "defined less by biological programming ... than at any other period of our lives, [and] not necessarily programmed at all by the social roles and norms that defined our youth and middle age." She calls this "at once the terror and the liberation of age."

Thanks to the women's movement, especially as it becomes the *older* women's movement, we are learning something that could only be convincingly experienced from the vantage point of a long life. Human qualities, whether good or bad, are *not gendered.* There is nothing genetically "male" about courage, forcefulness, daring, creativity, decisiveness — nor about harshness and insensitivity. There is nothing genetically "female" about caring, nurturing, gentleness, compassion. That is why we find young and middle-aged women these days up to their eyes in the cutthroat competition of boardroom politics. As much as insecure adolescent boys in various military academies may flinch at the fact, the U.S. Marines are training women for combat and finding they can do the job. On the other hand, I have known a surprising number of fathers and "house-husbands" who cook, do the dishes, and diaper the baby with no sense of humiliation. And in the streets and parks each day I see more and more young men tending their children with some delight. But even progress of this kind in the home and on the job may leave lingering vestiges of gender in the personality, the woman's concern for her femininity, the man's longing for virility. Maybe some sense of balance and civility in expressing those needs is the best one can expect at midlife. But beyond that initial insight lies the uncharted territory of deep maturity where all talk about "the mystery of gender" and "the ineradicable differences between the sexes" rapidly loses meaning.[15]

As we learn in every basic anthropology survey, gender roles vary from culture to culture. That is precisely what calls all the roles into question. But we also know that there have always been roles of *some* kind. It is as if our inborn division of reproductive labor has to be seen as more than a purely physical difference. All our fellow mammals respond to signals and cues in their mating; Arousal is the inevitable prelude to procreation. To that extent, gender game-playing may have been necessary for as long as fertility mattered. If fertility still mattered, then it might make biological sense to keep the old game of boy-girl going. But reproductive success has come to play less and less of a role on our overpopulated planet. Indeed, the very fact that people in the industrial societies — the women especially — have come to challenge gender roles, as I do here, is some reflection of our greater biospheric condition. We are at a point where discovering the person who lies beyond masculinity and femininity — as age offers us the opportunity to do — has become an ecological necessity. Longevity is becoming a greater fact of planetary life than fertility.

It is time to call off the game.

CHAPTER ELEVEN

_____

# THE DISRUPTIVE WONDERS OF BIOTECHNOLOGY

U p to this point the longevity revolution has been defined as a new
demographic order in which the old will inevitably outnumber the
young. But there is one way in which that revolution might be stopped in
its tracks.

What if old age were to be abolished?

Suppose physical aging — the wrinkles, the hardened arteries, the loss
of eyesight, teeth, hair — ceased to be our fate. Then those who grew older
by the calendar would show no outward sign of their age. The world would
then remain forever young because nobody would grow older by the measures that have always been most decisive: declining health and the death
of the body.

This sounds, of course, like the scenario for a science fiction movie.
But it is hardly that. As medical research intensifies its focus on the causes
of aging, we are coming to understand exactly how the organism grows
old. And just as knowledge of that kind has helped us tame so many other
diseases, we can only wonder if the disease of aging might also be healed.

Until the late twentieth century, our understanding of aging was frag-
mentary and largely anecdotal, if for no other reason than that there were
so few very old people available for study. Those that did survive as long as
eighty or ninety years were often so depleted that no one would have thought
it possible or desirable to keep them going much longer. Medical expertise
concentrated its resources on the young where it had the best chance of
success. Age, like death, was accepted as our fate, indeed a defining feature
of the human condition. Studying how it might be avoided would have
seemed comparable to asking how the body might avoid the force of gravity and be trained to levitate.

That is very much the spirit in which I started this book. However much the longevity revolution might reshape society, it never crossed my mind that old age itself might be eliminated as a stage of life. What I had heard about anti-aging research in biotechnology seemed to me too fantastic to take seriously.

Then I looked more closely.

The progress that has been made in solving the mystery of aging is among the great achievements of modern science. For the first time in history we now possess a theory that tells us why animals age. We now know where in the organism aging takes place; we have begun to unravel the intricate chemistry of the process. That process takes the form of a molecular rhythm, a metaphorical clock, that determines the life and death of cells. How soon this discovery can be used to modify aging in human beings, and how great that modification might be, remains to be seen. But biotechnicians are now working from a powerful paradigm and they have put out the warning. The research is under way; the results may be astonishing. In the words of Dwayne Banks and Michael Fossel, two major researchers, "The possibility of extending the maximum human life span has gone from legend to laboratory."[1]

## GENETIC ROULETTE

In the premodern period when aging was more legend than science, Luigi Carnaro might be regarded as the first celebrity elder. A Paduan who died in 1565 at the age of ninety-eight, Carnaro was a wonder of his age. As far as anybody knew, he was the oldest man since biblical times. When he reached the age of eighty, people across Italy wanted to know how he had managed to live so long. He obliged their curiosity by authoring periodic discourses on longevity. Since he had restored his health after living through a dissipated middle age, Carnaro's counsel was all the more coveted. He recommended temperance and moderation in all things. He also believed in preserving the "innate moisture" of the body, which, he felt, kept the humors in balance.[2]

Ever since Carnaro's day, the oldest old have been objects of popular interest. After all, the oldest among them define our life span, the maximum number of years that a fortunate few of us can hope to live. As of the turn of the twenty-first century, the consensus among physicians and actuaries is that the life span can reach no further than 125, and even so only for a very few. That estimate is based mainly on the remarkable Mme. Jeanne Calment of Arles France, the oldest known human being able to document her age. Mme. Calment could remember seeing the building of the Eiffel Tower in 1889. She died in August 1997 at the age of 122 years, 146 days. Though she remained lucid to the last, by the time she died she was seriously incapacitated physically. Her eyesight and her hearing were severely dimmed and she was barely able to move about. But until she reached 117, she was reasonably ambulatory and highly spirited. At the age of 120, Mme. Calment decided to give up smoking; she feared it might become a habit. While we can expect to see an increasing number of people reach 100 in the years ahead, few are expected to get as far beyond the century mark as Mme. Calment.[3]

In recent years, the oldest old have become a special medical study — and not just the oldest human old. Geneticists are carefully studying the longest living of every species, from rodents to elephants to see whether we share genetic factors with other animals. Even the lowly nematode has contributed a few "candidate longevity genes" for research. Some of the findings are astonishing. Among the oldest living individual entities is a lotus seed that spent most of its history in a state of suspended animation. Discovered in China, the seed was dated at 1,288 years; watered, it was still capable of putting out a shoot. The experiment is more than a botanical curiosity. Biologists wonder if the seed holds the secret to potentially new cellular repair processes that may delay aging in other species.[4]

So far, as remarkable as the endurance of the very old may be, it tells us little about our prospects in the years ahead. When doctors quiz the oldest old about their habits, the results are notoriously inconclusive, almost comically so. Probably bored by the question, elders over ninety tend to give flippant answers, as if they were beyond caring. Some say they smoke cigars, some (like Mme. Calment) that they drink wine, some lead active lives, some do not.[5]

The only conclusion researchers have reached about the oldest old from studying them directly is that most of them are female and most remain relatively lean. Their caloric intake is modest. Is this because abstemious eaters live longer, or simply because, with age, appetite drops off? George Roth, a molecular physiologist at the National Institute for Aging, has kept lab animals alive for abnormally long periods by underfeeding them until their metabolism drops to "survival mode." Though he believes caloric austerity alone might lengthen the human life span to well over eighty, it remains uncertain why this should be. Some researchers believe it has to do with slowing down cell division, others that it diminishes the damage done by free radicals in the cells — a hypothesis that receives support from other lines of investigation mentioned later in this chapter.[6]

In one respect, the longevity of the oldest old might be seen as discouraging. After all, these supremely senior people were born and raised before there was much reliable knowledge about nutrition or aerobics or the damage done by saturated fats and smoking. They knew nothing about cholesterol or antioxidants. Yet they have outsurvived millions of clean-livers. This suggests that long life is simply a matter of genetic roulette.

If that is true, then the natural human life span still remains to be discovered and will surely go beyond Mme. Calment. It was only after World War II that the population at large began to understand about the basic risks posed by saturated fats, tobacco, and toxins; it was only then that better nutrition and physical exercise became widespread. Thanks to these more enlightened practices, someone will manage to combine good genes with healthy habits (and enough good luck to avoid being run down by a truck) to push the limit further. That person may only be getting born today. He or she will not report in to the *Guinness Book of Records* until the beginning of the twenty-second century.

## The Last Older Generation

Both medical science and common sense have long shared a basic theory of aging and death. It might be called the "wear-and-tear" hypothesis. Bodies simply give out the way cars give out after a certain amount of mileage. One rheumatologist puts it this way: "You've got an automobile that has a carburetor, wheels, valves, a water pump and all these different parts that are built to last beyond a warranty period. ... The human body expires when enough of its components have collapsed."[7]

This mechanistic image of aging and dying has been with us since William Harvey first likened the heart to a pump in the seventeenth century. Call the heart a pump, and you can expect it to wear out as all pumps do. The venerable Thomas Jefferson writing to the more venerable John Adams in 1814 (both men were in their seventies), observed, "Our machines have now been running seventy or eighty years, and we must expect that, worn as they are, here a pivot, there a wheel, now a pinion, next a spring, will be giving way."

As this traditional imagery would have it, people run down and finally die of a "natural cause" called "old age." Eliminating those familiar phrases from the medical vocabulary has been a major advance in the science of gerontology. We have come to see that dying of old age is a self-fulfilling prophecy. The terms are left over from an era when no one troubled to perform autopsies on the very old. Doctors simply assumed that old people died of old age and would attribute their deaths to "natural causes." Statistics compiled from such records would therefore confirm the assumption that old people died of ... being old.

Today we can be more precise about the wear and tear our bodies sustain through a lifetime. We can trace the damage to numerous sources. In one respect, death may be a cosmic process: the radiation that streams in relentlessly from outer space may eventually scramble the genetic data in our cells; or all on its own, the DNA containing that data may, after years of replication, simply accumulate so many random mistakes in transcription that the result is an "error catastrophe" large enough to prove fatal. Once we have identified such causes, however, the mechanistic model of aging at once gives rise to the hope that we will be able to fix the damage the way we fix any machine.

As we learn ever more about the specific sources of senescence, the word has gone out: Future generations need not age as fast as generations past. To take one example, Dr. Steven Lamm, who practices "vitality medicine," prefaces his book *Younger at Last* with the admonition: "Discard the tired, outdated, and inaccurate notions of how we're supposed to be at forty, fifty, or sixty. You are not your parents; you are not doomed to age the same way." His prescription for fending off the incursions of age is a balanced combination of several new anti-aging medications: yohimbe (from the bark of an African tree), testosterone, L-arginine (an amino acid), pycnogenol (an anti-oxidant), plus some "nootropics" like ginkgo biloba and deprenyl to offset memory loss.[8]

Lamm's approach to rejuvenation is becoming ever more widely practiced. Find a substance that we produce naturally in youth but that drops off with age. Then replenish the supply or find a substitute. Several of our hormones diminish with age, among them testosterone, melatonin, and DHEA. In our youth, the adrenal gland secretes DHEA in high quantities; by the age of eighty, we have 90 percent less in our blood than at age twenty-five. Is one or another of these the substance that once kept us young?

Since the early 1990s, we have been involved in a massive, largely uncontrolled public experiment with just such a hypothesis. Female hormone replacement therapy (HRT) to replenish estrogen is now a routine procedure for postmenopausal women, and one of the most commonly prescribed treatments in American medicine. The benefits, which may include a declining incidence of heart disease and various signs of rejuvenation, are well documented. So too is the effect of estrogen on the brain's cognitive functions; it has been found to enhance learning and memory even in those suffering from Alzheimer's disease. Estrogen replacement seems, then, to retard aging.[9]

But there are other possibilities. Among other leading candidates as a cure-all for aging is human growth hormone (HGH). Ronald Klatz, president of A[4]M (the American Academy of Anti-Aging Medicine) believes that aging is essentially a pituitary deficiency disease. He points out that people who suffer from that deficiency manifest all the signs of age. The pituitary gland can, however, be revived by dosing on HGH, the "fountain of youth hormone." The result, he is certain, will be the reversal of natural aging. It is as simple as that. Klatz, who writes articles in the popular press under headings like "Can We Grow Young?" answers the question with an emphatic yes. Other researchers believe the most astonishing results with HGH have been placebo effects achieved with participants who were highly motivated to regain their lost youth.[10]

It is an odd feature of American medical culture that, for all its closely guarded professionalism, anti-aging, the most crucial of fields, remains in the realm of do-it-yourself folk medicine. The public usually learns about anti-aging medications from one of the television news magazines or from pop medicine best-sellers (bearing titles like *The Melatonin Miracle*) that now arrive in waves, always accompanied by extraordinary claims. Once a promising supplement has been publicized, it becomes a product. Since many hormones are not subject to FDA control, health food stores are free to stock and sell them; so too every local drugstore and supermarket. They are casually on sale alongside hair spray and aspirin tablets, or they can be ordered in bulk from merchants everywhere.

But self-medication can be risky. There have been few reliable tests on the effect of these hormones on human subjects; taken in large quantities, some have adverse effects in lab animals. DHEA, for example, can cause liver tumors in mice. Then there are the more benign immunity boosters, mainly antioxidants, that promise to arrest the aging process. Echinacea, an extract from the purple coneflower, cat's claw from the Amazon rain forest, shark's cartilage, goldenseal, ginseng, or plain garlic ... each has its following as a way to restore the vigor of our younger years.

Along this line of research, an astonishing new idea about aging has emerged. Rather than accepting old age as fate, researchers now define it as a *disease* — or rather, as a collection of mainly deficiency diseases. If that is so, then perhaps aging is also curable, if not all at once, then in the same piecemeal way we have gone about curing other sicknesses and extending life expectancy. It is simply a matter of going through a checklist of lethal or disabling ailments and eliminating them one by one, as we have very nearly eliminated smallpox and scurvy.

The ability of medical science to reverse or prevent diseases once thought to be invincible is very nearly an article of faith. Recently I came upon a children's AIDS project in the local YMCA. It was a quilt the children had sewn to wish AIDS sufferers well. At the center of the quilt was a large patch that said, "Hang on! Scientists will invent a cure." That conviction is among the major reasons we may never be able to agree upon the moral permissibility of euthanasia, even for the very ill. Who can say what medical miracle waits just around the corner? If we can believe what life-extension researchers are telling us, perhaps one day soon it will not be necessary to age at all. This generation will be remembered as the last older generation. And if aging can be cured, the same might be possible for the ultimate result of aging, death. People who do not grow old do not die — at least not of "natural causes."

Rejuvenation in its various modes is a "stochastic" theory of aging. That is, it holds that aging is due to the buildup of random damage in the organism. As optimistic as rejuvenation therapy has become in its claims, it is fast becoming the conservative position in life-extension medicine. There is another, more radical hypothesis. The extreme wing of anti-aging research sees the entire complex of characteristics we call "aging" as *a single physiological phenomenon* that is controlled by a core genetic mechanism. Rather than seeing aging as stochastic, this approach maintains that senescence is "programmed." The very terminology suggests a course of therapy. Find the flaw — or bug — in the program and fix it.

The guiding image here is the oldest model of nature in Western science: the clock. We are asked to imagine a genetically determined clock ticking away in the organism; it is fully wound at birth; it counts out our hours until it runs down and stops. The first researcher to use this image was the Russian biologist Vladimir Dilman, whose book *The Grand Biological Clock* was published in 1955. Dilman theorized that the metaphorical clock in question was a neuroendocrine mechanism based in the hypothalamic-pituitary axis of the body. This clock, which at first facilitates healthy growth and development, begins falling out of balance at about the age of twenty-five. To correct that imbalance, Dilman recommended the use of phenformin, an antidiabetic medication, plus several hormones, among them estrogen, to fine-tune the organism. Dilman's proposed cure did not work, but ambitious life-extenders have adopted his clockwork image, believing that it makes obvious what route medical science should take. Find that clock, reset it, and aging will be at an end.

As far-fetched as this sounds, the goal stems from a curious fact of life that calls the wear-and-tear theory of aging into question. Aging, as humans experience it, is *not* a universal phenomenon among living things. Some microbiologists have even suggested that the oldest of life forms — the microbes — are immortal, in the sense that they go on and on dividing with no sign of age. Do they ever die? It is a matter of definition. A cell lineage can stop reproducing and die out, but cells in another lineage, say, moved to another laboratory culture, may continue splitting and living on. At a more complex level of development, creatures do indeed die, but rarely by aging as humans do. With the exception of a few long-lived species like the elephant, the parrot, and the Galapagos tortoise, very few animals have the chance to grow old in the wild; they are hunted down or they die by starvation, freezing, or any number of fatal accidents.

Before zoologists began keeping animals alive to study them in captivity, aging was a rare experience in the nonhuman world. Before the twentieth century, there was probably never such an animal as a very old chimpanzee. We now know that rockfish, mollusks, sharks, tortoises, and sturgeons may go on for decades longer than humans, showing no signs of physical deterioration; even their fertility lasts to the end of their days. The flounder female grows larger rather than older; the male reaches a limit and then shows signs of age. The bristle-cone pine lives for millennia, though only at the growing edges. The creosote bush has clocked in at ten thousand years of age. Oddly enough, many of these creatures are distinguished by how primitive they are, as if a long life with minimal sign of aging were the original design from which "higher" types have deviated.

Can this human evolutionary departure, then, be reversed by reengineering the genetic apparatus?

In working with yeast cells, researchers have been able to identify fourteen genes that are directly related to aging. By manipulating the genes so that they "overexpress" or "underexpress," aging in yeast has been increased or decreased by as much as 30 percent. No one has yet discovered timekeepers that govern aging in the human cells with that precision, but progress in that direction represents one of the most impressive lines of research in modern science.

## The Disease Called Aging, the Mistake Called Death

Until the early 1960s, the dogma among microbiologists was that, given proper attention, a cultured human cell might live indefinitely. The implication was that cells do not themselves age; aging must originate in some other process. Then two researchers, Leonard Hayflick and Paul Moorehouse, discovered that cells do indeed register the passage of time. Freeze a collection of cultured cells after they have divided a certain number of times, thaw them, and they will only divide so many more times, as if somewhere in side there were a clock keeping track of their age. There is in fact a limit to how many times a cultured cell can divide. This finite replicative capacity gives out after about one hundred divisions. This means that the cells of a young person will survive in a petri dish longer than the cells of a much older person. Eventually, however, after a certain number of divisions — now called the Hayflick limit — the cells stop dividing, begin to malfunction, and soon die.[11]

Here we have a landmark discovery in modern medicine. *Aging happens at the cellular level* and presumably works out from the very foundations of life.

But if there is a cellular clock, where is it located? In 1978 the site of the Hayflick limit was discovered to lie at the tip of the chromosome. There we find an expendable stretch of DNA called the telomere. Each time a cell divides, a small amount of the telomere flakes away, leaving less to lose the next time the cell divides. The telomere is a buffer that protects the rest of the DNA from growing shorter. A great many of the effects we see as the aging of the body actually ensue when the telomeres begin to break down at their tips. In aging cells, molecular debris accumulates, membranes get ragged, some genes stop functioning, other genes, capable of doing great damage, begin to run rampant. The malfunctioning of senescent cells that have used up their quota of divisions causes brittle bones, parched skin, declining memory.[12]

This cellular model of aging is now the prevailing paradigm in medical research. It has that empirically mechanistic quality that always proves highly attractive in science: specific mechanisms causing specific effects by way of chemical reactions. Images like this invite tampering and possibly improvement. In a typically mechanistic metaphor, the gerontologist Vincent Giampapa puts it this way: "The blueprint of aging is in the DNA under the hood of the telomere."[13] Obviously, then, if the telomeres can be kept from breaking away — better still, if damaged telomeres can be repaired — aging might be stopped, even reversed. At the cellular level, this is called "immortalization."

There is an enzyme that does exactly that. It is called telomerase. In 1984 the microbiologists Carol Greider and Elizabeth Blackburn, working along the lines Leonard Hayflick had charted, discovered that telomerase can actually render a cell immortal by keeping it dividing seemingly forever. But there is a problem with telomerase. It is the enzyme that causes cells to grow beyond control. That is called cancer. In that case, the immortalized cell kills the all-too-mortal organism. Finding a way to make controlled use of telomerase is among the most active areas of anti-aging research.[14]

Early in 1998, biotechnicians at the Geron Corporation in California took the first significant step toward that goal. They identified the gene that manufactures telomerase and used it to "immortalize" aging human eye and skin cells. Once the gene had been inserted, the aging cells began to divide vigorously once again. Leonard Hayflick, whose limit had thus been surpassed, greeted the achievement as a "monumental advance in the understanding of the molecular genetics of aging."

At this point the most likely application for the new technique is in cell biology. Long-lived human cell cultures will diminish the need to use laboratory animals; they may also help grow customized tissues for spare parts surgery. At some still distant point such cultures may be used to rejuvenate selected organs and tissues, but the prospect that this method can be used to switch off aging in the entire organism before birth is still in the realm of fiction. As one critic puts it, "To think that aging is caused by a single clock ticking away inside cells is almost as naive as thinking that homunculus-like figures control your brain."[15]

Radically altering the genetics of aging lies a long way off, but in the meantime there may be ways to protect the telomeres from the daily damage they suffer and so keep the cell in good working condition. Some longevity researchers think this may be quite easy to do. Grace Wong of Genentech Corporation was among the first to suggest the deleterious role played by oxygen free radicals in our organism. The free radicals, molecules that lack an electron and go hunting for it in other molecules, eventually damage DNA and RNA. Wong showed that antioxidants like vitamins C and E tame the free radicals. Several other dietary supplements also do the job. Beta-carotene, selenium, and coenzyme-Q10 all block the extensive damage done by the cellular burning of oxygen and may be most effective when they are coordinated to work as a team. Selenium and CoQ10 can be synthesized by our bodies, but they are among the substances whose presence in our blood declines with age. Their deficiency may play a role in aging.

## IMMORTALITY INC.

If there was ever a line of scientific research that needed advice from outside science, it is biotechnology. Any significant advance in this field that abolished aging or simply gave us decades more life would radically alter the human condition. Youth would become a matter of some fifty years, and retirement would stretch out over as much as eighty years, not for a lucky few but for all who did not die of accidental causes. At that point, every death below the age of eighty or ninety would be as great a tragedy as we now regard the untimely death of a teenager. The economic disruption that would come about is obvious. The current entitlements debate asks us to worry about baby boomers who may live some twenty years longer than their grandparents. What if the entire human race were demanding access to medications that would *double* its life expectancy?

Medical professionals and biotechnicians have only lately begun to give serious thought to this daunting prospect. Dwayne Banks and Michael Fossel have called for a review of all public policy based upon conventional population projections. They have cautioned us to begin weighing the long-term economic and political consequences of life-extension research. "Predictions of the costs of aging will be hollow unless they factor in the ongoing, nascent, and fundamental changes in our understanding of aging and age-related diseases."[16]

But can we imagine calling a moratorium on life extension research, or fixing some limit to its pursuit? The rough rule of thumb that Leonard Hayflick has suggested will hardly do. He advocates calling off research when life expectancy reaches one hundred, long enough, he feels, for a good life. Pressing beyond that opens up "grotesque scenarios" of over-population.[17] But his choice is little more than arbitrary. That proposal might be endorsed by everyone below the age of fifty — and it would just as surely be rejected by any healthy ninety year old. Other researchers wash their hands of all responsibility for social consequences. Some make an optimistic appeal. A race of healthy elders, Ronald Klatz believes, will find the wisdom to solve any problems that arise.

Biotechnology could be the gateway to our evolutionary future. It might bring us an expanding repertory of scientific knowledge, medical skills, and social values that we culturally transmit to our progeny as the secret of longevity. Eventually, if we ever discover the biological basis for aging and incorporate that discovery into the human genome, the genetic transmission of longevity might take over from cultural transmission. Longevous traits would then become as much a part of our physical constitution as hair or eye color. Someday, looking back, our ancestors may regard the twentieth and twenty-first centuries as the great watershed when longevity made the transition from cultural ideal to genetic characteristic.

*Or ...* biotech may be summoning us to a delusionary and ultimately fruitless quest, rather like the search for the proverbial fountain of youth. But the quest could take a tragic turn; it might leave the human race impoverished and genetically crippled in ways that cannot be repaired.

How could this terrible result come about? One need only survey the growing literature of biotechnology to sense where the flaw might lie. It has to do with the very exuberance that drives research in the field. The hubris and hyperbole that now characterize popular writing in biotechnology, even that of leading professionals, comes worrisomely close to the commercial hype that surrounds computers and high tech. The reason is the same in both cases. The research, far from being "pure," stems from corporate sources. The lion's share of biotechnology is being financed by private laboratories. We are dealing here with entrepreneurial science. In search of venture capital, it is selling longevity like a product.

No, not *like* a product — *as* a product. The treatments and medications that yield longevity are taking the form of merchandise: pharmaceuticals, vitamin and nutritional supplements, lifestyle accoutrements, and, most controversially, patented genes. The result is exactly what we have come to expect in other dollar-driven fields: exaggeration, misleading advertising, and frenzied, competitive jockeying — none of which precludes the possibility of genuine research breakthroughs. High tech promises machines that will be smarter than people; biotechnology promises us the life of the gods. But in the case of longevity, we are dealing with a product that impinges upon the deepest yearnings of the human heart.

A television series on biotech takes the title *Man Immortal*. A survey of the field calls itself *No More Dying*. Ronald Klatz announces that we are in "a life-extension revolution" that "will soon make human life spans of 120 years and beyond a boring reality." These are intoxicating promises. They carry with them the resonance of an age-old cultural ideal that lends them almost religious significance. They are the life impulse raised to its highest power. Wisely or not, people want those promises to be true. If limitless longevity is now to be made available from corporate America, what charge is too high? And if the profits are also limitless, then what claim is too great to make?

But to pursue the evolutionary metaphor a bit further: Commercialism could prove to be the flawed gene in our *cultural* transmission of longevity. Profiteering may very well corrupt the message and produce a monstrous cultural mutation.

In August 1997, the front page of my daily newspaper carried a jarring juxtaposition of reports that illustrates the problem we may one day face. One story recounted a great new breakthrough in our understanding of telomerase, the enzyme that plays a central role both in cancer and in aging. The story indicated that we are getting ever closer to the ability to manipulate the aging process and thus extend life expectancy by many years.

That same day the news from Washington was that Congress had cut thousands of retarded, dependent children from the welfare roles as part of a budget-balancing campaign. The Social Security Administration explained that it had been mandated to save the money. In effect, our society was declaring that it could not afford to maintain these children. Consider what the burden would be if these children were the beneficiaries of a revolutionary enzyme therapy that gave them another century of dependent life.

Imagine that we achieve a dramatically increased life span, but not the health and vigor we want with it. To be sure, vitality is always intended to be an integral part of life extension. But can we be certain that we will get what we want? Will profitable advances in life-extending technology be kept classified and off the market until it can be demonstrated that the procedure guarantees twenty or thirty years of vigorous, disease-free life? If we are mistaken about a matter as consequential as this, there will be no obvious fix. The "mistakes" will be people clinging to a life that may not seem worth living to most of us, but not for that reason volunteering to take themselves off society's hands.

Or suppose we discover that there is an *older* old age waiting somewhere beyond the present life-span horizon; suppose it brings with it forms of disability we cannot imagine, a sort of hypersenility. In a recent survey of progress on the genetics of aging, the researchers conclude with a dark rumination upon the "polymorphism" of the genes. Polymorphism means the ability of genes to express themselves in unpredictable ways over the life span. "One might consider that, if the human life expectancy should approach the present record of 122 years, some existing gene polymorphisms that may be 'lying in wait' could rise up to challenge the quest for health in the advanced years."[18]

Hopeful as this progress is bound to seem as it is reported in the media, we should remember that enthusiasm can blind as readily as it can inspire. In their 1976 book *No More Dying*, Joel Kurtzman and Phillip Gordon confidently predicted "the conquest of aging" and "freedom from death ... the last enemy." Similarly, in *The Immortalist*, a bizarre but utterly serious paperback manifesto written in 1969, the novelist Alan Harrington announced that "death is an imposition on the human race" and called for its elimination. Given the powers of modern science, Harrington believed, it was time to "prepare for immortality, or the state of indefinite living." He called this "engineering man's divinity." Indeed, in Harrington's eyes the only significant obstacle to waging a "war on death" was the continuing influence of antiquated "death-worshipping" forms of religion and philosophy.[19]

*And ye shall be as gods.*

A breath-taking prospect. But one looks in vain in the pages of these books for any mention of Alzheimer's disease. Why is the disease not there? Because, as of the early 1970s, too few people had contracted the disease to make it a significant feature on the medical agenda. Indeed, as of the late nineteenth century, when life expectancy was much shorter, we did not even know that Alzheimer's disease existed.

Those who offer glowing predictions of an ever extending life span may be as wrong as those who predicted intelligent computers by the year 1990. But even to raise such possibilities has an impact upon the culture of longevity; indeed, research, investment, and development are rushing forward on the basis of those expectations.

Considerations like this return us to the dilemma of the ragged fringe: the declining physical condition that awaits even the most longevous among us at some point in the future. That dilemma is with us now and is already contributing to the rising cost of Medicare. Biotechnology could make that problem even worse. Currently, the oldest of the old — those who reach ninety and one hundred — seem to require little medical care and die quickly when their time comes. But biotechnology could allow many more people who reach the seventy- to ninety-year-old range to die very costly deaths. The result could be the ultimate nightmare: a society in which the hospitals and nursing homes are filled with decrepit but superlongevous seniors in need of ever more long-term, expensive care.

This is the "terrifying prospect" Sir George Pickering raised in the 1960s when he warned that "those with senile brains will form an ever increasing fraction of the inhabitants of the Earth."[20] That sad scenario is, of course, as speculative as anything the biotechnicians are brainstorming. Life beyond 125 is *terra incognita*. That does not mean the research should cease, but only that it ought to be guided by a certain prudence and caution. We should be feeling our way forward. We are not. Market forces are rushing us into the demographic frontier as if nothing could go wrong. The main reason for the optimism is money. Everybody involved in the research has an eye on the prospective profits and the glory of the discoveries to be made. This is hardly a prescription for objective scientific work.

## LIFE/DEATH, YIN/YANG

"To be" and "not to be" arise mutually.
Difficult and easy are mutually realized.
Long and short are mutually contrasted.
High and low are mutually posited.
Before and after are in mutual sequence.

— From the *Tao Te Ching*

There is a philosophical conundrum hidden away in the more optimistic lines of life-extension research. Some of the most promising ideas about reversing aging and staving off death share a perplexing characteristic. They link aging and death to otherwise necessary functions of the living organism.

Consider what we have discovered about glycosylation. Glycosylation results from the way sugars are metabolized, or caramelized, in our bodies. It is known to contribute to cataracts, the blocking of arteries, and the stiffening of joints — all characteristics of old age.[21] The same process underlies the wrinkling of the skin in old age. As we grow older, our aging cells do a less and less effective job of producing the enzyme that eliminates sugar, which then begins to gum up the functioning of the cells, and so the skin begins to age.[22] Perhaps, then, this most basic of cellular chemical processes is implicated in aging.

But cellular use of sugars, like the burning of oxygen, is the cell's main way of gaining the energy it needs to do everything. The wedding of oxygen and vitality is one of the great turning points in the evolution of life. By virtue of this ingenious cellular chemistry, it became possible for life to develop a complexity far beyond the microbial level. Now, at a much later stage of life's evolution, human beings have developed a science that can study the chemistry of our organism. What we have discovered is that, over time, the bonding of sugars and protein produces harmful side effects that resemble aging; so too the burning of oxygen produces free radicals, which eventually damage the cells of the body and kill them. Thus, while learning how to use oxygen was among the basic achievements of life on Earth, in the form of free radicals oxygen becomes a life-shortening menace to the organism. Our efforts to eliminate free radicals that come of oxygen combustion amount to reaching a few billion years back in evolutionary time and revising how life works.

While there are many other directions in life-extension and anti-aging medicine, I mention these for a particular reason. At least to my layman's eye, this situation has an intriguingly paradoxical character. We now know that one promising way of reversing senescence leads us to a process that both nourishes and kills. It is almost as if the human organism were booby-trapped. Our perception of death as an "enemy" leads us to believe that it can be eliminated as the "opposite" of life. But is it possible that life and death are intertwined, not as "opposites" one can choose between, but as a radically coupled, mutually defining phenomenon resembling the yin-yang relationship in Taoist philosophy?

Is it possible that life and death are not an opposition but a *polarity?* The answer makes a great difference. One can choose between opposites, but not between poles. One cannot, except under exotic experimental conditions, have a positive pole without a negative pole; the two are companions that define each other. So too one cannot strip certain quarks of their companion particles. What if death is rather like the shadowed ground that makes the bright figure upon it visible?

One new area of medicine seems to be flirting with just that ancient spiritual insight in its biological translation. Apoptosis is a process that accompanies life throughout its course, serving the needs of the living creature. It is defined as cellular suicide, or more colorfully as a "cellular death wish." Research now suggests that life is as much the beneficiary of that death wish as its victim. One of the experts in the field, Martin Raff, actually refers to the process as an "existential drama" and connects it with Albert Camus's conviction that suicide is "the only truly serious philosophical problem."[23]

Apoptosis is a process of self-destruction programmed into cells. It is there from the beginning of life; it appears in the embryo, where it acts systematically to kill off cells by the millions in order to shape the newborn. For example, the human fetal hand first appears with webs between the fingers. The cells that constitute the webs kill themselves so that the hand can have the right shape. This might almost be seen as a form of genetic sculpture in which chemicals work away at tissue the way an artist carves stone. Similarly, if a cell is infected by a virus or expresses mutated DNA, for safety's sake apoptosis sets in, nudging the cell toward self-destruction.

Throughout life, cells are constantly proliferating, but their numbers remain constant, again owing to apoptosis. Some scientists believe this process might be susceptible to manipulation for the purpose of saving lives, say in the case of heart attacks or strokes. Left alone in such crises, damaged heart muscle or brain cells may opt for self-destruction. But if that response can be stalled for days or even hours, it may be possible to preserve the cells and repair the damaged tissues.

Like all microbiological processes, apoptosis is intricate. It involves the production and carefully orchestrated interaction of enzymes whose behavior adds up to a suicide gene. The enzymes carefully repackage dead cells so that neighboring cells can consume them. Unlike necrosis, which is the untimely death of a cell due to trauma or disease, apoptosis is neat and efficient. It leaves so little waste behind that it wholly escaped the notice of scientists until the 1970s, and even then its function in the normal course of life was unremarked for another decade. In a sense, the role played in our healthy functioning by dying cells was invisible because there was so much of it going on.

Our bodies are filled with death, but the dead cells are neatly scavenged and recycled by the organism. It is now understood that without apoptosis, life would not be possible. In fact, when cells lose their ability to die, they run rampant, assuming that life-threatening form we call cancer. Thus, every cell has to be able to die for the good of the organism. The result is a cell carefully "balanced on a knife edge with death on one side and growth on the other."[24]

The process of apoptosis as a whole is profoundly communal, or cooperative — though, of course, such metaphorical terms have to be used with some caution. The signal each cell needs to keep growing and living comes from adjacent cells. Martin Raff speaks of this as a "social control" exercised by "cellular neighborhoods." He goes so far as to suggest that cells behave as if death were their "normal" state; suicide, he thinks, is their "default setting." Cells are kept alive as long as their "life-affirming partners" signal them to stay alive. That is why no cells — except for a cancerous one — can survive long in isolation. They need to be "encouraged" to live.

How did such a process get started in evolutionary history? Some scientists believe apoptosis is a primitive defense mechanism against disease that can be found very early in evolution; the process has been located in some microorganisms. Single-celled parasites have been observed performing apoptosis. The parasites apparently use apoptosis as a way of controlling their growth as a population in their host and thus surviving.

Because of its mysterious links with both cancer and aging, apoptosis is one of the most active areas of inquiry in medical biology. However complex the chemistry of the process, there is no doubt that apoptosis is a primordial feature of all organisms and deeply embedded in the evolutionary history of life on Earth. It bears a haunting resemblance to Sigmund Freud's purely speculative Thanatos, the death instinct, the deeply conservative psychic force that seeks to return life to the inanimate state from which it arose. Freud wrote quite lyrically about Thanatos; he called it the "equally immortal adversary of eternal Eros," one of the two "heavenly forces" that govern the human soul.

None of these thoughts is meant to suggest that we should not do all we can to control free radicals and harness the powers of apoptosis. As deeply ingrained as they are in the evolution of life, these may be processes that we can modify or put to use. On the other hand, they at least suggest that we may eventually discover, somewhere in the foundations of life, a figure and ground unity that so tightly combines the polar companions life and death that it cannot be altered.

This same distant, prehistoric background has been invoked in a new field called Darwinian medicine. It too has something to teach us about the paradoxical relationship between life and death.

Developed in the 1980s by Randolph Nesse and George Williams, Darwinian medicine raises the prospect that there may be a limit to age-reversal research that has yet to be fully appreciated. Darwinian physicians believe that some of the diseases and disabilities of our species may represent adaptations carried forward from the deep historical past.[25] These adaptations once served a good purpose; they allowed life to survive and prosper and so became embedded in our genes. Perhaps they still benefit us, but we have lost sight of that beyond the historical horizon and now see the adaptation as the symptom of disease. Fever, for example, may be the body's primordial way of making itself inhospitable to infectious agents. Stop the fever, as doctors are inclined to do, and the germs may do more damage, not less. Similarly, the swelling that surrounds a break or sprain may be the body's way of immobilizing the injury. Even some lethal diseases may have once played a very different role in life. A good example is sickle-cell anemia. A deadly disease among African-Americans, sickle-cell anemia evolved out of a beneficial adaptation to malaria. Those who carried the trait in certain malaria-infested areas of the world — mainly Africa — benefited and survived. But now, in other times and places, it shows up as an inherited liability. This is called "negative pleiotropy."

Is it possible that senescence has something of this same double-edged quality, a process that confers adaptive benefits early in life but later claims its price in the form of organic deterioration? Those pursuing this line of research have found creatures whose capacity for reproduction seems tied to traits that age them rapidly as soon as they have mated. The salmon and the Australian marsupial mouse are examples of this; they mate and reproduce in a frenzy, then almost at once show signs of age and die from an accumulation of diseases.

We cannot say. But if it should turn out that there are diseases linked to positive survival traits, we may find ourselves unable to remove them from our constitution. Darwinian medicine is still in its infancy, but it may lead to a new kind of medical science, one that works with evolution and so brings unexpected benefits. Among its discoveries may be one possibility that will undermine the most ambitious goals of biotechnology. The bodies we inherit out of the evolutionary process are intricately woven into the history of life on Earth. That history has been preoccupied with the evolution of life forms that are viable just long enough to reproduce and bring offspring into the world. In achieving that much, the process of evolution may have had to make compromises in the structure and function of organs — trade-offs as we might now call them — that limit our life span. That fact may be so deeply embedded in our development that it can never be changed short of replaying the entire process.

## The Readiness Is All

> If it be now, 'tis not to come; if it be not to come, it will be now; if it be not now, yet it will come; the readiness is all.
> — WILLIAM SHAKESPEARE, *Hamlet*

The current wishful fascination we are coming to develop for survival and longevity could be an invitation to staggering disappointment — like a rash investment in a highly speculative enterprise. That is literally so in the biotechnology industry, where the value of the companies fluctuates with each new breakthrough or failure. The more credence we give to such chancy prospects, the more we are distracted from the great truth: that all of us, long-lived or not, confront a common fate. Whether death comes sooner or later, it nevertheless comes. "The readiness is all," as Shakespeare wisely said. If that is so, then the wonders of biotech may be treacherous indeed. Once again, like so much of Western science, they pit us against nature as if we were face to face with an adversary whom we must outsmart. Moreover, with the promise of near-immortality somewhere in the future, how can we help but feel cheated that we do not live to see the time?

Playing upon that fear, some impresarios of immortality are hawking their cure-alls as if they were street-corner vendors applying the hard sell. One of the newsweeklies, sporting a cover picture of a glamorous young lady, runs a major feature titled "How Science is Searching for Ways to Keep Us Forever Young," and making that promise seem very close at hand. Ronald Klatz, whose research in longevity has a distinctly entrepreneurial bent, announces (as of 1996) that "within five to fifteen years ... we will have true age-reversal. ... But the train is leaving the station and anyone who is past age thirty-five or so will have to clamber on now." Another anti-aging enthusiast, Vincent Giampapa, warns that "if you don't limit cellular damage and treat the DNA now, ... you will have so much extra damage to chromosomes and DNA that you won't be able to benefit."[26]

Here is one respect in which earlier generations may have been more fortunate than us, despite their briefer life expectancy. They lived with no eager predictions of endless physical survival to inflate their expectations. They knew earlier on in life than we do that the time was at hand to prepare. *Memento mori* had a far more persuasive meaning for them.

In times past, people turned to great religious teachings to console and advise them as they advanced into their later years. There is a small library of literature that was written for that purpose. The biblical psalms, the wisdom of Lao Tzu and Confucius, *The Meditations* of Marcus Aurelius, Boethius' *Consolation of Philosophy*: Works like these face the great questions that all of us must face sooner or later. As boomers become the first older generation to age under pressure of commercial blandishments about age-reversal and even immortality, they may finish by giving more attention to pills and medications than to matters of mind and spirit. What a shame it would be if we became a society that spent more time combing through "how to live forever" best-sellers than acquiring the wisdom that is appropriate to elders and our only true consolation in the face of death. Fleeing mortality is no way to make ready for it.

CHAPTER TWELVE

# THE ECOLOGY OF WISDOM

In the year 1798, Thomas Malthus published a slender book that was destined to have more influence than any work of its size in modern times. Little more than a few hundred pages in length, his *Essay on Population* was hailed at once as a brilliant, if sobering contribution to economic theory. Read by the young Charles Darwin, the book would eventually launch the field of evolutionary biology. Moreover, as the first serious effort to connect a species to its environment in a dynamic and reciprocal way, it has come to be appreciated as a founding document in environmental science.

Working from nothing more than dour assumptions about human nature and a conservative distaste for the radical politics of his day, Malthus had discovered a superficially persuasive relationship between people and their food supply. Believing that people in their fallenness will fornicate and reproduce without limit, he foresaw no possibility that there can ever be enough food to provide for all. His conclusion that fertility must always outstrip sustenance was, he believed, a "fixed law of nature." Thus, there must always be a "struggle of existence." Kindness, altruism, charity — all these are no more than "mere feathers that float on the surface." In talking about population, Malthus seemed to be talking about matters of fact. But he was laying the groundwork for one of the most hard-hearted philosophies the world has ever known, a worldview based on selfishness, greed, and brutality. It was, in fact, the view of life that Charles Dickens would attribute to Ebenezer Scrooge. When asked what he would do about the starving paupers who would not endure the discipline of the workhouse, Scrooge answered, "If they would rather die, they had better do it, and decrease the surplus population."

## "MORE PEOPLE ARE LIVING LONGER ... GOOD!"

We now know that Malthus, despite his enormous impact on social philosophy, was wrong. In thinking about human beings the way one might more properly think about rabbits, he overlooked a basic cultural factor: Industrial societies become more cunning as they grow in numbers. The same scientific and technological genius that creates overpopulated industrial cities can be used to find solutions to overpopulation. As the last few centuries have shown, we have found myriad ways to increase food production and limit reproduction. But Malthus left out another factor, certainly among the most crucial when it comes to our long-term demographic destiny. He never touched upon longevity as an environmentally imperative phase in the history of modern society. Less still was he aware of the revolutionary changes longevity brings with it in ethics and economics. Yet just as deserts spread where land is overgrazed and rain forests flourish in a tropic climate, so industrial societies must age and, as they age, profit by their experience. That is what makes the campaign against entitlements so ludicrously misguided: It fails to grasp the magnitude of the phenomenon it seeks to alter.

Something vast and irreversible is happening in the demographics of the modern world, a revolution that permanently affects our relations with the Earth as a whole. But in contrast to other developments like acid rain or global warming, which threaten to diminish the quality of life, longevity is — potentially — the best thing that has happened since the advent of industrial cities. With all the force of a "fixed law," it confronts us with the prospect of an ultimate limit to growth based upon the changing values of a mature industrial society. If we might fancifully imagine the biosphere thinking about the antics of its troublesome human children, the thought that may loom largest in its mind at the beginning of the twenty-first century is, "More people are living longer ... Good! About time they grew up." Not only was Malthus wrong about population, he was *radically* wrong. Unable to foresee the longevity revolution, he was ignorant of the single most important social factor in our future. There is no guarantee that the baby boom generation will achieve environmental enlightenment, but the longevity revolution is the next best thing: a pressing cultural transformation that makes enlightenment all but obligatory.

I recall the words of a Sierra Club activist as he despaired for the fate of the Earth beneath the punishing assaults of urban industrial society. He was convinced, as so many environmentalists have been, that population will grow, and as it does, that consumption will increase, resources will dwindle, pollution will mount, species will perish — all as the result of human greed to which he could see no limit. He was, in short, a Malthusian. "There is only one solution," he concluded with wishful resignation. "We have to import a new human species that has some sense of eternal values." The baby boom generation in its senior years may be that population — or as close to it as we are likely to come.

That, at least, is the possibility we will explore in this analysis of the longevity revolution as a global, environmental factor.

## CULTURAL DEMOGRAPHICS

In the early 1960s, when our society was more daringly youthful, an American president who seemed to embody the exuberance of the period rallied the nation to spend billions of dollars to land a man on the moon. Today it is likely that the same Americans who, in their youth, cheered John Kennedy for his bold decision are preoccupied with less spectacular goals than colonizing outer space. One would not be surprised to learn that they are far more worried about holding their jobs in an unsettled economy and paying off their overworked credit cards.

Not much further down on their list of priorities might be a nagging anxiety about finding affordable medical insurance and providing for a secure retirement. Those who may be facing (as of the mid-1990s) upwards of $30,000 a year to pay nursing home costs for their aging parents may wonder, as they make each monthly payment, where their children will one day find the money to afford as much for them. Concerns like these are not limited to seniors; they implicate whole families and finally whole societies as matters of public policy.

Viewing the political and economic behavior of people in this way might be called cultural demographics — a head count that does not leave out the hearts and minds of the population. That is actually the way marketing analysts use the term "demographics" when they are sizing up a product. Raw numbers matter, but a refined evaluation of preferences, income, gender, ethnicity, and class is even more important. The intention is frankly commercial; it concentrates on obvious money questions. What will any particular public buy? How much will it buy? At what price? How can we get their attention and induce them to spend?

Environmentalists usually regard this approach to markets and audiences as the enemy's way of thinking. But there is something they might learn from the hucksters. It is as simple as recognizing that, in its relations with the natural environment, a human population cannot be dealt with in the same way as other species. Leave out tastes, values, ideals, sensibilities, and the numbers tell very little about the use that population will make of its space and resources — surely not enough to make sensible predictions or intelligent policy. How much pressure will a human population place upon its habitat? Is it not obvious that the answer has everything to do with whether the population in question is a community of medieval monks living a life of fasting and prayer or a suburban tract filled with swinging singles addicted to luxury cars and young marrieds who spend most of their leisure time at the mall?

Cultural demographics assumes that age is among the factors that most decisively shape people's collective environmental relations — even when the people themselves may have other things on their mind. Thus, for cultural demographics it is a matter of importance that many members of the baby boom generation are beginning to register the fact that they have provided poorly for their retirement years. A 1997 survey by the AARP concluded that the vast majority of middle-aged Americans had given little realistic thought to the cost of a lengthy retirement; many were only just waking up to what awaits them. Wishfully, almost desperately, an increasing number were placing their faith in the stock market. In the view of one researcher on the project, the survey found more "false confidence" than sound planning.[1] Some retirement counselors are now warning Americans in their forties that they will have to accumulate over a million dollars to guarantee a comfortable retirement. Whatever the truth of such intimidating estimates, they make for cautious choices.

Those choices can begin to influence values as early as midlife — about the time people begin to fear that losing their job could spell disaster. The fear is well founded. If they find themselves in dire straits, what will they have to fall back on? Welfare has ceased to be an entitlement; it has been stripped to the bone, and the unemployed are now identified (in the eyes of conservative leaders) as little better than a public nuisance. To go for any length of time without a job, a retirement plan, or medical insurance is to be performing without a net. All these fears mount as one ages out of the work force. At the age of sixty, one is too old to scramble, especially if there is nothing to scramble for but part-time jobs flipping hamburgers. Multiply personal hopes and fears like these by tens of millions and the result is a force that cannot help but change the economic agenda.

There is a workshop practice used by some environmental activists. It asks people to "think like a mountain." There is another more difficult exercise worth trying. *Think like a marketing analyst.*

In later chapters we will discuss the way maturity alters habits of consumption. Suffice it to say here that the senior market, as advertisers currently see it, has rotten "demographics." True, the numbers and the dollars are there, but so too is a sales resistance that advertisers find formidable. It is hard to sell grown-up people on the basis of hot copy and glossy imagery alone — and all the more so if that population has other things on its mind, like a heart condition, an ailing spouse, failing joints, the cost of supporting live-in children, or a far greater interest in courses at the university extension than in a dynamite new car. But for that very reason, the cultural demographics of seniors ought to look promising to environmentalists. The analysis of senior values may begin with simple statistics, but it will finally have to integrate the ideas and ideals that people take with them into their later years. Within such a perspective, matters that are often treated purely statistically can assume a very different force.

Death, for example. The death rate normally appears in demographic charts as a simple calculation: so many deaths per thousand. But in living experience, death is not a statistic; it is as profoundly personal as anything can be. How people deal with mortality as it closes in upon them has everything to do with their habits in life. Simpler creatures ask no questions of their ultimate fate. We do. For cultural demographics that is a significant point, because the answers we find prescribe meaning. And the meaning we find for our lives becomes a part of our greater ecology.

## How to Count a Population

The maturing of the baby boom generation confronts us with a new population problem, one that belongs to the industrial societies rather than the Third World. Heretofore, the image that has come to mind when we think of "overpopulation" is the back alleys of Calcutta or Kinshasa, filled with starving, jobless people — hungry, powerless masses whom the rich have seen fit to treat as invisible.

Population alarmists, viewing the plight of these impoverished societies, have urged aggressive population policies, but more than that, they have raised an impassioned moral appeal. In addition to achieving population control in the underdeveloped nations, they have called for consumption control in the affluent societies. They incorporate per capita resource use into their analysis, arguing that the citizens of First World nations consume far more than their share of energy and resources. In the words of Paul and Anne Ehrlich, "Americans are superconsumers and use rather inefficient technologies to service their consumption. ... America's total environmental impact is roughly six times that of the 900 million people of India." In this sense, the Ehrlichs see the United States as the "most over-populated nation in the world."[2]

The images that population alarmists have of First World consumption are the gas-guzzling automobile and expensive beef — luxuries that can be easily targeted for ethical condemnation. Suppose, however, there were *another* population in the First World that was large and growing, but whose need was not for luxury goods. Suppose this was a dependent population that required a reasonable provision of food, clothing, shelter, and medical care. And what if that population, unlike the propertyless and disempowered millions of the Third World, possessed rights that could not be ignored? What if it had the power to elect governments and demand the necessities of life? That would give us a new politics of population, one that could arise only in the developed economies. That is exactly what we see happening in the First World today, where active millions are living out a second life that frequently stretches twenty and thirty years beyond retirement, and where millions more, who are highly dependent on costly medical services, now fill hospitals and nursing homes.

Clearly, we need a new demographic calculus. We must ask what the age range of the population is and what effective claim its older members have upon care and sustenance. Life expectancy and life span must be added in. And more than that. Along with those purely quantitative factors, we must take into account the changing quality of life that comes with an aging society. In the advanced industrial societies, the economic impact of all population statistics must now be calculated as life expectancy multiplied by the cost of the social services and medical care that are likely to be necessary at each age. In the United States, this would be the cost of entitlements plus other forms of senior care, including private family care that may remove a husband or wife from paid labor outside the home.

Thus, when demographers predict that the population of the United States will stabilize at some 305 million by the year 2040, it is important to add that more than one-quarter of that number will be seniors over sixty and on their way out of the work force — many into volunteer services, higher education, and political activism, and some into intensive, long-term nursing care. Among the latter will be a small nation of some 14 million Americans suffering from Alzheimer's disease. With less than half that number stricken by the disease today, the annual cost of advanced Alzheimer's care is $100 billion. One estimate places the cost of the Alzheimer's population in the year 2050 at $1 trillion.

The new demographic calculus should also include the future shape of the population: namely, that it will continue trending toward age and away from youth for the indefinite future. That fact — especially if we take into account the mature ethical values associated with age — has everything to do with social policy and fiscal planning. For example, cultural demographics includes the growing use that retired citizens are making of educational resources and what they may be learning that makes a political difference. They may, after all, be reading a great deal of ecological literature with a view to becoming good environmental citizens.

## WILL THE LONGEVITY REVOLUTION SAVE THE PLANET?

If at any point over the past thirty years, one came upon a news story titled "Population Bombshell," the phrase could have meant only one thing. Overpopulation. Ever since Paul Ehrlich wrote *The Population Bomb* in 1968, fears of a Malthusian nightmare have haunted the environmental movement. But in the course of the final quarter of the twentieth century, the demographic doom the Ehrlichs foresaw from the heights of the baby boom has dramatically receded in the industrial societies. The "population bombshell" referred to by *New Scientist* as of 1998 is the surprising *decline* in population that the United Nations has discovered in its most recent studies. "With the world's population doubling in forty years, disaster seemed inevitable," *New Scientist* reports. "Yet now the population is beginning to stabilize or even fall in many parts of the world. So has the population explosion turned into a whimper?"[3]

In light of this "baby bust," the latest population projections by the United Nations now include a best-case scenario predicting that the world may number only 3.5 billion people in the year 2150. This is the most optimistic projection we have had for world population in over a century.

It would seem that environmentalists have achieved a victory they may never have expected. As of the year 2000, some seventy nations, including all the major industrial powers, are reproducing below the replacement rate, and some far below. Italy and Spain, Catholic countries where environmentalists never expected to make their voices heard against the authority of the Catholic church, which still condemns contraception, are running fertility rates that are half of replacement, which means they are shrinking rapidly. Italy, it is predicted, will shrink from a population of 57 million to 40 million by 2050; Germany will drop from 82 million to 73 million. In the European Union as a whole, it is expected that population will decrease steadily over the next five decades. There are governments today that have greater fear of a "birth dearth" than overpopulation. They worry that their work force will grow too small to maintain economic growth.

But now that we have at least the hint of a more hopeful demographic future, conservative economists are hardly cheered by what they see ahead. Indeed, they are gloomier than ever. In their eyes, the birth dearth has begun to loom as a major political threat to the global economy. Thus, in a front cover story on "The Global Aging Crisis" for March 1, 1999, *U.S. News and World Report* warns that "with the elderly population exploding, the social and economic costs could be staggering for all of us." Similarly, Ben Wattenberg of the American Enterprise Institute calls global aging "the real population bomb." As he puts it, "I am not a catastrophe-monger, but it is a hell of a lot bigger problem than too many people."[4] Why? Because Wattenberg believes aging costs too much. Like the conservative commentators who have been telling us since the 1980s that the United States cannot afford entitlements, Wattenberg sees fiscal catastrophe awaiting all the industrial nations that will have to pay for their growing senior numbers.

If fears like this prevail, we may see fiscally worried governments overreacting to the cost of the birth dearth as the Japanese, Czechs, and Germans have done by instituting programs to encourage population growth. Workers at the Bandai Corporation in Tokyo are now being offered a million yen bonus (roughly $10,000 American) for every baby after the family's second child. The Japanese government encourages such programs. It fears that at current levels of population replacement, it will not be able to afford the generous social programs that now support the elderly. Over the next decade, the number of young Japanese workers below the age of thirty will drop by 25 percent. Peter Schwartz of the Global Business Network wonders if Japan may not soon have to import young people to prop up their aging economy.[5] What Bandai and other employers are offering is now supplemented by official educational and child-care subsidies aimed at boosting the size of families.

Will such inducements work? Do they, for that matter, make any economic sense? Would the cost of bribing young couples to produce families of three, four, or five be any savings over entitlements? Or would this simply be exchanging one group of dependents for another?

Those who fret over the birth dearth may be up against another, greater obstacle. There is reason to believe that the longevity revolution is grounded in a law of population that is the exact reverse of Malthus. *Fertility and life expectancy may be inversely linked* in ways that make it biologically and sociologically impossible to expect a baby boom from long-lived societies. If that is so, then the longevity revolution has brought us a new law of population.

And as with most of what we know about population, the study begins with fruit flies.

As early as the 1970s, population geneticists began to notice a peculiar characteristic among *drosophila*, the fast-breeding fruit fly on which so much of our genetic knowledge is based. They recognized that flies that reproduce late in life and have fewer young tend to live longer. This finding gave rise to a hypothesis called the "disposable soma theory." The theory argues that there is a trade-off between fecundity and longevity. Animals that invest heavily in reproduction divert physical energy and resources from the maintenance and repair of cells and so age more rapidly. As one commentator puts it, using the economic metaphors that now dominate genetics, "It is as if our genes are unscrupulous factory owners, skimping on quality control and exploiting their workforce to earn the profits needed to spread their empires."[6] Or, in more technical terms, "the mechanisms underlying the increase in lifespan involved greater investments in somatic durability."[7] It would seem to follow, then, that the less energy a fruit fly puts into reproduction, the more it can devote to cellular repair and maintenance.

Do these mechanisms have anything to do with human beings? They do. It may seem a long reach from fruit flies to the lords and ladies of Great Britain, but a recent study of the English aristocracy over a thousand years of history indicates the same demographic pattern we find in *drosophila*. English aristocratic families can be traced back to the eighth century; that makes them one of the few groups for whom reasonably reliable long term vital statistics can be found. A December 1998 study published in *Nature* shows that parents who were barren or produced the fewest progeny lived longer than more prolific members of their class.[8] This corroborates a 1997 study indicating that American women who waited until they were in their forties to have their first, and usually only, child had a far better chance of reaching the age of one hundred.[9]

The striking aspect about this longevity-fertility trade-off is that it applies to males as well as females. Fathers among the barren aristocrats shared their wives' longer life expectancy. Why should this be? An August 2000 study in the journal *Human Resources* suggests an answer. Fecundity (meaning the ability to produce offspring within a given period of time) is governed in men as well as women by a biological clock. Men may remain fertile indefinitely, but from about age twenty-four on, a man's real chance of impregnating a woman drops by 3 percent each year. There is also a correlation between miscarriages and the father's age: the older the father, the more likely is miscarriage to happen.[10] Thus, the longer any couple waits to reproduce, the less likely they are to have young. But meanwhile, the maintenance functions of their bodies are free to keep their immune systems in better repair and so make their somas that much less disposable.

Is it possible, then, that *fertility is inversely correlated to life expectancy?* In fruit flies, the disposable soma may be the whole explanation for that astonishing fact. But in humans, there may another sociological factor at work. Women's liberation.

When overpopulation was first identified as an environmental threat, the women's movement had not yet achieved its full impact even in the highly developed societies. Those were the baby boom years when American women were running a record fertility rate and supposedly aspiring to little more than full-time home making. As soon as women began to re-think their role in life, their fertility rate slumped, reaching 1.7 by 1976 and staying somewhere between there and bare replacement level ever since. In a very real sense Betty Friedan's *Feminine Mystique* provided the solu-

tion population alarmists once thought could only be achieved by rigorously enforced contraception.

Environmentalists have been reluctant to admit it, but altering the
psychology of women does more than all the scare-tactics and coercive
public policy in the world to change reproductive habits. What could be
more obvious? Societies that educate girls raise their expectations. As their
skills improve, young women want full access to the good things of modern life. Inevitably, they grow up to marry and start families late. As their
earning power and personal independence increases, they find less and less
resistance to their views from the men in their lives. As a survey by the
National Marriage Project at Rutgers University has discovered, American
men and women in their twenties are steadily shying away from matri-
mony, instead choosing casual sex over courtship and marriage.[11] Or, if
they do marry, young wives and their husbands increasingly opt for an
upscale lifestyle, preferring to remain childfree: *Families of Two*, as Laura
Carroll calls them in her study of "happily married couples without children by choice." The result is what the demographic analyst Joel Cohen
calls "Methuselah's choice," a near stationary population based on long life
and low reproduction.[12]

Just as the old choose to live longer, the young choose to have smaller
families. *The longevity revolution is hardly a geriatric conspiracy. It is the result
of intergenerational choice, the combination of longer life expectancy and lower
fertility.* When the media report that Japan is "desperate" about its growing
imbalance between young and old, we should remember that this is not
the result of life expectancy alone, but the choices being made by young
Japanese women. Between the ages of fifteen and forty-nine, 30 percent of
Japan's women are unmarried; one in seven is expected to stay that way.
Similarly in the United States, *Time* magazine reports that, as of August
2000, 43 million adult women — 40 percent of adult females — are now
single, many of them digging into an unmarried lifestyle that involves buying their own home. Young and old, we are all in it together. If the young
choose to reproduce less, then they must necessarily have more elders to
support. Entitlements are the long-term cost of the lifestyle for which youth
is spontaneously opting everywhere. But then one should not leave out of
account the fact that the long life enjoyed by the old, far from being some
permanent class advantage, will one day belong to the young.

## THREE FEEDBACK LOOPS

The formulation that follows summarizes in a highly schematic way what we have said so far about the demographics of the longevity revolution. It then extends the analysis as a sort of environmental impact statement. What we have here is a set of three interconnected loops that feed into one another as they move forward in time. If the pattern they describe holds true, then it may represent the most important insight into population dynamics since Thomas Malthus opened the field in the early days of the industrial revolution.

### *The First Loop: Greater Longevity, More Costly Entitlements*

To begin with the obvious: Thanks to progress in public health, nutrition, and modern medical science, we have found ways to extend life expectancy and possibly the life span. As the number of senior citizens in the population increases, the need for and the cost of medical care rises. Both the need and the cost act as incentives for research and investment, encouraging more medical progress. Research in longevity becomes an ever livelier field. Health care (insurance, pharmaceuticals, hospitals, nursing homes) becomes a major enterprise, attracting steadily more capital, technical talent, and entrepreneurial skill, until it becomes as important to the economy as a whole as railroads, automobiles, and high tech have been in the past. As new techniques are discovered and applied, more people benefit from the advances. Accordingly, the ratio of older to younger in the population increases.

Entrepreneurial values contribute to longevity in other ways, some of them highly ironic. These days enlightened employers, seeking to hold down the cost of medical insurance, take pains to look after the health of their workers. They offer heart healthy foods in the company cafeteria, encourage regular physical checkups, perhaps open a gym on the premises to provide aerobic training. If the employer does not offer such care, insurers might, sending out literature or lecturers to pitch for better diets and exercise, and to warn against smoking.

No doubt the result is real immediate savings. But it is also longevity. The same healthy practices that save money on the payroll lead to a larger, more long-lived retirement population. So the cost of entitlements rises and with them the payroll taxes that employers must pay. At which point, the very companies that did so much to encourage good health may complain about the cost of Social Security. They may even contribute to one of the conservative think tanks that clamor for an end to entitlements. But if the cost of entitlements results in so great a fiscal burden, then employers would do better to discourage a healthy lifestyle. Why not serve lard sandwiches and french fries in the cafeteria and provide free cigarettes?

Unless we can imagine some reason why medical science and sound advice about health should be brought to a halt, it is difficult to see how longevity and entitlements can be kept from circling round and round and increasing with each cycle. Moreover, if we include in our calculations the effects of any single major biotechnology breakthrough in reversing the aging process, the circle might begin to accelerate, producing more older people who would extend their careers not only in literature, art, finance, but in medical science, thus increasing the medical expertise of our society. With each turn of the circle, more experienced and qualified scientists would give us more research in longevity and, very likely, more significant results.

### The Second Loop: The Growing Dominance of Senior Values

As the number of senior citizens grows, their collective voting power increases — at least in the democratic societies. Voting is, to be sure, a modest form of political action, but older citizens have ways to amplify their power at the ballot box. They have more money to contribute to political campaigns than younger voters and, perhaps most important of all, more time to make available in the political process. As the active years extend deeper into old age, we may expect to see more seniors working as campaign volunteers and lobbyists. We can also expect to see them running for office — and winning, especially if their rivals continue their granny-bashing ways. Accordingly, the influence of their needs and values upon the political agenda is bound to increase. While there is a wide range of opinion in the senior population, overwhelmingly their values clearly lead toward expanding welfare state benefits and all goods and services related to those benefits. Only the wealthy retired could afford to reject entitlements.

At some point, diverting resources to the welfare state sector serves as a brake upon entrepreneurial dynamism and conventional economic growth. This is already happening in Japan, whose population is aging faster than that of any other industrial society. As Japan registers the demand for the social services it must provide for its seniors, there is less capital to pump into the dynamic high-tech ventures that have kept the economy booming for so long. Because the Japanese are reluctant to run budgetary deficits, the dilemma shows up more dramatically with them, but it is only a matter of time before all of Japan's rivals face the same choices.[13] The entrepreneurial community may feel considerable ideological unease about the reordering of priorities that comes with an aging society. But ironically, it has only itself to blame for the result. As long as capital flows toward profitable returns in health care, pharmaceuticals, and biotechnology, smart investors are helping make us an older society.

In the ongoing debate over entitlements, liberals have charged conservatives with cutting back on senior entitlements in order to finance upper-income tax breaks. Conservatives, of course, hasten to deny the accusation, but were they more candid about the matter, they might frankly insist that holding down the taxes of the entrepreneurial class is a defensible concern. As they see things, unless the rich get richer, the wealth will not trickle down. Economic growth, after all, requires investment and expansion. In Laurence Kotlikoff's view, "Every dollar the Treasury has to borrow is a dollar denied to the private sector for investment. Over time, that diversion of resources will curb economic growth and leave America poorer."[14]

Conservatives might then warn that the capital we need to launch new industries is being used to keep the elderly ambulatory. Are hip replacements and cataract surgery worth what they are costing us? The high-tech future on which the investment community has its eyes fixed will at some point be gravely compromised if Medicare expenditures continue to grow. And what else can they do but grow?

### The Third Loop: The Vanishing Young

As younger couples register the increasing cost of entitlements or are forced to assume responsibility for aging parents, they are apt at some point to respond by seeking to reduce domestic expenses. The cost of elder health care is not the only pressure on them; they also need to provide for their own medical needs and their children's. That will grow more expensive regardless of any change in Medicare. By the late 1990s, it had become clear that managed care, once thought to guarantee cheaper medical services, had saved as much money as it could by imposing unaccustomed austerity on doctors and patients alike. The public's response to managed care, and especially that of retirees under Medicare, grows ever more critical. In response to public pressure, state after state has passed some form of a medical bill of rights that undermines frugality. Forced to spend more on their clients, HMOs see their profits falling and their stocks lose value. Their response is to raise premiums across the board for old and young alike, but the young, lacking Medicare, feel the pinch more acutely.

Such expenses may lead to smaller families in order to maintain a high-consumption standard of living. This effect is already visible in some societies. In Germany, the birth rate has become a matter of acute political concern. As of the early 1990s, it fell to 9.3 births per thousand people. In the European Union as a whole, only Spain and Italy have a lower birth rate. As a result, Germany is among the few countries that have adopted pronatalist policies aimed at turning back the demographic tide. The state of Brandenburg has undertaken to promote larger families by offering a cash subsidy for each new baby. The reward is in addition to other state benefits, including *Kindergeld,* substantial monthly payments to offset child-rearing expenses. As the government sees it, unless Germans can be bribed into higher rates of reproduction, by 2030 there will be nine German retirees "living off" every ten German workers. In Czechoslovakia, where births have fallen well below the replacement rate, the government has run anti-contraception ads advising couples to "stop taking care." Billboard ads show Johann Sebastian Bach as twenty naked clones.

It is difficult to imagine what the effect will be upon younger people in the industrial world who find themselves on the trailing edge of the longevity revolution. The situation is without precedent. At some point, they may resent being born into the senior dominance, but they also know that, without entitlements programs, they would become fully responsible for aged parents — a less financially advantageous choice. One result of this situation might be a high degree of demoralization among younger citizens. They may see less and less promise for their own lives in a society beholden to senior values. They may feel increasingly less inclined to participate in the political process or even to vote — a decision that would lessen their power still more. Meanwhile, the consumer demand associated with younger people is apt to become less effective as the youth market diminishes. In general, the daring, energetic entrepreneurial values that might win their support may begin to lose their influence.

While superior medical care is the most obvious force behind the shifting ratio of young-on-the-job to elders-in-retirement, other factors are at work. Some have an air of sociological inevitability about them. Families everywhere in the industrial nations are getting smaller. Couples are marrying later (if they marry at all), waiting longer to have babies (if they have babies at all), and then having fewer of them. That trend is intimately, perhaps inextricably, connected with aspects of the modern world that many identify as "progress" and "freedom." It may also be connected less desirably with features that are intended to make our lives safer, more efficient, and convenient. There is now an impressive body of evidence that suggests we are filling our environment with "a cocktail of pollutants," sometimes called "endocrine disrupters," that reduce the sperm count or cause testicular cancer. [15] Among the possible toxic culprits are chemicals widely used in ordinary detergent, floor polishes, plastic tubing, and food wrapping. If this is so, then a maturing industrial economy may "naturally" fluctuate toward lower reproductive rates as it increases the distribution of cheap, synthetic materials, many of which are valued for their "convenience" and seen as enhancing the standard of living.

Women especially experience diminished fertility as liberating. It is an opportunity to spend more of their lives exploring careers, traveling, learning. So they wait longer to begin families, or perhaps never do. As medical science progresses, women need not feel desperate about delaying motherhood into their late middle age; they can afford to wait as long as age forty-five — or, in at least one highly publicized Italian case, until sixty. It is even possible for younger women to store ova so that they can be fertilized at any point in their lives by the sperm of their choice. The biological clock has very nearly been put out of commission.

The option this creates is still in need of fine-tuning when it comes to planning parenthood within the limits of population control. Older women tend to produce more twins, especially if they are using fertility medications. In the course of 1990s the number of twins born to American mothers, many of whom waited into their forties to conceive, increased by 50 percent; the number of triplets by over 400 percent, not to mention record-breaking deliveries of six, seven, and eight babies, all of which resulted from fertility drugs. The American College of Pediatrics now recommends that fertility clinics monitor their clients more closely to eliminate the risk of multiple births that may produce more babies than women want. If the advice gets through, we may see many more single-child families, settling for the number of young that parents really planned to have.

This changing pattern in reproduction began to appear in the United States in the 1970s. In that decade, the number of childless women in their twenties doubled, followed, in the next decade, by a tripling of births for women between age thirty and thirty-five — the largest increased birth rate for any age group in the society. Most of the late-age mothers were working mothers who would have fewer babies, often no more than one. The change corresponded to a new vision of life. As one feminist psycho-therapist observes, "Most of today's women are not interested in going from the classroom to the diaper pail without having some time to achieve a certain amount of self-knowledge. The phrase 'giving birth to myself before I give birth to a baby' is one that more and more women are using to describe their approach to having children."[16]

These new reproductive habits are creating a social order that once might have seemed unimaginable. In the United States, the percentage of households that contain married couples with children has shriveled to just 26 percent in the late 1990s, down from 45 percent in the 1970s. These figures reflect the growing number of people who are waiting to have babies. Singles and domestic partners living together out of wedlock may never produce families at all. Twenty-six percent of boomer women have elected to remain childless. Even more striking, 40 percent of baby boom women between the ages of thirty-six and fifty-four have been ster-ilized.[17] Childlessness is becoming a far from unusual married condition, one that is less and less viewed as "unnatural." There are, in fact, support groups at work on the matter. They seek to change the image of those who are childless by choice so that they will pass as "normal."[18]

Lester Brown of World Watch Institute neatly summarizes the way the birth dearth is now playing out around the world.

> Declines in fertility flowed from economic gains and social improvements. As incomes rose and as employment opportunities for women expanded, couples chose to have fewer children. The improved availability of family planning services and the liberaliza-tion of abortion laws gave couples the means to achieve this. Population stabilization in these countries has been the result, therefore, of individual preferences, the product of converging economic, social, and demographic forces.[19]

Some analysts have flippantly, but perhaps accurately, characterized these preferences as a matter of parents having a refrigerator instead of having a baby. The assumption is that young working couples at some point choose to substitute consumer durables for extra children. Can the same transition to a stable population be expected in other countries? That is an open question until we know what demographic changes industrialization will bring about in major test cases like China, India, and Indonesia. China has been especially aggressive in enforcing its one-child family policy. In the 1990s, female sterilization surged forward to cut the national fertility rate to two births per woman. Ironically, the Chinese prejudice in favor of boy babies has produced a gender imbalance (roughly 114 boys for every 100 girls as of 2000) that will eventually work to lower the birth rate more: fewer females, fewer mothers, fewer babies.[20]

Another factor affecting family size may be the growing acceptance in high industrial societies of homosexuality households, single-parent households, and unmarried cohabitation. This is the "postmodern family condition," as the sociologist Judith Stacey has called it. Her studies assume that the classic Victorian family — the breadwinner father, the full-time mother at home with the children — is now a relic.[21] When that family prevailed, it was possible for women to specialize in pregnancy and homemaking — provided they did not die in childbirth along the way. And if they did, the husband could easily find another wife and carry on procreating. Hence, the prolific middle-class households of the nineteenth century. If that domestic arrangement were still with us, there would be no need to bemoan the declining ratio of young to old; we would have baby boom upon baby boom.

If that is indeed what conservatives want when they speak of "family values," then there is an ironic twist to the story of the waning classic family. Those on the political right may despair over the cost of entitlements and prefer to transfer that expense from the welfare state to families. But they have actually contributed to the very situation that makes that responsibility unaffordable for most people. The leaders of corporate America have behaved as one would expect them to behave. They have disempowered unions and depressed wages, placing American labor in competition with desperate workers in distant lands. That harsh reality has forced more and more women out of the home and into the work force. Many of the new jobs celebrated on the financial pages are part-time, low-paid second jobs for working mothers who are racing to stay ahead of the family's credit card debt, which, as of the 1990s amounted to upwards of $50 billion annually. But even with two paychecks, such costs as nursing home care for aged parents are well beyond the reach of working-class families. If something has to give in the grip of the tightening household budget, it is apt to be the number of children couples choose to have.

It would, of course, be a mistake to assume that family planning is always a rational matter, but insofar as it is, life in the longevous society is apt to reinforce all these influences. As younger couples try to stay afloat in the sea of consumer choices, they are likely to register the increasing demand of entitlements upon their paychecks and respond to it by trying to reduce domestic expenses. As the working population is taxed more heavily to pay for senior programs, it will tend to cut back further on reproduction in order to maintain a standard of living that advertising insidiously insists we must have. These factors make each successive younger generation smaller relative to the older, and that, in turn, diminishes the ratio of young to old. The result is a demographic circle from which it is difficult to see any way out.

Or can we imagine rebellious young marrieds deciding to produce another baby boom, even though they will be forced to live poorer?

There is one more form of population control that may appear in late industrial society, a direct link between sex and longevity. In the years ahead, the use of anti-aging medications is apt to increase greatly as word of miraculous possibilities spreads. But some researchers believe there is a trade-off between the sexual urge and longevity. Dosing on anti-aging hormones may diminish the sex drive and so the birth rate. Michael Rose, a researcher in aging at the University of California at Irvine, predicts that many of the hormones involved in mating will grow more quiescent in those who use life-extending medications. He says of our longevous future, "Randy teenagers will be a thing of the past. ... We'll lose the high-testosterone surge of insanity that so much American culture is based on."[22]

In such unforeseen ways, it becomes ever harder for industrial economies to keep their numbers growing, except perhaps by immigration. But in time, as immigrant families adapt to the prevailing values of the urban industrial mainstream, their demographics fall into the same pattern. The third generation of Hispanic migrants living in Los Angeles does not continue the lifestyle of a poor, newly arrived family of five or six from central Mexico. Immigrating turns into a form of population control. If prevailing, middle-class consumption standards are not enough to change old ways, then inadvertent hormone ingestion may do the job. One might almost believe there is an inherent restraint that connects affluence with diminishing fertility, as if the ecology of the planet uses our own synthetic chemicals against us, hitting us where it hurts.

## THE GREEN AMID THE GRAY

The environmental movement has done more to make us rethink our most basic values than any political program of modern times. It has done more than raise issues of justice and democratic participation; it has called into question the very rationality of industrial civilization. It has dared to suggest that industrialism has limits that can only be violated at the cost of our survival.

But environmentalism is itself a product of the civilization it addresses so challengingly; more specifically it is an outgrowth of the baby boom, a response to the misguided affluence of that generation. And like all political movements, it is beholden to its history.

In the early days of the movement, environmentalists saw the world from a very American perspective. The United States was regarded as the bellwether of the industrial future, the society that was setting the standard — the very bad, wasteful standard — other nations were tempted to adopt. The baby boom of that period seemed to pose the threat of runaway demographic growth. In reaction to the soaring fertility rate of the 1950s and 1960s, environmentalists adopted a neo-Malthusian stance, fearing that the future would swell the size of the population bomb. They also took the mindless consumerism of that time to be the inherent lifestyle of high industrial society. It never occurred to them that these menacing prospects might change and pass.

Thus, when Barry Commoner, in his classic work *The Closing Circle* (1971) castigated the bad consumption habits of his day, he focused on the gas-guzzling automobile and the ten-lane freeway as the major environmental offenders of the era, interpreting these as long-term, perhaps permanent conditions of life. Gloomy assumptions like this infected the movement with an air of desperation that sometimes reached the level of despair. As a matter of principle, environmentalists became doomsayers, even taking pride in being tough enough to face impending catastrophe without flinching.

But, as with every generation, the baby boom cannot be fairly evaluated until it has run its course. As boomers become the leading edge of the longevity revolution, they have much more to teach us. There may in fact be forces at work in this generation that will prove to be ecologically beneficial. Societies change because people change, and nothing changes people more surely than age. Even wars and bloody revolutions can fade from memory with the years. But age cannot be put behind us; every morning when we wake there is more of it waiting at our bedside to meet us. It waits with a bit more pain or fatigue, and it asks "So what is this day going to teach you about the meaning of life?" If Barry Commoner were writing today he might anticipate the demise of the automobile as we have known it. He might make much of the fact that older drivers have less interest in speed and eye-popping style, and that at some point they may want, or have to stop driving altogether. Retirement may bring them no greater reward than the chance to quit commuting to distant jobs. That very fact is already altering our living and transportation patterns. Indeed, city planners and architects now assume that older citizens, needing companionship and ready access to health care, will be moving into more compact urban residences where they can share transportation or use more economical cars that run on electricity, hydrogen, or compressed air. As the next generation of private and institutional retirement architecture makes its appearance, planners are already expecting senior residents to demand more green space.[23]

Commoner might also now foresee a declining interest in frivolous, resource-depleting consumption as boomers devote ever more of their income to health care. As we saw in chapter seven, seniors are a notoriously hard sell under the best of circumstances. That, more than money or numbers, explains why advertisers continue to pursue the young demographic.[24] The resistance of the over-fifty population to marketing has nothing to do with the superior virtue of the elderly. A slower pace, a thriftier lifestyle, a greater concern for health, leisure, and natural beauty are matters of necessity for an older population.

That is why senior organizations and gerontologists have begun to pay serious attention to the environmental impact of aging boomers with an eye to enlisting them in the cause. In 1991, the AARP, in league with the Environmental Protection Agency, set up EASI, the environmental alliance for senior involvement. EASI now runs as a nonprofit coalition of aging and environmental groups that draws on the expertise of retired volunteers to promote a heightened sense of stewardship, usually with a highly practical local focus: monitoring water quality, tracking endangered species, educating the young, public health problems in "brownfield" areas (underutilized urban property). The largest of these projects is a state-wide Pennsylvania water-quality monitoring effort funded at $200,000. At the national level, EASI has held conferences under such titles as "An Aging Population, An Aging Planet, and a Sustainable Future: Thinking Globally, Acting Locally."[25]

It is the thesis of this book that aging is the key contradiction in the history of industrial society. Longevity distances us from the entrepreneurial values and forces that helped make long-life and good health possible in the first place. At some point environmentalists may view such transformations as a form of subtle ecological balance. But I suspect that such a change of mind will be a long time coming. Environmental activists are apt to see that possibility as a philosophical concession they cannot allow themselves to make. That is because all the benign changes mentioned here come on the far side of industrial development and indeed are the result of the industrial process. It is only in modern societies that women have so many choices in life besides childbearing. Similarly the longevity revolution that transforms the way people understand wealth and use their resources stems from the science and technology one can only have in fully modernized cultures. For some environmentalists, granting that good things may yet come from our troubled industrial adventure may seem like giving aid and comfort to the enemy. But there is another way to view the matter. It may be that Dame Nature is gifted with powers that the science of ecology has not yet fathomed. She may have a resourcefulness that allows her to devise a hair's-breadth escape even from the darkest perils. And that resourcefulness may take the form of an alliance with the needs of elders.

That is the hope of Rabbi Zalman Schachter-Shalomi in one of the most searching philosophical examinations of longevity. Based upon the workshop he has been leading in "spiritual eldering," Schachter-Shalomi expects to see the coming older generation "foster a renewed relationship with our devastated planet Earth." He is convinced that elders have a stronger inborn sense of "organic connectivity to our environment." This is an expression of their "completing instinct," the dominant psychological reflex of our later years. "By exploring the spiritual dimension of life, [elders] encourage younger people not to equate standard of living with quality of living. As both older and younger people learn to find fulfillment in non-material ways and consume less of the Earth's resources, they reduce the damage inflicted on the environment and become willing collaborators in healing the planet."[26]

Schachter-Shalomi has called for councils of senior ecowardens who will monitor the local environment and a national environmental senior corps through which elders can serve as consultants. Whether boomers will become environmentally enlightened in so conscious and active a way is impossible to say. But the "organic connectivity" Schachter-Shalomi has in mind might express itself more humbly in ways that are not obviously ecological. It may make itself felt as the increasing influence of mature taste and common sense, a force that can work in many subterranean ways to tame the worst excesses of the industrial marketplace. There may be other subtle ways in which the longevity revolution will contribute to eco-logical enlightenment. It may represent the solution to what environmen-talists have long regarded as the most intractable problem of all, namely that there are simply more human beings than the planet can afford to support.

Human society has always been a blending of energy and wisdom — alas! more often too much of the first, too little of the latter. The young provide the energy to get things done, but it takes the wisdom of more experienced heads to know how best to use that energy. Industrialism has vastly expanded the energy of the youthful Western world, but it has con-tributed nothing to our wisdom. Machines have no souls. One need only look around to see where the power of that soulless technology has led us — into a global economy that heedlessly strips the planet of its riches and its dignity as if there were no tomorrow.

That leaves us with the paradox that the baby boom generation will have to resolve. For the whole of the modern period, we have thought of the future as the cultural property of youth. But when it comes to the deep future — the enduring health and beauty of the planet — it may be the old, precisely because they have fewer years ahead of them, whose wisdom has the most to offer. In thinking about the fate of the Earth we could do worse than to restore caring and sharing to their proper place in the hu-man story.

CHAPTER THIRTEEN

_____

# THE FUTURE OF DEATH

The idea of death, the fear of it, haunts the human animal like
nothing else; it is the mainspring of human activity — activity
designed largely to avoid the fatality of death, to overcome it by
denying in some way that it is the final destiny of man.
— ERNEST BECKER, *The Denial of Death*

When Becker wrote those words in 1972, existentialism was the reigning philosophical style in the universities. Like Sartre and Camus,
Becker saw the willingness to face our inevitable annihilation without flinching as the only dignified stance in life. He called it "cosmic heroism." But
as medical science finds ever more ingenious ways to keep the body alive,
the relationship between Sartre's "being and nothingness" is changing radically. We may soon discover a greater dread: *the fear of life.*

## LET ME DIE BEFORE I WAKE

In the context of the longevity revolution, death becomes a new kind
of problem. More people will have to choose when and how and at whose
hands they or those they love are going to die. Or they will have to choose
someone to make that decision for them if they cannot. For the first time
in human history, ordinary people — not existential philosophers — will
have to decide whether life is worth living. That is one hard result of having more life: the quantity of years we may have ahead of us forces us to
ponder the quality of the life we will be living in those years. No image
more typifies the meaning of philosophy than that of Socrates in his prison
cell electing to drink hemlock rather than live on as an exile from Athens.
Few of us may have Socrates' greatness of soul and acuity of mind, but we

are going to be *forced* to be philosophical about the greatest question of all.

That question has already passed beyond philosophy and into politics. Wherever euthanasia initiatives have been placed on the ballot in the United States, the debate that ensues reveals that many people (and I count myself among them) regard thwarting death at all costs as a frightening prospect, one that grows more horrifying as our power to keep people alive increases. While modern medicine can now stave off death longer than ever before in history, the result is not a dream come true but, beyond a certain point, a deepening nightmare.

During the 1990s Oregon voters twice approved doctor-assisted suicide ballot measures that legalized euthanasia for the terminally ill. The debate, which was heavily covered by the national media, rapidly became a bitter confrontation between "right-to-life" and "right-to-die" factions. Those who supported the proposition may have been defending "death with dignity," but not far below the surface of their appeal they were sounding a distinct note of terror. They protested passionately against being kept unwillingly alive and made a burden to all around them. In highly charged television commercials, they pictured themselves being trapped in a vegetative state with images that recalled Edgar Allan Poe's dread of premature burial.

The fear they were invoking is age-old. It is the fear of the dungeon and the rack that was once the stock-in-trade of Gothic tales. But the images evoked to express that fear are new: the hospital bed, the intensive care ward, the nursing home. They force us to imagine ourselves as prisoners of our own bodies, bound to an existence that must be lived out to the last gasp in pain and helplessness. Instead of thumbscrews and iron maidens, we have the IV tube and the respirator. Instead of hooded torturers, we have doctors and nurses in clean white uniforms at the bedside scrutinizing dials and gauges.

As long ago as the seventeenth century, Francis Bacon speculated that a day would come when the fluids and organs of an infirm body might be replaced by healthy ones. In this way, he believed life might be prolonged indefinitely. Since then, the "conquest of death" has been one of the defining features of scientific progress. Bacon actually flirted with the heresy that science would reverse the fall of man by lifting the curse of death under which the human race had groaned since being cast out of Eden. He referred to this as the "restitution of man to the sovereignty and power which he had in the first state of creation." By the age of the Enlightenment, champions of worldly progress had made the defeat of death and disease part of their revolutionary agenda. There was no telling how long life might be extended. "A period must one day arrive," proclaimed Condorcet, the great eighteenth century prophet of progress, "when death will be nothing more than the effect either of extraordinary accidents or of the slow and gradual decay of the vital powers; and that the duration of the interval between the birth of man and his decay will have itself no assignable limit."[1]

How ironic, then, that so many now live in dread of becoming the involuntary beneficiaries of the highest reward that science can offer.

I have had a firsthand encounter with Bacon's promise. I found it chilling. Several years ago I was caught in the sort of medical crisis that forces one to rethink the meaning of life and death. Told I was likely to be suffering from incurable malignancy, I was assured by my physicians that they would make every effort to save my life. I did not feel encouraged. What I saw ahead of me was months, possibly years, of medical dependency: an endless regimen of tests and procedures that would make the hospital my home, and all of it possibly leading to a protracted state of helpless delirium. The terror that gripped me was relieved by only one conviction: If it all became unbearable, I would take my own life.

I went out in search of a suicide manual (no easy item to find) and was relieved when I finally discovered Derek Humphry's *Let Me Die Before I Wake*, published by the Hemlock Society of England. I may have bought the only copy in stock in the San Francisco Bay Area. Grim reading though it was, I began to see death, not as a curse, but a deliverance. As for my concerned physicians, so heroically determined to keep me alive, they took on a most unpleasant aspect. Distorted in the mirror of my fears, they began to look like mad doctors, not because they were out to kill me, but because they were so intent on saving me — like it or not. Could I depend on them to take my worst fears into account? Or would I become an intriguing challenge to their medical expertise?

## GOTHIC MEDICINE

These days doctors can keep their patients alive under physical and mental conditions that approach the grotesque. They can prolong the lives of the disabled and demented for years. Their decision to do so may spring from many motives. They may honestly feel that there is reason to hope, perhaps that some unexpected cure or palliative will appear. They may fear that anything less than heroic measures will open them to lawsuits for malpractice. They may know of no way to explain the bad news to their patient or the patient's family. They may be doggedly determined to fight to the last as a matter of professional pride.

Sherwin Nuland, whose book *How We Die* offers a rare insight into how physicians deal with death, believes that many doctors take the death of a patient as a defeat. "Physicians accept the conceit (in every sense of the word) that science has made us all-powerful and therefore the only proper judges of how our skills are to be used. The greater humility that should have come with greater knowledge is instead replaced by medical hubris: Since we can do so much, there is no limit to what should be attempted — *today* and for *this patient!*"[2]

This fixation on success may finish by delivering patients into an ethical hell. Doctors can prolong the lives of hopelessly sick people who may be using up the financial, emotional, and spiritual resources of their families.

I had another occasion to reflect on these matters in the course of writing a sequel to Mary Shelley's *Frankenstein.*[3] As I worked back through the original text of this familiar classic, I realized that Shelley had anticipated the fears I speak of here. The dread of unnaturally extended life is the prophetical subtext of her novel, underlying the gore and violence of the tale. Seen in this light, the story becomes a moral analysis of the flight from mortality. Frankenstein's monster is monstrous not simply because he is ugly, but because he is a living corpse. The ultimate achievement in life extension, he is a collage of dead body parts stitched together and forced to return to life. Endowed with the high intelligence of his transplanted brain, the creature soon learns of his origin and rebels against his enforced immortality. The epigraph to the novel anticipates the horror of his condition. It is the poignantly rhetorical question that Adam asks of God in Milton's *Paradise Lost*: "Did I solicit thee from darkness to promote me?"

From this point of view, the horror of the story is first of all *his*; our fear is the prospect that we may become what he is.

Recalling my own condition as I once lay in intensive care with as many as five tubes plunged into my body to deliver and extract fluids, I realize how much like the familiar image of the monster on the laboratory table I must have looked. Yes, I was grateful to have survived the crisis. But what if this were to go on and on until I became the comatose appendage of some relentless machinery of survival? Before the child expired in 1998, doctors at a Virginia hospital managed to keep an anencephalic baby alive for over two years; in days past the child's life span might have been mere days. It was an astonishing achievement — and absolutely horrifying. In this instance, the doctors could claim they were simply following orders, since the mother had demanded that the child be kept alive. But in 1992 an anencephalic baby born in Florida was placed on life support against the parents' wishes until it died. In both cases, the disturbing fact is that such a thing *could* be done and was. How many of us would welcome having our bodies kept breathing and metabolizing years after we were brain-dead? In video reports, the poor brainless baby we are shown is an even more grotesque monster than Mary Shelley's brute. With no mind to register its condition, it has become a mere physical lump, completely helpless in the clutches of curious doctors.

Even more grotesque, in the fall of 1997 an American laboratory managed to engineer a headless frog that could be used to produce spare parts for other frogs. The "animal" was little more than a circulatory system used to keep the parts alive until they were harvested. There is no reason to believe the same might not be done with a headless human carcass. If it ever is, more and more people walking the streets of the world will be assemblages of borrowed anatomical equipment. A medical ethicist, asked about the matter, could see no issue, since nobody had been hurt by the procedure. Nevertheless, images like these strike me as exercises in Gothic medicine.

The same theme can be found in the work that has become *Frankenstein's* literary companion in horror: Bram Stoker's *Dracula*. *Dracula* works from the other direction. Frankenstein's monster survives as a crazy quilt of cadaverous parts: many dead bodies adding up to one live one. Dracula's victims are many who take their collective life from a single source: The legion of the undead is forced to share the demonic elixir of the master's blood. The terrifying effect is the same: the undead are denied the peace of the grave and driven to endure an anguished existence. Yet both the monster and the vampire cling desperately to life even when they despise what they must be to survive.

Several years ago, a cardiac patient with no chance of surviving more than a few weeks was attached to a huge artificial heart, a blood-pumping machine the size of a horse that he had to drag about his home to keep alive. The cruelest part of this is simply that such choices should be forced upon us in the first place. For how many can refuse the chance to ward off death a little longer? By the time the man's exhausted organism was ready to give out, he confessed to being relieved that his ordeal was over. Surviving had become hell.

That is the true underlying terror that the monster and the vampire embody. Both are torn between drives that work on two distinct evolutionary levels. At the most basic level, they are driven by an undiminished biological instinct for self-preservation. That instinct all but defines life itself; we assume it characterizes all living things. Except for the most sentient of the mammals, who have been known to will themselves to death in zoos, the "lower" animals struggle to survive under all conditions. Were it not for that drive, no individual, no species would have been selected for survival.

But at another level, intelligence comes into play. And at that point, our species, having evolved the capacity for foresight and aspiration, transcends basic biology; human beings set an independent cultural value upon survival. We can conjure up fears that our fellow creatures cannot — specifically, the fear of a valueless life. This intellectual gift introduces a terror that does not exist in our primal nature. At the level of instinct, human beings find themselves driven to survive like any other animal. But they can also find themselves longing to surrender their existence.

Such a divided state, psychologists tell us, is the essence of horror. In his analysis of nightmares, Freud observed that "anxiety is an indication that the repressed wish has proved too strong for the censorship and has accomplished or is about to accomplish its fulfillment in spite of it." We recognize this state vividly with sexuality. We experience horror when a deep sexual taboo begins to crumble in the face of an insistent desire to enjoy what is forbidden. Similarly, in the flight from mortality, horror sets in when we feel ourselves wanting what our instinct for preservation forbids us to want. The ghouls and walking corpses invented by an earlier generation of Gothic novelists were initially meant to frighten by their ugliness and menace. But now we can see them in a different light. They embody a tragically conflicted condition that is surely more real and more fearful to modern readers than their traditional fangs and claws.

Scientific progress has produced a painful division between our instinctual appetite for self-preservation and our intellectual desire for a life that has value. Oddly enough, in that conflict we find medical science in league, not with our more highly evolved rational faculties, but with our primitive biological nature. Each time I place myself in the hands of my well-intentioned doctors, nothing is more chilling than the possibility that the powers of modern medicine are out of touch with our highest human values.

Can science, which has created this dilemma, also find a solution? Can it perhaps live up to Bacon's promise that death will be eliminated? The human genome project promises the possibility of deleting all hereditary diseases and many constitutional weaknesses out of our DNA — or at the very least offering the chance to abort any pregnancy that might produce a less than long-lived specimen. Though the doctors may work Frankensteinian marvels, at some point the physical limitations of the body make themselves known, if not at 100 then at 200. And then we are face to face with the same existential dilemma our ancestors might have confronted.

Or perhaps there is another solution. It is offered not by medical science, but by high tech.

## A RACE OF SILICON IMMORTALS

Francis Bacon anticipated the possibility of life extension by spare-parts surgery. But why bother to preserve the perishing carcass at all? Why not simply extract the mind by copying it into a computer? As a disembodied electronic intelligence, the person might be sustained indefinitely. This fantasy of computerized mentality haunts the field of artificial intelligence.

Robert Jastrow of NASA looks forward to the time when, thanks to high tech, we shall become "a race of immortals." One day, he tells us,

> a bold scientist will be able to tap the contents of his mind and
> transfer them into the metallic lattices of a computer. Because mind
> is the essence of being, it can be said that this scientist has entered
> the computer and that he now dwells in it. At last the human brain,
> ensconced in a computer has been liberated from the weakness of the
> mortal flesh. ... It is in control of its own destiny. The machine is its
> body; it is the machine's mind. ... It seems to me that this must be
> the mature form of intelligent life in the universe. Housed in
> indestructible lattices of silicon and no longer constrained in the
> span of its years by the life and death cycle of a biological organism,
> such a kind of life could live forever.[4]

Jastrow's prediction is a high-tech variation on Manichaean themes that have long sounded through modern science: the hope of liberating pure reason from the physical facts of life — and incidentally from the messy bodily intimacies of sex. Note the assumption: "Mind is the essence of being." Delete the body and identity remains intact.

At the birth of modern Western philosophy, Pythagoras and Plato seized upon mathematics as the purest expression of deathless being. Two thousand years later, at the beginning of the modern era, Descartes echoed that same desire to rise above the flesh when he separated calculating mind from corruptible matter and made mathematics the official language of science. As an essentially computational machine, the computer has inherited the flight from mortality as a subliminal goal that continues to cast its spell. In Jastrow's formulation, we have the Cartesian dictum *Cogito, ergo sum* pressed to its literal and logical extreme. "I" become nothing other or more than my cogitating brain. If, therefore, that brain can be simulated in silicon, "I" survive.

The astrophysicist Frank Tipler has pressed these possibilities even further. In his book *The Physics of Immortality* he sets out to reinvent the scientific equivalent of the Christian resurrection. "The dead," he tells us, "will be resurrected when the computer capacity of the universe is so large that the amount of capacity required to store all possible human speculations is an insignificant fraction of the entire capacity." Following the Catholic evolutionary philosopher Pierre Teilhard de Chardin, Tipler refers to this as "the Omega Point," the grand climax of cosmic history. Humanity would then dominate the entire universe; we would have progressed "from Earth-womb into the cosmos at large."[5]

Long before that far horizon is reached, Tipler is certain that we will be able to simulate the body in all its most refined details — and improve upon it. It would then be unnecessary to preserve the carnal original; it might be cast aside in favor of its robotic equivalent. Such an "emulated person," Tipler argues, "would observe herself to be as real, and as having a body as solid as the body we currently observe ourselves to have." The simulated body would, however, have one very special quality: It would be deathless. Tipler sees the same great dividend in this that Jastrow finds in putting his brain in a box. In that form, disembodied minds of the future might be loaded aboard a spacecraft and fired off into the universe to explore the galaxies far, far away — needing no air, food, water, or exercise for the journey. Even boredom need not be a problem; a disincarnate intelligence could be placed in a comatose state for the thousands of years it would take to arrive at a destination light-years away.

Platonic mysticism continues to intrigue the world of high tech. Plato was convinced that it was the corruption of the flesh that separates us from the highest forms of knowledge. So he recommended the study of geometry as a sort of purgation of the senses; such a study would elevate the mind above the body's mortality. Mark Slouka has this same strange alliance of the ascetic and the mathematical in view when he characterizes high tech as "an attack on reality as human beings have always known it." Cyberspace, he reports, is getting crowded with scenarios uploading consciousness into electronic networks. Behind these high-tech fantasies he sees "a fear and loathing of the natural world, of physical experience in its entirety."[6]

In the pages of *Wired* magazine, silicon immortality is among the constant themes of the rising cyberpunk intelligentsia. This may in fact be the emotional subtext for the advanced claims of artificial intelligence. Interviewed in *Wired*, Chris Langton, one of the founders of artificial life research, puts it this way: "There are these other forms of life, artificial ones, that want to come into existence. And they are using me as a vehicle for reproduction and for implementation." Vernor Vinge, looking further into the future, tells us that, "if we ever succeed in making machines as smart as humans, then it's only a small leap to imagine that we would soon thereafter make — or cause to be made — machines that are even smarter than any human. And that's it. That's the end of the human race within the animal kingdom."[7]

Not everybody in the high tech world views this prospect favorably. Bill Joy, a leading computer innovator, cringes at predictions that we will achieve "near immortality" as "engineered organisms," but fears it may indeed happen by some combination of genetics, nanotechnology, and robotics.[8] Jaron Lanier, a principal creator of virtual reality and a maverick member of the computer community, is even more critical. He believes these fantasies are among the major attractions of cyberspace. Many hackers "nurture hopes of being able to live forever by backing themselves up onto a computer tape."

> Nanotechnology might be used to create a supercomputer that will quickly figure out how to make nanomachines that can repair the

human body and make old age an anachronism. ... Or, perhaps most tellingly, the contents of our brains will be read into durable computers, so that our minds will continue after our bodies cease to function.[9]

This, Lanier believes, is what accounts for that curious new psychological category we call "nerdiness." Intellectually, the nerd is one who searches for ways to digitalize away all distinctions of quality, feeling, and affect. Emotionally, the nerd is given over to a defensive blandness that wants to shelter from human intimacy and physicality. Why should anyone have such an insistent desire to erase the barrier between the human and the mechanical, even in one's own personality? Because once we believe we are beyond that barrier, we are beyond death. Machines do not die.

The idea that identity is mentality has received some skeptical attention from science fiction. In Curt Siodmak's classic tale "Donovan's Brain," the image of life as a lump of bodiless gray matter is made to seem even more horrific than Mary Shelley's patchwork corpse. In the story, the merciless and predatory Donovan gleefully finds his scope for villainy expanded and relishes his new status as a single-minded, domineering intelligence. Free of the flesh, he is also free of all moral responsibility. He envisions living forever as a parasitic brain taking over whatever organism he may need.

Similarly, HAL, the deranged computer in *2001*, is all the more monstrous precisely because he has no body. Knowing no community of the flesh with human beings, he has become all the more alien for lacking an organic dimension. He can murder with clinical dispassion. When he wipes out the crew members of the Jupiter Mission, their vital signs become so many flat lines on a computer terminal: For an entity without a body, the difference between life and death is a mathematical squiggle on a graph. HAL can only "die" when the modules of his electronic brain are disassembled one by one — at which point his last memory is of the tune "Daisy, Daisy," a wedding song about relations of the flesh that artificial intelligence can never know except as a data point.

In all these cases, science fiction remains true to Mary Shelley's dire warning. Life without this perishing body is as monstrous as ever the Frankensteinian original was. Or perhaps more so. The monster's carcass, though an unnatural creation, preserved at least some tenuous connection with humanity. In my sequel *The Memoirs of Elizabeth Frankenstein*, I imagine the monster's greatest suffering comes of pitying the unwilling many who have become his body. Elizabeth, in her encounter with the monster, records his words in her memoirs:

> Impatiently he all but growls, "Will you not understand? There are times when all the flesh and sinew of my body cries out to me with the voices of other beings, the dead that live again in me. This hand, this shoulder, this finger ... this brain. As if I walked through a graveyard and from every grave I could hear the muffled voices speaking their names. Can you imagine what it was like to learn what I am? A thing? An artifact?

Monsters that lack even so much as a cadaverous body, though less hideous in appearance, are a far more alien breed. They remind us that the body, this supreme organic puzzle, remains the basis of our human identity. In it spirit and matter mingle in a marriage that admits of no divorce except at the price of our humanity. Walt Whitman, poet laureate of the body electric, had a greater wisdom to offer us in celebrating death as evenhandedly as ever he celebrated life. For "to die," he believed, "is different from what any one supposed, ... and luckier."

## IN THE HOUR OF OUR DEATH ... WHO DECIDES?

It might seem that the solution to the problem of enforced living is obvious. *Just let people die when their time comes.* But neither living nor dying is simple any longer. Having so many skills and resources at hand to keep people alive has made a complex legal, financial, and technical affair of letting people die. There are tubes and wires to be removed from the body, monitors to be switched off, plugs to be pulled, papers to be filled out, reports to be filed, bills to be paid, accounts to be added up. None of this *just happens*. The patient's quality of life may have sunk to minimal; the patient may be comatose. Nevertheless, somebody must make the decision to end the heroic intervention that is making survival possible. But who should this be? The answer that leaps to mind is the patient, provided the patient is conscious and competent enough to give informed consent. But who decides that the patient is competent? Who decides if the patient is or is not "legally dead"? Who provides the information the patient needs for informed consent?

Obviously, physicians are bound to play some central part in these judgments. They already are, but in surreptitious ways that cloud the moral issues. There are, for example, "slow codes" that physicians invoke to back off from aggressive treatment of patients deemed beyond saving. The medical staff goes through all the necessary legal motions to save the patient, but with no real effort to achieve resuscitation. When the charade is done, everyone breathes a sigh of relief. Also called "show codes," "Hollywood codes," and "light blue codes," the practice has been condemned as unethical dissimulation.[10]

This is where a new ethical question arises. *Can physicians be trusted?*

This is more than asking if doctors are professionally skilled enough to offer advice. Let us grant that they are. But giving advice has become a matter of *business* because death has been assimilated to cost-benefit analysis. More and more doctors now work for HMOs or within health care corporations that have their institutional eyes on the bottom line. Keeping patients alive costs money, often a great deal of money. Can doctors who are company personnel working to the standards of their employer be trusted to ignore the costs and act in the patient's best interests?

In the fall of 1997 the *Journal of the American Medical Association* published a study of "medical care at the end of life." The survey compared the ways in which critically ill patients were treated under two modes of compensation: fee for service, under which there is every incentive to provide aggressive treatment to keep the patient alive, and managed care, which provides no such incentive. Under managed care, doctors earned no more by keeping the patient alive and giving more care. Indeed, doctors and hospitals could only lose money by wasting their resources on "hopeless" cases. The results of the study were clear. Critically ill HMO patients were likely to die sooner.

That sounds shocking. But some physicians believe it is a positive feature of managed care. HMOs do not waste time on hopeless cases; they withhold treatment and cut the suffering short. HMO patients avoid what the editors of *JAMA* call "ineffective, painful, expensive, and unwanted medical interventions that deprive them of their dignity, personal interactions, and family savings." Even advance directives like living wills frequently fail to spare the patient prolonged pain and financial loss. As one doctor put it, "If you don't want to die with a lot of tubes in you, then HMO care may be the place to be." To which a consumer spokesperson replied caustically, "HMOs are wonderful for people who want to embrace euthanasia."[11]

The difficulty with the choice this study presents is that money is the decisive factor *on both sides* of the question. One doctor may be acting to make money for himself; another doctor — or the supervisor who reviews the doctor's decision — may act to save money for her HMO. In either case, money distorts the morality of the choice. And money is no sensible measure of life. It might make some sense for critically ill patients themselves to choose fee-for-service treatment or managed care *after* they have decided either to prolong their lives or to accept a quick death. But to be committed one way or the other *before* the crisis arrives is ethically absurd.

Here, then, is where we stand. If people cling to life desperately, irrationally, out of fear or panic, who has the right to tear that life away from them? If people wish to cast their lives away, again irrationally, out of despair or fear or unbearable pain, who has the right to force that life upon them?

In a 1995 television discussion on National Public Radio, former Health, Education, and Welfare Secretary Joseph Califano raised a tough question. He observed that the largest single Medicare expenditure is for the strenuous measures undertaken to save the lives of hopelessly ill elderly patients, many of whom have only a few more weeks to live. In 1992 the intensive care units of the United States consumed $62 billion; a Stanford University study has concluded that a disproportionate amount of that money was spent on the terminally ill for "potentially ineffective care." Califano argued that this was the most obvious place to start saving money on Medicare.

One wonders what he had in mind. Perhaps he envisions a formula that combines medical cost, the age of the patient, the likely number of years the patient might survive following the procedure, with possibly some coefficient worked in to measure the quality of life. The calculation might be programmed in the same way that major investment decisions are now computer-controlled on the stock exchange. The patient would then be allowed to live or die depending on how the numbers came out.

To which the response might be, "Easy for you to say." In the abstract, we can work out tidy formulations relating age to chances for recovery to cost. But medicine, as every hospital soap opera tells us, is hardly a matter of dispassionate cash choices. Suppose you had to inform a loved one that you were stopping treatment because of the expense? Can you imagine telling your wife or mother, your husband or father that it just costs too much to try another bypass at this late stage? Can you imagine running the numbers for them to prove their lives are not worth saving? No matter how serious our budgetary troubles become, the answer to such questions is never likely to be a cost-benefit assessment — at least not openly.

Rationing health care in life-and-death situations is like belling the cat: a solution that may look good in the talking stage, but turns out to be utterly impractical because nobody is going to step forward to do what the solution requires. Even if the medical ethics of the matter could be worked out by way of a seemingly fair and dispassionate formula, there is another major obstacle. Medicine these days has as much to do with lawyers as doctors. Can anyone doubt that, in this era of obsessive litigation, there are malpractice attorneys who are already preparing to bring suit against the first doctor, hospital, or insurance company that announces it will withhold life-saving care to sick, old patients for financial reasons? Does anyone doubt how juries selected to include a representation of seniors would decide such cases?

Some entitlements critics have raised the same point about the rising cost of Medicare. Peter Peterson, for example, believes we must find the courage to invoke the "r word" — rationing. But suppose we suggest an even more courageous option: the "z word," meaning zero charge. Suppose, when medical costs rise beyond a certain point, treatment is offered without charge by physicians, hospitals, insurance companies, and pharmaceutical companies as an act of human kindness. One can predict the response. *Offer medical care for free? Unthinkable!* What does that leave us to conclude but that it is morally acceptable to sacrifice life for money, but not money for life?

## THE DUTY TO DIE

Is there a "duty to die"? The question was first raised, and with jarring aggressiveness, in 1984 by the then-governor of Colorado, Richard Lamm. Lamm went on record strongly suggesting that the elderly should, as a matter of ethical cost containment, consider making room in the world for the young by simply doing with less medical care and letting themselves die. The idea was taken up more comprehensively in 1987 by the medical ethicist Daniel Callahan in a study of "medical goals in an aging society."

Callahan's concern was essentially that of the generational accountants: The nation faced a "new social threat ... a demographic, economic, and medical avalanche."

Unlike the economists who tactfully restricted themselves to the fiscal implications of the issue, Callahan was prepared to take the next, fatal step toward philosophical consistency. Life-extending health care, he argued, should be denied to all those who have "lived out a natural life span." How long was that? About seventy or eighty years — an allowance that might have denied us the later-life contributions of Igor Stravinsky, Gandhi, Giuseppe Verdi, Michelangelo, Mother Theresa, Martha Graham, just to name a few of the more famous whose active lives continued well beyond Callahan's stingy limit.[12]

John Hardwig has pursued the same question, writing in the *Hastings Center Report,* a leading journal of medical ethics. His answer is yes health care should be withheld from the elderly, even for "those who want to live." The conclusion sounds harsh, but in fairness one must note that Hardwig raises the question as a matter of personal morality, not as a matter of public policy. In what situation would he impose the duty on himself? Rather too analytically, he maps out a set of criteria that he hopes would lead him to answer yes. Foremost among the criteria is cost and emotional strain. If prolonging one's life should become a burden to one's family, and all the more so if one has reached an advanced age (he suggests seventy-five) and had the benefit of a "full, rich life," then one is duty-bound to die.[13]

Hardwig's query may be legitimate enough as a matter of personal ethics. But issues of financial cost and emotional strain take us beyond the personal. His assumption is that health care costs are becoming too great for government programs to pay and so will soon have to be transferred to families. For Hardwig, money becomes a major ethical consideration. This, he believes, will "dramatically increase the number of Americans who will have a duty to die." Of course, by this criterion it would be a small step to concluding that the disabled bear the same duty, and perhaps even the children a family cannot afford. In the eyes of some, welfare policy might include such a criterion: The useless poor may as well be told they have a duty to vacate life and save the rest of us money.

Hardwig's argument is most persuasive when it is narrowly restricted to the family. For those lying hopelessly near to death, it does indeed tear at

261

the heart to know that they are imposing an ordeal on those they love. Framed in that way, who would not feel shamed into considering suicide? But by introducing the burdens of family cost and care as if these were insurmountable problems, Hardwig distorts the issue. There are, after all, other societies, no richer than the United States, where the community has assumed a major responsibility for paying the costs and providing the care that the very sick need. In the Scandinavian countries, medical care and home care for the chronically ill and the aged are simply taken for granted under state programs. Of course, such governmental responsibility makes for higher taxes; compassion costs. But it makes a mockery of social ethics to contend that the United States, of all countries, is at the end of its fiscal tether while gambling casinos and shopping malls are thriving. The priority Hardwig advocates accepts a wasteful and extravagant standard of living as so absolute and immutable that some must pay for it with their lives.

When it comes to deciding how much our society can afford for medical care, professional ethicists might set themselves a nobler task than counseling the elderly to commit suicide. Suppose we created a social category called "morally outrageous enrichment." Place in that category all those whose level of compensation is unquestionably exorbitant: corporate CEOs, movie stars, professional baseball players, talk-show hosts, television news anchors. Challenge these people to justify salaries that reach into the millions. For that is where the money our society saves by denying treatment to the elderly will go.

There is a cultural dimension to the issue that Hardwig overlooks. Every chronically ill patient being kept alive by strenuous measures is the result of a centuries-long historical development. In a real sense, these people are the living criterion of progress in modern life. What sense does it then make to say that the grand consequence of that progress is the duty to die? There may, of course, be a *desire* to die. In despair and with no future worth living for, an individual may elect suicide. That choice, if it must ever be faced, is hard enough to make on personal grounds without overlaying it with cost-benefit considerations.

What we have in the concept of a duty to die is an agonizing example of what generational accounting has brought us to in the discussion of medical ethics. By obscuring the fiscal truth about entitlements, it has created the false impression that we cannot afford one penny more for Medicare. The main service the generational accountants are doing for "our children" is to offer them a way to guilt-trip sick parents into taking their own lives.

On the other hand, suppose we were to reformulate the question and adjust the financial burden. *How much more are you willing to pay in order to free your loved ones — and yourself — of ever feeling you have a duty to die?* Rather than asking the sick to choose death, suppose we ask ourselves to choose taxes? After all, death is a universal fact of human life. Only the very young can be excused for not being aware of their mortality. The rest of us know full well that illness, age, and death await us. If we elect to leave these matters on the shoulders of families, then we are behaving like irresponsible children. But if we can see our way clear to revisioning our criterion of wealth — reconfiguring it into something like the "national life expectancy" we touched upon in chapter three — we would regard the kindness we show to the sick and dying as a far more human gauge of our affluence. Compassion would no longer be a burden, but a measure of our social maturity.

Once we remove money from this most delicate and authentically tragic of human situations, we can begin to devise humanistic alternatives to rationing medical care or shaming the sick into suicide. In a study of medicine and death, Marilyn Wells speaks of a new medical-philosophical skill that we are bound to see members of the baby boom generation exploring. She has called for "midwives to the dying," the sort of counseling that can be found in hospices and which has been vastly expanded as part of the AIDS crisis.[14] The day may not be far off when the words of Socrates, the works of Lao Tzu, Spinoza, and Montaigne, the teachings of all the great spiritual masters will be as much a part of modern medicine as the latest piece of diagnostic technology.

CHAPTER FOURTEEN

# POWERS OF THE MIND

A specter is haunting the senior community — and all those who wait on its borders. Its name is Alzheimer.

In the course of writing this book, every older person I interviewed from age fifty and up admitted to fearing this dreaded disease more than death. Those who work with the elderly as doctors, caregivers, or teachers describe concern over Alzheimer's as an obsession. Medical authorities who write on aging tell of patients as young as sixty asking anxiously if their minds are going. What occasioned the fear? A minor lapse of memory ... a name forgotten, a phone number misremembered, an appointment over-looked. But the lapse is immediately identified as a symptom of Alzheimer's. Ironically, for all the progress we have made in extending life expectancy, there may now be a greater anxiety about aging than ever before. The one fate all seniors fear the most — senility — has returned under a new name and with an even more ominous aspect. We have never had a more pressing reason to learn about the powers of the mind than now when longevity can sentence us to so long a term in the prison of dementia.

I had occasion to visit an Alzheimer's ward in a senior life care center. I was told that only a brave few of the several hundred older residents who lived there volunteered to help in the ward. The rest found it too disturbing. That part of the center was treated like the haunted wing of a Gothic castle. What I found there was understandably unsettling. There were fifteen people the day I visited, all of them frail, dozing in wheelchairs or staring vacantly into space. A few had suffered stroke; most were Alzheimer's sufferers. One or two were in minimal and episodic touch with the world around them; most were wholly withdrawn. Some mumbled to themselves, some sang, some wept. Walter, the only man in the ward, sometimes danced for the others. He had been an engineer but once taught for an Arthur

Murray studio. He was still ambulatory. I was introduced to him. He had no time for me. He was leaving.

"Where are you going?" one of the caregivers asked.

"Home," he answered.

"Tell me about home," the caregiver answered.

Walter had no time for that. He wandered off around the room, then sat down again and fell silent.

The two nurses who supervised the ward had refined their methods for dealing with their charges. "Never correct a mistake," they told me. "Don't expect them to learn. Pick up on whatever they say and ask them to tell you more. They like your company."

"What do they talk about?" I asked. "Can you tell what's on their mind?"

"Like Walter, they talk about home, the home they lived in as a kid. They ask about their mothers. They say they're waiting for their mothers to take them home. They go back in time. It's like everything from now back to their childhood is being erased. In their minds, they're growing younger. At night, when you help them into bed, they usually curl into a fetal posture."

"Would they be better off in the care of their families?" I wondered.

The caregivers were adamant. "No, absolutely not. They're a great burden. Their children have a hard time handling them well, unless they can hire round-the-clock help. Even then, it's heartbreaking. They remember how their parents once were. They try to bring them back. They can't."

"Do you get attached to them?" I asked.

"We try not to. They are all so close to death. We just wait with them and let them go as gently as we can."

That day the residents of the Alzheimer's ward had held a party with games and balloons and cake and prizes. Everybody won prizes. Everybody wore party hats. The scene looked like kindergarten. It might have seemed demeaning. But these people were beyond that. They were also beyond the fear that must have been there once as the specter approached. That was the one mercy this disease granted. It allowed them peace.

But those of us who remain observing from outside their world have no peace. We are left to wonder at nature's cruelty in allowing the body to outlive the mind. Some fear that Alzheimer's is only the swift and extreme form of the fate that awaits us all.

## "But That's Not Me!"

Senility is the besetting stereotype of old age. What the scatterbrained bimbo once was to women, what the Stepin Fetchit bootblack once was to African Americans, the doddering old codger is to seniors. Like all stereotypes, it is a blight upon one's life. Knowing that others are watching for the telltale traits to emerge — a moment of confusion or forgetfulness, a bad move behind the steering wheel — one spends each day seeking to prove, "That's not me!" But in the case of the elderly, the stereotype has always had some modicum of truth. There are disabilities and diseases of the brain that account for what was once called senility. We now know these disabilities are not a matter of fate, nor are they exclusive to age.

Most of the disabilities of age are a matter of challenging the odds. Like the soldier whose luck declines the longer he stays under fire, the longer one lives, the greater the chance that one or another mental weakness will have its chance to show up. If nobody had ever made it to the age of seventy, we might never know Alzheimer's disease existed. When Dr. Alois Alzheimer diagnosed his first patient in 1906, he described the condition he documented as "a peculiar, little-known disease process." He did not identify the process as a disease of age. Why should he? His first patient was in her forties and died at fifty-one. At first, the disease was thought to be a rare condition that was mainly found among people under the age of sixty. Now we know that this is one of the hazards that lies waiting along the distant reaches of the mortality slope.

How great is the risk? There are more than 4 million Americans with Alzheimer's disease today. The best studies available suggest that, as of the mid-1990s, about 10 percent of those who reach the age of eighty-five may suffer some form of "dementia" — the word that has replaced "senility" as an acceptable designation. For those who reach their nineties, that figure rises to between one-quarter and one-half. About 70 percent of all the cases of dementia after age sixty are due to Alzheimer's; most of the rest are due to stroke or Parkinson's disease. The most worrisome aspect of Alzheimer's is the fact that many of those afflicted with the disease can lose as much as one-third of their brain cells without displaying any symptoms of the disease before it kills them. This makes early detection and treatment almost impossible.[1] But there is a hopeful fact to be gleaned from studies of identical twins. Not all twin pairs come down with the disease together; about 50 percent of twin siblings escape Alzheimer's, which suggests that environmental factors may play some role in determining who will be stricken.

In July 2000, at the World Alzheimer's Conference the National Institute of Aging announced that a new Alzheimer's vaccine may be nearer than anybody had realized. Tested over a year's time on mice, the vaccine had altered the immune system of the rodents so that it cleared away the plaque that Alzheimer's disease spreads through the brain. Unless some cure of this kind is found, there could be 22 million cases of Alzheimer's disease worldwide by 2025 and 45 million by 2050. The incidence of the disease doubles every five years among those over the age of sixty. Statistics like these are both consoling and worrying. The percentage of those who have fallen victim to one form of dementia or another is high enough to cause legitimate concern. But at least we can now recognize that the worst cases are the result, not of inevitable degeneration, but of disease — a genetically determined disease that is being closely monitored. The mutated gene that seems to produce Alzheimer's has been identified and its action tracked. Like the assumed idiocy of the child who is born deaf and simply cannot hear, the senility once thought to be inescapable can now be seen as a birth defect, a corrupted gene visited unpredictably upon an unfortunate minority. If, by the time boomers have entered the Alzheimer's zone of life, the twisted logic of the gene can be corrected, they may be able to enjoy their long life expectancy free of the specter.

Everything we once thought we knew about the aging mind is in need of a radical revision which may help us understand minds both young and old. Previous studies of elderly populations were too often based on people who were, for the most part, poor, in bad health, and demoralized. Worst of all, they were frequently studied under institutionalized conditions. Samples were often drawn from a poorly educated population that had been treated as burdensome and dispensable. We now have significant longitudinal studies, the best known from the National Institute on Aging in the United States and from the University of Gothenberg in Sweden, that undercut all previous testing. These studies are unambiguous in their findings. Aging brings with it no automatic, genetically programmed decline in the powers of the mind. Even physical prowess can be maintained far longer than was ever thought possible in times past — as the remarkable performance of people over sixty in the senior games has shown.[2]

## MIND, MEMORY, AND MEANING

The aging brain is now a subject of intense scrutiny. But we need to be clear about what laboratory studies of the brain can and cannot tell us. Can they, for example, tell us anything about the "mind" as distinct from the "brain"? It is a matter of great philosophical dispute where one draws the line between the two. One commonsense distinction holds that the "mind" is what thinks; the "brain" is what the mind thinks *with*. The brain is the physical basis for a process that may be no more physical than the various forms of energy that hold the atom together. If it makes any sense to put the matter that way, then scientific studies of the brain can, at most, be credited with helping us understand where and how the mind can fail. They tell us how well the brain is serving the mind's full capacity. If the brain is damaged by injury or aging, the mind may be encumbered and fall short of its total potentiality. But no scientific study is sufficient to define the upper limit of that potentiality, especially when the mind is working against physical resistance. Nor can studies of the brain help us understand powers of the mind such as educability or aptitude, that are essentially social. Intelligence is often a matter of the company we keep.

Studies using new imaging techniques report that, thanks to the brain's massive interconnective redundancy, most seniors retain excellent cognitive capacity into their nineties. The overall brain shrinkage to which elders were once thought to be doomed is mainly a distortion introduced by the extraordinary effects of Alzheimer's disease.[3] Research along other lines, however, verifies the fact that older brains do tend to suffer from AAMI — age-associated memory impairment, or as one researcher calls it, the onset of the "Swiss-cheese memory."[4] Researchers now distinguish AAMI into normal forgetfulness and the more serious MCI, mild cognitive impairment, which shows up as an inability to recall visual imagery. That may be a signal of early Alzheimer's. Memory problems like these are age-related, but not *aging*-related. That is, it shows up more prominently in older people but has not been connected with some inevitable form of physical deterioration. Variation among the elderly in this respect is therefore very great, with many remaining able to outperform their juniors on memory tests.

The causes for AAMI are complex; some are totally unrelated to age. For example, many seniors use medications, especially sedatives and pain-killers, with the side effect of impaired mental functioning. Others, who are no more forgetful than younger people, experience a low-level panic whenever their memory fails — as it might fail for anybody. But when older people forget, they become fearful that they are growing senile, or that others will think they are. In a social situation where such a lapse produces winks and nods from those all around, the problem is aggravated and the anxiety mounts. These are the private battles older people fight in a society that demands quick, unerring responsiveness — a quality I have found as lacking among the smiling young people in shops and offices as among older people on the job. It is primarily for these younger workers, after all, that cash registers with pictures rather than numbers were invented, lest they need to memorize prices.

In the old, as in the young, memory deficiency can be treated. With training, AAMI can be reversed; teaching people how to do that is the subject of programs, some federally funded, that are bound to grow in the years ahead. Among the most ambitious of these efforts are the Aging and Dementia Research Center at New York University Medical Center and the Memory Assessment Clinics headquartered in Bethesda, Maryland.[5] Seniors trained in these techniques often outperform much younger people. Efforts of this kind are a godsend to the elderly, but they are also something more. They have political implications. With the inhibiting fear of AAMI brought under control, the next older population is apt to gain the confidence and competence it needs to assert itself in much the same way that consciousness raising studies once strengthened the civil rights and women's movements by breaking down disempowering stereotypes.

There is a curious feature about the mental anxiety of the old. A psychologist I know teaches courses for men and women over seventy to improve memory and problem-solving. She knows she achieves impressive results; her students tell her so and she sees it in their conduct. But when she seeks to administer a test so she can collect some numbers, most of her students refuse to cooperate. They have no interest in scores. They dislike grading and avoid competition. So she cannot give the tests that will prove the efficacy of her methods. But that in itself is a "finding" of value. With maturity, scoring points, proving oneself, and competition lose meaning. They are seen for what they are: ego games that belong in the schoolroom. She tells me the greatest problem she has in drawing out the latent or long-repressed mental capacities of her students is their dismal self-image. They have been convinced that they are no longer capable of learning or even thinking. So she must begin by boosting their self-esteem, after which they go on to learn all she has to teach them about problem-solving, memory, and planning. I asked whether she thought the next generation of the old would present the same problem. She was convinced that would not be so. The seniors coming along — she had the boomers in mind — are more confident, assertive, and better educated. They are gifted with a greater sense of security and purpose.

When it comes to mental impairment, many retired people may actually be suffering from their way of life rather than from physical decline. Consider the mental state of people in their eighties or nineties who have survived their friends and relatives and live in great isolation — the situation for elderly people in any community that has no senior center or services. The old often seem out of touch because they *are* out of touch. We easily overlook the social aspect of memory and alertness. On the job we are paced along by coworkers and a daily routine that helps us remember what needs to be remembered. Executives with a lot on their mind benefit from memory aids that are made up of secretaries, administrative assistants, and computerized "to-do" reminders that keep them on track and on time. It might be the case that retaining as much minutiae as most of us do in the workplace is a highly unnatural stunt, a skill that flags when the pressure is off. As soon as one drops out of the workforce, one loses this collective support ... and may well grow "forgetful."

Retired seniors may then be too deeply intimidated by the senility stereotype to ask questions or assert themselves. Still others, impeded by poor eyesight or hearing, make mistakes, fail to respond rapidly, and grow withdrawn. Finally — and most interestingly — some elders may simply have other, greater issues on their mind than younger people around them can understand: questions about life, death, meaning, sin, salvation. They have stopped caring about the 10:00 A.M. meeting or the 2:00 P.M. district manager's report because all this has become boring. If their thoughts wander, they may be wandering into more philosophical territory where they need education or a spiritual discipline to keep their minds focused.

I sometimes suspect the reason elderly people are marked out for scamming has to do with the fact that they have come to care less about money in the bank. They trust too easily, not worrying all that much about what may become of their worldly goods, especially if they have outlived family and friends. That leaves them vulnerable to exploitation by those who have their minds on lesser values or unworthy pursuits. It is easy to write off what they suffer at the hands of con artists as the result of senility, but here again we are at a juncture of the mental and the social. It is not incompetence that the scammers play upon; it is the same vulnerability they look for in all their victims — something, *anything* that creates enough momentary trust to allow them to grab the money and run.

In the case of the elderly, it is loneliness and fear they target, and the tendency of those who are alone and afraid to weaken in response to any gesture of kindness. Telemarketers have become especially adept at conning isolated seniors. They scout them out the way a hawk scouts for mice. In one newspaper report, a seventy-seven-year-old widow confessed that she had sent thousands of dollars to a telemarketer because she became "addicted" to the attention she was being offered. "They were nice on the phone. They became my friends," she explained. Telephone fraud like this takes in an estimated $40 billion a year, the bulk of it from the elderly who will pay to make real the sad, fond hope that somebody cares about them. They trust because a friendly gesture matters more to them than money.

Once again, we must realize that gerontology is a frontier field, long neglected on the assumption that people must not expect much in their senior years beyond an easy death. Just as techniques for toning and conditioning the muscles are giving seniors better physical ability, so too forms of mental exercise are lengthening the mental life span. New medications are being used to slow the brain's aging. Antioxidants called "nitrones" are proving to be of promise in not only preventing but reversing certain forms of AAMI.[6] More ambitious still is research on "cognitive enhancers," medications like ampakine drugs that boost the signals emitted by the neurotransmitters involved in memory and learning.[7]

No doubt there will be a succession of breakthroughs in the chemistry of cognition, but research of this kind can be misleading. At some point we must take another factor into account, something rather like the cultural bias that is now commonly recognized as a distortion of IQ and aptitude testing. Just as racial and ethnic factors may bias performance on standardized tests, so too age brings its peculiar influence to bear on the powers of the mind.

Most academic and professional work emphasizes details — facts, figures, skills — that can be quantified and tested for competitively. Even younger people of divergent intellectual ability may be quite poor at that kind of performance and yet have fine minds. Elders may bring to the task a different orientation, an instinct to go for the big picture, the controversial issue, the questions that require thought and tough judgment. What we mistake for poor memory may be a different focus, a shift of emphasis, possibly a more mature grasp of issues. Seeing the forest as well as the trees is not a weakening of the mind, but an advance toward wisdom.

## THE DYNAMIC BRAIN

There are many molecular changes in the aging brain that have been identified. Some result from the same destructive impact of free radicals that we have noted throughout the organism. Since the brain is one of the few organs that does not (except in some minor respects) replace its cells, losing neurons might seem more serious than the loss of other body cells. In a few parts of the brain, a sizable percentage of neurons do vanish with age. The brain may even shrink in size, but recent research shows that in those centers most relevant to the higher functions there is no significant neuronal loss in dementia-free elders. And where there is some loss, other healthy neurons take over the function of those that have died. This is because the brain is designed as a network with all the redundant circuitry of a telephone exchange. "The brain," Dennis Selkoe, a neurologist and Alzheimer's expert, tells us, "is capable of dynamic remodeling of its neuronal connections, even in later years. As is true of other organs, the brain appears to have considerable physiological reserve and to tolerate small losses of neuronal function."[8] Perhaps for this reason age-linked changes in the brain produce only modest alterations in performance.

Richard Restak reaches the same optimistic conclusion in his summary of findings in brain research. "The mature brain," he tells us, "performs as well as the younger one in tasks requiring planning, organization, and the manipulation of information. Thus, the mature brain is not a defective version of a younger one." Statistically speaking, older people may tend to be at a slight disadvantage when they are competing with younger people in tests of simple mental rapidity. There is a slowing down of the transfer speed in moving short-term memories between what Restak calls the brain's "storage compartment" and its "permanent store." But "with advancing years, the brain redesigns itself to compensate for decreases in reaction time and general slowing."[9]

Thanks to research on aging, we are learning a great deal about the amazing plasticity and dynamism of the brain at all age levels — and perhaps coming to a greater appreciation of its many modes. Restak reports a revealing study conducted by Richard Shimamura at the University of California, Berkeley, in which senior faculty members displayed a distinct slowing of raw reaction time to stimuli projected on a screen — the sort of skill that might be essential for an air traffic controller. They were also slower in processing certain kinds of data, especially arbitrary associations, such as connecting a name with a face or a name with a phone number.[10] But is this not exactly the kind of data we can now delegate to computers, which are far faster in working through a database than the quickest human brain?

That finding raises an intriguing possibility. In chapter eight, we discussed how high tech is invariably depicted as a technology that belongs to the young and leaves the old behind. But in a very real sense it is older people who might be most empowered by the computer. What older workers tend to lack is exactly what computers do best. For at least as long as we remain a data-intensive economy, computers can come to the aid of working memory in ways that make AAMI less detrimental.

If there were nothing more to be said about the powers of the aging mind beyond what gets lost along the way and how to compensate for it, we might be left with a dismal conclusion. But that is far from the whole story. The power of the aging mind in areas of interpretation, judgment, creativity, and imagination is undiminished and continues to benefit from educational stimulation. Even when Alzheimer's disease locks into the brain, there is some indication that mental exercise can diminish the damage.

At least that is the conclusion some researchers have drawn from the nuns' study, a research project that charted the cognitive powers of 180 nuns from the School Sisters of Notre Dame Order over several years. The sisters, a cloistered order living unusually uniform lives that effectively remove them from most outside influences, have agreed to bequeath their brains to medical science upon their deaths. Many of the sisters, whose age-range at death spreads from seventy-five to over one hundred years old, have kept autobiographical journals from the time they took their vows. Autopsies performed since 1991 reveal that those whose journals show them to be better educated and more intellectually active, were able to remain self-reliantly independent to an older age, despite any physical decline. Even more striking was the finding that one of the oldest nuns — she had lived to 102 — remained independent and mentally alert despite having advanced Alzheimer's disease. The researchers concluded that she had built up sufficient "brain reserves" to remain symptom free.[11]

"Use it or lose it." That result for cerebral as well as physical ability has been confirmed by numerous other studies. In summer 2000, two studies — one at Case Western University, another by the MacArthur Foundation — showed that education and a continuing high level of mental activity, especially reading, keep the brain agile and hold Alzheimer's disease at bay. The effects are enhanced when they are accompanied by steady physical exercise; activities that raise the oxygen level are particularly helpful.[12]

In August 2000, the American Association on Aging launched a program that will aggressively collect and disseminate current research on aging and mental fitness. Called MindAlert, the initiative recognizes that we now have evidence "that the brain is able to grow new cells that can keep the mind alert and capable of storing and retrieving memory as it goes. Mental function can be significantly improved by appropriate training and practice, even among older adults already showing signs of memory loss."[13]

The longevity revolution is producing as topsy-turvy new perspective on education. For generations we have thought of education as being the special province of children. Building schools has been justified on the basis of the contribution it makes to the careers of the young. Now we see that education has even greater value for the older population. The talents we are mining among the elderly are enriching in their own right. But in addition lifelong learning keeps people fit and alert in their later years in ways that will save society billions in medical costs.

## THE TROUBLE WITH WISDOM

This book is based on an assumption about the powers of the human mind that some will find controversial. I believe that as people grow older, they grow wiser — and indeed *want* to grow wiser, as if to make good use of life's final phase. We obscure that truth when we insist that wisdom is a rare and exalted quality that few can achieve. If we say that wisdom can be attributed only to a Socrates or an Albert Schweitzer, we run the risk of placing it beyond the reach of ordinary mortals. But I assume that wisdom is everywhere around us. *Wisdom happens.* It happens as simply and naturally as learning happens in children. Just as children cannot help but learn with every breath they take, so adults, as they age, cannot help but become wise. Wisdom is that same act of learning as we go forward in life, with one difference. It is sufficient for children to greet the world with wonder; elders must add reflection — and do, quite spontaneously, because they have a broadening base of experience to draw upon for comparison and questioning.

Wisdom is examined experience, examined in the same way Socrates examined all that his pupils said, helping them find their way through their thoughts, offering a word of criticism here, a word of encouragement there, bringing them to view the values and presuppositions that underlay their beliefs with discriminating distance. Wisdom grows from any ordinary life provided that life is taken seriously and brought under reflection. That is all wisdom is, yet it is infinitely precious and wholly indispensable to growing up. In our language, we speak of being "wised up." Learning in the sense of being wised up does not make us smart in ways that lead to writing books or winning awards, but it makes us competent. Unless we are in a coma, every day we live wises us up by bringing us how-to learning, hard-knocks learning, depression learning, pleasure learning, boredom learning, anxious learning.

Far from being rare, wisdom is what life gives us with every passing moment. If people need any help with wisdom, it is mainly to wake them up to the fact that wisdom is happening here and now, and that we need only learn to take our own experience seriously. If we are acting in the world, we are learning by that action. And if we are not acting, we are most likely thinking life over — or worrying about it, or regretting it, or laughing at it, or crying over it. That is when wisdom happens most importantly — in moments of reflection, when we go back over things, replaying what happened, coming up with all we might have said or done, wondering where we go from there. That is what I imagine people are doing as they go through the day, driving to and from work, walking the streets, loitering over lunch, lying awake at night. With a little self-awareness, with a companion to share the experience, and above all with the courage to speak and act on the basis of what they have learned, everybody becomes a practical philosopher. We all know this. We experience it every time we sit down with another person — friend, relative, workmate — and talk about the dilemmas and decisions that punctuate our lives. What we give and take in that simple encounter is the hard-won smarts of everyday life.

Wisdom is — at least potentially — the most common and plentiful human resource in the world. It is not in short supply. Why then do we think it is so rare?

Because there are forces that make wisdom unwelcome. They shame it into silence and so neutralize the role it has to play. As I suggested in chapter seven, the commercial interests that dominate the marketplace are out to infantilize us every hour of the day. But more generally, in an industrial world dominated by scientific precision and technological know-how, by specialists and technicians, by experts in every walk of life, wisdom is crowded out. It does not seem to know the right words, the formulas, the facts. It is not up on the latest. The trouble with wisdom is that we have, in a sense, become too smart for our own good in the modern world — smart in ways that seem to eliminate our need for the old Socratic project of self-examination. In the absence of self-examination, we lose touch with our true motivations and become rigid about values. We quite literally do not know what we are doing. And so we grow heedless and arrogant.

I have worked among academics and intellectuals all my life, some of them men and women of genius. Brilliant minds, but too often carrying a built-in resistance to wisdom. In their view, wisdom is an irritatingly fuzzy quality rather like judgment, interpretation, or taste. It is nothing that can be tested or objectively measured. There is no section on wisdom in the SAT exam; the Nobel committee makes no awards to the wise. Those who earn their living by using their brains feel more comfortable with performance that can be gauged by results, by clear logic, by numbers, by peer review. Professionals like qualities that can be identified by a title: M.D., Ph.D., M.S.W., R.N. But wisdom is among those virtues that need no license or degree. It is a quality of the person that cannot be taught. Proverbially, it can be an attribute of the unlettered, even of certain "wise fools."

To tough-minded intellectuals, talents that require no book-learning or special training smack of obfuscation and fraudulence. Up to a point, they are right. No society has been without its share of charlatans, fakers, and frauds. That was certainly true of our society in the past. Even today quacks and cults abound in the midst of our scientific civilization. I confess that when I find myself among the questionable gurus that gather along the New Age fringe, I grow as skeptical as any. I have been to anything-goes presentations on "spirituality" some of them by franchised teachers that finish by promising financial success, good-looks, cosmic bliss, and weight loss. Caught between the hard edge of skepticism and the slough of gullibility, wisdom has no good choice in either direction.

In the contemporary world, the discussion of wisdom runs into a special barrier. It is among those powers of the mind that cannot be imitated by a computer. There are no programs for making wise choices. Ours is called the information age, but wisdom has little to do with information. After all, the people who are most widely credited with possessing wisdom — Confucius, Jesus, the Buddha — predated the Internet. Socrates openly declared that he knew nothing; he would be the last person to ask for information. That simple fact, that our culture was created by people working with nothing more than their naked wits, has become a heresy in our time. It is actively ignored in ways that can be comic. In 1997 the Apple Computer Company ran an ambitious series of advertisements that featured the faces of eminent intellectuals and artists — Edison, Picasso, Einstein, Frank Lloyd Wright, Martha Graham, Gandhi. The ad was out to sell computers by associating them with people who were "mavericks." It might also have added that all these mavericks shared one trait. None of them had ever used a computer.

If there is one quality elders should be able to claim as peculiarly theirs, it is wisdom. Yet what is the real value of wisdom if specialized knowledge monopolizes the culture and the alternative to specialized knowledge is so often regarded as holy fakery? When an industrial population needs solutions for its problems, it turns to experts. Experts have their role to play. But just as one could draw up an endless catalog of mindless follies committed by the untutored and anti-intellectual, one could also assemble a sizable collection of stupidities perpetrated by the experts and technicians whom we trust so implicitly and reward so highly. Much of the Promethean recklessness that has animated modern technology stems from an expertise that has lost touch with ordinary prudence, a know-how that does not know why.

What wisdom needs is to be liberated so that it can flood the mind and freely flow between us. That is the true task of elders; it is what the elder mind seems especially empowered to do.

## An Education for Elders

As recently as the 1960s, medical science was dominated by a piece of scientific folklore about the aging brain. It was a matter of professional dogma that the brain actually shrank with age, losing cells at an accelerating rate with the passage of years. The loss was held to be most critical in the cerebral cortex, where the "higher functions" are quartered. Experts contended that aging people lost up to one-third of their cortical neurons, and that was taken to be the cause of senility.

Later research has shown this assumption to be quite wrong. What was mistaken for neuronal loss was another phenomenon, namely, the thinning out of the dendrites. The dendrites are connectors; they receive the impulses of surrounding neurons. We might regard them as the physical basis for the rich interplay of ideas and images that makes for a lively mind. Richard Restak uses a striking figure of speech to explain the role of the dendrites. "Picture in your mind a tree in its full summer bloom, when it has the greatest number of small branches and leaves. Now imagine that same tree in winter, when the branches are denuded and starkly outlined against a slate sky. That transition looks very much like what's seen when neurons from the young are compared to neurons taken from older brains."[14]

But this thinning is not a permanent loss; it is a symptom of disuse. It can be restored by putting the mind to work. Education is the tonic that restores dynamic neuronal connectivity. The active mind replenishes the brain with an expanding network of dendrites. That is good news for the individual, but it carries social and economic implications. If the most burdensome and costly disease among the elderly is dementia — including Alzheimer's disease — then the best prescription we have is *thinking*. The more subtle and complex, the better. And quite spontaneously, that is what is happening as a form of cultural self-medication. Older students — now more and more understood to include students over sixty-five, rather than just over forty — are returning to school in numbers sufficient to shift the economic basis of higher education in the United States.[15] That is hardly surprising. Education is one of the major activities people take up in their retirement. As of the late 1990s, there were nearly 4 million elders over sixty-five enrolled in university courses, or 13 percent of the total in the age group. Everybody in higher education expects that number to rise steadily. One educator describes the rising enrollment of reentry baby boomers as a "windfall" for universities alert to the opportunity at hand. The elder hostel movement has burgeoned into a worldwide community camped at many universities. Similarly, continuing education has developed a growing stake in senior enrollments. But older students are also enrolling in standard courses, sitting in among the young to take degrees and with each passing year taking up more space in the classroom. A local campus can be an ideal place to spend retirement time. It comprises art galleries, libraries, theaters, and physical education facilities. Older students, especially those resuming their higher education, may create a new teaching ambience; they can function as aids and assistants for instructors, offering better judgment and more long-term continuity.[16]

In my teaching experience, I became aware of the growing prominence of older students as long ago as the late 1970s. The students were mainly women in their fifties and sixties, some newly divorced, some widowed, all of them beyond their child-rearing years. Many found their way to school through a local counseling facility called the Center for Displaced Homemakers. I learned that women who found themselves "displaced" thought first of all of returning to school. Their main reservation was that they were not sure they "belonged" there, and so might not be welcome. Some of my colleagues, trained to teach the standard eighteen-to-twenty-four-year-old "prime-time" audience, did resent having older students in the class. They had no idea why these people should be enrolled in a university. Most of the women had no career plans; they often did not care about finding jobs and found no meaning in grades and credits. They were notoriously noncompetitive when it came to grade point averages. All they seemed to want to do was attend and learn.

They were, in short, ideal students. They came for the love of learning. I soon came to value having them in my classes and went out of my way to draw them in. In their presence, the demands on me as a teacher became more challenging and mature. The older students were not brilliant; they were simply more experienced. They had a sense of significance about things. They asked big questions about life, death, love, purpose. They took to great literature and philosophy because they saw its value. Teaching *King Lear* or *Madame Bovary* to older and then to younger students was like teaching in two different universes. That also created pedagogical problems. As senior students grew more assertive and outspoken — mainly with my encouragement — they tended to take over the class. The younger students felt at a disadvantage in the presence of mature minds. Some withdrew into silent resentment. The trick was to keep both groups in touch and learning from one another — a skill I was never offered in my training as a university teacher.

As the years have gone by, the number of older students has increased rapidly at my university, as it has at all schools. There are now more older men, many of them retired or downsized out of their jobs. Older students have begun to entertain career plans, so they come to learn employable skills as well as arts and letters. But whatever they study, they retain their maturity. That makes teaching them a joy. It is also a groundbreaking adventure. Just as students of the baby boom decades transformed higher education by bringing an air of dissent and experimentation to the campuses, older boomers may well become the beginning of a similarly innovative spirit at the universities. We are approaching a time when the universities will have to make a generous place for the mature and the elderly. That will be where the numbers and the money can be found to rejuvenate the schools. At some schools, the older students outnumber the undergraduates, and so the campuses will have to grow up. They will become, at least in large measure, senior academies, in some respects resembling the famous Danish folk-schools of the nineteenth century.

The Fromm Institute for Lifelong Learning in San Francisco has served as the model for senior education of that kind. Established as a philanthropic endeavor in the 1970s by Hanna and Alfred Fromm on the campus of the University of San Francisco, a private Catholic school, the Institute functions as a "school for the sages," bringing together retired teachers (almost all of them university professors emeriti) and retired students ranging upward from age sixty-five. With several hundred students now enrolled, the school answers the question I'm sure many teachers have asked themselves: what would education look like if we got rid of competition, required courses, grading, exams, and credentials? Answer: a gathering of peers who come together for the love of learning. With what other student population could that be said with the same purity? Fromm teachers are invited to teach what they want to teach; the students choose freely among courses with no career objectives hanging over them. "Our students never graduate," has been one of the school's mottos. Since Fromm was founded, many universities have added a program or an adjunct senior school.[17]

There may be another front in elder education waiting to be opened: the Internet. Over one hundred web sites are maintained by SeniorNet Learning Centers in nearly every state. For shut-in elders, this presents a valued opportunity. Nicholas Negroponte of the MIT Media Lab sees online communications as a chance for the old to give as well as receive. He reminds us that "the 20 million members of the AARP constitute a collective experience that is currently untapped. Making just that enormous body of knowledge and wisdom accessible to young minds could close the generation gap with a few keystrokes."[18] He might also have mentioned that the Internet could use a strong infusion of maturity to save it from sinking further into commercial inanity.

As the boomers return to college campuses, many may come to learn job skills, fully intending to remain in the job market. Others — the middle and senior old — may come to sign up for course work that alleviates age-associated memory impairment. But it is also likely that the traditional *studium generale,* the heart of the humanities, will have a special value for mature students. The classics, the hundred great books, the art treasures of the world — all these are still the most effective way to stimulate the dendrites that keep the gray matter alive. It will be an appropriate marriage of minds. Plato and Dante, Montaigne and Spinoza, after all, never wrote to be read by sophomores. I doubt there is a teacher alive who has not more than once wondered whether it makes any sense for us to be struggling to force the "greats" — as the English call the classics — upon students whose mental energy is so tied up with thoughts about grades, careers, success, sex, marriage — all the distracting preliminaries of adulthood. The effort is well intentioned, but it betrays the work. For what does the finest undergraduate curriculum produce in young minds but, too often, the kind of brittle facility one needs to pass exams or make smart conversation?

Great minds, whatever the field — the humanities or the sciences — demand mature minds to be fully appreciated. Yet in times past those few undergraduate years between eighteen and twenty-one were the last chance educators had to teach the high culture to the next generation. So we did the best we could. But now we have another, better chance. Students are coming back to us on the other side of youthful distraction, bringing a lifetime of experience into the classroom. What a grand opportunity this is! It is our chance as educators to salvage the wisdom of elders.

# CHAPTER FIFTEEN

## RITES OF PASSAGE

L eo Tolstoy's *Death of Ivan Ilyich* may be the greatest short story ever written. It has certainly proved to be the most powerful reading experience I have known, a work of literature that captures the pulse-beat of life more convincingly than one would believe possible for words on a page. Whenever I assign it to my students, I give them careful instructions. They are to read the story at one sitting, with no interruptions. They are to read every word, slowly, skipping nothing, pausing along the way to let each section of the tale sink in. And when they are finished, they are to sit quietly, imagining that Ivan's story is their story. Certainly nobody who ever lived to tell about it has done a more persuasive job of presenting the experience of death than Tolstoy achieved in this work. The final moments of Ivan's life leave you convinced that Tolstoy has been through the ordeal and come back to tell about it.

While the assignment is frequently lost upon younger students, who tell me they find the story demanding or morbid, its impact upon more mature students has invariably been enormous. They have no trouble seeing themselves as Ivan and learning from his experience.

If I could, I would at this point make that same assignment to those of you who are beginning this chapter. Find the story. Read it. Instead, I will offer a brief, and of course inadequate summary.

Tolstoy's Ivan is a minor government functionary in czarist Russia, one of thousands of "superfluous men" of that era. As remote as that period in Russian history may seem in every other respect, Tolstoy brilliantly develops Ivan as a modern Everyman, one who has spent his life building a tidy career of little more than personal importance, seeking to make himself moderately successful in one of his society's many bureaucratic niches.

He is the essence of ordinary, a man who has never taken life to be more than routine, one who has carefully isolated himself from strong experience. One day, while hanging drapes in his home, he injures himself. The injury grows worse. A doctor is called. The doctor discovers that there is a serious condition, which is never clearly defined in the story. It is, in fact, death approaching. That is all that matters. The doctors cannot heal what ails Ivan; he becomes sicker and finally realizes he is doomed, though nobody will confirm his fears. The story traces his last days, hours, minutes of bewilderment, anger, self-pity, and finally resignation. The moment of his death becomes the only moment he has truly *lived*. The story builds until we reach that terrifying moment; it leaps from the page and takes you by the shoulders and shakes you. "Wake up!" it says. *"This man is you."*

## The Far Side of the Ordeal

As a teacher, I have valued Tolstoy's story over the years because it uses death so powerfully to teach the magnificence of life. Yet as universal as Ivan's experience is, the very fact that his plight deals with illness and doctors and patients now limits it to a certain historical period. A century later, the tale may need to be rewritten to capture the defining life-and-death experience of our time. What we need in order to make the story relevant to our era is a "death" that does not happen — not yet. We need the story of an Ivan who comes just that close to dying — but then *survives*. Death pauses; it waits, longer for us than for any previous generation. That is becoming more and more the special experience of our time. By the thousands people now undergo medical miracles that rescue them from diseases and disabilities that would have killed them a generation ago. They pass through the shadow — and are then sent back into the world to start their lives again. As one member of a cardiac support group described his experience, "It was as if the angel of death drove by my house and waved. 'I'm busy now,' he said, 'but I have your address. I'll be back.'" That experience is becoming as commonplace as marriage or divorce, a routine part of the modern world.

Today Ivan Ilyich would be likely to confront a greater trial. *Life.* He would return to take up his career, his family life, his ambitions. But how would life look to someone who has been on such close terms with death? What would it then mean to "wake up"? Tolstoy would have to deal with an Ivan who might not be willing to continue being a bureaucratic zombie, but who insisted on making his life *mean* something.

We have learned to recognize these great revelatory moments that punctuate the course of life as rites of passage, moments that shake people out of their accustomed routine and elevate them to a new level of existence. In traditional societies, these rites are highly structured occasions that usher people into a new phase of existence: from childhood to adolescence, from adolescence into maturity, from maturity into old age, and finally from old age into death. In this respect more than any other, primary people have proven themselves wiser than us: They take the course of life seriously, seeing it as an educational progression. Where rites of passage fade from the cultural repertory, as they have in the modern Western world, maturing into a true elder becomes all the more difficult.

In many rites of passage, episodes of great fear are designed to capture the full sense of crisis that faces us at the main turning points in life. Sometimes death is mimicked, as if one were dying to one's old self and being reborn into new life. Young boys in some tribal societies are put through the moment of their own death and taken into the terrors of the underworld — and then ushered back. Outside of religious communities, we have few rites of passage that retain the dignity and depth of these traditional practices. To that degree, we have cheapened the quality of life. Perhaps that has something to do with the cult of youth. We cling to youthfulness with no desire to move on, even though the effort to hold back is futile.

But now a new kind of rite of passage is upon us. It is highly structured and involves the threat of death, even to the point of literally, physically endangering our lives. It is not make-believe. Like the rites of the past, this one too calls upon expert practitioners, high priests of a sort, to guide us through to the far side of the ordeal. And when we emerge, we are in a different stage of life. The rite is medical crisis. It usually happens in a hospital, perhaps an emergency room, at the hands of doctors. What happens all around in this strange ambience — the blood tests, the X-rays, the CAT scans, the medications — can be almost ceremonial in its solemnity and precision. Often the procedures hurt: One is jabbed, cut, shaved, scrubbed, made nauseated. They can certainly frighten. Being inside a CAT scan is a nerve-wracking experience of mystification. Episodes like this can jar, rend, batter ... but they may have no spiritual meaning, at least not yet. It is simply a close call.

That is how I recall thinking about the medical crisis I once passed through. When, after emergency surgery that came close to costing me my life, I returned to my senses, I woke feeling as if I had hit rock-bottom: feeble, dazed, unable to eat or drink or move. I learned I had lain in the intensive care unit hallucinating for hours at a stretch. My body felt shattered to pieces — as I have heard shamanic apprentices feel after they have been through one of their vision quests. But for them the experience is one of transcendence. For me it was nothing but numbness and confusion. I wanted desperately to take hold of a friendly hand as if that would keep me in one piece. Slowly, I came to realize I had been through a close call.

A phrase came to mind: I had *dodged a bullet*. But I knew I had been through far more than that. Or at least I felt I *should* make something more of it than a lucky break. I *wanted* this to count for more. But it was up to me to supply everything the hospital and doctor could not. I almost felt cheated. After suffering all this, I should have become wiser. My life should have been turned around. But I saw no way that was going to happen. The doctors came to check me out; nurses came to take my vital signs. I was in the hands of caring experts; I was grateful. But nobody came to minister to my soul.

With the best intentions, medical professionals often take it to be their duty to return those they have saved to their "normal" life — that is, to the routine they had before. In their view, medical crisis is a bad patch in the road; the sooner you get over it and put it behind you, the better. Their goal is to make us as good as new. If patients can resume their job and their family responsibilities, that is ideal. It is as if the upshot of the exercise is to gloss over the terror and anguish of the crisis. Nothing could be further from the purpose of a rite of passage: to stand as a landmark along the way. In some tribal societies, the body is marked during the rite; blood is taken, a scar is left, a part cut away, to serve as a reminder. Our medical rites of passage often seek to eliminate any reminder of that kind. If possible, the body is left whole and unmarked, or perhaps repaired by cosmetic surgery later on. In my case, it was not. The scar, an ugly one, remains as a chapter in my life etched upon my flesh.

Yet seen from another angle, the medical crisis has features that could be of the highest therapeutic value if used in the right way. It is above all a deviation from all normal routines that is sanctioned by an air of emergency. Work and family responsibilities are postponed; bills wait to be paid;

appointments are canceled. Bedridden and largely incapacitated, patients are left with a great deal of time on their hands to think. If they are given nothing better to do, they while away the time watching television. But that need not be the way the occasion is used. It is, after all, a situation where social conventions are put on hold as if to clear a space. One's food is prescribed, like it or not; everybody under care dons the same ridiculously awkward and revealing gowns; nurses, who will take no nonsense, appear with bedpans, esoteric equipment, and medications at all hours of the day and night. They expect their patients to do as they are told, to eat what they are served, to undress and be washed with no great show of modesty. Of course it is an ordeal; one comes to deplore it. And the healthier one becomes, the more agonizing it all is. But this is exactly what many rites of passage are designed to be: a suspension of the ordinary, a time of tribulation when one's fate is entrusted to the judgment of others who know what is best.

In the years ahead, more and more of us are going to be leaving hospitals after a brush with death that subjects us to a crisis like this. We will have a story to tell; but if all it comes down to is the excitement of a hair's-breadth escape, the story will soon wear thin. My experience led to an odd result. Though I am a writer and teacher somewhat skilled in words, I discovered with some embarrassment that there was not much I had to say — at least nothing that sounded earthshaking. One cannot expect others to make much of phrases like "glad to be alive"; they do no justice to the event. Yet that was what I felt. That was all I felt. For me, it was a discovery that yearned for expression. Perhaps this is what religious people find at church testimonials: the chance to stand up and say what everybody has heard a hundred times. "Praise the Lord! I am saved." The words are a formula; one utters them knowing that everybody present will be able to fill in the full feeling behind them.

The modern world provides some techniques for articulating ineffable moments in life. Support groups were created for that purpose. As a self-help, therapeutic invention, the support group dates back to the creation of Alcoholics Anonymous in the 1930s, a movement based on local associations of people who shared the suffering of a common condition. Those who gather at AA meetings do not come expecting to hear eloquent declarations. They listen for the emotional subtext from which they judge the authenticity of what is said. A perceptive therapist might see the possibility of using the medical crisis in somewhat the same way, as an occasion for building the kind of camaraderie that keeps the experience alive.

In the longevous society, we will need therapists who know the value of deepening the medical rite of passage. They will want to work with that moment, not as a trauma to be talked away but as the beginning of a quest. Very little current therapy has that skill or intention. Most therapists, after all, take their degrees in "marriage, family, and childhood," relationships that belong to early and midlife. Death transcends those relationships; it reaches out for the solitude that lies beyond society. What may be more appropriate than therapy is a heavy application of philosophy. The medical rite of passage cries out for the sort of "support" that only great minds and great hearts can offer.

## Near Death ... Or Near Enough

The publication in 1970 of Elisabeth Kübler-Ross's *On Death and Dying* struck an important new note in medical science. The book opened for frank discussion what had been among the most unmentionable of subjects. Initially, Kübler-Ross's interest was limited to the medical care of the dying. What she had to say on this score was of great importance. She was able to document the fact that medical people and hospitals were seriously insensitive to the special needs of the dying. Doctors in particular posed a problem. They rarely got around to the task of comforting those they could no longer help; they knew no way to prepare their patients for death. So they tended to write off the terminally ill as a black mark on their record.

Kübler-Ross, who had worked among the casualties of the Nazi death camps, suggested a simple but brilliant idea: Treat death as you would any well-defined stage of life — the final stage. Examine how people face their mortality and work with that. She was able to identify a pattern in the emotional life of the dying that presented distinct phases: denial, anger, bargaining, depression, and acceptance. Each requires special handling and above all patience. If dying people are allowed, or better still helped, to move through these phases, their death becomes more bearable, even welcome. Along the way, they might require painkillers like morphine, perhaps in heavy doses. Give them, Kübler-Ross recommended. Because their needs are special, it might even be a good idea to move the dying to a hospice where people skilled in their treatment can give them the attention they need.

The seminars Kübler-Ross offers on these techniques have helped transform our thinking about death. There was always a subtext to her work. She believes our treatment of the terminally ill is of great benefit to the live and healthy who are nowhere near dying. Simply knowing that such care exists can make everybody's life more secure. Soon after the publication of her book, workshops on "The Art of Dying" were being offered as adult education courses. A new field of inquiry opened at universities: thanatology; and entirely new medical protocol was being invented from scratch.

At a certain point, however, Kübler-Ross's work began to take on mystical and occult overtones that strayed from professional respectability. Some of her patients described what they had been through on the brink of dying as an out-of-the-body sensation. Strange beings might appear to them, or colored lights. On the basis of her research with the terminally ill, Kübler-Ross portrayed the experience of dying as an altered state of consciousness. In later writing, she endorsed these more sensational ideas about death, even claiming to have had out-of-the-body experiences of her own and contact with a spirit guide. On the basis of her patients' experience, she professed to have proven the reality of life after death and the validity of reincarnation. When she began working with California channelers in the late 1970s, she lost a great deal of her credibility among doctors — who did not, it should be noted, even try to find a professionally acceptable equivalent for her techniques.

But by then death had gone from the status of a distasteful subject to a sort of craze, especially along the New Age fringe. The counter culture of the 1960s may have been a youth movement, but oddly enough the discussion of death and dying became one of the great topics of that period, and especially among the young. Writing in the English journal *Encounter* in 1970, Melvin Maddocks mordantly asked, "Has death become the supreme authenticator for a generation that craves more than anything to be authentic?" In a period when young people were hunting for exotic forms of experience, anything that sounded even remotely psychedelic was sought out. The field of inquiry rapidly grew into a sensational fad. Movies on the subject (for example, *Resurrection, Ghost, Sixth Sense*) have invariably proved to be good box office.

Later still in her career, after she had suffered a debilitating stroke and was sadly incapacitated, Kübler-Ross repudiated many of these extreme claims and became quite bitter. She felt convinced that medical science was falling far short of her expectations for dealing with death. Her own hospital experience had been miserable.

If some of her more aberrant beliefs have discredited her in the medical establishment, that is an overreaction. Her research and her methods for dealing with the dying have much to offer. Frankness on the subject is to be welcomed. But in one respect, her fascination with dying cheapened the experience she set out to reclaim. Whatever her intention, the more mystical turn her thinking took in the 1970s was a move in the wrong direction. Not all near-death experiences are accompanied by exotic visions, dazzling lights, and communications from beyond. It is wrong to arouse such expectations. Being near death may bring pain and insecurity and finally the sense of a life that has been left unraveled. For many what remains of their medical crisis is a vivid sense of mortality. That is all there is. One awakens thinking *I nearly died ... I might not have come back ... this moment might never have occurred.*

Devaluing that simple but jolting insight — just that and nothing more — leads to an unfortunate result. It discourages people from making all they can of the near-death experience that most of us are apt to go through. Every heart patient who has been put on a heart-lung machine during surgery has been closer to death than any shaman ever was. There may be no psychedelic light show, but there is much to ponder when one returns from the anesthetic depths. One has brushed against one's own mortality. This is not an extravagant or euphoric high; it is simply what one knows as a fact. Yet that fact can be the occasion for philosophical reflection.

## *ARS MORIENDI:* THE ART OF DYING

In the ancient world, every religious tradition offered a body of wisdom whose purpose, if time and circumstance allowed, was to encourage the contemplation of mortality before death was suddenly at hand. The advice was collected into "books of the dead" that summoned up courage, counseled serenity, and often graphically described what the dead would experience beyond the grave. Modern nonbelievers like to think that religion is an emotional crutch for the weak and fearful. But the books of the dead are not always comforting; there might be terrors and testings in the afterlife as well as consolations. In the Western world, most books of the dead date from the time of the Black Plague in the later Middle Ages, when death was an object of constant fear. In that age of the *danse macabre*, entire villages were wiped out. With death waiting in ambush around every corner, tracts were written to meet the needs of the time. They were called *ars moriendi* - studies in the art of dying. Their central teaching was that "in the midst of life we are in death."

Much of this literature was morbid in the extreme. Its strategy was to prepare people, young and old, rich and poor, beautiful and ugly, for death by teaching disgust and contempt for the corruptible flesh and the pursuits of this world. Many came to believe life was not worth living. Once again, the strategy was not always meant to subdue fear with false hope. Most *ars moriendi* tracts, as was only realistic at the time, held out no promise of recovery or of easy salvation beyond death. Downplaying the threat of death is a distinctly modern deception, using the scientific mystique of the doctor to mislead. As one student of the subject observes,

> The approach to the dying ... was thus diametrically opposed to the practices that until recently dominated modern western medicine. In hospitals, it used to be a common practice for the attending physicians and other medical personnel to use all possible means to conceal from the patients the diagnosis and prognosis of serious diseases and to join with the relatives in elaborate games to obscure the reality of the situation.[1]

In the classic books of the dead, supernatural figures identified as psychopomps, leaders of dead souls, mercifully waited for the dying individual like guides at the border of a new land. The god Hermes was among these, the deity of twilight, of wind, and of travelers. The attributes are all spiritual symbols: wind for the spirit, twilight for death, travel for the road of life. In another of his attributes, as the god of thought, Hermes represented the transcendent quality of mind, that which outlives the perishing body. In traditional cultures, there were also human guides who claimed the powers of the psychopomp. These were the shamans, advisers whose authority was derived from the experience of having symbolically died and returned to the body. The shaman was one who had wandered in other worlds, above the Earth or below, scouting out the perils and pitfalls. When the shaman sought to heal the sick, it was with the intense awareness that a cure might not be found; then it was the shaman's job to escort the soul forward.

The healing part of the shaman's calling has been taken over by physicians who, as specialists, may know little about their patients' whole anatomy. As for the soul ... that is for psychologists to deal with. But few therapists have studied the art of dying. Many confine themselves to childhood traumas and troubled marriages, sexual dysfunction and career pressures. Those who hire them for their services are still in the midst of life, struggling and scuffling, taking their jobs and marriages very seriously. They would not gladly pay to be told there are matters of greater concern even than love or money. I suspect they come to therapy to have their worries validated. Therapy continues, but the calling of the psychopomp has been forgotten. Yet that is the figure our new medical rites of passage call out for, one who is ready to guide toward death, but also back into life, one who knows the spiritual value of crisis.

## THE POLITICS OF HEALING

Healing has not always been practiced as a form of science. For that matter, it has not always had that much to do with medicine understood as mending the body or dispensing pharmaceutical concoctions. The legendary medicine man of tribal lore was more a priest than a doctor. "Medicine," as Native Americans understood the word, was a global capacity that might include making rain, exerting personal power, hexing one's enemies, invoking the fertility gods, having great visions, as well as healing the sick and consoling the dying.

When it comes to counseling the dying, it is enough of a problem that modern medicine restricts itself to the limits of science. It is even more of a problem that the science of medicine has been overtaken by the *business* of medicine. Science makes knowledge important; business makes money important. Where, in this mix, does the task of the psychopomp fit in? It is not a service one can sensibly bill for by the quarter-hour. What HMO would be willing to pay for a service called *ars moriendi?* All this may have to change in the years ahead as doctors and medical counselors find themselves meeting a new public, one that has outlived (though not necessarily solved) the dilemmas of youth and midlife.

Imagine a different paradigm borrowed from an earlier era. Once the most learned physicians in the Western world were monks. The monasteries were the best hospitals one could find. Often all the monks could do was comfort rather than cure, though comfort is hardly to be underestimated as a healing quality. Healing was then practiced by men — and sometimes by nuns too — who were spiritually trained, people who could prescribe for the soul as well as the body. They were contemplatives rather than men of a worldly calling. Can we imagine something like this re-emerging in our time: medicine practiced as a spiritual discipline within the setting of an intentional community of men and women who see their work as a vocation?

That hope may seem outlandish as long as the vision we have of modern medicine is that of television dramas like *ER* or *Chicago Hope*. But medicine was once so pursued; the monks even carried on a kind of research, exploring the medicinal powers of herbs. If something of that spirit could be reinvented in our time, many of the financial issues surrounding medicine would be far less urgent. Physicians would not need to evaluate themselves by the money they make. And from such a stance, they might be better positioned to challenge the obscene profiteering of the health care industry. Vocational healers could be fully trained in their science; they surely would not need to be ascetics or mendicants, but neither would they be entrepreneurs. The honor due them would not depend upon their earnings, but upon their role as true therapeuts, healers of the body and soul.

As strange as this must sound, I can imagine medical practice attracting a new kind of caregiving talent, the same sort of talent that volunteers for the Peace Corps or rescue work in troubled places around the world. There are those highly motivated to provide service like this; many are already toiling in clinics and emergency rooms, under the pressure of marketplace medicine. Others are on the job now as medical missionaries and relief workers where famine, plague, and war have struck. These are the people whom television reporters seek out when they cover great disasters in distant places. They may be interviewed anonymously; we have no idea who they are or how they came to be where they are. As often as not, they are Americans. We can be sure of only one thing. They are not taking these risks and making these sacrifices for money. They are skilled and caring people and they do more to hold our world together than politicians or financiers.

Marc Freedman, in his study of nonretired retirees, gives special and hopeful attention to health-care volunteers now running affordable clinics for low-income families. These efforts — he gives special attention to Volunteers in Medicine headquartered in South Carolina and Good Samaritans in San Mateo, California — stem from the initiative of doctors and nurses over the retirement age whose skill and vitality have not been diminished by age. He believes there are many more medical volunteers to be found among the 140,000 retired physicians in the United States.[2]

What if we provided people like this with the support and opportunity they need to band together in medical orders, keeping a common house, maintaining a nursing home and hospice, offering the medicine appropriate to the living and dying needs of a growing senior population? We might be creating a new cultural category: compassionate heroism.

The training of vocational healers would be rich in the *ars moriendi*. It would include the ability to stand by the terminally ill as a psychopomp, or to draw upon those who have that special sensitivity, whether they are medically trained or not. In Tolstoy's story, Ivan Ilyich's psychopomp turns out to be an unlikely choice: It is the peasant lad Gerasim who waits patiently at the bedside to do what little he can to comfort the dying man. "We must all die," the lad replies when Ivan apologizes for putting him to so much trouble. Gerasim's simple compassion and candor are Ivan's first glimpse of the truth he must accept. There are centers and communities that have formed already around the needs of the dying where the talents of a Gerasim could be of great value. What we still lack are ways to deal with the near-death crisis that does not kill but leaves us shaken to our foundations and in search of a new beginning that may stretch out across the years.

There are at least a few people exploring that frontier. One of them, Rachel Remen, both medical doctor and therapist, works from the premise that the negative aspects of crisis, the pain, the anxiety, even the desperation, can be precisely the most effective means of deep transformation. She is the healer who helped bring me through the medical crisis that was my rite of passage. "In avoiding all pain and seeking comfort at all costs," she writes, "we may be left without mercy and compassion. In rejecting change and risk, we often cheat ourselves of the quest. In denying suffering, we may never know our strength and our greatness."[3]

Currently, Remen is teaching "The Healer's Art" at the University of California Medical Center in San Francisco. She describes the course as "an experiential and didactic curriculum in relationship-centered care which presents the human and sacred dimensions of both the physician and the patient." "What we tell the students," she says, "is that who they are is as important as what they know, and that what they are bringing with them to medicine is as central to their physicianhood as anything they will learn in med school." The course has led to a new Center for Integrative Medicine on the campus that will add wholistic and humanistic values to the standard curriculum. That is a welcome sign of maturity in health care, though not one that will easily be assimilated into the prevailing system of managed care, where the economic bottom line is rapidly becoming the top line, cruelly restricting the time physicians can spend with their patients as well as the trust that patients can place in their doctors.

I have argued that longevity leads to wisdom. But even so, wisdom needs to be midwifed and given the courage to speak what it knows. For many, the decisive point in getting beyond the follies of senior life may lie in making skillful use of the medical crisis. But if that crisis is to function as an authentic rite of passage, it requires structure and guidance, a good professional ear for the telling nuance, an ability to work with and through fear. Counseling of this kind should not be a casual aspect of medicine left to some informal, catch-as-catch-can procedure. It should be respected as an integral aspect of medicine, not only as part of geriatric care or the management of terminal illness, but as a way to bring people back from the brink of death with a sense of life-enhancing insight.

In one of the few contemporary efforts to re-create the *ars moriendi*, the pastoral counselor Robert Neale devised a number of exercises for dealing directly with the anxieties that surround death, especially for the old. Writing in the early 1970s, Neale felt that death had become almost "pornographic" with respect to the secrecy and shame that surround it. His conclusion was that "death is an ultimate mystery. Such a mystery makes an excellent screen on which to project all our concerns about life. The fear of death is a projection of our most basic fear. Our fear of death is really our fear of life."[4]

In effect, Neale discovered that death, the silent presence, elicits the ultimate psychological transference. Skillfully presented, it is the ideal blank screen that every therapist seeks to become for the client. Before this dark witness, one's entire life comes under examination. The anxieties that Neale found to be most domineering in many of his clients are instructive. There was, for example, the fear of "incompleteness and failure." People feared they had not measured up to the demands of life and saw death as "a forced retirement." If we are tied to values like that until the end of our days, we will always see age and death as evils.

It may seem odd to put it this way, but the compassionate use of medical crisis as a rite of passage might be a politically significant act of the highest order. Searched to its full philosophical depth, the near-death experience has enormous transformative power. Unless people are aggressively encouraged to forget what they have been through, it is difficult to imagine that many would return from that existential ordeal without caring more about the simple pleasures of life and about one another. As folklore teaches us, "death levels all ranks." It "lays the shepherd's crook beside the scepter."

Only the very young are apt to emerge unchanged from a scrape with death, simply because life, with its insistent demands for performance and achievement, closes in so rapidly after the crisis. But where that does not happen, there is the possibility of wisdom, that deeper dimension of knowledge born of suffering and self-examination. My conviction is that those to whom this rite of passage does bring wisdom will find it impossible to take acquisitive habits and egotistical values as seriously as they might once have done. Competition and selfish interest will mean less and money will be seen for the sad illusion it is.

I cannot say exactly what sort of politics might follow from the careful instructional use of the medical crisis; it would very likely be a politics that transcends the categories of conservative or liberal or radical, none of which were created to delve into the eternal questions. Ideology is ephemeral, a matter of issues and arguments. Underlying all the issues is the tone in which we address life and one another. To know that we are all mortal as powerfully as Ivan Ilyich came to know it, to understand that all have experienced heartbreaking loss, is to know ourselves as Everyman. "Winning" matters most when contenders have little time to take stock before the game is over. So politics has always been a matter of choosing sides in the fury of the passing moment. But with a bit more time on their hands, the boomers have the chance to find the common humanity that all sides share.

## CHAPTER SIXTEEN

---

## THE SURVIVAL OF THE GENTLEST

Recently, out of curiosity, I visited a local video arcade. What I saw as I walked through brought many of the themes of this book into sharp focus.

I was, as I expected, a stranger in the place. The arcade was filled exclusively with boys in their early and mid-teens, all of them fiercely concentrated on the games before them. I stopped at the machine that had drawn the largest gathering. Its title *Killer Instinct* flashed above the screen in crimson lights. While one boy played, the others, intent as a young war party, looked on, totally absorbed in the animated mayhem before their eyes. Along with a complete martial arts repertory (jump, jab, kick, duck, punch), the game featured an armory of gruesome weaponry: sabers, grenade guns, rockets. Video games give no quarter. With a flick of the trigger, a player can slice off a head, disembowel a rival, knock down a building, blow up a city. The results register on the screen with maximum gore and screeching explosions.

Philosophy gets taught in many ways, and never more effectively than when it comes disguised as mere entertainment. The boys, so earnestly at play, were surely not aware of the cultural genealogy behind the games that held them mesmerized. *Killer Instinct* might just as well be called *Survival of the Fittest*. That was the theme behind the electronic violence in this arcade; all the games were adolescent exercises in social Darwinism, that harsh philosophy of life that dominated our society through the early centuries of industrialization. Here was the heritage of Darwinian natural selection being played out among the young as shoot-outs, street-fights, hand-to-hand combat. A battle to the death with no holds barred, and may the best man win. One must say "man," because this is exclusively masculine terrain, no women in sight. Some games include a female martial artist, but she — a bosomy, bikini-clad caricature — is hardly there to enlist female interest.

As I watched this garish contemporary pastime, I wondered: Do these games not reveal how childish this philosophy has always been? *Little boy* childish. How good it would be if these electronic simulations were the last, sad remnant of social Darwinism in our culture, a marginal adolescent amusement that boys would soon outgrow as they became men.

## THE STRANGE PERSISTENCE OF RUGGED INDIVIDUALISM

But that is not what has happened. Social Darwinism, with its infatuation for ruggedly competitive individualism, has seen a recrudescence. At the 1984 Democratic convention, then-governor of New York Mario Cuomo used his keynote address to warn the nation about this unexpected twist of fate. The survival of the fittest was back in force in our national policy. The Reagan administration, so Cuomo contended, believed that "the wagon train will not make it to the frontier unless some of our old, some of our young, some of our weak are left behind by the side of the trail. The strong will inherit the land!"

The reasons for the reemergence of social Darwinism are many, not least of which is the timidity of an American liberalism that continues to stray from its rich historical roots in populist and progressive tradition. This failure of the liberal center has allowed conservative opportunists to target all the most humane social programs of the past century for destruction. The boomers bear a heavy responsibility for this turn of events. The major thrust behind the contemporary conservative backlash is distrust of government. In a painfully ironic sense, the protest movement of the 1960s is the source of that backlash and has played into corporate hands. It taught America how easily power corrupts a nation's leaders. Accusations of high crimes on the part of ruling elites that once had to be screamed in the streets to an incredulous public finally proved to be true — and continue to be documented as the CIA and FBI release more secret documents each passing year.

But by a devilishly clever editing of that lesson, conservative elements have focused the public's wrath exclusively on government, leaving the expanding corporate establishment all but invisible to criticism — as if it were not also a form of "government," a private, usually secret government whose activities are literally and legally "nobody's business" but its own. Like the feudal barons of the Middle Ages, the great corporations rule fiefdoms of enormous wealth, some now worldwide in their outreach. In the 1960s and 1970s, when protesters attacked the "power structure," it was hardly welfare mothers, the post office, or the National Park Service they had in mind, less still the efforts of the Justice Department and the federal courts to defend civil rights. And yet the lesson that has endured is big government, no! Big business, yes!

This opportunistic attack on the federal government often advertises itself as "populism." But if this is populism, it has nothing to do with the great battle cries of its historical namesake: "Soak the rich" and "Share the wealth." Nineteenth century populism, the protest of brave, impoverished farmers, was clear about the great issue: "the people versus the interests." And no interest was more virulent than "the money power." Today one may still be able to arouse anger in people, but hardly the political acumen that once gave that anger a sensible moral target. Instead, animosity is deflected away from the global corporate heights and *downward* — against the disempowered: welfare mothers, immigrants, gays. It becomes scapegoating, and at last that scapegoating has reached the nation's seniors, now seen as parasitic dependents who will be our fiscal ruin.

Not since the 1920s has Darwinian competitive toughness run so rampant in the land or commanded so much public admiration. In a 1997 PBS documentary dealing with the stock market, the central figure was a mutual fund manager, a celebrity financier who had at the time run up a moneymaking record of astounding proportions. His every word and appearance were being carefully tracked by thousands of admiring investors. Watching him on the job, I was struck by how much he resembled the boys playing *Killer Instinct*. He too was computer-obsessed. Like a lion in a cage, he paced the floor between desks crowded with video terminals. He wore a telephone headset that put him in touch with New York, London, Tokyo. As calls came in, he flashed a look at the screens and snapped decisions. "Buy, sell, buy, sell! Five thousand, a hundred thousand, sell at fifty, buy at one hundred," he barked, peppering his words with aggressive invectives. "Wipe 'em out! Ka-bam! Nuke that! Rat-a-tat-tat!" He too was jabbing and ducking and punching. He had become a financial street-fighter, a Dow Jones warrior, one of the fit who had earned his survival. And what was the proof of his fitness? Money. Nothing but money.

## Darwin, Farewell

As a moral concept, the survival of the fittest has a curious history. Many people assume the phrase was coined by Charles Darwin to explain his theory of evolution. Darwin used the words, but he did not invent them. In a late edition of his *On the Origin of Species*, he reached outside the field of biology to borrow the phrase from the then-prominent social philosopher Herbert Spencer. Spencer, who had politics on his mind, not biology, patterned his ideal of fitness on the dog-eat-dog competition of the industrial marketplace. He saw the world as a jungle where the strong devour the weak.

Spencer was a mediocre thinker, hardly Darwin's equal. But Darwin did borrow that one memorable phrase from him, and that gave Spencer a prominence he never deserved. In effect, the survival of the fittest was a hoodlum idea that managed to stow away on an intellectual luxury liner disguised as reputable science.

No real jungle was ever as brutish as the early industrial cities of the modern world. No beast of prey was ever so voracious as the early industrial entrepreneurs were for money and power. But that made no difference to Spencer. In his view, it was a law of nature that the strong should prevail and the weak sink into poverty. He went further. The poor, being unfit, had to be eliminated. *Literally* eliminated. "The whole effort of nature," Spencer believed, "is to get rid of such, to clear the world of them, and make room for better." On these grounds, Spencer opposed not only private charity but public sanitation, public education, public housing, pure food and drug regulation. If his society had offered entitlements, he would have advocated ending them, the better to sweep away elderly parasites. Were he still with us today, Spencer would surely be taking sides with those who are laboring to end Medicare and insisting that it is the duty of the old to die as soon as possible if they cannot pay their own bills.

By associating his theory with Herbert Spencer's politics, Darwin attracted a public he might not otherwise have reached. The business community at once latched onto his theory and turned it into the ideology called social Darwinism. The great captains of industry fancied themselves to be the "fittest" — and thus deserving of all the money they could lay their hands on. Darwin had given them a way to justify their brutality and avarice. Nineteenth-century America, the historian Richard Hofstadter comments, "was like a vast human caricature of the Darwinian struggle for existence and survival of the fittest. Successful business entrepreneurs apparently accepted almost by instinct the Darwinian terminology which seemed to portray the conditions of their existence."[1]

With the advent of the welfare state and other more humane forms of social policy in the twentieth century, one might have expected social Darwinism to pass from the scene as the self-serving social ethic of the wealthy few. The Great Depression, a monumental failure of the free market, made such capitalist bravado ring hollow. More discreditable still, there was the association between social Darwinism and Nazism. Along certain lines, Darwinism has always lent itself to brutally racist and sexist interpretations, a morality of male supremacy and the master race. No political movement has ever been as biologically based as the fascism that gave us death camps and final solutions for supposedly inferior millions. All this is the dark side of the folklore of fitness, the cult of competition.

And yet, with the collapse of Soviet power in Europe in the 1980s, those who speak for market economics, especially in the United States, have been quick to claim victory in the cold war. And to the victor belong the spoils, including the philosophical spoils. From Eastern Europe to China, national economies, including those that were committed to socialism only a decade before, are turning to ruthless corporate and political elites, those who claim to know the secret of rapid development.

The global economy, so filled with the opportunity for quick riches, has given social Darwinism a temporary new lease on life. It has placed a premium on toughness, avarice, and rapacity. Around the world, "development" has come to mean the recrudescence of sweatshops and wage slavery, the same evils that were the blight of early industrial America. Sometimes we are told bluntly by corporate leaders that profiteering and selfishness are good, that only hard-charging entrepreneurs deserve to prosper and the rest must hustle or suffer. Welfare "as we know it" must end; entitlements must be terminated; security is a thing of the past. More euphemistic versions of the survival of the fittest appeal to "self-reliance," "competitiveness," and "personal responsibility." It all comes down to the same remorseless creed: the world and its wealth belong to the strong, and the devil take the hindmost. Ironically, just as the world industrial economy has grown affluent enough to provide a decent standard of life for all, we are hearing the war cry of rugged individualism again.

In a world dominated by entrepreneurial zealots, one might despair of expecting an appeal for gentler values to be heard. Nevertheless, the industrial societies of the world will be forced to leave the Darwinian jungle, if not as a matter of abstract philosophical preference then as a matter of objective demographic necessity. The Darwinian struggle for existence simply has no place in a maturing world. The need for kindness and cooperation is built into the very bones and sinews of a senior population. As societies mature, hard competition ceases to be a viable choice in life. The old are no audience for philosophies of toughness.

To some — the alpha males who still sweat to build their fortunes bigger — that will seem a loss, but many of us have been praying for the day, including the wisest economists, for whom the central issue has been not the production but the use and distribution of wealth. A generation before the baby boom, in the depths of the Great Depression, John Maynard Keynes, the premier economist of the twentieth century, allowed himself to envision some highly utopian vistas on the far side of the economic crisis. His words lead us to that critical line where the abstractions of the marketplace end and the life of the soul begins.

> When the accumulation of wealth is no longer of high social
> importance, there will be great changes in the code of morals. We
> shall be able to rid ourselves of many of the pseudo-moral principles
> which have hag-ridden us for two hundred years, by which we have
> exalted some of the most distasteful of human qualities into the
> position of the highest values. ... All kinds of social customs and
> economic practices affecting the distribution of wealth and its
> rewards and penalties which we now maintain at all costs, however
> distasteful and unjust they may be in themselves ... we shall then be
> free, at last, to discard.[2]

The great changes that Keynes presaged now lie before us. All we need do is awaken to the true magnitude of our industrial affluence in order to make those changes real. A "new code of morals" is already in the making among us as we explore the deeper ethical dimensions of longevity.

The old need help. They must be free to say they need help. Ethically speaking, it is hitting below the belt to make that appeal seem weak or unworthy and it is a lie to say it is unaffordable. What neither we nor the living planet can afford is the fiercely rapacious vision of life that has for so long driven industrial civilization. Demographics and the logic of progress are against it. Our marvelously productive industrial economy has for far too long been entrusted to the control of men who are still no more than tall children — overly rich, overly pampered, twelve-year-old boys playing with the lives of whole societies and the resources of the Earth as if these were mere counters in a great global video game. The heated imperatives that we are all expected to obey — "We must remain competitive!" "We must keep the economy growing!" "We must increase our market share!" — are no more than the arbitrary rules of that game. It is time for our fate to be taken into the hands of adults.

In the era of the longevity revolution, the "fittest" are the gentlest, those who touch the lives of others with kindness and strive to strengthen our sense of community. Whether they know it or not, boomers who survive long enough to join the next senior generation are voting with every breath they take for a compassionate social order.

## SECOND CHILDHOOD

In the hands of conservative economists, Darwinian biology might almost be seen as an attempt to talk people out of their own common sense and experience. Market economics makes self-reliance a matter of life-and-death importance, as if there were no question but that all of us are committed from birth to a war of each against all. But in fact we are born into total dependency and remain dependent through the first several years of life. Our need of others is the most formative experience in our lives; and indeed, modern civilization lengthens that period of dependency. The whole thrust of the industrial period has been to extend the semidependency of children through adolescence into the college years. What do we mean by the phrase "disadvantaged" but that someone has sadly lacked the care and support to be prepared for a successful career?

Independence is a status we are introduced to in measured steps. As we grow out of childhood, we take on more responsibility for ourselves, but the process is gradual as if to keep us aware of the debt we owe to others. Then, at some point in early adulthood, most of us assume responsibility for the lives of our children, once again binding ourselves to the needs of others by ties of love and conscience. In the course of a lifetime, the amount of time in which we can pretend that we are free, competitive agents looking out for number one is limited to a brief period of years during our youth and midlife. But even then, though we may try to hide the fact, we live in a dense fabric of needs and responsibilities in which our ethical and emotional relations with others — in the home, the school, the workplace, the community — place strict boundaries on selfish individualism.

Finally, in our senior years, as careers wind down, as physical vitality fades, and as earning power drops off, we return to a greater state of dependency than we may have known in many years. That is exactly what people, especially men, have been made to fear about age and fight against: a need for help that can no longer be ignored or wished away. In the later years, friendship, family, medical care, spiritual counseling become matters of high urgency. In this sense, age recapitulates the needs of childhood. It not only reminds us of the transiency of self-reliance, but of how illusory individualism can be.

There are biologists who see human beings as a walking collection of "selfish genes"; there are social scientists who argue strenuously that there is no such virtue as altruism. But the greater evolutionary truth about human beings stands out clearly in every anthropology textbook. We descend, not from sharks or tigers, but from primates, animals who live in families, clans, and hordes with a tight sense of kinship. Social Darwinism has been at war with human nature since the day it was invented as a philosophical alibi for the anti-social antics of the robber barons.

## An Evolution for Elders

The issue we raise here has a long history. It reaches back to the turn of the twentieth century when the Russian naturalist Peter Kropotkin touched off one of the great debates in modern science. Kropotkin noted that far more animals live as members of groups than as loners. For every species that survives as a lone predator (and even these need to be mothered into adulthood) there are many more whose lives are bound to the herd, the flock, the hive, the colony, the pack. Kropotkin generalized that truth to human beings, emphasizing the extraordinary degree to which traditional societies are based on cooperation and mutual aid. Kropotkin rejected social Darwinism as a gross distortion of biological reality. "Mutual aid is as much a law of animal life," he insisted, "as mutual struggle." Notice that Kropotkin did not rule out competition as a factor in evolution; he simply balanced it against sociability. Even so, his theories, despite the careful research that went into them, never received the same academic and journalistic attention as the Darwinian "struggle for existence," certainly not in market-based economies where winners trumpet their own predatory virtues.

Perhaps a personal word would be appropriate here. I have, over my lifetime, been a highly successful competitor, whether for grades, or awards, or pay-raises, or money. I have done reasonably well at the careerist rat-race, even though I have always felt competition brought out the worst in me. The selfish values of competitive individualism always seemed false to me; they blind us to the favors, support, advice, and resources we have received from others. Then, several years ago the medical crisis I write about in chapter one utterly wiped out whatever validity I might still see in the individualistic stance in life. I was forced to ask for help, to lean on those around me, to offer thanks on so many sides for so many favors that I could no longer pretend that any of us stand alone or make it through life on our own.

Aging, the physical loss and trauma that come with it, the need for support that arises from it, will, I suspect, teach our society at large what each of us learns from the experience of medical crisis. How did the poet W. H. Auden put it? "We must love one another or die." The love he had in mind was not Romantic love or even family love. It is the capacity for caring deeply, though impersonally about others because we see our fate reflected in their trials. Maybe "loyalty" would be a better word for that capacity to support, defend, and nourish.

At the level of living experience, we all know the importance of mutual aid. But there are always forces of mystification at work in society that confuse and mislead. Once common people timidly accepted the claims that lords and ladies made to social superiority. It took bloody revolution to tear down those claims and replace them with democratic institutions. In much the same way that blue bloods once intimidated ordinary people, so the pervasive force of the marketplace, with its sway over the media and the educational system, easily persuades many people that the rich and the powerful must know better. They are, after all, self-proclaimed victors in the game of life. That image of self-reliance eclipses the fact that the strong were also born dependent and have needed the help all their lives. They may have received that help for love or for money, but they did not succeed on their own. And as the years advance upon them, they too will finish needing the care of others.

Darwinism is not the whole story of evolution. It offers a plausible account of that part of the story where competition, selection, and survival matter. But as human beings build a second nature around themselves in society, cultural values take over from the struggle for existence. We begin to see other possibilities. Most remarkably, we recognize that aging may be the most important chapter in the human story. For if one believed that philosophical insight were the true purpose of evolution, then longevity and what it permits us to learn about the powers of the mind might be seen as the pivot on which the process turns.

Evolutionary biologists will not, of course, feel free to endorse such a notion. They play the game of explanation by the rules of their guild, and those rules reject all reference to purpose. Scientists think purposes can reside only in a mind, and they think a mind can only exist inside a skull. Aldous Huxley once challenged that set of assumptions by observing how many natural phenomena, especially those of some great intricacy, resemble well-shaped ideas. He believed the universe might better be modeled on a thinking mind, which he called Mind At Large. Scientists may not find that an acceptable model, but they should at least recognize that excluding purposes from nature produces a strange paradox in our understanding of evolution. Since there is no convincing way to account for the magnitude and diversity of the human mind and the wealth of culture it has generated, evolutionary theory has been forced to regard this entire line of development, including the appearance of science itself, as a sort of quaint sideshow outside the main tent, a mere accidental spinoff. The science of evolution has found no way in which science itself is adaptive. But to belittle so remarkable a development as the human mind is a high price to pay for theoretical orthodoxy. It is at best arbitrary, and at worst cowardly.

That was the charge George Bernard Shaw, a philosopher as well as a playwright, levelled at Darwinism. In his play *Back to Methuselah*, Shaw boldly links evolution and aging. He raises the possibility that our understanding of evolution may be age-biased. Darwin and his followers may be thinking within a life span that still belongs to the youth of our species. And for the young, sex and reproduction are paramount. But, Shaw asks, what if life expectancy stretched well beyond the concerns of midlife? The biologist who speaks for Shaw in the play insists that evolution might best be described as "Eternal Life" that "wears out Its bodies and minds and gets new ones like new clothes." The purpose? "The pursuit of omnipotence and omniscience. Greater power and greater knowledge: These are what we are pursuing at the risk of our lives and the sacrifice of our pleasures. Evolution is that pursuit and nothing else. It is the path to godhead. A man differs from a microbe only in being further on the path."

Evolutionary theorists wince at ideas like this, even if the rhetoric makes for exuberant literature. But then they can see no evolutionary reason why any animal should write exuberant literature, let alone dramas about evolution. How would they understand Shaw, who spent his life producing literature rather than producing babies? His life would seem to be a pure waste of time that should have been spent on more usefully adaptive behavior.

Shaw's view of evolution was teleological, meaning he believed evolution was aimed at a goal in the future like an arrow pointed at a distant target. Scientists dismiss all reference to purpose in evolution because they think (mistakenly) that teleology has to be a religious principle; they sense God is lurking somewhere in every teleological argument. That is why they seek to trounce teleology as often as they come across it. But as rational a thinker as Aristotle held that nature acts in purposive ways. He saw forms and forces in nature that work toward completion. He was not particularly religious about the idea; it simply seemed apparent to him in the order of things. And in fact whenever scientists use phrases like "in order to" and "because," they are speaking the language of teleology. They would not get very far in making themselves understood if they omitted such words from their vocabulary. They explain by way of purpose and then say there is no purpose.

Whatever biological orthodoxy may require, what we can say for certain is that some rather important things about human beings seem to have little to do with competitive survival and reproductive advantage. Our massive brain, with all redundant curls and loops and folds, is hard to explain on the basis of survival alone. Survival may be enhanced by tool-making, but why are we left with enough surplus brain-power to produce symphonies and scientific theories? The very mind that Darwin employed to explain evolution seems sheerly excessive in its size and power.

Yet it is the mind that people spontaneously value most in their later years and see as the locus of their human identity. People as severely incapacitated as Stephen Hawking are still in touch with life, still part of our culture because there is a thinking mind at work inside the withering shell of the body. But if the mind goes, we become "vegetables" and life ceases to be worth living. That is when most people seem willing, perhaps eager, to pull the plug. "Brain dead" means *dead*, whatever else still twitches and pulses. Mind is what keeps going as the physique grows old; it endures long after agility, beauty, sexuality have faded. Aging teaches us its supreme value. At last, that may be the greatest and most transformative truth that longevity has to teach us.

We find in nature the things we look for. When evolutionary theory was new, it sought for the sort of physical causes and utility that were appropriate to the technologically based science of that period. Evolution started its career as a tough-minded idea. It was a theory that could be used like a club on all sentimental ideas about life. Now, in more mature minds, evolution may take on a new formulation. Older, wiser heads look for meanings and purposes, not power and profit. It may be that the mature, alert, and well-educated brains we are producing in the longevous society will rethink evolution, especially now that we have begun to find the power to intervene in the process and revise it.

CHAPTER SEVENTEEN

# GRANDPARENT POWER

> Grandparents need grander ideas, especially about their evolutionary
> roles. Altruism supports the grander parenting that can motivate
> elders. "Higher evolution" can imagine the whole world as a
> servicing organism tacitly maintained by human decency.
> — JAMES HILLMAN, *The Force of Character* (1999)

G randparents Day (the second Sunday in September) has one of those folksy origins that warms the heart. It started in the United States in 1978 as a grass roots campaign launched by Marian McQuade, a grand-mother from the mountains of West Virginia. Mrs. McQuade, who was eventually to have over forty grandchildren of her own, saw the holiday as a way of encouraging kindness for the elderly, especially shut-ins and nurs-ing home residents who normally live in the shadows. It featured an "Over-Eighty Day" for visiting the frail elderly. Greeting card and flower-delivery companies moved quickly to get in on the event, though Mrs. McQuade refused to make commercial endorsements.

Showing appreciation for grandparents is a commendable idea, but by the time the holiday took hold in the 1980s, it was very much a sign of days gone by. In spirit Grandparents Day was a throwback to the early Social Security era when the old were marginal and needy dependents. But as the United States moved into the years of the Reagan presidency, a con-servative backlash was under way whose goal was to root out every linger-ing remnant of the Roosevelt New Deal including Social Security. For the first time in the country's history, senior citizens were being cast in the role of a predatory, selfish interest. Far from believing older Americans deserved some flowers and candy, political leaders were targeting the country's greedy geezers for hard knocks and cut-backs..

Not only had many politicians changed their perception of grandparents, but by the 1990s older Americans were beginning to regard themselves very differently. As baby boomers move into their retirement years, they are taking the nation's demographic center of gravity with them. Indeed, many boomers have shown a stubborn reluctance to growing old at all, if by "old" one means dowdy looks, the rocking chair, and the retirement home. With the benefit of aerobic workouts, anti-aging medications, and heroic face-lifts, boomers, if they retire at all, are more likely to be seen heading for the senior Olympics than for Sun City. Whatever sort of grandparents they are going to become, they are certainly not going to retire into Mrs. McQuade's Hallmark greeting card image of granny and gramps.

In the century ahead, grandparenting is destined to be a growth industry. We will be adding more grandparents to our numbers than newborn children. By 2050, there will be ten seniors over sixty for every child under four. Already today grandparents may be doing more for the younger generation than their children are doing for them. As divorce becomes more common, grandparents have begun taking over more responsibility for children in single-parent homes. A 1997 study of grandparenting in the United States concluded that grandparents were spending as much as $8 billion annually to help feed and clothe their grandchildren.[1] The money they are spending within the family is sufficiently large to attract the attention of merchandisers, who see grandparental generosity as a lucrative market. Even more important is the free day care and baby-sitting they provide, a service that the Commonwealth Fund estimates may be worth as much as $29 billion a year. That is the sort of unpaid work entitlements critics conveniently overlook when they pretend that retirees are not to be found anywhere except on the putting green. [2]

Under the RSVP program discussed in chapter five, grandparenting has started to receive a bit of professional structure and official status. RSVP's Foster Grandparents program offers day care to working parents at minimal cost. There are nearly twenty-four thousand foster grandparents on the job in the United States; their work has been valued at $262 million, but with little in the way of personal remuneration. In some states, as of the mid-1990s, foster grandparents (who are almost invariably foster grandmothers) received $9 a day plus carfare. In short, they are underpaid labor, but with time on their hands, they do the job with good cheer.[3]

But numbers alone, whether demographic or financial, are not the most important part of the story. The major changes we face are matters of cultural style and moral tone. The thesis of this book has been that industrial society is maturing beyond the values that created it. The rise of grandparent power is a sign of that transition. With the steady thrust of a demographic glacier moving through the history of modern times, every assumption that men of power have held (and they have with rare exceptions all been men) will feel the pressures of change. How we measure the wealth of nations, what we mean by progress, the value we place on those fuzzy powers of judgment we call "wisdom," the criteria of leadership, the meaning of life — all these will shift with a decisiveness and yet with a subtlety that will make the transition seem inevitable.

## THE GRANDMOTHER HYPOTHESIS

The political implications of the longevity revolution are only just dawning on the modern world. But even more difficult to appreciate is the way in which our new demographic reality is forcing us to reassess the biology of aging, and with that the history of our species: where we come from, how we got here, what our deep biological and moral identity is. Grandparent power may have had more to do with shaping our human identity than we have cared to realize.

As stereotypes give way to science, we are learning that aging is a radically gendered phenomenon. The longevity revolution represents, as one gerontologist puts it, "a wave of estrogen" washing through the body politic. The leading voice in this cultural transformation is the new generation of menopausal women that appeared in the mid-eighties. Once an unmentionable topic, menopause has all but become an ongoing national conversation, replete with books, study groups, workshops, and all the media-savvy frankness we have come to expect from those who come out of the countercultural 1960s. The females who once brought us women's liberation are setting the pace in changing our image of aging.

So when we ask: Does old age make any biological sense, it is women who are overturning the conventional wisdom. And in doing so, they are challenging orthodox science with a new reading of evolution that links age and gender.

As Darwin saw it, the only traits that matter in life are those that parents can pass along to their children. That makes it easy to understand why quick wits, rapid reflexes, and sexual attractiveness get selected by nature. The smart and the fast are more likely to survive in the struggle for existence. And since they survive, they produce more young. So their qualities are preserved and inherited by the next generation. Interestingly, the entire theory is formulated to suit the sexual interests and competitive values of youth and midlife.

But once an individual has outlived the capacity or the opportunity to reproduce, why should it make any difference how much longer he or she survives? Living to a ripe old age would seem to have no value if the twilight years are childless. That leaves us to wonder why longevity should be one of the most distinctive and durable features of the human species.

Women are at the heart of this mystery. Human females are the only members of the primate family to live so long after they cease to ovulate. As average life expectancy grows steadily longer, women may now outlive menopause by another thirty years. But why should that be? Female chimpanzees who have used up the last of their reproductive power rapidly decline, showing all the signs of age. But look around you. In our world, we see women well beyond the age of fifty living fully active lives. They have left behind neither sex nor careers. Why should nature have given them that capacity? What role could so many years of non-reproductive life play in human evolution? Even more interesting: Why did evolutionary biologists take so long getting around to that question?

Evolutionary theory has long tended to focus on the role played in human development by the rugged, competitive qualities most associated with men: strength, cunning, agility. Maybe that is because in the past most biologists and anthropologists were men; so they tended to think of evolution in stereotypically masculine terms. But now some anthropologists have begun to recognize the enormous contributions that have been made to our species by the least rugged people in human society: grandmothers.

In the mid-1950s, the evolutionary biologist George C. Williams was first to suggest that menopause had adaptive value. "Adaptive" is the god-word of evolutionary theory. An adaptive trait, whether physical or mental, contributes to survival. Adaptive traits accumulate and finally shape the basic features of a species. In what sense, then, is menopause adaptive? Williams speculated that the midlife cessation of childbearing in women gives mothers the chance to stop having babies. That means they can pay more attention to their young, thus giving their characteristics a better chance to survive. We might think of this as prehistoric "quality time" for parenting. Providing more care for the young may have helped evolve the longer infancy during which human babies grow a larger brain, learn to speak, and master a complex culture.

Williams' thesis has been much debated since it first appeared. Some anthropologists dismissed it completely. They used the evidence of age. They were quick to point out that long-surviving humans, whether female or male, are all but impossible to find in prehistory. Judging by their surviving bones, early humans were lucky to live to their mid-forties. Women simply did not live long enough for the postmenopausal years to come into play. If they are living longer in our time, perhaps that is because of superior diet and health care, not because of a distant evolutionary adaptation.

That is a strong argument, at least for the prehistoric period. But we now have reason to believe that Williams' thesis, with some variation, does apply to traditional societies that can be studied in our own time. That is what the University of Utah anthropologist Kristin Hawkes has concluded from her research among the grandmothers of the Hadzas of Tanzania. Her thesis runs like this:

If it is an advantage to have an attentive mother, how much more so to have a caring grandmother as well? A grandmother who has nothing better to do with her time can help feed and protect her daughter's young. With a grandmother (or any helpful postmenopausal female relative) to help gather food, a mother can stop breast feeding earlier and bear her next baby sooner until she reaches her own menopause. As Hawkes sees it, "natural selection favored menopause because only grandmothers who are not busy feeding their own children have time to provision grandchildren." Her studies of the hunting and gathering Hadzas show that postmenopausal women contribute significantly to the health and growth of the young, offering help when it is needed most by pregnant and lactating mothers. *Science* magazine calls this "the first serious challenge to the widely accepted view that the human family evolved because males were needed to provision mothers."[4]

Having given grandmothers a greater role to play in human evolution than man the hunter, Hawkes goes on to give her hypothesis a dazzlingly ambitious sweep. Menopause, she believes, was a "watershed event in human prehistory." It gave rise to "the original division of labor ... between childbearing women and postmenopausal women. Mothers bred what grandmothers fed. Through that compact, human fecundity and human mobility knew no limits." At which point, Hawkes believes, grandmothers may have empowered the human species to become the planet's dominant animal. As Natalie Angier summarizes it, "older women invented youth. They made human childhood what it is today: long, dependent, and grandiose. And in inventing childhood, they invented the human race. They created *Homo imperialis*, a species that can go anywhere and exploit everything."[5]

But why exclude the possibility that grandfathers may have been every bit as helpful to the family as their wives? In his extensive studies of tribal elders, the anthropologist David Gutmann concludes that elders both male and female have been an enormous, but now largely unrecognized advantage to our species.[6] He calls grandparents, "the wardens of our precious human heritage." In hunting and early agricultural societies where young men provide the agility to chase big game or the muscle needed to guide the heavy plow, older men may be of little use in the primary economy. What are we to imagine they were doing after injury, age, or illness forced them to give up hard physical labor and risky exploits? Was there perhaps a kind of stone age retirement that left them home to join with the older women at gathering food, telling tales, and passing on the lore of the group?

## Aging and Altruism

Not all anthropologists agree that grandmothers gave evolution the opportunity it needed to make us fully human. Attributing so important a role to grandparent power is highly speculative, though no more so than all the scenarios anthropologists dream up to account for human origins. There is no good evidence for believing that prehistoric humanity was a collection of wily brutes formed in the image of Attila the Hun. That is only what one generation of anxious and ambitious men decided to read into our ancestral past. But this much is certain: Even when the theories we devise to explain evolutionary development are pure fantasy, they reveal a great deal about who we are here and now. The early industrial society of Darwin's day was a jungle where it was every man for himself. In that dog-eat-dog world, it was easy to believe that our ancestors must have survived by being as ruthless as John D. Rockefeller or J. P. Morgan. Similarly, there is no such thing as a "selfish gene" except as a lame metaphor. But in the context of a global economy based on fierce profiteering, selfishness looks for a biological justification.

In contrast, the grandmother hypothesis appears at a time when we are reappraising the importance of aging and gender in our society. We are beginning to bestow dignity on other, gentler human qualities. As Professor Hawkes observes, "If there is a group we have paid no attention to, it's old women." But now we are coming to see that "grandmothers matter!"

The grandmother hypothesis shifts our understanding of evolution away from compulsively masculine competition toward more nurturing, family-based virtues. It embodies the values that are going to matter most in our aging, postindustrial future, a world where, as a matter of political necessity, kindness will have to count for more than predatory cunning. If paleolithic grandparents did make themselves useful as caring childminders, then we may be at the point of seeing their generosity and gentleness regain its place in a society where there are going to be a lot more grandparents than ever before.

As Natalie Angier observes in discussing the grandmother hypothesis, "The lengthening of childhood opens a window of opportunity for cerebral experimentation." If the extended childhood we enjoy as humans does trace back to grandmothering, then our most defining characteristic — the mind — is the result of altruism. The human mind unfolds from the convivial practice of sharing food between older and younger, grandparent and grandchild.

## In Grandpa Vanderhof's House

It has always been the role of elders to raise the great questions of meaning and purpose that loom large as death approaches. As we grow older, we naturally become more inward and contemplative, wondering what it has all been for: the effort and the anxiety, the hard pursuit of success and acquisition. *You can't take it with you.* As familiar as the phrase may be, it is one of those clichés that we all come to accept as indisputably true.

In the famous American comedy of that title by Moss Hart and George S. Kaufman, the central figure is Martin Vanderhof, the *grandpater familias* of an odd New York household. Around him he has gathered a small utopian ménage of madcap artists, crackpot inventors, amateur scientists, assorted layabouts, and social misfits. In the living room of Grandpa Vanderhof's community, meals are eaten, plays are written, snakes collected, ballet steps practiced, xylophones played, printing presses operated — if there were room enough there would probably be ice skating. In short, the brood presided over by Martin Vanderhof goes about the business of living in the fullest sense of the word.

Grandpa Vanderhof, far from being a character role reserved for a crotchety old geezer, is a sophisticated and ingratiating philosopher. He is described as "a man who made his peace with the world long, long ago, and his whole attitude and manner are quietly persuasive of this." He is, in short, one of the few true elders to hold a place in modern literature.

At the climax of the play, Grandpa has reason to explain to Mr. Kirby, the harried, gratification-deferring businessman, what his bizarre household is all about.

> GRANDPA: You've got all the money you need. You can't take it with you.
>
> KIRBY: That's very easy for you to say, Mr. Vanderhof. But I have spent my entire life building up my business.
>
> GRANDPA: And what's it got you? Same kind of mail every morning, same kind of deals, same kind of meetings, same dinners at night, same indigestion. Where does the fun come in? Don't you think there ought to be something *more*, Mr. Kirby? You must have wanted more than that when you started out. We haven't got too much time, you know — any of us.
>
> KIRBY: What do you expect me to do? Live the way *you* do? Do nothing?
>
> GRANDPA: Well, I have a lot of fun. Time enough for everything — read, talk, visit the zoo now and then, practice my darts, even have time to notice when Spring comes around. ... See?
>
> KIRBY: Yes I do see. And it's a very dangerous philosophy, Mr. Vanderhof. It's — it's un-American.

Un-American, perhaps, but profoundly, marvelously wise. A modest, communal way of life filled with family, friendship, and the joy of the inspired moment — things of infinite worth, but no cash value. Later in the play, Grandpa prevails, and Mr. Kirby, admitting that he has been keeping a saxophone hidden away in his closet, decides to revise his way of life. A CEO who opts for fun ... at that point we know we must be in the realm of pure fiction.

When *You Can't Take It with You* was written in the depths of the Great Depression, people like Grandpa Vanderhof were marginal figures in our society, few in numbers and feeble in power. Even so, one could not imagine Grandpa Vanderhof's part being assigned to anybody but an elder. The play voices an elder's vision of life even if, in that troubled time, few Americans were likely to subscribe to it for more than the two hours they were in the theater. In effect, Grandpa Vanderhof was sixty years ahead of his time. His dialogue with Mr. Kirby distilled the ethical thrust of grandparent power long before anybody could see it coming.

At times, when I allow my mind to wander among utopian vistas, I like to imagine that Grandpa Vanderhof's make-believe conversation with Mr. Kirby represents an encounter of historic proportions. I envision it as the wise elder confronting the frenetic entrepreneur. Two contrasting visions of life: the vision that drove the industrial revolution meeting the vision that anchors the longevity revolution. Instead of a future devoted to ever more joyless money-making, ever more ruthless development, I imagine the world Grandpa Vanderhof would create, a community of bright spirits where there is time enough to notice when Spring comes around, a world that has nothing to do with money.

How sad that so many supposedly practical people still regard Grandpa Vanderhof's world as an impermissible prospect. The makers and shakers of modern times like to boast that they have enhanced our freedom. They tell us we are swimming in a sea of choices. Yet this one choice, the choice every child and every elder would make, remains forbidden except as a flight of the literary imagination. Children will never have the power to make that choice. But elders are fast becoming so numerous that they very well might, if they cared to use their power to teach the Mr. Kirbys of the world what the true wealth of nations is.

As a demographic fact — as mere numbers on a page — the longevity revolution guarantees that the future belongs to elders. But will grandparent power turn out to be any different from so many other political transitions in the past, an electoral shift that benefits one group at the expense of another? In the modern world we have seen many movements bid for power. Sometimes they bring more justice into the world, a fairer share of wealth, a broadening of the political process. Grandparent power may do at least that much for the rights of the elderly. But will it make any greater difference than that?

There are certain aspects of the demographics of longevity that give reason to hope it will. Aging is touched by a sense of the universal that raises us above lesser loyalties. Grandparent power, by definition, belongs to the family. It is a role within the family. The relationships it plays upon are the gentle bonds of love and loyalty, ties that exist within the home, around the dinner table, among people who suffer through or take joy in one another's experience. Whatever changes about society from time to time or place to place, family — the continuity of flesh and blood across generations — remains as constant as things can be for our species. All other belongings — nation, church, race, class, gender, ethnicity — become pale abstractions when placed beside the tangible reality of a baby held in arms. Maybe that is why these great fictitious collectivities must often whip their members up to such a fever pitch of dedication. They lack the simple, immediate reality of the flesh. They are culturally fabricated rather than biologically given.

There is also the fact that age is defined at its extreme by death. Grandparent power is practiced under the shadow of mortality and in the presence of the spirit. Elders may come in all the usual class and ethnic varieties, but age still serves to provide a common perception of the human condition that transcends all the parochial commitments that divide people.

And finally longevity is a shared gift — or at least so it promises to be as the healing arts make good health available to ever more people. It need not be rationed. Provided we insist that the right to life entails the right to health, longevity is not a property that a select few can monopolize or that armed camps need fight over. There is enough to go around. One just has to live long enough to get there.

Grandparent power, let us hope, is the one kind of power that is wise enough to know how little power weighs in the scales of eternity And so it asks, "Don't you think there ought to be something *more*, Mr. Kirby?"

NOTES

INDEX

# NOTES

## Introduction: The Approaching Senior Dominance

1. John Dewey, Introduction to E. V. Cowdry, *Problems of Ageing: Biological and Medical Aspects*, Baltimore, Williams and Watkins, 1939. Dewey's introduction remains one of the most incisive overviews of gerontology yet written.
2. Since publishing *America the Wise*, I have learned that the phrase "longevity revolution" was coined in the 1980s by Robert Butler, whose many books and articles on issues of aging have been among my best and wisest sources. See his "The Longevity Revolution," in Forum of Aging Report, *Your Aging Future 1985-2030*, Racine, WI, Wingspread Press, 1985. My use of the phrase overlaps his formulation at points but has a more historical orientation connected with the dynamics of the industrial revolution.

## 1. Boomers' Destiny

1. Theodore Roszak, *The Making of a Counter Culture*, New York, Doubleday, 1969, p. 40. The book was reissued in an updated edition by the University of California Press in 1996.
2. Richard Suzman et al., eds., *The Oldest Old*, New York, Oxford University Press, 1992.
3. Cynthia Taeuber and Ira Rosenwaike, "A Demographic Portrait of America's Oldest Old," in Richard Suzman et al., eds., *The Oldest Old*, New York, Oxford University Press, 1992, p. 17. Thomas Perls, "The Oldest Old," *Scientific American*, January 1995, pp. 70-75.
4. Robert Binstock, "The Oldest Old and 'Intergenerational Equity'," in Richard Suzman et al., eds., *The Oldest Old*, New York, Oxford University Press, 1992, p. 399.
5. *DARE to Be 100*, New York, Simon and Schuster, 1997 is by Walter Bortz, former president of the American Geriatrics Society. DARE stands for Diet-Attitude-Renewal-Exercise, Bortz's long-life formula. He has also written *We Die Too Long and Live Too Short*, New York, Bantam Books, 1991. *Stop Aging Now!*, New York, Harper Perennial, 1996 is by Jean Carper. *You're Not Old Until You're 90*, Nevada City, CA, Blue Dolphin, 1997 is by Rebecca Latimer. *How to Live to 100 Using the Brain-Body Connection* is the subtitle for David Mahoney, *The Longevity Strategy*, New York, John Wiley & Sons, 1998. There is also Michael Fossel, *Reversing Human Aging*, New York, William Morrow, 1996.
6. Robert Binstock, "Older People and Voting Participation: Past and Future," *The*

*Gerontologist*, February 2000, 40, no. 1, 18-31.

7. Mike Males is particularly bitter in his indictment of the senior population, including the baby boomers. See his *Scapegoat Generation: America's War on Adolescents*, Monroe, ME, Common Courage Press, 1996

8. William Frey quoted in Jonathan Tilove, "Generation Gap Becoming Racial Gap," *San Francisco Examiner*, November 23, 1997, p. A17. Also see Peter Brimelow, *Alien Nation*, New York, Random House, 1995, and Frederick Lynch, *The Diversity Machine: The Drive to Change the White Male Workplace*, New York, Free Press, 1997.

9. Mireya Navarro, "The Silver Haired Legislature: A Political Powerhouse in the Making," *New York Times*, October 19, 1997, section 1, p. 10.

10. Robert Binstock, "The Oldest Old and 'Intergenerational Equity'," in Richard Suzman, et al., eds., *The Oldest Old*, New York, Oxford University Press. 1992, p. 404. Also see Laurie Rhodebeck, "The Politics of Greed? Political Preferences Among the Elderly," *Journal of Politics*, May 1993, pp. 342-364.

11. Robert Binstock, "Older People and Voting Participation: Past and Future," *The Gerontologist*, February 2000, 40, no. 1, 18-31. Binstock notes that "the empirical evidence from European nations is similar." On the subject of senior political power, also see Susan MacManus, *Targeting Senior Voters*, Lanham, MD, Rowman and Littlefield, 2000, and Glenn Ruffenbach's study of senior voting in *Encore*, September 11, 2000.

12. Janet Novack, "Strength from Its Gray Roots," *Forbes*, November 25, 1991, pp. 89-92.

13. Gerald Larue, *Geroethics: A New Vision of Growing Old in America*, Buffalo, NY, Prometheus Books, 1992, pp. 265-266.

14. See, for example, Paula Brown Doress-Worters and Diana L. Siegal, *The New Ourselves, Growing Older*, New York, Simon & Schuster, 1994, chapter thirty, "Changing Society and Ourselves."

15. Maggie Kuhn, *No Stone Unturned*, New York, Ballantine Books, 1991, pp. 132, 138.

## 2. The Attack on Entitlements

1. Sidney Gulick, *The American Japanese Problem*, New York, Scribners, 1914, p. 68.

2. Richard Leone, "Supporting Retirees II: Stick with Public Pensions," *Foreign Affairs*, July/August, 1997, p. 39.

3. Krugman quoted in *San Francisco Chronicle*, December 22, 1995, p. B2.

4. Peterson's books are *Will America Grow Up Before It Grows Old?: How the Coming Social Security Crisis Threatens You, Your Family, and Your Country*, New York, Random House, 1996, and *Gray Dawn*, New York, Times Books, 1999. For a pro-entitlements review of Peterson, see Dean Baker, "Granny Bashing," *In These Times*, December 23, 1996, pp. 32-35.

5. Smith quoted in *San Francisco Chronicle*, November 21, 1995, p. C6.

6. See Laurence J. Kotlikoff, *Generational Accounting: Knowing Who Pays, and When, for What We Spend*, New York, Free Press. 1993. Also see Rob Norton, "Cheating Tomorrow's Children," *Fortune*, July 10, 1995.

7. For a persuasive critique of generational accounting, see Dean Baker, *Robbing the Cradle?*, Washington D.C., Economic Policy Institute, 1995.

8. See the ASA's journal *Generations* for Winter 1993, which replies point by point to the "sky is falling" conservative scenario.

9. Robert Ball, "A Secure System," *American Prospect*, November/December 1996, p. 34. In the same issue, see Jerry Mashaw and Theodore Marmor, "The Great Social Security Scare."

10. Jane Bryant Quinn, "Staying Ahead," *San Francisco Chronicle*, July 15, 2000.

11. Mark Weisbrot and Dean Baker, *Social Security: The Phony Crisis*, University of Chicago Press, 2000.

12. Peterson quoted in John Cassidy, "Spooking the Boomers," *New Yorker*, January 13, 1997, p. 31.

13. Mary Deibel, "Few Rolling Over 401(k)s," *San Francisco Chronicle*, August 16, 2000, p. C-2.

14. Editorial, *Wall Street Journal*, January 8, 1997, p. A18.

15. For the full story of this remarkable case, see the *Wall Street Journal*, July 9, 1998.

16. Dean Baker and Mark Weisbrot, *Social Security: The Phony Crisis*, University of Chicago Press, 1999, p. 150.

17. Trudy Lieberman, *Slanting the Story*, New York, New Press, 2000, pp. 34-35. Also see Lieberman's article "Social Insecurity: The Campaign to Take the System Private," *The Nation*, January 27, 1997.

18. Lester Thurow, "The Birth of a Revolutionary Class," *New York Times Magazine*, May 19, 1996, pp. 46-47.

19. Meredith Minkler, "Guest Editorial: Scapegoating the Elderly: New Voices, Old Theme," *Journal of Public Health Policy*, vol. 18, no. 1.

20. David Wessel, "The Outlook: As Populations Age, Fiscal Woes Deepen," *Wall Street Journal*, September, 11, 1995.

21. On China's geriatric crisis, see Jason Dean, "Chinese Find Options Limited in Caring for Aging Population," *San Francisco Chronicle*, June 7, 1999, p. A10.

22. Government estimates cited in Andrew Rosenbaum, "The Medicare Brawl," *New York Times*, October 1, 1995.

23. Richard Leone, "Supporting Retirees II: Stick with Public Pensions," *Foreign Affairs*, July/August 1997, pp. 40-41. Also see W. Crown, "Some Thoughts on Reformulating the Dependency Ratio," *The Gerontologist*, 1985, 25, 166-171.

24. Third Millennium's *Declaration* is available from Box 20866, New York, NY, 10023. Its web site at www.thirdmil.org features a clock that totals up the national debt by the minute.

25. See Jean Davies Okimoto and Phyllis Stegal, *Boomerang Kids*, Boston, Little Brown and Company, 1987. The 1993 national census reported that eighteen million adult children between the ages of eighteen and thirty-four were living with their

parents up from thirteen million in 1970. As of the mid-1990s, fifty-three percent of the eighteen- to twenty-four-year-old population was living with their parents; that number was forty-seven percent in 1970.

26. G. Pascal Zachary, "Parents' Gifts to Adult Children Studied," *Wall Street Journal,* February 9, 1995.

27. Frances and Calvin Goldscheider, *Leaving and Returning Home in Twentieth Century America,* Washington, D.C., Population Reference Bureau, 1994.

28. As of 1993, only twelve percent of the elderly were estimated to be below the poverty level: about $7,000 for a person living alone, $8,700 for a couple. In contrast, before Medicare was adopted in 1965, those above sixty-five made up more of the poor than any other group in the United States.

29. Christina Duff, "Profiling the Aged: Fat Cats or Hungry Victims?" *Wall Street Journal,* September 28, 1995.

## 3. The Coming Health Care Economy

1. Richard Scott, CEO of Columbia/HCA Healthcare Corporation in Nashville, has been called "the Bill Gates of health care." The Justice Department broke the story of its investigation in September 1997. See Kurt Eichenwald and N. R. Kleinfield, *New York Times,* December 21, 1997, section 3, p.1, for a full report on the scandal.

2. See the report by Robert Pear in the *New York Times,* November 4, 1999.

3. Malcolm Sparrow, *Licence to Steal: Why Fraud Plagues America's Health-Care System,* New York, Westview Press/HarperCollins Inc., 1996. See the interview with Sparrow in the *National Retired Teachers Association Bulletin,* October 1997. Sparrow's estimate is higher than the government's estimate of $23 billion. He recommends a number of reforms in the Health Care Financing Administration which governs Medicare, among them a schedule of rewards for reporting fraud.

4. In July 1997, a report by the Inspector General of the Department of Health and Human Services detailed the loss of $23.2 billion from Medicare in 1996 alone due to waste and fraud. At the time, the Congress was debating the need to raise Medicare deductibles for seniors to keep the system solvent. The higher deductibles would recover some $4 billion, far less than a crackdown on the cheating that goes on in the system.

5. "Health Care System Denounced," *San Francisco Chronicle,* December 3, 1997, p. D1.

6. *Journal of the American Medical Association,* reported in *San Francisco Chronicle,* November 13, 1996, p. A4.

7. Jonathan Cohn, "Live a Little," *New Republic,* June 7, 1999, p. 6.

8. Charles Morris, *The AARP,* New York, Times Books, 1996, pp. 165-169.

## 4. Entitlements and the Ethics of Affordability

1. Roy Lubove, *The Struggle for Social Security 1900-1935,* Cambridge, MA, Harvard University Press, 1968, pp. 39.

2. John Blum, et al., *The National Experience*, 6th ed., New York, Harcourt Brace, Jovanovich, 1985, II, 685.

3. Michael Harrington, *The Other America: Poverty in the United States*, New York, Penguin Books, 1963. Chapter six, ironically titled "The Golden Years," covers the plight of the aged.

4. Quoted in Sharon Curtin, *Nobody Ever Died of Old Age: In Praise of Old People, In Outrage at Their Loneliness*, Boston, Atlantic Monthly Press, 1972, p. 33.

5. Richard Calhoun, *In Search of the New Old: Redefining Old Age in America, 1945-1970,* New York, Elsevier, 1978, covers senior politics through the Great Society period.

6. David Hackett Fischer, *Growing Old in America*, New York, Oxford University Press, 1977, p. 192.

7. Robert Butler, *Why Survive? Being Old in America*, New York, Harper & Row, 1975, p. xi-xii.

8. Eric Bates, "The Shame of Our Nursing Homes: Millions for Investors, Misery for the Elderly," *Nation*, March 29, 1999.

9. Miles Benson, *San Francisco Examiner,* August 18, 1997.

10. Rachel Filinson and Stanley Ingman, eds., *Elder Abuse: Practice and Policy*, New York, Human Sciences Press, 1989.

11. In 1995, twenty-four thousand Americans above the age of sixty-five attempted suicide; six-thousand of them succeeded — a 32 percent increase over 1980. Eighty percent of the suicides were white males. The AARP makes literature available on the subject. For the pamphlet "Suicide of Older Men and Women," write to AARP Fulfillment, EE01180, 601 E Street, NW, Washington, D.C. 20049. Also see Caryl Stern, "Why Depression Is a Silent Killer," *Parade*, September 28, 1997.

12. Townsend's political autobiography can be found in *New Horizons: An Autobiography*, Chicago, J. L. Stewart Publishing Co., 1943.

13. Diana Walsh, "The Fear Merchants," *San Francisco Examiner*, February 8, 1998, p. A1.

14. James Riley, *Sickness, Recovery, and Death: A History and Forecast of Ill Health*, London, Macmillan, 1989.

15. Anthony Smith, *The Body,* New York, Viking, 1985.

16. David Perlman, "Research on Genes and Diseases of Aging," *San Francisco Chronicle*, November 7, 1995, p. A3.

17. Gina Kolata, "New Era of Robust Elderly Belies the Fears of Scientists," *New York Times*, February 27, 1996, p. 1.

18. Leonard Hayflick, *How and Why We Age*, New York, Ballantine Books, 1994. p. 335.

19. Bernard Starr, "This Longevity Is Killing Us: Healthy Choices for Sick Health Care," *Barron's*, January 15, 1996.

20. Sharon Bernstein, "HMOs Face Fundamental Changes to Survive," *San Francisco Examiner*, April 9, 2000, p. A4.

## 5. Retirement: How *Not* To

1. William Graebner, *A History of Retirement*, New Haven, CT, Yale University Press, 1980, pp. 10-17.

2. Quoted in Marc Freedman, *Prime Time: How Baby Boomers Will Revolutionize Retirement and Transform America*, New York, Public Affairs, 2000, pp. 60-61. Freedman's study is an incisive discussion of changing styles in retirement.

3. Stephen Pollan, *Die Broke: A Radical Four-Part Financial Plan*, New York, HarperBusiness, 1997.

4. Marc Freedman, "The Aging Opportunity," *American Prospect*, November-December 1996. Also see Lori Simon-Rusinowitz et al., "Grandparenting at Century's End: Grandparents in the Workplace," *Generations*, Spring 1996, and Robert Butler, "Living Longer, Contributing More," *Journal of the American Medical Association*, October 22, 1997, 278:1372-1374.

5. Gene Koretz, "Wiggle Room in the Workforce," *Business Week*, October 27, 1997, p. 34.

6. Randall S. Jones, "Japan: Population Aging," *OECD Observer*, December 1997. Wanda Menke-Gluckert, "Aging Population Creates Critical Situation," *Europe*, February 2000. Suvendrini Kakuchi, "Japan Desperate for a Baby Boom," *IPS World News* (online), November 16, 2000.

7. On Chile's pension system, see Richard Leone, "Supporting Retirees II: Stick with Public Pensions," *Foreign Affairs*, July/August 1997, pp. 40-41.

8. Milton Friedman, "The Case for the Negative Income Tax," *National Review*, March 7, 1967.

9. See the report "Guaranteed Annual Income: A Hope and a Question Mark," in *America*, December 11, 1971, p. 263.

10. U.S. Chamber of Commerce, *The National Symposium on Guaranteed Income*, Washington, D.C., 1966.

11. Robert Theobald, ed., *The Guaranteed Income: Next Step in Socioeconomic Evolution?*, New York, Doubleday Anchor, 1970, pp. 16-18. By far the most imaginative analysis of postwar affluence is Paul and Percival Goodman's *Communitas: Means of Livelihood and Ways of Life*, New York, Random House, 1947.

12. Jane Holtz Kay, *Asphalt Nation*, New York, Crown Books, 1997 estimates the cost of road repairs at $200,000 to $400,000 per mile. But the figure can soar well beyond that in some urban areas. In my vicinity, a recent freeway construction job occasioned by an earthquake in 1989 was reported to cost $400 *per inch*. Kay's book is a persuasive plea for devehicularization.

## 6. The Compassionate Economy

1. Arlie Russell Hochschild, *The Unexpected Community*, Englewood Cliffs, NJ, Prentice-Hall, 1973, p. 19.
2. Bill McMillon, *Volunteer Vacations*, Chicago, Chicago Review Press, 1993.
3. A 1997 survey by the National Alliance for Caregiving estimates that between the late 1980s and late 1990s the number of households in which an elderly relative, usually a parent or grandparent, had become a dependent rose from 7 to 22.4 million. For an excellent survey of care giving in all its aspects, see Beth McLeod, *Caregiving: The Spiritual Journey of Love, Loss, and Renewal*, New York, John Wiley & Sons, 1999.
4. H. M. Zal, *Sandwich Generation: Caught Between Growing Children and Aging Parents*, New York, Plenum Insight, 1992. Also see James Atlas, "The Sandwich Generation," *New Yorker*, October 13, 1997.
5. Harriet Sarnoff Schiff, *How Did I Become My Parent's Parent?*, New York, Penguin Books, 1997, Kenneth Scileppi, *Caring for the Parents Who Cared for You*, New York, Birch Lane, 1995, Sheelagh McGurn, *Under One Roof: Caring for an Aging Parent*, New York, Parkside Publishing, 1992, Claude Amarnick, *"Don't Put Me in a Nursing Home!"*, New York, Garrett Publishing, 1996. Also see Rosalynn Carter, *Helping Yourself Help Others: A Book for Caregivers*, New York, Times Books, 1994 and Thomas Cassidy, *Elder Care: What to Look For, What to Look Out For!*, New York, New Horizon Press, 1997. Parent Care Advisor, a helpful newsletter, is available from LRP Publications, P.O. Box 980, Horsham, PA 19044. Web sites include Eldercare Web and Eldercare Web/Aging, Dying, and Death at http://ice.net/~kstevens/ELDERWEB.HTM, and Geropsychology at http://www.premier.net/~gero/geropsyc.html.
6. See Ken Dychtwald, *Age Wave: The Challenges and Opportunities of an Aging America*, Los Angeles, Jeremy Tarcher, 1989, p. 243.
7. See Rodger McFarlane, *The Complete Bedside Companion: No-Nonsense Advice on Caring for the Seriously Ill*, New York, Simon & Schuster, 1997, Cappy Capossela and Sheila Warnock, *Share the Care: How to Organize a Group to Care for Someone Who Is Seriously Ill*, New York, Fireside Books, 1995.
8. David Tilson, ed., *Aging in Place: Supporting the Frail Elderly in Residential Environments*, Glenview, IL, Scott, Foresman and Company, 1990 is a survey of the many forms that on-site aging takes. The book was published through the American Association of Homes for the Aging.
9. On NORCs and other forms of caregiving, see David France, "The New Compassion," *Modern Maturity*, May-June 1997, pp. 33-41.
10. Marc Freedman, "The Aging Opportunity," *American Prospect*, November-December 1996. As of 1997, RSVP was funded under the Corporation for National Service at $35 million and was running 460 local groups. Call (800) 424-8867 for information. The National Senior Service Corps has a web site: www.cns.gov/senior-a.html.

11. Reagan quoted in *Time*, October 19, 1981, p. 47. Of course, neither Reagan, who took Calvin Coolidge as his presidential ideal, nor George Bush, whose model was Herbert Hoover, ever inquired into how well volunteerism during the Coolidge-Hoover era of the 1920s was dealing with poverty on the farms and in the slums of a prospering economy.

12. Figures from Jeremy Rifkin, *The End of Work: The Decline of the Global Labor Force and the Dawn of the Post-Market Era*, New York, G. P. Putnam's Sons, 1995, p. 241. Rifkin's study is a thought-provoking defense of Third Sector economics. Also see Jon Van Til, *Mapping the Third Sector: Volunteerism in a Changing Social Economy*, Washington D.C., Foundation Center, 1988.

13. Deets quoted in Maggie Kuhn, *No Stone Unturned*, New York, Ballantine, 1991, p. 208.

## 7. The Senior Follies

1. Robert Butler, *Why Survive? Being Old in America*, New York, Harper & Row, 1975, p. 417. Also see Robert Butler and Herbert Gleason, eds., *Productive Aging*, New York, Springer-Verlag, 1985.

2. Lucy Scott, with Kerstin Joslyn Schremp, Betty Soldz, and Barbara Weiss, *Wise Choices Beyond Midlife: Women Mapping the Journey Ahead*, Watsonville, CA, Papier-Maché Press, 1997, p. 6.

3. Betty Friedan, *The Fountain of Age*, New York, Simon and Schuster, 1993, pp. 29, 199.

4. Carl Jung, *Memories, Dreams, and Reflections*, New York, Vintage Books, 1961, reviews Jung's discovery of the Child archetype. Also see Joyce Mills and Richard Crowley, *Therapeutic Metaphors for Children and the Child Within*, New York, Brunner/Mazel, 1986, pp. 32-36, and W. Hugh Missildine, *Your Inner Child of the Past*, New York, Pocket Books, 1963.

5. John Bradshaw, *Homecoming: Reclaiming and Championing Your Inner Child*, New York, Bantam, 1990. Also see Lucia Capacchione, *Recovery of Your Inner Child*, New York Simon & Schuster, 1991. The work of the German therapist Alice Miller focuses on forms of child abuse, especially abuse of gifted children. See *Prisoners of Childhood*, New York, Basic Books, 1981.

6. James Hillman and Michael Ventura, *We've Had a Hundred Years of Psychotherapy and the World's Getting Worse*, San Francisco, HarperSanFrancisco, 1992, p. 6.

7. Thomas Harris, *I'm OK - You're OK*, New York, Avon, 1967, p. 17.

8. Robert Bly, *The Sibling Society*, New York, Vintage, 1997.

9. Thomas Gordon, *Parent Effectiveness Training: The No-Lose Program for Raising Responsible Children*, New York, P. H. Wyden, 1970.

10. David Gutmann, *Reclaimed Powers: Toward a New Psychology of Men and Women in Later Life*, New York, Basic Books, 1987, pp. 4, 5, 7. See especially chapter ten, "Deculturation and the Passing of the Elders."

11. Daniel Levinson, *The Seasons of a Man's Life*, New York, Alfred A. Knopf, 1978, p. 46.

## 8. Maturity and the Media

1. Marc Freedman, "The Aging Opportunity," *American Prospect*, November-December 1996, p. 40.
2. Thomas Frank, *The Conquest of Cool: Business Culture, Counter Culture, and the Rise of Hip Consumerism,* University of Chicago Press, 1997, pp. 5, 26.
3. John Dewey, Introduction, E. V. Cowdry, ed., *Problems of Ageing: Biological and Medical Aspects*, Baltimore, Williams & Watkins, 1939.
4. In the 1990s, some seventy-five percent of population growth in the United States was immigrant-derived, the major part of that increase coming from births to immigrant families. Some demographers fear that immigration could raise the United States population to one billion by 2150, mainly concentrated in a few job-rich sectors of the nation. This has become a contentious issue in the environmental movement. The Sierra Club has, for example, refused to take the "elitist" position that immigration be sharply curtailed. In doing so, the club falls into line with many political and corporate leaders who encourage immigration as a source of cheap labor. See B. Meredith Burke, "Sierra Club Schism: The Limits of Sharing," *Christian Science Monitor*, April 21, 1998, p. 11.
5. These figures come from a report on the senior market carried by National Public Radio's *Marketplace* (produced by KUSC in Los Angeles), June 27, 1996. On the economic status of seniors in America, Ken Dychtwald's books, *Age Wave*, Los Angeles, Jeremy Tarcher, 1989, and *Age Power*, Los Angeles, Jeremy Tarcher, 1999, are excellent sources.
6. Virginia Munger Kahn, "How to Make Money from Those Aging Baby Boomers," *New York Times*, June 16, 1996, p. F3.
7. Cheryl Russel quoted by Ken Dychtwald, *Age Wave*, pp. 276-277.
8. J. Walker Smith and Ann Clurman, *Rocking the Ages*, New York, HarperCollins, 1997.
9. Jerry Della Femina, "When Will Madison Avenue Get It?" *New York Times Magazine,* March 9, 1997, p. 74.
10. For a darkly dissenting view on the American job market, see William Wolman and Anne Colamosca, *The Judas Economy: The Triumph of Capital and the Betrayal of Work,* New York, Addison-Wesley, 1997. The authors predict that high-tech workers will eventually suffer the same job insecurity and degradation of wages as blue collar labor has.
11. Marilyn Zeitlin, "The Hollywood Greylist: Too Old to be Hired, Too Young to be Retired," *DGA NEWS*, September-October 1991, pp. 15-19.
12. For a revealing report on how programming decisions are made in television, see Susan Champlin Taylor's article "Primetime's Big Sleep," *Modern Maturity*, November-December 1995, pp. 38-43. Taylor sets out to investigate why the still-popular program *Murder She Wrote* was cancelled by CBS. The answer had little to do with demographics or money. Advertisers and media consultants simply felt embarrassed to be connected with a program that appealed to an over-fifty audi-

ence. What can one call this except ageism?

13. Malcolm Caldwell, "The Coolhunt," *New Yorker*, March 17, 1996.

14. Jon Herskovitz, "High School Girls Fashioning Japan's Pop Culture," *San Francisco Chronicle*, November 29, 1997, p. 1.

15. Some enterprising people in advertising and the media are already in touch with the demographic facts of life. See David B. Wolfe, *Serving the Ageless Market*, New York, McGraw-Hill, 1994. Also see Peter Weaver, "Opportunity Knocks as America Ages," *Nation's Business,* August 1996, pp. 30-32. For statistics on population and income, a good source is Age Wave Inc. (1900 Powell Street, Suite 800, Emeryville, Calif. 94608), a public relations firm that consults with media and advertisers about the senior generation.

## 9. In The Absence of Elders

1. Paul Goodman, *Growing Up Absurd,* New York, Random House, 1960.

2. Don Tapscott, *Growing Up Digital: The Rise of the Net Generation*, New York, McGraw-Hill, 1998.

3. For my purposes here, I have used samples from several newsgroups. They include alt.society.generation-x, alt.punk, alt.slack, alt.drugs, alt.drugs.culture, alt.cyberpunk, alt.cyberspace.rebels, alt.rave, alt.destroy.the.world, alt.life.sucks, alt.bitterness, alt.angst.

4. Some computer-friendly social commentators celebrate these seemingly neurotic features of online communications. Sherry Terkel, *Life on the Screen: Identity in the Age of the Internet*, New York, Simon & Schuster, 1995, sees many grand postmodern possibilities in the multiple personalities people create at the keyboard. I leave it to the therapists to decide whether lying about yourself to strangers who are lying to you about themselves is the best way for adolescents to work out a sane and stable identity. Some might say that the many opportunities we are offered for role-playing — on the Internet, over CB radio, on talk-show call-ins, or in singles bars — is a troubling measure of urban alienation. In contrast, how many ways do we have for people to know themselves and others for who they really are?

5. Sheldon Turner, *San Francisco Chronicle*, August 13, 1996.

6. "Generation War a Myth: Seniors and Gen-X, It's Time to Unite!" *Solidarity, the United Auto Workers Magazine*, September 1996.

7. Carolyn Lochhead, "The Issue Clinton, Dole Won't Touch," *San Francisco Chronicle*, October 21, 1996, p.1.

8. The phrases are Stewart Brand's and Nicholas Negroponte's. See Brand's *Media Lab: Inventing the Future at MIT*, New York, Viking Books, 1987.

9. Elaine Aron, *The Highly Sensitive Person: How to Thrive When the World Overwhelms You*, New York, Carol Publishing Group, 1996.

10. Lewis Mumford, *The Pentagon of Power*, New York, Harcourt, Brace, & Jovanovich, 1970, p. 435.

## 10. Longevity and Gender

1. Among the groundbreaking studies of senior sexuality are Alex Comfort, *A Good Age,* New York, Simon & Schuster, 1978, and Robert Butler and Myra Lewis, *Love and Sex After Sixty*, New York, Harper & Row, 1988. More recently, there is David Gutmann, *Reclaimed Powers: Men and Women in Later Life*, Evanston, IL, Northwestern University Press, 1994, P. B. Doress-Worters and D. L. Siegal, *The New Ourselves, Growing Older,* New York, Simon & Schuster, 1994, and Joan Elizabeth Lloyd, *Now and Forever Let's Make Love*, New York, Warner Books, 1997. For more philosophically oriented discussions, see Susan Griffin, *The Eros of Everyday Life*, New York, Doubleday, 1995, George Leonard, *The End of Sex: Erotic Love After the Sexual Revolution*, New York, Bantam Books, 1984, Morris Berman, *Coming to Our Senses: Body and Spirit in the Hidden History of the West*, New York, Bantam Books, 1990. Betty Friedan's *Fountain of Age*, New York, Simon & Schuster, 1993, is a thorough critical survey of love among the elders.

2. Royda Crose, *Why Women Live Longer Than Men, and What Men Can Learn from Them*, San Francisco, Jossey-Bass Publishers, 1997, pp. 20-21.

3. Betty Friedan, *The Fountain of Age*, New York, Simon and Schuster, 1993, p. 165.

4. David Gutmann, *Reclaimed Powers: Toward a New Psychology of Men and Women in Later Life*, New York, Basic Books, 1987, p. 236.

5. Paul Shepard, *Nature and Madness*, San Francisco, Sierra Club Books, 1982.

6. Catherine Keller, *From a Broken Web: Separation, Sexism, and Self,* Boston, Beacon Press, 1986, p. 122.

7. Jean Baker Miller, *Women's Growth in Connection*, New York, Guilford Press, 1991, pp. 25, 26.

8. Fione Hobbs and Bonnie Damon, *Sixty-Five-Plus in the United States*, U.S. Department of Health and Human Services, Washington, DC, 1997. Also see Silvia Sara Canetto, "Gender and Suicide in the Elderly," *Suicide and Life-Threatening Behavior*, 22, no. 1, 1992.

9. Royda Crose, *Why Women Live Longer Than Men, and What Men Can Learn from Them*, San Francisco, Jossey-Bass Publishers, 1997, p. 74.

10. Erik Erikson, "Identity and the Life Cycle," *Psychological Issues*, 1, no. 1, New York, International Universities Press, 1959.

11. Daniel Levinson, *The Seasons of a Man's Life*, Alfred A. Knopf, 1978, pp. 98-99.

12. James Hillman, *The Soul's Code*, New York, Random House, 1996, p. 121.

13. Robert Bly, *The Sibling Society,* New York, Addison-Wesley Publishing Company, 1996, pp. 44-45, 180.

14. Jed Diamond, *Male Menopause*, Naperville, IL, Sourcebooks, 1997, though from an out-of-the-way press, is among the few works that provide an honest and illuminating survey of male aging from both the medical and psychological perspective. There is also a fine work of fiction: Isaac Bashevis Singer's *Old Love* (1979). Women, in contrast, have many wise works to draw upon, among them Simone de Beauvoir, *The Coming of Age*, New York, W. W. Norton, 1973, Charlotte Painter,

*Gifts of Age*, San Francisco, Chronicle Books, 1985, Paula Brown Doress, *Ourselves Growing Older: Women Aging with Knowledge and Power*, New York, Simon & Schuster, 1987, Paula Brown Doress-Worters and D. L. Siegal, *The New Ourselves, Growing Older*, New York, Simon & Schuster, 1994, Janet Ford and Ruth Sinclair, *Sixty Years On: Women Talk About Old Age*, London, Women's Press, 1987, Caroline Bird, *Lives of Our Own: Secrets of Salty Old Women*, Boston, Houghton Mifflin, 1995, Letty Cottin Pogrebin, *Getting Over Getting Older*, Boston, Little, Brown, 1996, Carolyn Heilbroner, *The Last Gift of Time: Life Beyond Sixty*, New York, Dial Press, 1997.

15. The phrases "the mystery of gender" and "the ineradicable differences between the sexes" are from Sam Keen, *Fire in the Belly: On Being a Man*, New York, Bantam Books, 1991.

## 11. The Disruptive Wonders of Biotechnology

1. Dwayne Banks and Michael Fossel, "Telomeres, Cancer, and Aging," *Journal of the American Medical Association*, October 22/29, 1997, p. 1345. For an accessible review of research on aging, see Scientific American Presents, *The Quest to Beat Aging*," summer 2000.

2. Gerald Gruman, *A History of Ideas About the Prolongation of Life*, Philadelphia, American Philosophical Society, 1966, pp. 70-71.

3. For a collection of Mme. Calment's wit and wisdom at the age of 122, see Michel Allard et al., *Jeanne Calment, From Van Gogh's Time to Ours*, New York, W. H. Freeman, 1998.

4. Associated Press report in the *San Francisco Chronicle*, November 14, 1995, p.1.

5. For example, see Thomas Perls, "The Oldest Old," *Scientific American*, January 1995, pp. 70-75.

6. On George Roth's research, see the report in the "Forever Young" cover story, *Time*, November 25, 1996, p. 93. Also see Richard Weindruch, "Caloric Restriction and Aging," *Scientific American*, January 1996, pp. 46-52.

7. Quoted in "Simple Question: Why Do We Die?" *San Francisco Examiner*, November 24, 1991, p. B7.

8. Steven Lamm, *Younger at Last: The New World of Vitality Medicine*, New York, Simon and Schuster, 1997.

9. "Estrogen Stakes Claim to Cognition," *Science*, May 2, 1997, pp. 675-678.

10. Daniel Rudman at the Medical College of Wisconsin in Madison was able to achieve a remarkable result with HGH. He reversed the aging effects of sixty-year-olds, bringing them the physical condition of forty-year-olds. When the HGH was withdrawn, the gain was lost. But further tests were then unable to duplicate that result. See Richard Restak, *Older and Wiser*, New York, Simon & Schuster, 1997, pp. 41-43.

11. See the preface to Leonard Hayflick, *How and Why We Age*, New York, Ballantine Books, 1996, for a brief description of research on telomeres. Also see the summary in *Time*, November 25, 1996.

12. David Concar, "Death of Old Age," *New Scientist*, June 22, 1996, gives a good summary of the role telomeres play in aging.

13. Giampapa quoted in Ronald Klatz, *Grow Young with HGH*, New York, HarperCollins, 1997, p. 53.

14. Malcolm Gladwell, "The New Age of Man," *New Yorker*, September 30, 1996, pp. 56-70. As is so often the case in biology, however, research suggests that telomeres are more devilishly complex than the original model indicated. As of 1997, later studies have called into question the function of telomerase both in the production of tumors and in the immortalization of cells, as least in experimental mice. Peter M. Lansdorp, "Lessons from Mice without Telomerase," *Journal of Cell Biology*, 139, no. 2, October 20, 1997, pp. 309-312.

15. Editorial, *New Scientist*, January 24, 1998, p. 3.

16. Dwayne Banks and Michael Fossel, "Telomeres, Cancer, and Aging," *Journal of the American Medical Association*, October 22/29, 1997, p. 1345.

17. Leonard Hayflick, *How and Why We Age*, New York, Ballantine, 1996, p. 335.

18. Caleb Finch and Rudolph Tanzi, "Genetics of Aging," *Science*, 278, October 17, 1997, p. 411.

19. Alan Harrington, *The Immortalist: An Approach to the Engineering of Man's Divinity*, New York, Avon Books, 1969.

20. Pickering quoted in Alvin Toffler, *Future Shock*, New York, Bantam Books, 1970, p. 208.

21. *Time*, November 25, 1996, p. 92.

22. *New Scientist,* October 7, 1997.

23. Martin Raff, "Death Wish," *The Sciences*, July-August 1996, pp. 36-40.

24. Kate Douglas, "Making Friends with Death-Wish Genes," *New Scientist*, July 30, 1994, pp. 31-33. Also see Richard Duke, David Ojcius, and John Ding-E Young, "Cell Suicide in Health and Disease," *Scientific American*, December, 1996, pp. 80-87.

25. Roger Lewin, "Shock of the Past for Modern Medicine," *New Scientist*, October 23, 1993, pp. 28-32.

26. Ronald Klatz, *Grow Young with HGH*, New York, HarperCollins, 1997, p. 58.

## 12. The Ecology of Wisdom

1. The poll in question was commissioned by the AARP and several insurance and mutual fund companies. It was reported by the Associated Press on October 17, 1997.

2. Anne and Paul Ehrlich, "Growing Beyond Our Limits," *Triumph of Discovery*, published by Scientific American, New York, 1995, p. 182.

3. Fred Pearce, "Population Bombshell," *New Scientist*, July 11, 1998. Also see "Counting Down," *New Scientist*, October 2, 1999, p. 20-21, which concludes that "gloom about a population explosion is probably misplaced. ... Next century we may have to worry about falling birth rates, not rising ones."

4. Stevenson Swanson, "Population Crowding Edges of Age Spectrum," *San Francisco Examiner*, October 2, 1999.

5. Steve Proffitt, "Peter Schwartz: Bright Future's Prophet," *Los Angeles Times*, October 4, 1998, p. M3.

6. James Kingsland, "Golden Oldie," *New Scientist*, June 12, 1999, p. 46.

7. On the "disposable soma theory," see Thomas Kirkwood, *Time of Our Lives*, London, Weidenfeld and Nicholson, 1999.

8. Rudi G. J. Westendorp and Thomas B. L. Kirkwood, "Human Longevity at the Cost of Reproductive Success," *Nature*, December 24, 1998, pp. 743-746.

9. T. T. Perls, L. Alpert, and R. C. Fretts, "Middle-Aged Mothers Live Longer," *Nature*, 389, 133, 1997.

10. Emma Ross, "Biological Clock Ticks in Men Too, Study Says," *San Francisco Chronicle*, August 1, 2000, p. A5.

11. Associated Press, "Young Adults Wary of Marriage," *San Francisco Chronicle*, June 8, 2000.

12. Joel Cohen, *How Many People Can the Earth Support?*, New York, Norton, 1995.

13. See the analysis by Stephanie Strom, "Japan Growth Plan Delayed; Doubts Abound," *New York Times*, December 17, 1997, pp. 1, 7.

14. Kotlikoff quoted in *San Francisco Chronicle*, December 22, 1995, p. B2

15. Gail Vines, "Some of Our Sperm Are Missing," *New Scientist*, August 26, 1995, pp. 22-25. Also see Theo Colborn, *Our Stolen Future*, New York, Dutton/Signet Books, 1996, and Lawrence Wright, "Silent Sperm," *New Yorker*, January 15, 1996.

16. Lucy Scott and Meredith Angwin, *Time Out for Motherhood*, Los Angeles, Jeremy Tarcher Inc., 1986, is an authoritative survey of late-mothering in the United States.

17. On the marriage and childbearing patterns of boomers, I am grateful to have the research of Suzanne Reynolds-Scanlon of the Florida Policy Exchange on Aging at the University of South Florida.

18. One of these groups is Childless By Choice (P.O. Box 695, Leavenworth, WA 98826, e-mail: 76206.3216@compuserve.com). It works to "dispel the negative stereotypes surrounding childless couples so that there can be greater acceptance of our choice by others." It issues a newsletter and distributes literature.

19. Lester Brown, et al., *State of the World*, New York, Norton, 1984, p. 2.

20. Lena Sun, "China Lowers Birth Rate to Levels in West," *Washington Post*, April 22, 1993.

21. Judith Stacey, *Brave New Families*, Boston, Beacon Press, 1991, and *In the Name of the Family: Rethinking Family Values in the Postmodern Age*, Boston, Beacon Press, 1996.

22. Rose, quoted in Malcolm Gladwell, "The New Age of Man," *New Yorker*, September 30, 1996, p. 67.

23. As an example of city planning with an aging population in mind, see B. Kweon, et al., "Green Common Spaces and the Social Integration of Inner-City Older Adults," *Environment and Behavior*, 1998, 30: 832-858. Also see the periodical

*Sustainable Communities Review*, published by the Center for Public Service at the University of North Texas in Denton, Texas.

24. A. Pebley, "Demography and the Environment." *Demography*, 1998, 35: 377-389.

25. For a perceptive survey of the role boomers are apt to play in environmental politics, see Scott Wright, "Gray and Green? Stewardship and Sustainability in an Aging Society," *Journal of Aging Studies*, Fall 2000, 14, no. 3. The essay offers an excellent bibliography. Also see Stan Ingman, Tom Benjamin, and Richard Lusky, "Environment: The Quintessential Intergenerational Challenge," *Generations*, Winter 1998-99, and AARP SCAN, *Environmental Issues and an Aging Population*, vol.1, Washington D.C., Forecasting and Environmental Scanning Department of the American Association of Retired Persons, Research Division, 1992.

26. Zalman Schachter-Shalomi and Ronald Miller, *From Age-ing to Sage-ing*, New York, Warner Books, 1995, p. 47.

## 13. The Future of Death

1. Condorcet quoted in Jacques Choron, *Modern Man and Mortality*, New York, Macmillan, 1964, p. 135.

2. Sherwin Nuland, *How We Die: Reflections on Life's Final Chapter*, New York, Alfred A. Knopf, 1994. p. 259.

3. Theodore Roszak, *The Memoirs of Elizabeth Frankenstein*, New York, Bantam Books, 1996.

4. Robert Jastrow, *The Enchanted Loom: Mind in the Universe*, New York, Simon & Schuster, 1984, pp. 166-67.

5. Frank Tipler, *The Physics of Immortality: Modern Cosmology and the Resurrection of the Dead*, New York, Doubleday, 1994.

6. Mark Slouka, *War of the Worlds: Cyberspace and the High-Tech Assault on Reality*, New York, Basic Books, 1995. I explore this philosophical theme in computer science in *The Cult of Information*, University of California Press, second edition, 1995.

7. Vigne quoted in *Wired*, June 1995, p. 161.

8. Bill Joy, "Why the Future Doesn't Need Us," *Wired*, April 2000.

9. Jaron Lanier, "Agents of Alienation," *Journal of Consciousness Studies*, 2, no. 1, 1995, pp. 76-81.

10. For a full discussion of slow codes and a survey of the literature, see the *New England Journal of Medicine* web site at www.nejm.org/public/1998.

11. "Saving a Few, Sacrificing Many — At Great Cost," *New York Times*, August 8, 1989, p. 23.

12. Daniel Callahan, *Setting Limits: Medical Goals in an Aging Society*, New York, Simon & Schuster, 1987. Also see his *What Kind of Life? The Limits of Medical Progress*, New York, Simon & Schuster, 1990.

13. John Hardwig, "Is There a Duty to Die?" *Hastings Center Report* 27, no. 2, 1997, pp. 34-42.

14. Marilyn Wells, *The Good Death*, New York, Bantam Books, 1997.

## 14. Powers of the Mind

1. For a good recent overview of Alzheimer's disease around the world, see the special issue of *Time* for July 17, 2000: "The New Science of Alzheimer's." Some good sources for current data are The Alzheimer's Disease and Related Disorders Association, Chicago, phone (800) 272-3900, web site: www.alz.org; and Alzheimer's Disease International, London, phone: 00 44 171 620 3011, web site: www.alz.co.uk

2. The results of the latest research on both the mental and physical aspects of aging are summarized in Betty Friedan, *The Fountain of Age*, New York, Simon & Schuster, 1993, pp. 71-103. Also see Robert Butler and Herbert Gleason, *Productive Aging*, New York, Springer-Verlag, 1985.

3. Daniel Goleman, "Studies Suggest Older Minds Are Stronger Than Expected," *New York Times*, February 26, 1996, p. 1.

4. Dharma Singh Khalsa, *Brain Longevity: The Breakthrough Medical Program that Improves Your Mind and Memory*, New York, Warner Books, 1997, p. 151.

5. The Memory Assessment Clinics can be contacted at 8311 Wisconsin Avenue, Bethesda, Maryland 20814. The clinic makes pamphlets and teaching aids available. Also see Daniel Lapp, *Don't Forget: Easy Exercises for a Better Memory at Any Age*, New York, McGraw-Hill, 1995. Dr. Lapp runs a memory research program at the Stanford Medical School. Mind Works, "the Mental Fitness Connection," teaches courses at senior centers in California using remarkably effective cognitive techniques. Contact Connie Lynch, Mind Works, 228 Cambridge Avenue, Kensington, California 94708, for advice and materials.

6. "Novel Antioxidants May Slow Brain's Aging," *Science News*, January 25, 1997, p. 53.

7. David Concar, "Brain Boosters," *New Scientist*, February 8, 1997, pp. 32-35.

8. Dennis Selkoe, "Aging Brain, Aging Mind," *Scientific American*, September 1992, pp. 135-142.

9. Richard Restak, *Older and Wiser*, New York, Simon & Schuster, 1997. See especially chapter two.

10. The research by Richard Shimamura is summarized at length in Richard Restak, *Older and Wiser*, New York, Simon & Schuster, 1997, pp. 70-73.

11. D. A. Snowden, "Linguistic Ability in Early Life and Cognitive Function and Alzheimer's Disease in Late Life," *Journal of the American Medical Association*, volume 275 (7), 1996, pp. 528-532. Also see "The Nuns' Story," *Science*, May 22, 1998, p. 1199.

12. Reported by NBC Nightly News on August 1, 2000.

13. For information about MindAlert, see the ASA web site www.asaging.org.

14. Richard Restak, *Older and Wiser*, New York, Simon & Schuster, 1997, p. 106. The research he quotes on dendrites is by Guy McKhann of Zanvyl Krieger Mind/Brain Institute at Johns Hopkins.

15. The Institute for Higher Education Policy of Washington and the Boston-based Education Resource Institute report that, between 1970 and 1993, the number of

Americans above the age of forty in our universities rose from 5.5 to 11.2 percent. The number of over-forties in adult education courses tripled during the same period.

16. Stephen Joel Trachtenberg, "Preparing for the 'Baby Boomers': Older Students Will Bring New Opportunities to Colleges," *Chronicle of Higher Education*, March 21, 1997, p. B7.

17. On the history and philosophy of the Fromm Institute, see the documentary film *Old Enough to Know Better,* produced by Ron Levaco for Trans Film and Video, 1192 Page Street, San Francisco, CA 94117.

18. Nicholas Negroponte, *Being Digital*, New York, Vintage Books, 1996, p. 203.

### 15. Rites of Passage

1. Stanislav Grof, *Books of the Dead: Manuals for Living and Dying,* London, Thames & Hudson, 1994, p. 26.

2. Marc Freedland, *Prime Time: How Baby Boomers Will Revolutionize Retirement and Transform America*, New York, Public Affairs, 1999.

3. Rachel Naomi Remen, *Kitchen Table Wisdom: Stories That Heal*, New York, Riverhead, 1996, p. 75. Also see her *My Grandfather's Blessings*, New York, Riverhead, 2000.

4. Robert Neale, *The Art of Dying*, New York, Harper and Row, 1972, p. 37.

### 16. The Survival of the Gentlest

1. Richard Hofstadter, *Social Darwinism in American Thought*, Boston, Little Brown, 1955, p. 74.

2. John Maynard Keynes, *Essays in Persuasion*, New York, Harcourt, Brace and Company, 1932, pp. 369-370.

### 17. Grandparent Power

1. "Gifts to Grandchildren," *American Demographics*, vol. 18, number 8, August 1996, p. 512. A 1997 study of grandparent giving that indicates the same generosity was reported on *NBC Nightly News*, September 20, 1997.

2. Lori Simon-Rusinowitz et al., "Grandparenting at Century's End: Grandparents in the Workplace," *Generations*, Spring 1996, pp. 41-45. This paper was researched for the American Society on Aging in 1996. Also see Robert Butler, "Living Longer, Contributing More," *Journal of the American Medical Association,* October 22, 1997.

3. The Foster Grandparent program has a web site: www.cns.gov/fgp-a.html.

4. *Science,* April 25, 1997.

5. Hawkes quoted in Natalie Angier, "Theorists See Survival Value in Menopause," *New York Times*, September 16, 1997. Angier offers a balanced evaluation of the grandmother hypothesis in *Woman: An Intimate Geography*, New York, Houghton Mifflin, 1999, chapter thirteen. Also see Sarah Blaffer Hardy, *Mother Nature,*

New York, Pantheon, 1999, chapter eleven. For a report on Kristin Hawkes' version of the grandmother hypothesis, see *Proceedings of the National Academy of Sciences*, February 1998.

6. David Gutmann, *Reclaimed Powers: Toward a New Psychology of Men and Women in Later Life*, New York, Basic Books, 1987, p. 7.

# INDEX

# The Author

Theodore Roszak is Professor of History at California State University, Hayward, and the author of eighteen books. He has been a Guggenheim Fellow and has been nominated twice for the National Book Award. His published works include *The Making of a Counter Culture*, *The Voice of the Earth: An Exploration of Ecopsychology*, *The Memoirs of Elizabeth Frankenstein* and *The Gendered Atom: Reflections on the Sexual Psychology of Science*. He lives in Berkeley, California.